INDIAN LITERARY CRITICISM

Indian Literary Criticism

Theory and Interpretation

Third Edition

Edited by

G. N. Devy

Orient BlackSwan

INDIAN LITERARY CRITICISM: THEORY AND INTERPRETATION, THIRD EDITION

ORIENT BLACKSWAN PRIVATE LIMITED

Registered Office
3-6-752 Himayatnagar, Hyderabad 500 029, Telangana, India
e-mail: centraloffice@orientblackswan.com

Other Offices
Bengaluru, Chennai, Guwahati, Hyderabad,
Kolkata, Mumbai, New Delhi, Noida, Patna

First published by Orient Blackswan Pvt. Ltd. 2002
Reprinted 2004
Second edition 2010
Reprinted 2011, 2012, 2015, 2016
Third edition 2020
Reprinted 2024

Cover and book design

ISBN 978-93-90122-57-8

039312

Typeset in Adobe Garamond Pro 11.5/13.5 *by*
Shine Graphics, Delhi 110 094

Printed in India at
Yash Printographics, Noida

Published by
Orient Blackswan Private Limited
3-6-752, Himayatnagar, Hyderabad 500 029, Telangana, India
e-mail: info@orientblackswan.com

Also by G. N. Devy

G. N. Devy Reader
A Nomad Called Thief
Of Many Heroes
The Question of Silence
After Amnesia
Countering Violence

For
Prakash and Anagha

Contents

Part II: Interpretation

Publisher's Acknowledgements

G. K. Bhatt, 'On *Natya* and *Rasa*: Aesthetics of Dramatic Experience' from *Bharata-Natya-Manjari. Bharata on the Theory and Practice of Drama—A Selection from Bharata's Natyashastra.* Pune: Bhandarkar Oriental Research Institute, 1975. Reproduced with permission of the Bhandarkar Oriental Research Institute.

S. Ilakkuvanar, 'On Diction and Syntax' from *Tholkāppiyam* (in English)*: with Critical Studies*, Madurai: Kuraḷ Neṛi Publishing House, 1963. Reproduced with permission of Maraimalai Ilakkuvanar.

K. Raghavan Pillai, 'On Syntax and Meaning' from *The Vākyapadīya: Critical Text of Cantos I and II*, pp. 44–132. Delhi: Motilal Banarsidass, 1971. Reproduced with permission of Motilal Banarsidass Publishing House.

K. Krishnamoorthy, '*Dhvani*: Structure of Poetic Meaning' from *Dhvanyaloka* (of Anandavardhana), edited and translated by K. Krishnamoorthy, Karnatak University, Dharwad, 1974. Reproduced with permission of K. Leela Prakash.

K. Krishnamoorthy, 'Language of Poetry and Metaphor' from *The Vakrokti-jīvita* (of Kuntaka)*: Critically Edited with Variants, Introduction and English Translations*, Karnatak University, Dharwad, 1977. Reproduced with permission of K. Leela Prakash.

R. Nath and Faiyaz 'Gwaliari', 'Multilingual Literary Culture' from *India As Seen by Amir Khusrau in 1318 A.D.* Historical Research Documentation Programme, Jaipur, 1981. Reproduced with the permission of Ajay Nath.

K. P. Bahadur, 'Kinds of Poetry and Defects of Poetry' from *The Rasikapriya of Keshavadasa: Translated into Verse*, pp. 239–47. New Delhi: Motilal Banarsidass, 1972. Reproduced with permission of Motilal Banarsidass Publishing House.

Sardar Jafri and Qurratulain Hyder, 'Poetry as Freedom' from *Ghalib and His Poetry*. Bombay: Popular Prakashan, 1970. Reproduced with permission of Sardar Jafri and Saif Hasan.

K. Krishnamoorthy, 'Sanskrit Poetics: An Overview', from *Comparative Indian Literature*, vol. 2, edited by K. M. George, pp. 1109–26. Trichur: Kerala Sahitya Akademi, 1984. Reproduced with permission of the Kerala Sahitya Akademi.

A. K. Ramanujan, 'On Ancient Tamil Poetics' from *Poems of Love and War: From the Eight Anthologies and the Ten Long Poems of Classical Tamil*, selected and translated by A. K. Ramanujan, pp. 235–68. New York: Columbia University Press, 1985. Reproduced with permission of Columbia University Press.

Bimal Krishna Matilal, 'Bhartrhari's View of Sphota', from *The Word and The World*, pp. 84–89, Oxford University Press. Reproduced with permission of Oxford University Press © Oxford University Press 2001.

R. B. Patankar, 'Aesthetics: Some Important Problems' from *Journal of Arts and Ideas*, vol. 6, Jan–March, 1984, pp. 44–66. Reproduced with permission of Jyotsna Naware.

Introduction to the Second Edition

Language is, perhaps, the most distinguishing feature of the human species, the most marked difference between other forms of life and the human consciousness. Language itself is made of such ephemeral material such as verbal modulations and entirely arbitrarily generated signs that, by its very nature, it is not capable of functioning within a framework of fixed correspondence between forms and significance. The perpetually shifting relationship between the verbal container and the content it is supposed to hold, as well as the semblance of a predictable relationship between them, provide human language their innate ability to be a versatile medium of creative expression. Thus, practically every linguistic utterance is 'creative' in essence. The marvel that is human speech largely vanishes into thin air, while some of it manages to remain embedded in the collective reception by a given speech community. A small part of this acquires staying power not only in its own time and context but beyond. Expression which is capable of transcending culture and time comes to be recognised as 'literature'. The notion of what constitutes literature keeps changing from one era to another, from one culture to another. The notion of what constitutes literature should probably be the most rudimentary definition of 'Literary Criticism'. But since the perception of what makes literature keeps changing, the norms and the idiom of literary criticism also continue to change from period to period; and there can be very distinct differences between the idea of literary criticism prevailing in one culture and that prevailing in another culture within the same historical period. This is not to say that there are no points of convergence and accidental or justified similarities between a given set of period-styles or cultural-styles of critical idioms. Such convergences or similarities are natural since the interdependence between the human consciousness and the external world, which language attempts to describe, is the very essence of human existence. Hence, while approaching any specific tradition of literary criticism it is desirable to keep in view the large backdrop of the relation between reality, language, literature and criticism.

Indian students of literature, particularly those who are exposed to western traditions of literary criticism, generally tend to think that there are, or should be, points of convergence between one or many of the western traditions of literary criticism and the one or many Indian traditions. Since higher education in India as it exists at present was shaped within the crucible of the colonial transactions of knowledge, Indian students of literature in English, as well as students of Bhasha literature to an extent, come to expect that the transition of the idiom of criticism from ancient times to our time in India has been akin to the transition in western tradition(s). If dissimilarities are noticed, they are read more as indicative of philosophical flaws or cultural inadequacies within the Indian tradition(s). Historians of ideas have pointed out that within the tradition conceived by ancient Greek philosophers like Plato, and Aristotle and partially revived and modified by British thinkers like Dryden, Coleridge, Arnold, Eliot, etc., literary criticism has run through four major phases: the mimetic phase, the didactic phase, the expressive phase, and the autonomous phase (M. H. Abrams, *The Mirror and the Lamp*, 1953). It would be a frustrating task to figure out if literary criticism in Arabic, Chinese, Tamil or Hebrew has precisely the same progression. Clearly, it will be inappropriate to read a given tradition of literary criticism in terms of the progression of another tradition, however rich in thought or dominant in terms of its influence the one or the other may have been.

I was required to reflect on these issues as someone engaged professionally with the field of literature teaching and research. As a young scholar of literature, I started thinking some there decades ago about the nature of literary criticism appropriate for Bhasha literature. At that time, I was not quite aware of how numerous the literary traditions and the speech communities have been in the Indian sub-continent. Though I had gone through the Census statistics on mother tongues (1652 as in the 1961 Census data), I had not quite imagined that many among those would really be surviving in our time as literary languages. Hence, I had no hesitation in arguing that an Indian student can propose for herself or himself an Indian intellectual tradition that would provide her or him a cultural space to engage in creative expression. In order to assess the viability of the enterprise, I undertook a scrutiny of the resources available in the library collection at the Baroda University. Fortunately, as I thought at that stage in my life, the Baroda University library had a rich enough stock of works in the field to keep me thrilled over several years.

During those years, I undertook to gather similar materials from other libraries in India, particularly those specialising in Oriental Studies, and in Britain and the United States whenever I visited those countries. As the material started piling up on my desk, I began to realise that the field had far too many challenges, and that it would be unwise to postulate any single tradition of literary criticism for the entire gamut of Bhasha literature. The realisation prompted me to write a long essay discussing the complexities involved in the enterprise, which appeared in the form of a book under the title *After Amnesia* (Orient Longman, 1992). However, I felt that it would not be inappropriate to select some of the texts out of the materials I had gathered and share them with other Indian teachers of literature who may have gone through a similar process of reflection and doubt. Therefore, I spent two long summers in preparing a typescript. When I typed the manuscript of this anthology, I had no idea as to its fate. For various reasons the actual publication got delayed. Therefore, though this anthology was first published at the beginning of the twenty-first century, I appeal to the reader not to overlook the fact that it is a twentieth century work by a young teacher of literature trying to define his own tradition of literary thought for himself. If I had compiled the volume when it was published, it would have been somewhat different in its orientation. In my 'Preface' to the first edition of the anthology, written in 1993, I had stated:

> It is hoped that the reader will find this volume useful, if not completely satisfactory, and that some other critic-editor will bring out an improved and more inclusive version as a sequel to it. It is also

hoped that this volume contributes, in however modest a measure, to curing our collective cultural amnesia.

Since the publication of the anthology, it has been reprinted twice, and is now being issued once more in a slightly modified format. One may be permitted to see this as an indication that there still is a need for a volume of this kind, at least for post-graduate students and college teachers of literary criticism.

As the editor of the anthology I feel pleased that it is being used today, but I would like to state that I am acutely aware of the major literary and contextual changes that have occurred during the two decades since I prepared the volume. Of these, one is a literary change, the second pertains to the structure of higher education, and the third is related to the political context. During the 1980s, Indian departments of literature had as yet not been fully exposed to post-structural and post-modern theory. The English translations of Jacques Derrida, Michael Foucault, Jacques Lacan, Roland Barthes, Louis Althusser, Jean Baudrillard, Gilles Deleuze and Jean-Francois Lyotard had just started appearing and Indian departments of literature had not as yet introduced their ideas in the curriculum. Those were the years when English Studies, in India as well as in other post-colonial countries, had started making initial moves towards decolonising literary studies. Obviously, the focus in criticism courses had not yet started moving from England and the United States to France, Germany and Italy. That change, and a truly substantial change, occurred in India mainly during the last decade of the twentieth century. As it happens, whenever a new philosophical or literary trend emerges with originality and force, several path-breaking studies written by Indian scholars start appearing during that decade. Moreover, as the disciplinary boundaries blurred, the critical idiom started receiving fresh concepts and insights from the fields of cinema and media studies, painting and sculpture, psychology and political thought. A future edition of the anthology stands to gain immensely by the inclusion of a whole section drawn from the rich wealth of criticism produced in India since the nineties.

Another contextual change that has occurred since I first made this compilation is related to the near disappearance of scholarship in the classical Indian languages. During my student days, at least some of my teachers had an acquaintance with Sanskrit and a few had learnt Pali. Besides, a majority of literature teachers in English departments had an intimate involvement with the literature in their own languages. As a result, it was not uncommon among academics to allude to the *rasa* or *dhvani* theory without any sense of unease. Though it is possible to raise serious questions about the propriety of speaking of Bharatamuni and Aristotle in a single breath—and I have myself questioned this practice—the teachers of literature during the first two or three decades after independence were able to pass on to their students at least some awareness about ancient and medieval Indian texts in literary theory. That situation has changed substantially. It is rare to find a literature teacher in India now who can offer students any sustained discourse or analysis of texts in Sanskrit or Pali. One notices that the tremendous gain in the form of exposure to the postmodern post-structural theory is sadly off-set by an equal loss of access to parts of the Indian intellectual tradition(s). In this changed context, I tend to think that there is an enhanced justification for an anthology such as the present one.

The most notable change, however, is neither pertaining to theory nor to the system of higher education. It comes from the political ethos. When I was struggling to gather texts from various ancient, medieval and modem sources and put them together in a single volume, I did not have to think that a given thinker would be labelled as a Hindu thinker (or otherwise). I am not able to say with any certainty if I was politically naïve or if the cultural atmosphere in India a quarter century ago was more liberal. My aim in presenting a volume of Indian thinkers on literature was primarily aimed at rescuing the field of literary studies from the undue dominance of irrelevant colonial baggage. But now I fear that my idea of tracing the literary thought back to ancient times may stand the risk of being seen in part as politically retrogressive. Therefore, I would like the user of this volume to bear in mind that I have neither included in this volume nor excluded from it any thinker for reasons of his/her religious affiliation. I do not think of religion as a matter of 'affiliation' but as a matter of purely personal pursuit. Besides, the rich tapestry of Indian literary traditions over the last three thousand years stands out for its profound spirit of tolerance and its immense ability to accept and nurture diversity.

It is important for Indian students of literature to know that most of the seminal theoretical positions proposed by thinkers in the Indian past had drawn upon a variety of linguistic, cultural and spiritual traditions. Beginning with Bharat Muni's description of *nāṭya,* Daṇḍin's theory of *riti* and Abhinava's concept of *rasa-dhvani* to Aurobindo's understanding of 'aesthesis' and Bhalchandra Nemade's definition of the novel, the theorists have invariably invoked the plurality of voices, tones, world-views, languages and styles as a value in creative expression. In preparing an anthology of an extremely complex and varied intellectual spectrum it is almost impossible to follow rigid guidelines. I was aware of the difficulties when I set out to make my choices. I had stated the difficulties in making the choices I made in the Preface to the first edition:

> In our own times, quite often the contemporary critical texts of significance tend to remain hidden in the pages of obscure periodicals, or are blocked by obscure publishers. Added to this is the problem of availability of good translations of critical materials. In a country where even literary works do not get translated in good time into all Indian languages, it is too much to expect to find translators committed to such a specialised activity as literary criticism. The combined result of this situation is that an Indian student of literature does not have easy access to India's critical tradition. She may show an emotional solidarity with the cause of Indian criticism, but may not be able to mention even one Indian text of literary criticism with any degree of familiarity, excepting those texts which are the most contemporary. Therefore, many of us have wished that there was a series of volumes giving Indian students modem renderings, of important Indian critical texts from the past, to be put to use in the present. To prepare such a series of scholarly volumes would be a project worthy of being taken up by a committee of scholars or a literary academy. The volume being

> offered here is a small substitute aimed at fulfilling that long-felt need. This volume tires to bring under one cover some of the most significant literary thinkers in the Indian tradition of the last two millennia. It is being offered in the hope that it will provide teachers, students and scholars-in-the-making easy access to some of the key concepts, terms and ideas from various Indian traditions of literary theorising. Besides, it will give students a convenient text in which they can find first-hand some of the most significant literary thinkers. It is with these modest aims that the present volume is put together though I am fully aware of its deficiencies.

Having said that, I will at once point out the deficiencies in this volume. The most striking one is that the excerpts selected from the Tamil classic *Tholkāppiyam* are all too brief. Unfortunately, the translation of order relevant sections available to us is so poor in quality that however sympathetically I looked at it, it was impossible to decide in favour of its inclusion The parts translated by Prof. Zvelebil of Holland, though the translation is very lucid, would not have fitted into the present scheme of the volume. Next, no text from Pali or Prakrit has been included. Two very able candidates that merited consideration were Ananda Coomaraswamy's translation of Milinda, and Nagñajita's treatise on structural aesthetics. Coomaraswamy's rendering of the concept of *samvega* is erudite; but the original is difficult to extricate from the translator's comments. On the other hand, Nagñajita's treatise on painting, which has so miraculously survived translation from Pali to Chinese to German to English would have been quite a valuable addition to this volume. However, the difficulty comes from the fact that not even one historian of ancient Indian poetics/aesthetics takes it into cognisance. In our collective amnesia it still exists at the level of fantasy! I decided to go by consensus. Though Abhinavagupta completed his life-mission by the first quarter of the eleventh century, the tradition of Sanskrit poetics continued till the middle of the seventeenth century. Jagannātha was, probably, the last important theorist in that tradition. However, the post-Abhinava theory was an abstract exercise with little reference to any contemporary living literature in modern Indian languages and not in Sanskrit.

When one thinks of literary criticism in medieval India, one experiences the difficulty caused by a relative absence of theoretical documents. What the medieval poets created was a fresh and powerful set of conventions, styles and metres; but they do not indicate that they felt the need to articulate the literary and theoretical premises guiding these styles, metres and conventions. Several passages from Jñānadevā's *Bhāvārthadīpikā* are included to exemplify the manner in which the orientation of creative literature was shifting during the medieval centuries. I am happy that an excerpt from Amīr Khusrau and three passages from Badāonī's literary history could be included here. However, it was not possible to include examples of the work of Hemachandra, the thirteenth century lexicographer and bilingual critic, for want of a suitable English translation. The availability of translations has in fact been one of the major limiting factors of this anthology.

Many texts included are translations from Sanskrit, Persian, Hindi, Marathi and Gujarati. Translations always have a way of misbehaving. They may say more than the original, or even less than the original; but they rarely say exactly what the original says. The difficulty is greater with English translations of ancient and medieval Indian texts, for they have a long and entrenched habit of being obscure and unreadable. I have retained most of the translations used here in their exact form, since they are done by eminent scholars. And, in a form of literature where ideas are more important than the way in which they are presented, it is preferable to have 'faithful' translations even if they are not charming. Yet, occasionally, I have touched up the translated versions so that they do not become entirely unintelligible.

In our times, Indian literary criticism seems to have been facing a profound crisis of identity. Philosophically speaking, this crisis originates in the uncertainty of perspective about basic aesthetic premises: should they be 'logical' and 'universal', or should they be 'native' and 'relevant'? These questions cannot be answered with any degree of certitude in the context of a multi-ethnic, post-colonial culture. Historically speaking, the crisis in criticism can be traced back to the beginning of the last millennium, to those pre-colonial centuries when Bhashas were emerging as languages of literary expression. In those new languages, and in literature written in them, there was a richness of creative expression but practically no critical writing and articulation. The split was perhaps a matter of a conscious cultural decision by the heterogeneous community of writers. There is no evidence that the decline of literary criticism was ever perceived as a crisis in any of the Bhashas during the pre-colonial centuries. The awareness of an imaginary or a real crisis in criticism in perhaps a gift of the colonial experience. During the last hundred and fifty years there has been an unprecedented rise in the status of criticism as an essential aspect of literary culture.

The importance of literary criticism increases when literary education becomes institutionalised and literature becomes a 'subject' in schools and universities. A natural consequence of this shift is the increase in importation of critical concepts, tools and perspectives. Another consequence is the spread of revivalist tendencies. At the time of the inception of colonial education in India during the early nineteenth century, the debate between the Orientalists and the Anglicists occupied the centrestage of the elite culture in India. The same debate, in infinite new varieties, continued to control and guide critical and metacritical thought in India throughout the twentieth century. Quite often the fact is completely overlooked that these two positions are non-starters in the context of modern Indian literature. The result is that we have critics who wish to modernise and westernise criticism, as well as critics who wish to purify and revive the mainstream native tradition of criticism. Considering that criticism, at its best, is produced for and by specific periods and styles in a literary tradition, this turning away, or turning back has not resulted in any significant contribution to the upkeep of contemporary creative literature in Indian languages. As such, literary history, practical criticism, theoretical formulation and the related philosophical speculation have remained inadequately developed in modern India. In any case, the development in these areas has not equaled, during any decade of the twentieth century, that in the field of creative writing.

Whether as a cause or a consequence of the above, contemporary Indians seem to be afflicted by a sense of amnesia in relation to literary history. Within the sphere of literary criticism, the affliction becomes more severe owing to the general unavailability of the older critical texts, and, in part, due to the alienation from the intellectual ethos within which these texts were generated. To a large extent, modern India has lost touch with the Sanskrit language. Similarly, there is not much awareness, outside the small circle of specialists, of the literary and critical texts produced in medieval India. And, though many of the texts continue to survive through oral transmission in the cultural transactions of sects founded upon those texts, there is little rapport between the classes involved in the sects and the class of intellectuals that has monopolised the contemporary literary culture.

The more debatable sections of this anthology are those in which the reader finds materials from the twentieth century. As we move closer to our own times, the difficulties in making the best choice increase. Should one include literary credos by creative writers? Should the views on art and literature of a philosopher like J. Krishnamurti be included? Which of the twenty or so languages used for creative expression should be given representation? Should one represent literary movements such as the Progressive Movement, Dalit literature, Nava-Kavya, Magical Realism, etc.? And finally, the most tricky of all questions, how much and whether any space should be given to modern Indian thinkers like Ashis Nandy, M. N. Srinivas, Sudhir Kakar and so on? In the face of all these questions, I have used my own judgement, inevitably with its subjective preferences, in selecting the more significant critics of this century: Sri Aurobindo, Tagore, B. S. Mardhekar, Krishna Rayan, Suresh Joshi, Bhalchandra Nemade, Gayatri Spivak and Aijaz Ahmad. There can be little doubt that each one of them has made a significant contribution to the modern critical discourse in India. Some more thinkers could have been included. In particular, I was keen on including a translation of Ram Vilas Sharma's writing on literary history. However, for entirely non-academic reasons, this did not become possible. Similarly, I should have liked to reproduce one of Homi Bhabha's essays here. I tend to think that he has been among the post-independence Indian literary critics one highly original in his arguments. A translation of his work in a few major Indian languages may cause a deep impact on critical writings in those languages. Yet, Bhabha's intellectual engagement has been primarily with post-structural theory in the context of post-modernism rather than with Bhasha literature. However, at a future date, when diaspora literature has received a greater acceptance within Bhasha literature, an extended version of this anthology, or another anthology such as this one, needs to include Homi Bhabha's work as an important contribution to 'Indian' literary criticism. I also have a feeling that a quarter century from now if a similar anthology of criticism is to be compiled, it will be necessary to include in it the activist writings of Mahasweta Devi, Arundhati Roy and cultural essays by Shivram Karanth and Dilip Chitre. The overlap between literature and history is overwhelmingly transforming our perception of creativity.

It has been the attempt here to represent the work of every Indian critic who can be claimed to have founded a school of thought or a literary trend: *rasa* (Bharatamuni), *riti* (Daṇḍin), *dhvani* (Ānandavardhana), *vakrokti* (Kuntaka). Abhinavagupta is included as a great philosopher with an original interpretation of the *rasa* theory. Jñāneśvara was the founder of the Marathi tradition of poetry, and an able spokesman for bhakti poetics. Rupa Goswami in Sanskrit and Keshavadasa in Hindi continue his work, but with significantly differing emphasis. Al-Badāonī represents the movement towards literary historiography in Persian. Besides, his text should show the reader that, contrary to the generally held assumption, literary history is not entirely of Western origin. Sri Aurobindo represents the most idealistic in Indian Romanticism. Tagore stands as a colossus among modern Indian writers. Mardhekar is, probably, the first Indian critic to turn to the area of pure aesthetics. Aijaz Ahmad indicates the directions in which Marxism was and is put to use in Indian literary history and criticism. Nemade is the founder of the Nativism movement, and Suresh Joshi is perhaps the most remarkable among Indian Formalists. Gayatri Spivak is the chief exponent of subaltern gender-justice. All of them, together, should provide very exciting reading to Indian students of literary criticism.

The second part of this volume, entitled 'Interpretation', consists of celebrated comments on Indian criticism. Not all of them were written as essays in literary criticism. Sudhir Kakar's analysis of the psychology of bhakti, and B. K. Matilal's commentary on Bhartṛhari belong to other discourses but are included in this volume as it illuminates some of the texts included in the first part of the volume. K. Krishnamoorthy and M. Hiriyanna have been the most significant during interpreters of Sanskrit poetics the twentieth century. Their commentaries should make a student's passage to Sanskrit poetics much less difficult. R. B. Patankar's provocative essay on modern Marathi aesthetics is included for two reasons. One, his contribution to the field of aesthetics in India is so significant that no anthology of this nature can overlook it; and two, his analysis of the situation in Marathi should be applicable with varying degrees to criticism in other Indian languages. However, the section on interpretation has been kept somewhat exclusive by bringing in it only the most essential and the most celebrated of commentaries. This is of course, not to deny that a great wealth of comments on ancient and modern Indian criticism exists today, though it is not properly classified in anthologies and bibliographies so far.

G. N. Devy
October 2009

About the Third Edition

The manuscript of the first edition was prepared in 1990. In 2020, in the third edition of the book, some essays could not be reproduced for want of affordable reprint permissions from the authors and publishers. The omission is regretted. The consequence of including these essays would have meant a significant increase in the price of the book. Since the book is widely used by students, I thought it proper to let the costs remain as affordable as possible.

G. N. Devy
2020

Part I

Theory

1

Bharatamuni

Tradition considers the *Nāṭyaśāstra* as an additional Veda, so important has it been in the history of Indian literary thought. A version of the *Nāṭyaśāstra* had been in existence before the third century; but by the third century, it had taken a definitive shape, as the references of later critics indicate. The authorship of *Nāṭyaśāstra* is ascribed to Bharatamuni. Our knowledge of him is so little that it is impossible to think of his literary philosophy in the context of his other probable works. It is not even certain whether or not he, the author of this great work, ever existed.

The *Nāṭyaśāstra* a is a compendium of performed arts: drama, music, dance. It presents in a great wealth of detail descriptions of the prevalent modes of these art performances; and the extraordinary precision with which the multiple facets of these arts have been defined and analysed is indicative of the sophistication of the art practices as well as art-criticism of Bharata's age. The *Nāṭyaśāstra* was used through the fifteen hundred years of Sanskrit literary thought as the bedrock of literary theory. Whether it was Abhinavagupta, Mammata, or Viśwanāth, discussing poetry and literature during the subsequent centuries, they inevitably turned to Bharata's formulations as the polar star of Indian aesthetics.

To many revivalistic Indian critics during the last two hundred years, Bharata has been the maker of the *rasa* theory. While there is no denying that his fascinating insight in the psychology of aesthetic reception was a phenomenal triumph of intellect, it is necessary to remind ourselves that the *Nāṭyaśāstra* is not devoted solely to the exposition of *rasa* theory. That is but a fragment of the entire compendium. It is also necessary to remember that the intervening centuries have altered both the concept of *rasa* (as in *bhaktirasa* during the middle ages) as well as the philosophic context within which it was originally couched. Hence, any easy revival may be impracticable.

There are many renderings of the *Nāṭyaśāstra* or parts of it in modern Indian languages, translation of concepts and terminology being easier in these languages. However, there is no satisfactory rendering of it in English. It must be added, immediately, that Monomohan Ghosh's rendering, which is its only available translation in English, has generally been praised by modem Sanskrit scholars. But it does not make easy reading for the non-Sanskritists. A quarter-century ago, G. K. Bhatt produced a *Bharata-Nāṭya Manjiri* (1975). It is a digest of the great work, and is aimed at the beginner, probably the undergraduate student of Sanskrit poetics. However, it is built upon Monomohan Ghosh's translation, and is slightly less archaic. Excerpts from it are used here, with occasional syntactic modifications. The materials used are the English sections from pages 11–16, 75–107, 153–154 and 265–268 of the *Bharata Nāṭya Manjiri* (1975, Bhandarkar Institute, Pune.)

On *Naṭya* and *Rasa*: Aesthetics of Dramatic Experience

....The *nāṭya* (in fact) is depiction and communication pertaining to the emotions of the entire triple world;
occasionally piety, occasionally sport, occasionally wealth, occasionally peace of mind, occasionally laughter, occasionally fighting, occasionally sexual passion, occasionally slaughter;
the pious behaviour of those who practise religion, the passion of those who indulge in sexual pleasure, the repression of those who go by a wicked path, the act of self-restraint of those who are disciplined;
creating boldness among those who are impotent, enthusiasm among those who consider themselves brave, comprehension among those who lack understanding, as also wisdom among the learned;

> graceful pleasures for those who wield power, steadiness and comfort for such as are afflicted with pain and misery, the ways of earning wealth for those who live by money, courage for those whose mind is despondent;
> rich with different kinds of emotions, built on the stuff of many stages and situations (*avasthā*) and imitating the conduct of the world: that is what this *nāṭya* is, which I have produced.

Based on the actions of men, high, middling and low, this *nāṭya* will produce wholesome instruction, create courage, pastime, entertainment and pleasure.

This *nāṭya* will be instrumental in producing restfulness, at the proper time, for such as are afflicted with misery, fatigue and sorrow and for poor wretches (*tapasvin*).

It will conduce to piety, glory, healthy life; it will be beneficial, promote intellectual growth. The *nāṭya*, in brief, will be the instrument of instruction for the world.

There is hardly any knowledge, any artist's craft, any lore, any fine art, any design, in which art, lore and emotions are interconnected, any activity, that will not be seen in this *nāṭya*.

So, you should not entertain any sense of resentment towards the gods. The *nāṭya,* I assure you, will be an imitative presentation of all the Seven Islands.

The *nāṭya* should be understood to be an indicator of happenings in the life of gods, demons, kings, family men and sages who have spiritual knowledge.

In fact the nature and behaviour (*svabhāva*) of the world, intimately connected with happiness and misery, as rendered by physical and other forms of acting, is to be called *nāṭya*.

The eight rhetorical Sentiments (*Rasas*) recognised in drama and dramatic representation are named as follows: the Erotic, Comic, Pathetic, Furious, Heroic, Terrible, Odious, Marvellous.

The high-souled Druhina (*Brahmā*) proclaimed these eight rhetorical sentiments.

I shall now mention the emotional states (*Bhāva*) as arising from the abiding (*Sthāyin*), the transient (*Sancāri* or *Vyabhicāri*) and the psycho-physical conditions (*Sāttvīka*) of the mind.

The abiding mental conditions (*Sthāyibhāva*) are mentioned as follows: love, laughter, sorrow, anger, energy, fear, disgust and astonishment.

Despondency, sinking or weakness (*glāni*), apprehension, jealousy or envy (*asūyā*), intoxication or pride (*mada*), fatigue, indolence, depression (*dainya*), anxiety, infatuation or distraction (*moha*), recollection, steadiness or courage (*dhṛti*), shame, impulsiveness or inconstancy (*capalatā*), exhilaration or joy (*harṣa*), agitation or impetuousness (*āvega*), stupor or inactivity (*jaḍatā*), conceit, despair (*viṣāda*), eagerness or impatience (*autsukya*), sleep, epilepsy (*apasmāra*), dreaming (*suptam*), awakening inner emotion or dissimulation (*avahittha*), menace, ferocity or cruelty (*ugratā*), thoughtfulness (*mati*), disease or sickness, madness or insanity (*unmāda*), death-fright (*trāsa*), wavering or hesitation (*vitarka*): these thirty-three emotional states are enumerated by their names (as transient mental states).

Paralysis (*stambha*), perspiration, horripilation, voice-breaking, tremor, change of colour (*vaivarṇya*), tears, complete loss of consciousness or fainting (*pralaya*): these eight are spoken as *sāttvika* or psycho-physical conditions.

Four kinds of *Abhinaya* or histrionic representations are recognised in *nāṭya:* they are: physical gestures, expressions and movements (*āṇgika*); voice-modulation in delivery of dramatic speeches (*vācika*); costume and make-up (*āhārya*) as also props and drapery; and *sāttvika* conveyed by physical reactions of inner emotional states.

The *Dharmi*, or the mode of dramatic representation, is recognised as twofold: *Lok-dharmi*, following the practice of peoples, or realistic, and *Nāṭya-dharmi*, following theatrical modes, or conventional, symbolic.

The four styles in which dramatic representation is established are: *Bhārati* or Verbal; *Sāttvatī* or Grand; *Kaiśikī* or Graceful; and *Ārabhatī* or Energetic.

The success of dramatic representation is twofold: heavenly and human.

The musical notes like *ṣaḍja* etc., are seven and belong to two groups: produced from the human voice (*śārīra*, literally, from the body) and from musical instruments like *vīṇā* (*vaiṇa*).

The musical instruments (*ātodya*) are of four kinds. Their characters are: stringed (*tata*), covered (*avanaddha*), solid (*ghana*) and with holes (*suṣira*). *Tata* is known to be connected with the stringed lyre; *Avanaddha* is connected with drum; *Ghana* is cymbal or gong; and *Suṣira* is flute.

The songs pertaining to the *Dhruvās* sung in the course of dramatic representation are of five kinds: songs to indicate entering (*praveśa*), unexpected or interposed happening (*ākṣepa*), leaving (*niṣkrāma*), propitiating or pleasing (*prāsādika*), filling the gap (*āntara*).

The theatre is defined as square-shaped, oblong and triangular.

* * *

[Tr.n.: The term *rasa* has a twofold significance: It means the 'aesthetic content' of literary art and also 'aesthetic relish' which the reader-spectator enjoys.]

... we shall first of all explain the rhetorical sentiments (*asas*). No literary import can ever proceed without rhetorical sentiment and aesthetic relish. Now, *asas* arise from a proper combination of the stimulants (*vibhāva*), the physical consequents (*anubhāva*), and the transient emotional states (*vyabhicāri bhāva*).

What is the illustrative case? There we say: Just as by a proper combination of different spicy foodstuffs (*vyānjana*), leafy vegetables (*ausadhi*) and other articles of food (*dravya*), there is a flavour and taste (*rasa*) produced, in the same way when different emotional states come together, aesthetic flavour and relish are produced. Just as again, on account of such articles of food as molasses, and spicy and vegetable-stuff, the six (food) flavours and tastes are produced, in the same way when various emotional states reach the abiding mental conditions, the latter attain the quality of rhetorical sentiment, or become aesthetically relishable.

Now, one may ask: what is this thing that you call 'rasa'? We say: it is so called because it is capable of being tasted or relished. How is *rasa* tasted? Just as people in a contented state of mind (*sumanasah*), eating the food prepared well (*samskṛta*) with various spicy things taste the (various) flavours (enjoy the various tastes) and obtain delight and satisfaction (*harṣādin*), in the same manner spectators, in the right (receptive) frame of mind (*sumanasah*), taste the permanent mental conditions, suggested (*vyānjita*) by the representation (*abhinaya*) of various emotional states, the *abhinaya* carried out by speech-delivery (*vāc*), physical gestures and movements (*anga*), and by the physical acting of physical impacts (*sattva*); and obtain pleasure and satisfaction It is for this reason that they have been explained as *nāṭya-rasa*: aesthetic contents and their relish arising from dramatic representation.

In this context there are two traditional couplets:

> Just as connoisseurs of cooked rice or food (*bhakta*), when they eat it as prepared with many articles of food and with many different spicy things enjoy the flavour and taste,
>
> in like manner, the wise (spectators) taste and enjoy in their mind the permanent mental conditions rendered through [lit. well connected with] the acting of emotional states (*bhāvābhinaya*).

Inter-relation of Bhāva and Rasa

One may ask: Are the emotional states turned out from the rhetorical sentiments or is it that the sentiments are turned out of the emotional states? Some opine that they arise from mutual contact. But this is not so. Why? Because it is a matter of actual perception that the rhetorical sentiments are turned out of the emotional states, and not that emotional states are turned out of the sentiments.

There are traditional couplets about this:

> The emotional states are so known by the designers of dramatic art because they (the *bhāvas*) bring to the spectators (*imān*) an emotional awareness (*bhāvayanti*) of the sentiments as connected with various modes of acting or dramatic representation.
>
> Just as, by many articles of food (*dravya*) of various kinds, the spicy foodstuff (*vyanjana*) like vegetables, meat, fish is brought to a distinct

flavour (*bhāvayate*), in the same way, the emotional states bring the sentiments to the level of actual experience (*bhāvayanti*) when helped by different finds of acting or histrionic representation (*abhinaya*).

There can hardly be the experience of sentiment without the previous presentation of an emotional state; nor can there be an emotional state which does not lead to the experience of a sentiment. During the process of histrionic representation the two (*bhāva* and *rasa*) accomplish their status and function by dual interaction.

As the combination of spicy foodstuffs and vegetables lends the cooked food a distinct relishable taste (*svāduta*), in the same way the emotional states and sentiments lead each to the distinct level of an experience.

As from a seed a tree grows, and from the tree flower and fruit, so all the sentiments stand as the root; the emotional states have their settled position for the sake of (*tebhyāh*: i.e., for the purpose of manifesting) the sentiments.

Now we will expound the origin, colours, (presiding deities) and illustrations of these Rhetorical Sentiments. The sources of origin of these (Sentiments) are the four basic sentiments: these are as follows: the Erotic, the Furious, the Heroic and the Odious.

The Comic Sentiment becomes possible from the Erotic, and the Pathetic from the Furious; the origin of the Marvellous is from the Heroic, and of the Terrible from the Odious.

A mimicry or imitation of the Erotic is fittingly (*tu*) described as the Sentiment of Laughter. And the consequence of the Furious is to be known as the Pathetic Sentiment.

In the same way the consequence of the Heroic is properly described as the Marvellous. And the presentation of the Odious is to be known likewise as the Terrible.

Now the colours:

The Erotic Sentiment is light-green (*śyāma*); the Comic is described as white (*sita*); Pathetic is grey (*kapota*) and the

Fearful is described as red (*rakta*). The Heroic is to be known as yellow-red (*gaura*); the Terrible as black; the Odious on the contrary is blue (*rāla*) and the Marvellous is yellow.

Now the Deities:

The Erotic (Sentiment) has Viṣṇu as its presiding deity; the deity of the Comic is Pramatha; the deity of the Furious is Rudra; the Pathetic has Yama as its deity. The deity of the Odious is Mahākāla; the Terrible has Kāla as the god; the Heroic, the god Mahendra; the Marvellous has Brahma as its deity.

* * *

Bhāva

We shall now explain the emotional states (*Bhāvas*):

> One may ask here: why are the *bhāvas* so called? Are they so called because they exist, denote existence of things (*bhavanti*), or because they bring about the existence of something (*bhavayanti*)? We reply: The *bhāvas* bring about poetic contents (*kāvyārtha*) through words, physical gestures and movements and psycho-physical representations; hence, the name *bhāvas.*

'Bhu' is a root denoting instrumentation or causation (*kāraṇa*); it follows that *bhāvita* caused to be made, brought about, *vasita*, made to live, *kṛta*, caused to be made or produced, are synonyms. Such expression as the following is quite well-known even among common folk: 'Oh, all this is *bhāvita* (made to possess infused or pervaded) by this fragrance or juicy taste!' The meaning in such expressions is that of 'pervading'.

About this there are some traditional verses:

1. The content which is brought forth by the stimulants (*vibhāva*) becomes a matter of awareness (*gamyate*) to the spectators by the manifestation of the consequents (physical impacts produced, *anubhāva*) and by the concentrated acting modes (*sattva-abhinava*) of words and physical gestures: such content is given the name *bhāva* or emotional state.

2. The *bhāva* is so called as it brings about (reveals, *bhāvayan*) the inner idea of the poet and makes it pervade (*bhāvayan*) the mind of the spectator through the representation of words, physical gestures, colour or emotional expression of the face, and through the acting (*abhinaya*) which is the result of complete concentration and absorption (*sattva*).

* * *

Vibhāva

Now, why the term *Vibhāva*? This is answered (as follows): *Vibhāva* has the meaning of distinct, specific knowledge. *Vibhāva*, *kāraṇa* (cause), *nimitta* (instrument), *hetū* (reason) are synonyms. As words, physical gestures and the psycho-physical acting connected with the representation of stable and transitory mental states are specifically determined by this (*vibhāvyante*) it is therefore called *Vibhāva:* Determinant or Stimulant. So that, *vibhāvita* has the same meaning as *vijnāta* (clearly known, determined).

Here, there is a verse:

> As many matters based on verbal and physical acting are determined by this for the actor, and as many matters arising through the verbal and physical acting are distinctly comprehended by the spectator this causative, stimulating or determining factor is given the name *Vibhāva*.

* * *

Anubhāva

Now, wherefore the name *Anubhāva*? The reply is: by it the particular acting rendered through words, physical gestures and *sattva* is made to be felt (*anu-bhāvyate*) as an after-effect (*anu*) of the impact of the emotional stimulant.

There is a verse about this:

> Since the emotional content of art (*artha*) is made to be felt by the particular acting through words and physical gestures, the term *anubhāva* (consequents or physical reactions) is therefore used; it is

> connected with the flourish of hand-gestures (*sakha*) as well as the gestures of the major and minor limbs of the body.

[Tr. note: *sakha* is a technical term of *āṅgika abhinaya*: it denotes the flourish of hand-gestures . . . which an actor makes before reciting a particular dramatic speech.]

* * *

Emotional States and *Rasa*

The emotional States (*bhāvas*) are explained in this manner as connected with Determinants or Stimulants (*vibhāva*) and Consequents (*anubhāva*). These emotional states achieve their existence only thus. Therefore we shall explain the characteristics and examples of these emotional states connected with Determinants and Consequents.

In this connection the *Vibhāva* and the *Anubhāva* are quite familiar among the common people. Besides, as they closely follow human nature their characteristics are not defined; and this is for avoiding verbal prolixity.

There is however a verse in this connection:

> The wise should know that the *Vibhāva* and the *Anubhāva* are such matters in the art of acting as are actually created (*sam-siddha*) by human nature and as closely follow the ways of human nature and worldly conduct (*lokatraya*).

Now in the matter of emotional states, the Stable or Permanent mental states (*sthāyinah*) are eight and the Transitory states (*vyabhicārinah*) are thirty-two. There is a further separate group of eight psycho-physical states (*sāttvikah*). These forty-nine emotional states should thus be recognised as the causal factors for the artistic revelation (*abhivyakti*) of the poetic content (*kriya-rasa*: its charm and relish). From these arise the *rasas* by (i.e., when the presentation acquires) the quality of universality.

The verse in this connection is:

> The emotional state pertaining to the art-content (*artha*) which evokes a hearty communion is the source of *rasa*; by it the body is pervaded as dry wood is enveloped by fire.

A question is asked in this connection: If the *rasas* are turned out by the forty-nine emotional states which are connected with the content of poetic compositions and which are manifested or suggestively conveyed (*vyāñjita*) through the Stimulants and Consequents, and by the fact of the presentation acquiring the quality of universality, how is it that the Permanent mental states (*sthāyinah bhāvah*) alone are said to obtain the status of *Rasa* (aesthetic charm and relish)? This is to be said in reply: Just as some particular human beings, though they have common characteristics, similar hands, feet, bellies and bodies, and major and minor limbs common with everyone else, acquire the status of king on account of their excellence (*vilakṣaṇatva*) of birth or family, moral character, learning and skill in arts (*karma*) and crafts (*śilpa*), while there, among the human beings, others possessed of limited intellect become attendants of those very beings who attain kingship: in a similar manner the Determinants, Consequents and the Transitory states remain under the wing of the Permanent mental states. Being the shelter of many mental states, the Permanent mental states appear as masters. Like the men who become subordinate (*guṇabhuta*) to the human being who occupies the position of a master commanding them (*tadvatsthāniya-puruṣa*) the other emotional states take the shelter of the Permanent states by being subordinate to them (*guṇataya*) and on account of their (i.e., of the *Sthāyibhāvas*) excellence (*guṇataya*). The Permanent states attain the status of *Rasa*. The Transitory emotional states become their retinue.

One may ask: Is there any illustrative example? Yes. Just as the Lord of men, although surrounded by a retinue of many men, alone gets the name (king), and no one else however great he may be, in a similar manner the Permanent mental state surrounded by Stimulants, Consequents and Transitory states gets the name of *Rasa*.

There is a verse in this connection:

> Just as the king is great among men and the preceptor among the pupils, likewise among all emotional states, in the context of art (*iha*), the Permanent mental state is decidedly (*hi*) great.

Vyabhicārī-bhāvas

We will now explain the transient emotional states. One may ask here: wherefore are they called *vyabhicārīns*? It may be replied: *vi* and *abha* are two prepositions; *car* is a root employed in the sense of movement or motion. The *vyabhicārīns* are so called because they (the transient emotional states) move (*caranti*) prominently towards (*abhi: abhimukhyena*) creating the poetic sentiments in a variety of ways (*vi: vividham*). Equipped with the acting based on speech, body and concentrated mind, these lead or carry the spectator, in actual dramatic performance, to the poetic sentiments; hence they are called *vyabhicārīns.*

Here one may ask: how do they carry him? The reply is: this is a proven matter in the world. Just as when People say: 'The Sun carries this day or the constellation of stars', it is not meant by that statement that these are carried on arms or shoulders. However, this a well-known saying among the people of the world. Just as the Sun is supposed to carry the constellation of stars or the day, in the same way these *vyabhicārīns* should be understood to carry the sentiments and lead the spectators to them.

Sāttvika bhāvas

Here one may ask: are these states called *Sāttvika,* because others (like *Vibhāva, Anubhāva, Vyabhicārī*) are represented on the stage without *sattva*? The reply is as follows:

In the context of discussion *sattva* is something that originates in the mind. It is so called on account of the equipoised state of mind. When the mind attains perfect concentration *sattva* is produced. Now, whatever its nature, manifesting itself as horripilation, tears, loss of colour and the like, according to the association with a Particular emotional state, that cannot be represented by one whose mind is distracted. And *sattva* is desired for *nāṭya* as the latter imitates human nature.

Any example to illustrate this? Here the emotional states produced by the experience of happiness and misery are set in accordance with the theatrical conventions; they should be so rendered with pure *sattva* as to be identical with emotional states in real-life experience. Now sorrow or misery is in the main weeping; how could it be acted on the stage by one who is not sorrowful, and happiness which is mainly joy be acted by one who is not happy? This, in fact, is the actor's (*tasya*) *sattva*, engrossment or concentration of mind, that, whether he be really sorrowful and happy, he should be in a position to show tears and horripilation. Having regard to this aspect of stage presentation the emotional states are expounded *sāttvika bhāvas*.

These *sāttvika bhāvas*, which are substantially connected with different kinds of histrionic representation, are all to be included (lit., understood) in these poetic sentiments by the producers of plays. A poetic composition cannot ever be supposed to arise out of one sentiment only. Whether it is an Emotional State, a Sentiment, Dramatic Style or Local Usage (*pravṛtti*): when many of these are assembled together, the one which is represented in many ways should be considered as the dominating sentiment, the rest as transitory states.

... Those emotional states should be regarded as Transitory (*sancārībhāvah*) which move pointedly illuminating the dominating sentiment; they have reached stability (in the sentiment).

The *Bhāva* is to be presented through the single character of *Dhurta* or *Vita* and is to comprise his various conditions. The wise should always construct the *Bhana* as depicting varied activities but having only one act.

The entire character of *Bhana* has been explained by me as it has come down by tradition (*āgama*).

Now, O Brahmins, 1 will state in due order the whole character of *Vithi*.

Vithi

The *Vithi* should have one act; it has the character of all the sentiments and it comprises thirteen aspects (lit., limbs); it is to be acted by one or two characters; it may include three kinds of dramatic *prakṛti*, high, middling and low.

The thirteen limbs of the *Vithi* are stated as follows: *uddhatyaka, avalugita, avaspandita, nali, asat-pralāpa, vāk-keli, prapanca, mṛdava, adhibala, chala, trigata, vyahara, ganda.*

I have spoken about the *Vithi.* I will now explain the characteristics of these thirteen aspects.

When dramatic characters (lit., men) connect words, uttered out of due respect but not understood in their correct meaning, with other words not intended by the original speaker that is called *Uddhatyaka*: Thrust interpretation.

Something connected with another context serves to accomplish some other result, that is to be known as *Avalugita*: Transferred connection by the designers of drama.

When a certain matter (*artha*) which has been stated (*ākṣipta*) from which good or evil may arise unintentionally, is skilfully interpreted to give another meaning, that will be *Avaspandita*: Ominous suggestion.

When a riddle-like, enigmatic reply is followed by laughter, that is to be known as *Nalika* (or *Nali*: Riddle and laughter).

That is *Asat-pralāpa* (incoherent chatter) where the statement or question and the reply are both inconsistent, where the statement made by a learned man in the presence of fools, although beneficial, is not accepted.

In this representation (of *Vithi*), the *Vikheli* (Sportive speech, Repartee) is a single or twofold reply.

A statement which is untrue but which looks like mutual praise of two, which is intended in the interest of one of the two and which evokes laughter, will be *Prapanca*: Comic exposure.

* * *

Model Spectator

A person who can watch the dramatic performance with all his senses undistracted, is pure and honest, is expert in judging the pros and cons, who can ignore a fault, and lovingly appreciate merit is to be regarded as a spectator in a dramatic performance.

All those qualities can never be properly expected in every single spectator.

Since the topics of knowledge are unlimited, from among the mixed crowd in the assembly of spectators, whatever particular craft, costume, deed or action a person is familiar with, that, with reference to his own activity, he should try to witness and judge.

Men have different characters and natures. The drama is created in (i.e., on the basis of) human character as belonging to old and child like men and women, and of high, low and middling status.

Young men derive satisfaction in the representation of love, the learned in things based on some religious or philosophical principle, those intent on money, in wealth, and the passionless, in topics concerning spiritual salvation.

Brave men delight always in personal combat and armed fight (*ahava*) and thus in the representation of Heroic and Terrible sentiments; and the aged people in religious stories and *purāṇas*.

It is not possible for the low people to understand the actions and behaviour of exalted persons. The wise are always pleased with (the representation of) all matters of principle. Children, untutored men (*murkha*) and women are always pleased with things evoking laughter and with costumes, make-up and scenery (*nepathya*).

One who experiences delight (lit., satisfaction; *tuṣṭi*) when he sees the delightful, experiences sorrow when pathetic things are presented (*śoke*), anger in the presentation of anger, fear in fear, such a person is to be known as the ideal (lit., most superior) spectator. Thus, a person who is able to enter in the particular imitation (*anukaraṇa*, i.e., dramatic representation) of an emotional state, and is endowed with these qualities, is to be known as a 'spectator' of that particular presentation.

In the stage performance of the ten types of drama, the spectators are to be recognised in this manner.

Bharatamuni, from the Nāṭyaśāstra
translated by G.K. Bhatt

2

Tholkāppiyar

Tholkāppiyar, conventionally considered the author of the first Tamil grammar, is more a name used for historiographical convenience rather than the name of a person. The historical truth as well as the cultural importance of this personage are comparable to that of Vyāsa in the tradition of Sanskrit literature. It is the work, *Tholkāppiyam,* which has given its supposed author his name, Tholkāppiyar. One modern commentator, S. Ilakkuvanār, likes to fix the date of its composition as being somewhere between the sixth century BC to the tenth century BC. On the other hand, Kamil Zvelebil, another sympathetic commentator, likes to think of the text of the *Tholkāppiyam* in terms of a gradually growing body, which took, after the initial nucleus was formed, about eight centuries to acquire the final shape. In Zvelebil's account, the sections dealing with prosody and diction belong to the fourth to the fifth century AD. Probably, the latter account seems closer to the truth of the matter, for there are distinct echoes of the *rasa* theory of Bharata, together with the description of a *sahṛdaya rasika* in the *Tholkāppiyam.* What is important, of course, is not the comparative historical placement of it, but its place in the tradition of Tamil poetic literature and the Dravidian poetic sensibility. Unfortunately, it has not been available to students of literature outside Tamilnāḍu: the translations that have been attempted so far are either incomplete or inadequate. In this respect too, *Tholkāppiyam* vies with the *Nāṭyaśāstra.*

The main bulk of the *Tholkāppiyam* is concerning the descriptive linguistics of Tamil. The descriptive apparatus appears to be far too sophisticated to be neglected by any modern linguist. A small, but by no means insignificant, part of it is devoted to the discussion of styles, metres, diction, and poetic sentiments. Many of these chapters involve meticulous cataloguing of themes, locales, conventions and symbols. Leaving these aside, the most original contribution to the field of literary theory that the *Tholkāppiyam* makes is in developing the antithesis between the poetry dealing with the themes of the 'interior' and the poetry dealing with the themes of the external world. The corresponding terms used in the original are *Aham* and *Puṛam*. It is impossible to bring out the fascinating psychological insight and the intellectual sophistication displayed by the author of this theory, for want of a lucid English translation. However, the essay by A. K. Ramanujan included in the present volume, together with Kamil Zvelebil's *The Smile of Murugan: On Tamil Literature of South India*, (E.J. Brill, Leiden, 1973, pp. 131–154), will be found useful in understanding the intricacies of the founding text in Tamil poetics. It must be added immediately, however, that it is somewhat surprising that the *Tholkāppiyam* did not exert much influence on the prosody and diction of the three major languages that branched off from Tamil, namely, Kannada, Malayalam and Telugu. Yet, it is certain that it has a vital link with the *Nāṭyaśāstra*; perhaps, the two share a now missing common ancestor? At the present stage of our knowledge about India's literary past, one must inevitably stop at that question.

The translation used here is by S. Ilakkuvanār, from his *Tholkāppiyam in English with Critical Studies*, Kuṛaḷ Ṉeṛi Publishing House, Madurai, 1963.

Excerpts used are: *Ecca Iyal*, 397–409; *Ahaththiṇai Iyal*, 3–13 and 53–55; selections from *Puṛaththiṇai Iyal*, *Meyppāttu Iyal*, 249–259 & 275.

On Diction and Syntax

Words used in poetry are *Iyaṛcol*, *Thirisol*, *Thisaiccol* and *Vadasol*. Of them, the *lyaṛcol* words are those which are used in conformity with the usage of Tamil and without change in their meanings.

The *Thirisol* words are of two kinds which are synonyms and homonyms. *Thisaiccol* or the dialectal words are those which are spoken with their meanings unchanged in the twelve divisions of Tamil land where correct Tamil is in use. The words of Northern language, *Vadasol*, become fit to be used in Tamil when they adopt the Tamil phonetics discarding their northern ones. Even if they become deformed in usage to suit the Tamil phonetics, they are not excluded. The poets say that when those four kinds of words are used in construction of poetry, sonant may change into surd and vice versa, phoneme may be added or elided, and phoneme may be lengthened or shortened; these changes are inevitable. The scholars say that the syntax in poetry is of four kinds which are *Niral Niṛai*, *Suṇṇam*, *Adimaṛi* and *Moḷimaṛṛu*. Of them, *Niral Niṛai* is the mode in which the words stand in a group of verbs and nouns separately in such a way as to join the predicates or governing words to the subjects or the words governed in respective order. *Suṇṇam* is the mode in which two lines of eight *sir* (measured word) grammatically formed may split up and join in such a way as to express the proper meaning of poetry. *Adimari* is the mode in which the position of the lines may be altered without changing the place of the *sirs* (measured words) and the lines may exchange places. When knowing the meaning of the stanza it is not forbidden that the final *sir* of the last line of the stanza may be connected with the penultimate line of the stanza. The mode of *moḷimaṛṛu* is changing the position of words to bring out the correct meaning of the stanza and placing them before and after as need be.

... On examining the content of poetry, it is found, *Muthal, Karu* and *Uri* are the three which excel in order in the act of composing. Space and Time are said to be *Muthal* by scholars who know their nature. Forest World occupied by *Māyōn*, mountainous world occupied by *Seyon*, water-logged world occupied by *Veṇdhan*, sea-shore world occupied by *Varunan*, these are said to be *Mullai, Kuṛinji, Marutham* and *Neythal*, respectively. The rainy season and evening belong to *Mullai* and the cold season and midnight to *Kuṛinji*. The dewy season also belongs to *Kuṛinji*, say the scholars. The last hours of the night and the dawn belong to *Marutham* and the sunset to *Neythal*. The middle placed *thinai* is being thought of when the midday and summer occur jointly. The scholars say that the later part of snow-season also belongs to it. The scholars say that when two kinds of separation take place permanently it is suitable. The intermingling of *thinai* is not prevented. The intermingling of regions is not allowed—poets well versed in literature say so. Those other than *Uripporuḷ* may overlap.

> ... The poets say that the usage of poets which consists of imaginary usage and factual usage as found in day-to-day life will have *kali* and *paripādal* as the metre-forms (which are specially suitable for describing the love aspects). In the literature of five love-aspects belonging to *Aham* having people as objects, the name of any particular person finds no place. The mentioning of any particular person by name may take place in *Puṛam* only....

... *Vetci* is the *Puṛam* of *Kuṛinji*; it has fourteen divisions of dreadful nature ... *Vaṉji* is the *Puṛam* of *Mullai*. It is aimed at marching in advance to frighten and conquer the king who is greedy to have lands of others ... *Ulināi* is the *Puṛam* of *Marutham*. They say that to besiege a well-guarded fort and to have it conquered, is the feature of the theme of *Ulināi* ... *Thumbai* is the *Puṛam* of *Neythal*. It is the greatness of a king who comes to fight having the object of exhibiting his might ... *Vāhai* is the *Puṛam* of *Pālai*. It is said to be one which is to improve one's own avocation, with great distinction without being a hindrance to others ... *Kānji* is the *Puṛam* of *Peruñthinai*. It is the ephemeral nature of the world in all phases of life ... *Pādañ* is the *Puṛam* of *Kaikkiḷai*....

They say that thirty-two concepts, evolved out of plays, may be calculated into sixteen. They may be calculated into eight also. They say laughter, weeping, despisedness, wonder, fear, fortitude, anger and delight are the eight *meyppādus*. They say that laughter has reproach, youth, foolishness and feigned ignorance—these four, as its source.

Weeping has inferiority, loss, suffering and poverty—these four, as its source. Despisedness has agedness, illness, pain and weakness—these four, as its source. Fear has the objects of fear, beasts, thieves and the king—these four, as its source. The much praised fortitude has education, fearlessness, fame and sacrifice—these four, as its source. Anger, born of hatred, has cutting the limbs, conspiracy, inflicting injury and speaking ill—these four, as its source. The delight freed from trouble, has enjoyment of wealth, knowledge, intercourse, and plays and games—these four, as its source.

It is difficult to understand the significance of *meyppādu* for the people other than those who have the capacity of understanding well by means of eyes and ears.

Tholkāppiyar, from the Tholkāppiyam
translated by S. Ilakkuvanār

3

Bhartṛhari

The most impressive achievement of ancient Indian thinkers, perhaps, was in the field of linguistics. Pāṇini has already been universally recognised as a phenomenon in the history and development of linguistics. Following Pāṇini, there was a long and rich tradition of linguistics till the period of emergence of the modern Indian languages. In this post-Pāṇini tradition, probably the most memorable contribution was by Bhartṛhari. His opus, the *Vākyapadiya* is the earliest scientific work on syntax. Scientific rigour and precision are evident in his presentation of the concepts of *sphoṭa* and *dhvani* included here. The concept of *sphoṭa,* which formed the basis of Indian Semantics, was also to become the cornerstone of Śankara's Vedantic philosophy, for he perceived the relationship between the visible and the invisible universe in terms of *sphoṭa.* On a comparable scale, the concept of *dhvani* was used by literary critics and poets. Ānandavardhana's entire theory of poetry was based on Bhartṛhari's interpretation of the concept of meaning. Thus, Bhartṛhari's contribution to literary criticism, and to metaphysics which formed the context of the post-classical aesthetics, can hardly be overstated.

His work has attracted so much scholarly attention that the *Vākyapadiya* is one of the most-translated Sanskrit works. In recent years, Western philosophy too has started taking interest in Bhartṛhari's linguistics as may be evidenced from B. K. Matilal's publication. *The Word and The World* (OUP, 1991). The selection presented here is from the translation of *Vākyapadiya* by K. Raghavan Pillai (Motilal Banarsidass, 1971). It may be necessary to note for those readers who may not be familiar with the ancient Indian style of discursive writing that all philosophical texts had a two-tier system of presentation.

The main formulas were called *kārīkās* or *sutras* and the elaboration on them or a subsequent commentary was called *vritti*. Included here are only the *kārīkās* (44–132 from Cantos I and II) without their *vrittis*.

On Syntax and Meaning

Grammarians consider that there are two 'word-entities' in functional words; one, i.e., the *sphoṭa*, is the cause of the production of words and the other, the speech-sound, is used in connection with meanings. Some, among the teachers of old, considered that there was a difference in essence between these two. Others on the other hand speak of the same undivided entity being thought various, through a difference in conceiving it. Just as the light which is in the fire-stick acts as the cause for further lights, similarly the Word (*Om*) which is in the mind is the cause of speech-sounds. The Word is examined in the mind, is then fixed to a specific meaning and then through the instrumentality of the speech-sounds produced through their causes. The Word is neither a 'previous' nor 'a subsequent', because it is the speech-sounds which are produced in sequence.

But the non-sequential is revealed as sequential as if it were divided. Just as a reflection formed elsewhere appears, due to the activities of the water, to partake of the movements of the water, similar is the relationship between the Word and the speech-sound. Just as in perceptual knowledge, there can be seen both itself, i.e., the act of perceiving, and the object of knowledge, the thing perceived, so in the Word there appears the meaning-element and the formal element.

The inner principle called 'speech' which exists egg-like, evolving into speech-activity, assumes sequence through its parts. Just as a shape which is a copy of another shape, after it has become the object of a unified perception having been first received by the senses as a complex-pattern of parts, is then painted in stages on the canvas, so likewise there are seen in the comprehension of speech.

Just as the mind of the speaker first dwells on the words, and not on their parts when he wants to convey their meaning, similarly, the activity of the hearer first arises out of the words and not their parts in his attempt to understand their sense. When certain meanings are conveyed the forms which convey them, having thus become accessories to such meanings, and having their purpose thus fulfilled, they are not perceived as accessories to action, because they are uttered for the sake of another meaning. Just as light has two powers, namely, the power of being perceived and the power of causing perception of objects, similarly all words have these two distinct powers. Meaning is not understood from words which themselves have not become objects of the sense of hearing. Without being thus received, they do not express meaning by their mere existence. Therefore when the form of the uttered word is not clear, the question 'what did you say' is asked of the speaker. But the nature of the sense-faculties is not similarly grasped when an object has to be revealed by them. These two aspects of the word, analysed and comprehensed separately, act without opposition as causes of different effects. Just as the words '*vṛddhi*' and the like besides expressing their own form are also related to the sounds named by them ... so the word '*agni*' besides being related to the word '*agni*' (meaning fire) is also related to that referred to by the word '*agni*', namely the form *agni.* A word which is uttered in everyday use is never linked with grammatical operations. But its capacity to, that is, its own form as the meaning, is not obstructed. The word which is pronounced in ordinary speech being secondary since it is for the sake of the other, namely, the thing-meant, is not linked with grammatical operations, and hence we adopt the convention that the grammatical operations are attached to words which symbolise themselves. Whatever common attributes there exist in the object with which anything is compared and the thing which is compared to it, some attributes other than them also exist in the object to which the comparison is made. Whatever quality which is the cause of the excellence of an object is itself mentioned in the form of an object, its own excellence is caused by the qualities residing in it.

When a word (like '*agni*' in the Sutra *agnerḍhak*) which has its own form as its meaning is pronounced for conveying its form, then from that word is discriminated another word (namely, the word '*agni*' which has 'fire' as its meaning). Before being connected to the thing it means, a name is capable of genitive and nominative constructions, because it has as its own form as its meaning. The nominative is prescribed to a name because it is meaningful with its form as its meaning, and it is from the same meaning that the genitive construction in the form 'of it' arises. Some consider that in the Sutra '*svam rupam*' a name as a particular is meant; the universal attached to the particular undergoes grammatical operation. Others think that what is meant by the Sutra is a particular instance of the named, and that it is the class which is the name, and that in any given instance one finds only a particular, the understanding of which is brought about by the universal. Both among those who uphold the eternity theory of words, and those who hold that words are created, there are some who uphold its sameness in all instances of its occurrence. Again among the upholders of the doctrine that words are created there are those who uphold the plurality of words, i.e., that every occurrence of apparently the same word is really the occurrence of a different word.

(The doctrine of an opponent school is stated regarding the comparative reality of letters, words and sentences): Even when the word is a different word, the identity of the letters is not impaired; and in the same way in different sentences the same word is observed. Therefore the word does not exist as more than its letters; nor is there a sentence existing as more than letters and the words. (The grammarian's doctrine is given): Just as there are no parts in letters, there are no letters in the word. Nor is there any reality in abstracting the word from the sentence. People follow customary usage and talk of 'words' and 'letters' though basing their theories on different views and on this question what is considered as primary by one school is taken as an opposite way by others. People talk of difference of diction as belonging to the utterance of the Word, which itself is of undivided time, but appears to follow the time-pattern of the speech-sounds, in accordance with the differences in the causes of its being perceived. With regard to the short, long and prolated vowels, since a speech-unit is essentially timeless, and therefore fundamentally different from the speech-sound which reveals it, it is the time of the primary sound which is metaphorically considered as belonging to the speech-unit. It is however after the word has been revealed by the primary sound that the modified sounds are presented to the mind as distinctions of diction, and hence *a fortiori* the self of the Word is not divided into parts by them.

There are three views among those who held the theory that words are manifested: (1) the sounds act upon the sense-faculty; or (2) they act upon the word or, (3) they act upon both. The first theory would be analogous to the theory of sight-perception which held that only the sense-faculty of sight is acted upon, namely, by attention and application of ointment.The second theory would be analogous to a theory of smell-perception which held that only the thing (for instance, the earth) is acted upon in order that its smell might be received. According to the third theory, where however, the eye effects the reception of a cognition, it is clear that both the object and the sense-faculty are acted upon by the light; and speech-sounds operate in the same form. Certain theorists maintain that reception of the sound takes place without any separation of it from the form of the Word (*sphoṭa*); others hold that the sound is not perceptible. According to yet others it is an independent manifesting agent. Just as a chapter or a single verse is apprehended as a unit by means of saying over its component parts in order, but of course the book is not defined at each component part, so likewise the form of a word is apprehended as a unity when the word is revealed by the sound through the agency of causal factors which are appropriate to the cognition of the word, but which are not themselves as such apprehended. Simultaneously with the last sound, the word is apprehended by the mind in which the seed has been sown by the physical sounds, and in which ripening of the speech has been brought about by the telling over of the sounds. As far as the non-existent forms, which a hearer considers as existing in the interval before the complete word has been pronounced, are concerned, this is merely incapacity on the part of the hearer; they are in fact only means to the apprehension of the complete word. There is the semblance of distinction in cognition; similarly the attributing of distinctions on words is always seen. The word appears to be produced in stages and cognition seems to be dependent on the cognised. Just as earlier numbers in a series should be apprehended for the apprehension of subsequent ones, although the latter are different from the former, so is the apprehension of parts in a unit of speech an aid to the apprehension of the whole.

When in reality revealing units in the syllable, word and sentence function independently of each other, they appear to function in combination, although they are entirely different. Just as looking from a distance or in the dark, one at first misunderstands an object, and later on understands it otherwise in its true nature, similarly during the manifestation of the sentence by its causes, namely, the smaller units like letters and words, the mind first functions as comprehending the component units as real units. Just as there is a fixed sequence in the stages of the transformation of milk into curds and the seed into the tree, similarly there is a fixed sequence in the series of the hearer's perception of the intervening words, phrases, etc. And when they are made up of real parts, the difference in form is really due to the sequence of their sounds. And where words, etc., are considered as not made up of real parts the fancying of parts is a means to the realisation of the total unit.

It is considered by some that the Word is a universal suggested by a number of individuals and these individual speech-sounds, according to them, constitute the sound-pattern of the Word. Just as light reveals objects, the speech-sounds produced by their causes become the cause of the immutable Word. If the Word is revealed like this, does it not mean that it is not eternal? The answer is in the negative; Being revealed is not established as invariably pertaining to non-eternal things. Universals which are eternal are also considered to be revealed by those in which they inhere. In life only concrete objects are found to have relation to place and the like (for instance, time). And even accepting the alternative—that difference in place, etc., applies also to those that are not concrete objects—there is no such difference between the speech-sound and the word it reveals.

Just as there exists an inevitable competence of the revealed and the revealer between a perceiving sense-organ and the things it perceives, so does it exist between the word and the speech-sounds. And it is seen that in the case of various smells and the like which are perceived by the same sense-organ, there is a separate causal factor for each substance.... The object revealed partakes of the attributes of the reflecting medium. This is obvious in oil, water and the like. And surely, concrete objects of the type of mountains cannot have existence except as their reflections in stones, a mirror-surface and the like of incompatible size. Therefore the period of the speech-sounds and of their secondary variations in the form of diction is assigned to the syllable, word and sentence which are themselves without time-distinctions.

The definitions of *sphoṭa* and *dhvani* by another school are given:

The *sphoṭa* is that which is produced by the union and disunion of the speech-organs like the vocal cords. And *dhvanis* are sounds born of this *sphoṭa*. Whether the speech-sound is short or long, the measure of the word does not change. The subsequent sound, i.e., the modified speech-sound, which arises out of the primary speech-sounds is expanded or contracted in its form. Like light from a lamp, merely the speech sound undifferentiated as primary and modified is heard from a distance. But in the sound of a bell and the like the distinction is clearly noticed. The long and prolated sounds which are different from the short sounds are produced by the striking of the organs of speech. And the sounds which modify diction arise after the cessation of the movements of the organs. Another school holds that even before the vibrations of the speech-organs have subsided, other sounds are formed from the word as *sphoṭa* itself, as one flame from another.

Now regarding what constitutes the substance of speech: It is held by some that air, the atoms or consciousness become speech. There is an endless number of variant views in this matter. The air which is stirred by the speaker's effort following his desire to speak strikes the speech centres and produces speech. Even powerful objects are broken by air which possesses the attributes of speed and accumulation, blowing with the capacity to cause such breaking. The atoms, which unite and separate, transform themselves into shadows, light, and darkness and also into speech on account of their possessing all possible capacities, i.e., capacities to be transformed into all things. When their capacity is being revealed these atoms which are called speech, prompted by the effort of the speaker, collect together like clouds in the sky. Finally, regarding the consciousness theory: Again, the inner knower who exists in the subtle quintessential speech transforms himself into audible speech for the purpose of revealing his nature. It, taking the form of the mind and ripening in the fire of the stomach, enters the life-breath, and it is then uttered. The breath which has become the substratum of the mental principle is suffused with the mind's attributes and manifested after it passes through the fire of the stomach. Breaking up its inherent knots, i.e., its continuous currents, the breath reveals the syllables through different and distinct speech-sounds and merges into those syllables themselves. Yet another view about sound ... Sound, though it is ever existing, is not experienced because it is too subtle. It is realised through the appropriate causal factors just as air is through fanning.

The view of yet another school is that the powers of speech resident in the breath and in the mind undergo transformation into speech at the centres of speech-production and assume the distinctions of revealed speech. The power which is based on words controls this universe. This universe which has a single Intelligence its soul is perceived as manifold through the word as the eye. Since it is seen that distinctions between two things, for instance between a *ṣaḍja* and another musical note become clear when explained in words, therefore all manner of things are determined as being only understood through words. Those who are versed of the *Vedas* know that this Universe is the transformation of speech. It was out of the *Vedas* that this universe was first evolved. In this world the knowledge of the proper action entirely depends on speech. Even a boy has this knowledge of the proper action, having in him the accumulated experience of the past. That first movement of the organs of speech, the upward sending of the breath and its contact with the centres—these would not be possible but for verbal imagination in the child. In this world no comprehension is possible except as accompanied by speech. All knowledge shines as permeated by speech. If it is denied that the permanent stuff of knowledge is speech, then that light, namely knowledge, will not shine in the form of recollection. It is speech which makes recollection possible. It is speech which binds all branches of knowledge of arts and crafts. Everything, when it is produced, is classified through it. This speech exists within and outside all living beings. Consciousness can exist in all creatures only after it is preceded by speech. It is speech which prompts all mankind to activity. When it is gone, man, dumb, looks like a log of wood or a slab of stone. It is when the distinctions such as subject versus object obtain in the state of wakefulness that the agent functions in connection with an object. But when such distinctions do not obtain, in the state of sleep, speech itself remains in the form of an object.

Whether things are identified with the self, or with the Supreme, they become established in the form in which they are introduced by words. It is words which establish things. Even when the cause for verbal expression, i.e., an object, is entirely non-existent, descriptions of the forms of such a thing through words is found, as in the case of a circle made by a fire-brand. Further, speech which exists within the speaker as his self is said to be the great Bull, identity with which is desired. Therefore, attainment of faultless speech is the attainment of Brahman. He who knows the secret of its functioning enjoys the immortal Brahman.

Bhartṛhari, from the Vākyapadiya
translated by K. Raghavan Pillai

4

Daṇḍin

Daṇḍin's *Kāvyādarśa* is considered to be one of the very earliest texts in literary theory. Edwin Gerow argues in his critique of Sanskrit poetics that Daṇḍin is the pioneer of Sanskrit literary theory. The claim is difficult to establish, but cannot be brushed aside lightly. Whatever the chronological eminence, *Kāvyādarśa* is certainly an illuminating text, mainly on account of its clarity of exposition of the idea of *Alaṇkāra.* Daṇḍin's text offers a minutely detailed catalogue of the linguistic virtues of poetry, giving closely discussed illustrations for each type and sub-type of *Alaṇkāra.* It is impossible in the space available here to indicate how exhaustive his treatment of the subject is. The main contribution of Daṇḍin is the concept of *mārga-riti,* regional variations of poetic language, and the description of the *Gauḍa* and *Vaidarbha* varieties of literary diction. Another major contribution of his, which was later elaborated upon by Bhoja in the eleventh century, is the definition of epic poetry that Daṇḍin proposes. Sanskrit literature abounds in examples of epic and episodic poetry. Daṇḍin, therefore, did not have a single prescriptive idea of the epic. Apart from his comments on the subject matter and the hero of epic, he also comments on the structural principles of the genre, a unique achievement for him. In the selections presented here, I have used the translation of *Kāvyādarśa* by Vavilla Vénkateswara Sastralu (Madras, 1952). While the first two passages have been retained in their original form, the third passage is a closely edited version of the original translation.

Sarga-bandha: Epic Poetry

A *Sarga-bandha* is a *Mahā-kāvya.* Its characteristics are told here. Its beginning (mouth) or preface is either a blessing or a dedication or an indication of the contents.

It has its source either in a story told in the *Ithiāsas* or good (true) material. It deals with the fruit (or goal) of the four kinds (*Dharma, Artha,* K*āama* and *Moksha*). It has a great and generous person as the hero. It is embellished with descriptions of cities, oceans, hills, the seasons, the moonrise, the sunrise, of sports in the garden and of sports in the waters, of drinking scenes, of festivals, of enjoyment (love), of separation (of lovers), of (their) marriage and their nuptials and birth of princes, likewise of consultation with the ministers, of sending messengers or ambassadors, of journeys (royal progress), of war and the Hero's victories; dealing with these at length and being full of *Rasa* and *Bhāva* (flavour and suggestion): with *sargas* (chapters) which are not very lengthy and which are well formed with verse measures pleasing to the ear; everywhere dealing with a variety of topics (in each case ending each chapter in a different metre). Such a poem being well-embellished will be pleasing to the world at large and will survive several epochs (*kalpas*).

A poem does not become unacceptable even when some of these parts are wanting, if the structure of the parts incorporated in the poem is pleasing to those who know how to judge.

At first describing the hero by his good qualities and by that very description despising his enemies; this method is naturally beautiful.

After describing the lineage, prowess and scholarship etc., of even the enemy, depiction of the excellences of the hero by his victory over such an enemy is in our opinion also pleasing.

* * *

[On Regional Styles in Poetry]

. . . literature, the great men say, is divisible into four classes—*Samskritam*, *Prākritam*, *Apabhramśa*, and *Miśra*. *Samskritam* is the name of the celestial language which has been used by the great sages; *Prākritam* is divided into many ways as *Tadbhava*, *Tatsama* and *Deśi*. They consider the language pertaining to the *Māharāshtra* as the best *Prākritam*. In such language is the ocean of gem-like sayings, *Setubandha* and other works. Similar languages are Souraseni, Gouḍi, Lati and the rest. In discussions, these are treated as *Prākritam* itself. In poems, languages like the *Abhira* and the like are considered as *Apabhramśa*; but in the *Śāstras* (grammars) any language other than *Samskritam* is considered as Apabhramsical. *Sarga-bandha* and other such are *Samskritam*; *Skandha* and other such are *Prākritam*; *Asara* and other such are *Apabhramśa; Nāṭaka* and other such are *Miśrakam*. *Kathā* may be composed in all languages as well as in *Samskrit*; they say that the *Bṛhatkathā* which is in the *Bhuta* language is of wonderful merit. The twofold classification that *Prekṣārtham* and *Śrāvyam* is illustrated by *Lasya, Chalika* and *Śalya* and such like on the one hand and on the other hand by the rest. Manifold is the path of words. And their mutual distinctions are very fine; therefore these two alone—the path of *Vidarbha* and the path of *Gouḍa* are here described, as they have radical differences. *Śleṣa* (compact), *pasada* (clarity), *samatā* (evenness), *mādhuryam* (sweetness), *sukumārata* (elegance), *artha-vyakti* (expressiveness), *udāratvam* (excellence), *ojas* (vigour), *kānti* and *samādhi* (structure)—these ten characteristics are considered to belong to the *vidarbha* path. In the *Gouḍa* path, the opposite of these characteristics is often found.

* * *

[On *Alaṇkāra*]

They give the names of *alaṇkāras* to the characteristics which render *kāvyas* attractive. These characteristics are even today diversified anew; who then can treat of them exhaustively?

But the rudiments of these divergent characteristics have been indicated by the old masters. This our effort is merely to formulate those rudiments again.

Some *alaṇkāras* have already been mentioned by us for the purpose of distinguishing between the *mārgas* (schools). The entirety of the remaining *alaṇkāras* which are common to all the schools is now expounded.

The old masters have shown the following *alaṇkāras* (figures of speech): Realistic expression, simile, metaphor, light, repetition, objection, illustrative citation, differentiation, cause, terseness, hyperbole, conceit, reason, subtlety, minuteness, sequence, felicity, provoking sentiment, vigour, paraphrase, unison, sublimity, denial, paronomasia, speciality, equation, direct praise, concealed praise, conjunctive expression, exchanges, benediction, confusion and expressiveness.

Realistic expression, also called *jāti* or group description, is the first *alaṇkāra* and describes the actual forms of different conditions of objects ... it alone is supreme in the fields of sciences (*śāstras*), and it is desired even in literature (*kāvyas*).

Where any kind of similarity is felt in anything, that *alaṇkāra* is called simile ... Simile itself, where the difference is implicit, is called metaphor ... There are two classes of metaphors desired (by poets) which are known as metaphor stating similarity and metaphor stating contrast, because they indicate respectively the similarity and the contrast between the principal and the secondary objects ... If by remaining in one place, a word, indicating *jāti* (the genus), *kriyā* (action), *guṇa* (quality) or *dravya* (the subject matter), can help the entire sentence, then it is called *dīpakam* (light).

... The repetition in meaning, the repetition in word, the repetition in both—these three *alaṇkāra*s are desired in the place of *dīpakam*. *Ākṣepa* (or objection) is a statement of denial and according to the three divisions of time (past, present and future) it is divided three-fold; and again its variety is endless, if the difference in the objection is considered.... In desiring a certain object, the citation of another object which is capable of conveying the same meaning as the original object must be considered *arthāntara-nyāsa* or illustrative citation. When the similarity between two objects has been suggested or expressed in words, a statement of the difference between them is called *vyatireka* or differentiation ... Where, after denying the generally accepted causes, another cause is stated, whether that cause is stated as natural or whether it is attributed, then that *alaṇkāra* is called *vibhāvana* or attributed cause. Having in mind a certain object, the statement about another object which is similar to it is because of its making for terse expression called terseness in expression' or *samāsokti*.... Expression transgressing the limits of usage about a particular thing is *atiśayokti* or hyperbole.... When the condition or action of an animate or inanimate object is in a particular manner and it is fancied by the poet in a different manner, they call that figure of speech *Utprekṣā* or conceit. Reason (*hetū*) and subtlety and minuteness (*sukṣma* and *lesa*) constitute the best *alaṇkāras* of words; the *hetū* is twofold, *kāraka* and *jnāpaka* or causal reason and reason which helps to know ... Where the meaning is indicated by *ingita* or facial gesture and *ākāra* or the condition of the body then it is considered to be *sukṣma* or subtlety ... *Samkhyanam* or *Krama* or sequence is where the intended words follow in their proper order. It is also called *Yathāsamkhyām* ... *Preya* or felicity is felicitous expression and *Rasavant* (or provoking sentiment) where *Rasa* (sentiment) abounds; *Urjasvi* is where pride dominates or where vigour or excellence is appropriate. Without stating directly a particular meaning, for the accomplishment of that very meaning what is told is another manner is considered to be *Paryāyoktam* or paraphrase. When a person is about to commence a piece of work, he gets an additional ally for the accomplishment of that object by good fortune; that they say is *samahitam* or union. Wise men call that *alaṇkāra Udattam* or sublimity which expresses the pre-eminent greatness of a person either in the qualities of his heart or in his riches ... Where something is denied and another meaning is made clear, then it is *Apahnuti* or denial. *Sliṣtam* or paronomasia is defined as a group of words which have one form but many meanings ... When in the quality, genus, predicate etc., an alteration or variation is shown, that makes for the pointing out of its speciality and is known as *Viśeṣokti* or speciality ... That is considered *Tulyayogita* or equation where, for the sake of praising or blaming a thing, a statement is made making it equal with things possessing the particular quality pre-eminently ... Where opposed objects are mentioned together with a view to emphasise their specialities, then it is considered *Savirodha* or opposition. Where the praise of an object with which one is not concerned is made then it is *Aprastuta-Praśamsā* or indirect praise ... If there be praise in the form of despair, it is considered to be *Vyājastuti* or concealed praise; here virtues appear in the form of vices. Where a similar good or bad consequence is exhibited by connecting a thing with another object, then it is *Nidarśanam* or illustrative example. *Sahokti* is the statement conjunctively of the qualities and actions of things; where there is an exchange of things, that (figure of speech) is *Parivṛtti* or exchange. *Aish* or benediction is where the desired object is extolled ... Of the *alaṇkārasamsṛṣṭi* or confusion of *alaṇkāras* there are two modes to be seen: (1) where there is a relationship of part (*anga*) and whole (*angi*) between the *alaṇkāras* and (2) where there is no interdependence among the *alaṇkāras.*

Daṇḍin, from the Kāvyādarśa
translated by Vavilla Venkateswara Sastrulu

5

Ānandavardhana

The *Dhvanyāloka* of Ānandavardhana (eighth century AD) is, with Bharata's *Nāṭyaśāstra,* the most central theory of literature in Indian tradition. *Dhvanyāloka* itself is a huge compendium of poetry and poetic styles, which refers to numerous views, scholars and poetic texts, mostly by way of illustration. The theory proposed by Ānandavardhana is known by the name *Dhvani*, which means the suggestive quality of poetic language. He has the distinction of introducing in Sanskrit poetics the semantics of poetic language; but more important is the contribution in terms of turning the focus of critical discussion from the outward linguistic style and poetic embellishment to the more complex issue of linguistic structure in poetry. In Ānandavardhana's view it is this structure, which is the total effect of the suggestive quality of language, that distinguishes poetry from the ordinary usage of language. His theory, appropriately, exerted an abiding influence on the succeeding generations of theoreticians in India. Among those who attempted a re-statement of Ānandavardhana's views in one form or the other were Bhattanāyaka, Kuṇtaka, Mahimbhatta, Dhananjaya, Bhoja, Pratiharendurāja, Rājasekhara, Viśwanātha. In the twentieth century, Ānandavardhana's theory has found a new lease of life, mainly under the impact of Western stylistics and Structuralism. Critics like Krishna Rayan and C. D. Narasimhaiah have been very enthusiastic about the practical utility of the *Dhvani* theory in the context of modern Indian literature. Though Ānandavardhana has been a theoretician of such a crucial importance, a good translation of his work was not easily available until Prof. K. Krishnamoorthy published his critical edition with translations of the *Dhvanyāloka* (Karnataka University, Dharwar, 1974). The text included here is selected from this translation by bringing together in their proper sequential order the main principles (i.e., the *Kārikās*) propounded by Ānandavardhana.

Dhvani: Structure of Poetic Meaning

Though the learned men of yore have declared time and again that the soul of poetry is suggestion, some would aver its non-existence, some would regard it as something (logically) implied and some others would speak of its essence as lying beyond the scope of words. We propose, therefore, to explain its nature and bring delight to the hearts of perceptive critics.

That meaning which wins the admiration of refined critics is decided to be the soul of poetry. The 'explicit' and the 'implicit' are regarded as its two aspects.

Of these, the explicit is commonly known and it has been already set forth in many ways through figures of speech such as the simile by other writers; hence it need not be discussed here at length.

But the implicit aspect is quite different from this. In the words of first-rate poets it shines supreme and towers above the beauty of the striking external constituents even as charm in ladies.

That meaning alone is the soul of poetry; and so it was that, of yore, the sorrow of the First Poet (i.e., Vālmiki) at the separation of the curlew couple took the form of a distich.

The speech of first-rate poets streaming forth that sweet content reveals clearly their extraordinary genius which is as unearthly as it is ever bright.

It is not understood by a mere learning in grammar and in dictionary. It is understood only by those who have an insight into the true significance of poetry.

That meaning, and that rare word which possesses the power of conveying it, only these two deserve the careful scrutiny of a first-rate poet.

Just as a man interested in perceiving objects (in the dark) directs his efforts towards securing a lamp since it is a means to realise his end, so also does one who is ultimately interested in the suggested meaning proceed by first evincing interest in the conventional meaning.

Just as the purport of a sentence is grasped through the meaning of individual words, the knowledge of that sense is got at only through the medium of the explicit sense.

Though by its own power the word-import is responsible for conveying the sentence-import, just as it escapes notice once its purpose is served—So also that suggested meaning flashes suddenly across the truth-perceiving minds of perceptive critics when they turn away from the literal meaning.

That kind of poetry, wherein the (conventional) meaning renders itself secondary or the (conventional) word renders its meaning secondary and suggests the (intended or) implied meaning, is designated by the learned as *dhvani* or 'Suggestive Poetry'.

Suggestion does not bear identity with indication because there is a difference between the two.

Nor is this a differentia of that as both the fallacies of Too Wide and Too Narrow would result (if one were to hold such a view).

Only that word, which conveys a charm incapable of communication by any other expression and which is pregnant with suggestive force, becomes a fit instance for the title 'Suggestive'.

Words which signify by common usage meaning other than what they primarily denote, as for instance the word *lāvanya*, do not become instances of Suggestion.

If one gives up the primary denotative power of a word and understands a sense (secondarily conveyed by it) through its indicative power, it is because of a purpose. In conveying this purpose, the word does not move falteringly at all (as it moves falteringly when indicating a meaning secondarily).

The fact is that indication is grounded on the primary denotative force of words. How can it ever be a definition of suggestion whose sole support is suggestivity?

At the most, it might serve as pointer to one of the aspects of suggestion.

If one were to say that the definition of suggestion has already been propounded by others, it would only substantiate our own position.

II

'Merged in the other meaning' and 'Completely lost'—these are the two kinds of the expressed in 'Suggestion with intended literal import'.

The nature of suggestion 'with intended literal import' is also two-fold: (i) 'of discernible sequentiality' and (ii) 'of undiscernible sequentiality'.

Sentiment, emotion, the semblance of sentiment or mood and their (rise and) cessation etc., are all of 'undiscerned sequentiality'. It is decided that when we have the prominent presence of this variety, we are having the very soul of suggestion.

Only that, wherein all the several beautifiers of the expressed sense and the expression exist with the single purpose of conveying sentiment and so on, is to be regarded as coming under the scope of suggestion.

But if in a poem the chief purport of the sentence should relate to something else, and if sentiment and so on should come in only as auxiliaries to it, it is my opinion that sentiment and so on are figures of speech in such a poem.

Those which in here in this principal element are regarded as qualities. And figures are to be known as those that are associated with its parts even like ornaments such as the bracelet.

The Erotic indeed, is the sweetest and the most delectable of all sentiments.

The quality of sweetness is grounded securely on poetry which is full this sentiment.

In sentiments viz., Love-in-separation and the Pathetic, sweetness will be uppermost. It is so because the mind is moved very much in such instances Sentiments like the Furious are characterised by great exciting power in poetry. The quality of forcefulness is that which inheres in sound and sense which produce this effect.

That quality in poetry by which poetry throws itself open to the entry to the all sentiments may be taken as perspicuity. Its applicability is universal.

Defects like 'indelicacy' which have been shown to be impermanent (by the ancient writers) have been in fact illustrated as blemishes only with reference to the erotic sentiment when its nature is suggestion.

The sub-division of its parts and its own sub-divisions become endless indeed if one were to take into account their mutual permutations also.

Hence their broad indications only will be given here. But it should be enough to educate refined critics. Their minds will have received the light which would enable them to guess aright everywhere.

In none of the varieties of the principal erotic sentiment does alliteration become a source of suggestion since it involves great effort at achieving similarity.

Even if the poet should be an expert in the use of figures like assonance, his employment of them in the erotic sentiment which is of the nature of suggestion, and particularly in that love-in-separation, would amount only to a lapse on his part.

Only that is admitted as a figure of suggestive poetry whose employment is rendered possible just by the emotional suffusion of the poet and which does not require any other extra effort on his part.

The galaxy of figures like metaphor becomes truly significant (i.e. will be real ornaments) when they are employed with great discrimination in instances of the Erotic Sentiment which is intrinsic to *dhvani*.

The sole consideration that it is only a means to the delineation of sentiment and never an end in itself, the necessity of employing it at the right time and of abandoning it at the right time; the absence of over-enthusiasm on the poet's part in pressing it too far, and finally, his keen watchfulness in making sure that it remains a secondary element only—these are the various means by which figures like metaphor become accessories (of the suggested sentiment).

The other element of this suggestion manifests itself in the same way as resonance and the temporal sequentiality of the two meanings will be discernible.

It is also two-fold:—'that which is based on the power of the word' and 'that which is based on the power of sense'.

Only that instance wherein is present a figure that is not expressed directly by any word but conveyed solely by the suggestive power of the word itself, should be regarded as suggestion based on the power of the word.

The other variety of suggestion is based upon the power of sense and it is instanced in places where the second meaning is conveyed only by way of implication by the first meaning and not by the expressed words at all.

A context wherein even an idea suggested by the power of the word and sense is again expressed directly in so many words by the poet, will instance only a figure far removed from suggestion. The sense which suggests another sense is also two-fold: 1. Existing only in ornate expression and 2. Naturally existing.

Contexts where a new figure of speech is seen to result from the mere power of sense and is suggested in the form of resonance should be deemed as instances of another variety of suggestion.

It has been shown effectively (even by the ancient writers) that the assemblage of figures like metaphor though generally found to be expressed only, also become suggested quite often.

Even it there should be found a suggested figure, unless there is also a singleness of aim towards it on the part of the expressed, it cannot be considered as a mode of suggestion.

Those very figures which do not possess invariably even the capacity of forming the body of poetry when they appear in their expressed state, will be found to assume extraordinary beauty when they become participants of suggestion.

When figures are suggested only by the idea itself, they are invariably participants of suggestion; for the very procedure of poetry is dependent upon it.

If other figures are suggested they will become participants of suggestion in case the principal importance of the suggested is discernible in respect of extraordinary charm.

If an instance of the implied sense is such that it can be caught only with great difficulty or if it is only subordinate to the expressed sense, in either case, it will not be an instance of suggestion.

The usage of a word with faltering denotation either because of the poet's want of education or because of his lack of genius, should not be regarded by the learned as a way of suggestion.

The full definition of suggestion in all its varieties includes clarity of manifestation and principal importance of the suggested element.

III

Both the varieties of suggestion with unintended literal import and resonance-like suggestion are suggested by individual words and by whole sentences.

Suggestion with undiscerned sequentiality will flash forth in letter, word etc., sentence, composition, and finally the work as a whole.

The (Sanskrit) letters 's', and 'ş' letters conjunct with 'r' and 'dh'—all these become deterrents of the erotic sentiment. Hence those letters are not conducive to a particular sentiment.

When these very letters are employed in relation to the sentiment of disgust and so forth, they will only intensify them. Hence also letters suggest sentiments.

'Texture' is said to be of three kinds: (1) without compounds (2) with medium-sized compounds, and (3) with long compounds.

The propriety or decorum of the speaker and the spoken is the consideration which governs it.

Another consideration which governs the usage of a texture is its decorum with regard to the literary medium adopted. Texture thus becomes different in different forms of literature.

The consideration of decorum detailed above will also govern all prose works which are not governed by the rules of metre.

Texture with decorum in the delineation of sentiments will shine out wherever it might be found. It will, however, assume a shade of variation coupled with the decorum of literary medium.

Construction of only such a plot, either traditional or invented, as is charming with its decorum of (the accessories of sentiment, viz.,) stimuli of setting, abiding emotions, emotional response, and passing moods:

If, in a theme, adapted from a traditional source, the poet is faced with situations conflicting with the intended sentiment, his readiness to leave out such incidents and inventing in their place even imaginary incidents with a view to delineating the intended sentiment:

The construction of divisions and sub-divisions of the plot only with a view to delineating sentiments and not at all with a desire for mere conformity to rules of poetics:

Bringing about both the high tide of sentiment and its low ebb appropriately in the work; preserving the unity of the principal sentiment from beginning to end:

A discreet use of figures of speech even when the poet is capable of using them in any number;

Such are the conditions which underlie the suggestiveness of a whole work of literature in regard to sentiments, etc.

Of this suggestion, the variety which is of the form of resonance and which has been already illustrated is found often in entire works of literature also.

Case-terminations, conjugational terminations, number, relation, accidence, primary affixes, secondary affixes, and also compounds—all these become conveyers of suggestion with undiscerned sequentiality.

Whether it is the whole work or a single stanza, a good poet who is desirous of incorporating sentiments etc., in what he writes should take pains to avoid hindrances to them.

Sketching the setting etc., of an opposite sentiment, describing something whose connection with the subject on hand is only very remote.

Stopping the delineation of sentiment abruptly as also elaborating it when not required; over-elaborating it again and again though it has already received sufficient elaboration, and indecorum in respect of behaviour—all these hinder the course of sentiment.

After the intended leading sentiment has been established on a secure footing, there will be no defect in including even hindrances provided that these come either as foils or as ancillaries.

Though there is a convention that more than one sentiment should find a place in entire works of literature, one of them alone should be made principal by the poet who aims at greatness in his works.

The importance of an intended sentiment which is shining throughout the work abidingly cannot be marred by the inclusion of other sentiments.

Just as one plot is made to remain major in a work as a whole, so also one sentiment can be made to remain major and it will not at all lead to a discrepancy.

When a sentiment is delineated in a work as the principal one, no other sentiment, whether unopposed or opposed to it, should be treated elaborately. This will ensure one that no opposition between them will remain any more.

If a sentiment opposed to the principal one happens to occur in the same substratum as that of the latter itself, the opposed sentiment should be given a different substratum; (once this is done) there will be no defect even if it should be treated in full.

A sentiment which has no opposition due to the sameness of substratum but which becomes an opposite of another (i.e., principal) sentiment coming closely beside it should be so conveyed by the intelligent poet that a third sentiment will intervene between the conflicting ones.

By the intervention of another sentiment, even the opposition of two sentiments in the same sentence will disappear.

The opposition and non-opposition of sentiments should be clearly noticed in the above manner, particularly so in the Erotic sentiment, for it happens to be the most delicate of all (sentiments).

A good poet should be extremely careful so far as that sentiment is concerned. Otherwise, the slightest inattention (or lapse) on his part will appear glaring at once.

Either for the sake of winning the attention of people who deserve to be instructed or for the sake of endowing the work with unique charm, a touch of the opposite sentiments may be brought into the accessories of the Erotic sentiment. It will not then be a fault.

When a good poet composes his poem bearing in mind these concepts of non-opposition and opposition of sentiments etc., he shall never blunder.

The main task of a first-rate poet lies in a proper marshalling of all the contents and the expressions in the direction of sentiments etc.

Vṛttis (literally, Modes) are said to be of two kinds only because they relate to appropriate employment of senses and sound in keeping with sentiments, etc.

We can see another variety of poetry viz., poetry of subordinated suggestion, wherein the artistic excellence of the expressed is greater than that of the suggested, though the latter also happens to be present alongside of the former.

In all poetic compositions that look delightful by reason of their lucid and elegant words, only this variety of poetry should be recognised by the intelligent critic.

The whole host of figures is seen in many an instance to put on a new charm when it is brought into touch with the suggested element.

Even for such expressions of poets as are already adorned by figures, this shade of suggestion will be a most important ornament even as bashfulness will be for women.

Of course we see the communication of a new meaning by the agency of Ironic Tone. Even this will come within this variety of poetry so long as the suggested element happens to remain secondary.

Instances which can reasonably be brought under this class of poetry should not be classed under *dhvani* by refined critics.

This class of poetry viz., that with subordinated suggestion will also assume the form of *dhvani* or that with principal suggestion if one views it from the standpoint of exclusive purport of sentiments etc.

These two classes of poetry are decided thus on the principle of importance or unimportance of the suggested content. That which is other than both is given the name of Portrait (*Citra*).

Portrait-like poetry is also seen to be two-fold inasmuch as it is based either on word or on meaning. The first variety is word-portrait and the second meaning-portrait.

It shines in diverse ways with its several varieties of subordinated suggestion figures, its own sub-varieties, their inter mingling and collocation.

Such are some of the different ways of principal suggestion and some of the minor classes of the major ways. Who can ever count them exhaustively? We have just indicated therefore, their direction only.

Principal suggestion which we have defined hitherto should be attentively studied not only by all the poets who aspire after writing good poetry but also by all the critics who aspire after understanding it well.

Those who were unable to explain properly this essential principle of poetry as they had only a glimmer of it (and nothing more), have brought into vogue the theory of styles.

Once this theory of poetry is fully understood, even the so called 'Modes' relating to the nature of sounds as well as to the nature of meanings will become intelligible.

IV

By the ways of principal suggestion as also subordinated suggestion shown thus far, the quality of creative imagination in poets will assume endlessness

By a mere touch of even a single variety of suggestion (among the many that have been enumerated), the poet's expression will acquire novelty though it might perhaps embody only a trite idea.

The sentiments, etc., whose scope is very wide should be followed along the said course. The otherwise limited range of poetry has become so unlimited only because of their influence.

Even trite subjects in poetry will put on a new freshness if they get into touch with sentiment just as the same trees appear quite new with the advent of spring

Though several varieties of the suggested-suggester relationship are possible the poet should be most intent upon one of them in particular, viz., that relating to the delineation of sentiments etc.

So long as these varieties of principal and subordinate suggestion are utilised in a work and so long as the poet has the gift of creative imagination (in so utilising them), there can be no dearth of poetic themes.

Infinitude is achieved by the expressed content also even when it remains in its pure and natural state by reason of the considerations of circumstances, place, time, etc.

We find in plenty examples of utilising the expressed content with variations of circumstances etc. But it will shine out only in the association of sentiment if only the real nature of objects in the world, differing as it does according to place, time, and so on, is utilised in such a way that it is imbued with sentiment, emotion etc., and that it is in keeping with the demands of decorum.

Like the resources of primordial Nature herself, the infinite possibilities of poetic themes can never be drained off even by a million Brhaspatis composing with all their might simultaneously.

There are bound to be plenty of coincidences amongst great minds.

But all of them should not be regarded by the wise as being identical (in respect of plagiarism).

Coincidence means correspondence with another. It may be like that of a reflected image or like that of a painted picture or like that of two living persons resembling each other.

Of these, the first has no separate existence at all of its own; the existence of the second is no more than a non entity; while the third has a definite existence of its own. A poet need not reject such similarity in themes.

So long as there is a separate life of its own, even a poetic theme bearing a close correspondence to an earlier one will acquire exceeding beauty, just as the delightful face of a woman will appear exceedingly charming in spite of its strong resemblance to the moon.

Even when the already existing elements of poetic themes such as arrangements of letters etc. are utilised, it will certainly not smack of a flaw so long as the poetic theme as a whole is shining with novelty.

Whatever theme it might be, so long as it produces the impression in the minds of people: 'Yes, this is a lovely and unique flash'.

Though it might smack of earlier usages, a theme can very well be utilised by a good poet. He will never become an object of censure by so doing.

May words that appear (to critics) as full of manifold ideas and ambrosiac sentiments be freely spread out. Poets need have no compunctions in the flawless realm of their own.

The Goddess of Speech, Saraswati, herself will provide the desired ideas of a good poet whose mind is averse to borrowing the belongings of another.

Ānandavardhana, from the Dhvanyāloka
translated by K. Krishnamoorthy

6

Dhananjaya

Dhananjaya has received less attention than he deserves from students of literary theory in India. His special contribution cannot be appreciated in terms of his theoretical formulations in isolation from their cultural context. He is important because he happens to be the most notable opponent of Abhinavagupta's concept of *śāntarasa*. He was also an opponent of Ānandavardhana's *dhvani* theory, his argument being that aesthetic experience is a function of its reception, as Bharata had argued, rather than of the art-structure as Ānandavardhana had argued. The ruling passion of Dhananjaya's theoretical work was to return to Bharata as much as to return to his contemporary literary practices.

Dhananjaya's work is called the *Daśarūpa* since it discusses the ten types of drama known in his times. Bharata, some seven centuries before him, had intended to discuss the ten types as stated in the *Nātyaśāstra* (chapter 20, verses 1, 2). Dhananjaya accomplished that plan by presenting an exhaustive catalogue of drama, though he is more partial towards the *Nātak*-drama and *Prakaraṇ*-drama.

If one had to think of a single critical text within the Indian tradition devoted entirely to drama, one has to point to the *Daśarūpa*. It is exhaustive in its treatment of the subject. It is naturally a great help to historians of Sanskrit literature. Dhananjaya's work, together with that of his contemporary Rājasekhara, indicates that the theorists had the supporting branches of literary study, literary history and literary criticism, at their disposal. The details offered by him while building the network of definitions and descriptions in his compendium of drama presuppose a rich fund of critical and historical comment.

Daśarūpa started attracting the attention of Indologists from the nineteenth century: and in 1912 George Hass produced an impressive edition with translation of the *Daśarūpa*. The excerpts given here are from Hass's translation.

Definitions and Descriptions in Drama

CLASSIFICATION OF DRAMA

Dramas are classified according to subject-matter, Hero and Sentiment.

The Subject-matter (*vastu*) is twofold. The main is known as the Principal Subject (*ādhikārika*), the subordinate as the Incidental Subject (*prāsaṅgika*). The possession of the desired result is called *ādhikāra*, and its possessor is called *adhikārin*; that which contains an incident connected with him is called *ādhikārika* (Principal Subject). The Incidental Subject (*prāsaṅgika*) is a purpose of another person by means of which one's own purpose is incidentally furthered. When it is continuous it is called Episode (*patākā*, lit., 'banner'); when of short duration, Episodical Incident (*prakarī*). An indication by the mention of something extraneous, of a matter that is begun or is about to happen is called an Episodical Indication (*patākāsthānaka*), which is characterised by similar situations or attributes. This is also threefold, owing to a threefold classification into legendary, invented, and mixed subjects. The legendary variety of subject-matter is derived from legends of the past and the like; the invented is devised by the poet; the mixed arises from a combination of these two in accordance with a classification into gods, mortals, and the like.

ELEMENTS OF THE PLOT

The Denouement (*kārya*) of the action consists of one of the three objects of human existence (*trivarga*); it is either simple or connected with one or both of the other objects. The cause of this Denouement is the Germ (*bīja*), at first manifested as very small, but expanding in manifold ways as the action proceeds. when the secondary matter of the drama interrupted, the cause of its being resumed (*accheda-kāraṇa*) is the Expansion (*bindu*). The elements designated as the Germ (*bīja*), the Expansion (*bindu*), the so-called Episode (*patākā*), the Episodical Incident (*prakarī*), and the Denouement (*kārya*)—these are declared to be the five Elements of the Plot (*arthaprakṛti*).

THE FIVE STAGES OF THE ACTION

There are five stages of the action which is set on foot by those that strive after a result: Beginning (*ārambha*), Effort (*yatna* = *prayatna*), Prospect of Success (*prāptyāśā*), Certainty of Success (*niyatāpti*), and Attainment of the Result (*phalāgama* = *phatayoga*). Beginning (*ārambha*) is mere eagerness for the obtaining of the more important result. Effort (*prayatna*) is exertion attended with great haste, when this result has not been obtained. Prospect of Success (*prāptyāśā*) is the possibility of succeeding, with mean at hand, but also with fear of failure certainty of success (*niyatāpti*) is the assurance of succeeding because of the absence of risk. Attainment of the Result (*phalayoga*) is the accomplishment of the entire result, as previously mentioned.

THE FIVE JUNCTURES

There are five Elements of the plot (*arthaprakṛti*), parallel with the five Stages (*avasthā*) of the action; from these respectively arise the five Junctures (*samdhi*), beginning with the opening (*mukha*). Juncture (*samdhi*) is the connection of one thing with a different one, when there is a single sequence of events. The five Junctures are: the Opening (*mukha*), the Progression (*pratimukha*), the Development (*garbha*), the Pause (*avamarśa*), and the Conclusion (*upasaṃhṛti* = *nirvahaṇa*). The Opening (*mukha*) is the origination of the Germ (*bīja*), giving rise to various purposes and Sentiments; it has twelve subdivisions, because of its connection with the Germ and the Beginning (*ārambha*).

The twelve subdivisions of the Opening are: Suggestion (*upakṣepa*) Enlargement (*parikara*), Establishment (*parinyāsa*),

Allurement (*vilobhana*), Resolve (*yukti*), Success (*prāpti*), Settling (*samādhāna*), Conflict of Feelings (*vidhāna*), Surprise (*paribhāvanā*), Disclosure (*udbheda*), Incitement (*bheda*), and Activity (*karaṇa*).

[These verses are followed by Dhananjaya's definitions of each of the above twelve types of the Opening.]

CHARACTERISTICS OF THE HERO

The Hero should be well-bred, charming, liberal, clever, affable, popular, upright, eloquent, of exalted lineage, resolute, and young; endowed with intelligence, energy, memory, wisdom, skill in the arts, and pride; heroic, mighty, vigorous, familiar with the codes, and a just observer of laws.

THE FOUR TYPES OF HERO

... the Hero is of four kinds, being light-hearted (*lalita*), calm (*śānta*), exalted (*udātta*), or vehement (*uddhata*). The self-controlled and light-hearted Hero (*dhīralalita*) is free from anxiety, fond of the arts, happy, and gentle. The self-controlled and calm Hero (*dhiraśānta*) is a Brahman or the like, possessed of the generic merits of a hero. The self-controlled and exalted Hero (*dhīrodātta*) is of great excellence, exceedingly serious, forbearing, not boastful, resolute, with self-assertion suppressed, and firm of purpose. The self-controlled and vehement Hero (*dhīroddhata*) is altogether dominated by pride and jealousy, wholly devoted to magic practices, and deceit, self-assertive, fickle, irascible, and boastful.

THE HERO AS LOVER

When he has been captivated by another woman, the Hero may be (act) clever (*dakṣiṇa*), deceitful (*śatha*), or shameless (*dḥṛṣṭa*) towards his previous love. A clever Hero (*dakṣiṇa*) is one that is kind to his previous love. A deceitful Hero (*śaṭha*)is one that hides the unfaithfulness. A shameless Hero (*dḥṛṣṭa*) is one that lets the disfigurements on his body show. A faithful Hero (*anukula*) is one that has only a single lady-love.

COMPANIONS OF THE HERO

The Hero of the Episode (*patākā*) is a separate person called Attendant (*pithamarda*), intelligent, assisting him, i.e., the principal Hero, devoted to him, and possessed of his qualities in a lesser degree. Another companion is the parasite (*vita*), who has but a single accomplishment, and the Jester (*vidūṣaka*), who is the fun maker.

THE OPPONENT OF THE HERO

The opponent of the Hero is avaricious, self-controlled and vehement, stubborn, criminal and vicious.

SELECTION OF THE PRINCIPAL SUBJECT

In a play in which the Hero is endowed with attractive qualities of the type known as self-controlled and exalted (*dhīrodātta*), glorious, eager for fame, of great energy, a preserver of three vedas (*trayi*), a ruler of the world, of renowned lineage, a royal seer or a god—in that the incident for which he is renowned is to be made the Principal Subject (*ādhikārika*).

ADAPTATION OF THE STORY

Whatever in it, i.e., in the original story, is at all unsuited to the hero or inconsistent with the Sentiment is to be omitted or arranged in some other way. After determining upon the beginning and end of the play in this manner and after dividing it into five parts, the author should furthermore break up into small sections the division called Junctures (*saṃdhi*). The subdivisions should be sixty-four in number. In like manner, moreover, one should divide the incidents of the Episode (*patākā*), which should have one or more sub-junctures (*anusaṃḍhi*) less than the principal subject.... one should insert the Episodical Incident (*prakarī*) without any Juncture. At the beginning of the play one should put an Explanatory Scene or an Act, according to the Appropriateness of the action when after omitting an extensive part of the subject-matter that is required, but is without Sentiment, one wishes to present the rest, then one should put an Explanatory Scene (*viṣkambhaka*) at the beginning.

When, on the other hand, the subject-matter proceeds with sentiment right from the start, then there should be at the beginning an Act following up the hints given in the Introduction. An Act visibly represents the doings of the Hero, is attended with inherence of the Expansion, and is based on the purposes, contrivances, and Sentiments of various kinds.

The principal Sentiment (*aṅgin*) is to be furthered by means of the consequents (*anubhāva*), the Determinants (*vibhāva*), the permanent State (*sthāyin*), and the Transitory States (*vyabhicārin*), taken up and dropped in turn. One should not make the Subject-matter too disconnected by the excessive use of Sentiment, nor should one overwhelm the Sentiment with matters relating to the Subject matter or its embellishment. One Sentiment, either the Heroic or the Erotic, is to be made the principal Sentiment; all the other Sentiments should be made subordinate. The Marvelous Sentiment should be employed only in the Conclusion.

SENTIMENT AND ITS PRODUCTION

Sentiment (*rasa*) results when a permanent State produces a pleasurable sensation through the operation of the Determinants, the consequents, the Involuntary states, and the Transitory states. Among these a Determinant (*vibhāva*) is that which causes the development of the States by its being recognised. Determinants are of two kinds, being divided into Fundamental Determinants (*ālambana*) and Excitant Determinants (*uddipana*). A Consequent (*anubhāva*), on the other hand, is an external manifestation that serves to indicate a feeling.... A State (*bhāva*) which is brought about by emotional states such as pleasure and pain, is the realisation of such states. The Involuntary States (*bhāva sāttvika = sattvabhāva*) are separate, for, although in the category of Consequents, they are different from these just because of their arising from the inner nature (*sattva*); and this is the reason for the realization of such states. The eight Involuntary states are: Paralysis (*stambha*), Fainting (*pralaya*), Horripilation (*romāñca*), Sweating (*sveda*), Change of Colour (*vaivarṅya*), Trembling (*vepathu*), Weeping (*aśru*), and

Change of Voice (*vaisvarya*) . . . The Transitory States are those that especially accompany the Permanent State in cooperation, emerging from it and again being submerged in it, like the waves in the ocean.

Dhananjaya, from the Daśarūpa
translated by George Hass

7

Kuntaka

Kuntaka is known as the originator of the *vakrokti* school of Sanskrit literary theory. Historically, he occupies a place between Ānandavardhana of the ninth century and Abhinavagupta of the later tenth century. These dates indicate that Kuntaka lived at a time when literary criticism in India was acquiring great sophistication. Among his other able contemporaries were Dhananjaya and Rājasekhara. Considering the presence of these literary geniuses in his generation, the originality of Kuntaka critical persuasions acquires a special significance. *Vakrokti* and *Alaṇkāra* are the two schools of Sanskrit criticism which come very close in spirit to twentieth century's Western Formalism and New Criticism.

Vakrokti is a theory of poetry which perceives poetry essentially in terms of the language of its expression. It sees the poetic language as language of metaphor and suggestive communication. It is amazing to see how much Kuntaka (and his contemporary critics) knew about the language of poetry, and the sophistication and rigour of logic and argument in his writing.

The text reproduced here is from K. Krishnamoorthy's translation of the *Vakrokti-Jivita* (Karnataka University Press, 1977). Only the main points of Kuntaka argument, the *kārikās*, have been included, without giving the elaborations of these points—the *vrttis*. For a commentary on the concept of *Vakrokti* refer to Krishnamoorthy's *Sanskrit Poetics: An Overview* in this volume.

Language of Poetry and Metaphor

My salutations to the goddess of speech, the dancer on the stage, of the moonlike face of master-poets, and giving a brilliant and beautiful performance with gestures, artful turns of speech.

In order to set forth the nature of beauty conducive to extraordinary delight, a fresh study of poetry is offered here, like an added ornament to it.

A poetic composition created with an eye to beauty is not only a means for the inculcation of values like righteousness, but also a delight to the hearts of the elite.

Participants in the affairs of life can come to appreciate the beauty of life-activity in a new light, viz., an appropriate pattern imposed by the poet, only by means of good poetry.

Apart from the enjoyment of the benefits of the four-fold values, there is the immediate sense of delight produced in the reader as a result of his enjoying the nectar of poetry.

The 'adornment' and the 'adorned' are distinguished artificially for the purposes of our enquiry, because this would be the only means to attain the ultimate goal. The truth of the matter, however, remains that the two together constitute poetry.

Poetry is that word and sense together enshrined in a style revealing the artistic creativity of the poet on the one hand and giving delight to the man of taste on the other.

That 'meaning' is what is signified, and 'word' is that which signifies, is so well known that it needs no elaboration. Yet, in the province of poetry, their true nature is as follows:

That unique expression which alone can fully convey the poet's intended meaning out of a hundred alternatives before him is to be regarded as 'word'. Similarly, that alone which possesses such refreshing natural beauty as to draw the appreciation of delighted readers is to be reckoned as 'meaning'.

Both these are 'adorned'. Their adornment consists in the poetic process known as 'artistic turn of speech'.

For those rhetoricians who hold that 'natural description' is an ornament, what on earth remains for being ornamented?

It is impossible to state anything except in terms of its nature. An object without it is tantamount to a nonexistent idea.

If the body itself should be reckoned as ornament, what would be the other thing which it can adorn at all? Never does one climb upon one's own shoulder.

In the event of nature-description itself being regarded as an ornament, when another ornament is also added, the question arises whether the distinction between the two is manifest or unmanifest.

If manifest, there should be only 'separable union of figures', and if unmanifest only 'inseparable union of figures' everywhere. There should be no scope at all for the remaining figures of speech.

When it is so obvious that word and meaning are ever experienced jointly, what is the special import of mentioning it (in the definition)?

The *sāhitya* or mutual coherence between word and meaning in respect of beauty is nothing but a unique poetic usage, involving neither more nor less than the exact form of word and meaning required to make the whole beautiful.

Art in the poetic process is divisible into six categories. Each one of them may have numerous subdivisions, every subdivision striking one by a new shade of beauty.

Art in the arrangement of syllables, art in the base form of substantives, and also art in their inflection forms.

And art in a whole sentence admits of a thousand varieties. In it is included the whole lot of figures of speech.

The beauty of section and the 'beauty of work' will be treated now under the two heads, 'natural' and 'artificial', both yielding artistic delight.

Diction is the name given to the art of sentence-construction which is congenial to heighten inner and outer charm of both 'meaning' and 'word' and which is at the same time a partaker of the poetic process.

The quality delighting men of taste is something over and above the three elements so far considered, namely, 'meaning', 'word' and 'artful expression'. It has a unique beauty of unfailing appeal.

There are three styles which serve poets as high-roads. They are: (1) 'the element', (2) 'the brilliant' and (3) 'the mixed'.

> That charming style where fresh words and meanings both blossom forth by virtue of the poet's undimmed imagination,

> where ornaments are few and yet lovely as they come in without efforts;
> where studious technical skill is superseded by the prominence given to the inner nature of things, where beauty is felt due to sympathy by men of taste who are experts in enjoying sentiments, etc.;
> where the beauty is such that it eludes the critic's power of analysis, where the wealth of beauty reminds one of the supreme artistic creation of the universe by the Creator himself;
> wherein every element of beauty is a result of the poet's imagination alone and succeeds in conveying flashes of gentle grace;
> such is the style called 'the elegant' which master-poets follow like bees roving along the grove of full blown blossoms.

The first and the foremost excellence of the 'elegant' style is sweetness. It is vivified by the use of expressions which are lovely inasmuch as they are uncompounded.

The excellence called 'perspicuity' is that which brings out the poet's intent without any effort on the reader's part, which conveys the meaning in an instant as it were, and which is concerned with sentiments and artful speech.

When even a little beauty in respect of alliterative syllables and in the choice of diction results in the charm of syntax and contributes to the strikingness of style, we have the excellence called 'grace'.

That which is smooth on the ear, and capable as it were of intimate embrace by thought and which is a naturally sparkling shade of loveliness, is spoken of as having the excellence called classicality.

> Wherein artistic beauty appears to be radiating brilliantly from within, in respect of both word and meaning, even at the time of the first manifestation of the creative imagination;
> wherein poets pile up tropes upon tropes without a sense of satisfaction, like necklaces inlaid with gems;

> just as the ornaments dazzling with lustrous beams of gems conceal a beloved's body and produce beauty;
> so also, wherein the 'adorned' is made to acquire brilliance by virtue of the tropes brilliant in themselves and reflecting it through their own excessive beauty;
> wherein even a trite subject is raised to a unique height of excellence merely by dint of artistic expression;
> wherein everything is made to acquire altogether new features at his sweet pleasure by a master-poet in his vision by the power of his inventive genius;
> wherein, further, the intended purport of the whole is communicated by a suggestive use of language which is distinct from the two well-known uses, viz., the communicative use of meanings and the denotative use of words;
> wherein the real nature of things pregnant with sentiments is augmented with a novel beauty which is unique;
> that style, whose life-breath is, verily, artistic beauty of expression, is termed the 'brilliant'. An element of imaginative flight or exaggeration will be invariably striking in it.

Such is the extremely impassable way trodden by learned poets. It is just like the path of sword-blades traversed by the cherished desires of brave warriors.

In this style a verbal 'sweetness' is maintained which is conducive to artistic brilliance. Relieved of loose texture, it becomes a means of producing compact beauty in diction.

The perspicuity contained in this style is nothing but the use of uncompounded expressions which is well known in the tradition of poets, but which mostly assumes a touch, however slight, of 'floridity'.

When in a sentence other sentences are made to fuse with a coherence usually possible only in the case of the constituent words, we have another variety of perspicuity'. By words without elision of the final aspirates and in euphonic combination with each other, and by syllables which precede conjuncts, 'grace' is enriched.

'Classicality' in this style is a product of great artistic skill. Neither too tender nor too harsh, it wins the heart all the same.

> Wherein the two styles, viz., the 'elegant' with its natural beauty and the 'brilliant' with its decorative effect both come to be blended,
> where the whole host of qualities like 'sweetness' become grounded on the 'middling' mode of style so as to nourish a unique stylistic effect,
> we get a third style, pleasing all tastes, and containing the best of both the other styles in competition as it were, which may be termed 'middling'.

It is this style which fascinates a class of fastidious poets who are fond of mixed variety in their art, like men-about-town, who are fond of fashionable dress.

That quality is known as 'propriety' by virtue of which the poetic subject gains in value in a most lucid manner; in fact it may be regarded as the vital essence of all poetic description.

An instance, wherein the matter on hand is concealed as it were by reason of the exquisitely charming nature of either the speaker or the listener, also deserves being regarded as an example of 'propriety'.

In the wide-ranging material before the poet, that which is pitched upon by the genius of the poet for its activity endows the whole with the quality of 'splendour'.

It is something attained by the full co-operation of all the constituent elements and it is something which surely results in an extra-ordinary aesthetic effect in the mind of connoisseurs; in short it is the whole and sole essence of poetry.

These twin literary qualities, very appealing in all the three styles permeate every element of poetry like word, sentence and the work as a whole.

Such are the three styles perfected only by a few poets in their earnest quest after perfection, after long, assiduous practice. The attainment of even a modest grounding in them has brought great reputation to them. Hereafter will be taken up for treatment the nature and scope of that unique and charming word-usage which is at once a happy sporting ground for all good poets and also an index of good taste.

II

One, two or more syllables used again and again at short intervals constitute the three forms of 'art in the arrangement of syllables'.

And consonants classified (i.e., 'ka' to 'ma' 25 in number) might combine with their nasals in alliteration; 'ta', 'la', 'na' etc. might be doubled and reiterated; or the rest might become conjunct with 'ra' etc., in alliteration. These also will shine by their harmony with the theme.

Sometimes alliteration without any interval too, employed artistically by the poet, contributes to high poetic charm because of variation in vowels.

When alliteration is effected without extra effort, when it is adorned with syllables which are not harsh, when it becomes appealing by discontinuance of earlier sound repetitions and by new choices for reiteration.

This alliterative art which directly exploits the beauty of syllables is seen to serve the cause of 'qualities' as well as 'styles' too; and it is this again which is meant by the ancients when they use the expression 'beauty of literary mode' (*vṛttivaicitrya*).

Rhyme (*yamaka*) is a special type of it which consists in words of similar sound with different meaning, perspicuous and pleasing to the ear, and endowed with decorum, and which shines in specific places of the verse such as the beginning. Since its beauty is not of a different kind, it is not treated here at length.

When common denotation of words is seen to expand to include connotation of even impossible attributes imagined by the poet, or to include a hyperbolic excess of even an existing attribute as a result of the poet's intent to shower extraordinary belittlement or extraordinary glorification of the theme, we get what is called 'art in beautifying conventional sense'.

> The use of a synonym which approximates most to the meaning intended, which can add to the beauty of meaning considerably, which can embellish the meaning by itself or its epithets coming to assume other shades of figurative body;
> which by itself, contributes to a new lease of excellence, which hints at a meaning having almost inconceivable elements;
> which contains embellishing figurative elements conducive to beauty, comes to be termed a 'superior art in the use of synonyms'.

Wherein even when the two are far from each other, a common attribute, however slight, is metaphorically superimposed in order to indicate that the resemblance is very close . . .

. . . and which forms the basis for various pleasing and inventive figures headed by metaphor—such a type of poetic beauty is designated by the name 'beauty of metaphorical expression'.

If, as a result of the excellence of the epithet, beauty is added to the verb or the noun (in a sentence), it is to be classed as 'beauty in epithet'.

In order to achieve excellence of expression, when the subject of description is screened as it were by the use of pronouns and so forth, we have what is designated as 'beauty of concealment'.

The affix in the middle of a word often adds to the beauty of decorum in the subject described, by virtue of its own excellence. This may be regarded as another type of poetic beauty.

Beauty of augment and so forth contributes a new charm to style by making for a striking originality in respect of composition.

A usage where beauty of word-forms such as adverbial compounds shines forth may be deemed as an instance of beauty of '*vṛtti*'.

An example wherein an activity yet to be accomplished is described as already accomplished, illustrates 'beauty of *bhāva*'.

When two words in different genders are used to signify an identical object, a new kind of beauty will emerge which we may characterise as beauty of gender.

Even when other genders could be used, if the feminine is preferred, it contributes to beauty; since even the name of a woman is pleasing.

Although other genders are possible, when a specific gender is significantly used by a poet in harmony with the idea to be conveyed and this contributes to beauty, we have another form of this type.

Extreme capability of the subject, superiority to another subject who could perform the same action, a significant qualification of the action itself, beauty of metaphorical superimposition and concealment of the direct object etc.—these five which add charm to the idea described are regarded as the five forms of beauty in action.

When there is remarkable beauty due to the utmost propriety of time described, we have what is called 'beauty in the speciality of time'.

Treatment of one and all auxiliary 'instruments of action' as if they were pre-eminent by superimposing primacy on them and reducing the status of the really pre-eminent into that of an auxiliary so that some special shade of charm is infused into the artful poetic expression—a treatment which thus involves a reversal of status in 'instruments of action'—comes to be designated by the phrase 'beauty of instruments of action'.

When poets intent on achieving special poetic charm resort to transposition of numbers, we have what is known as 'oblique beauty of number'.

When the (grammatical) first person or second person is required logically, instead of using it, the third person is used obliquely in order to gain poetic beauty, it should be regarded as 'oblique beauty of person'.

When both the *Atmane-* and *Parasmai-pada* affixes are possible for a root, if a poet is seen preferring the one as against the other because of an aesthetic purpose, that may be designated as arresting beauty of *'upagraha'* or verb-affix.

Apart from the usual affix, when a new affix is superadded with an eye to striking beauty, it constitutes 'unique beauty of affix'.

In a poem where the preposition and indeclinables are employed only to suggest *rasas* as the sole essence of a poem as a whole, we have what may be called another type of 'word-beauty'.

When several forms of such literary turns occur together in such a way as to enhance the beauty of one another, they go to produce artistic charm reminiscent of myriad-faceted beauty.

Poetic speech is a veritable creeper, with words as leaves, forming the bases for (symmetrical) beauty striking with artistic turn adding to the wealth of feelings and sentiments in a most striking manner. May the bee-like connoisseurs appreciate it and collect the profusely fragrant and sweet honey, from the sentence-blossoms, and enjoy it with ever-increasing zest.

III

When the subject-matter is described in a way conducive to beauty by virtue of its own infinite natural charm and by means of exclusive artistic expressions, we may take it as an instance of creative beauty relating to content.

There is also another kind of artistic beauty. It glows with the natural as well as the acquired skills of the poet. It results in imaginative original creations which are extraordinary.

The artistic beauty of a sentence is something quite distinct from the wealth of beauty due to qualities and figures of speech in so far as they relate to artistic word and content belonging to one or the other of the (three) styles. In fact expressiveness of the sentence-form should be regarded as the essence of this beauty. It is an index of the unique skill of the poet even as the unique total appeal of a painting which is something quite distinct from the beauty of the individual elements that go to fashion it such as lovely canvas, lines, and colour shades.

Subjects of poetry described in all their undimmed propriety and beauty of nature come to be classed under two heads, namely, the sentient and the non-sentient.

Of these, the first class can be subdivided again under two heads—'gods etc.', and 'lions etc.' These may be either primary or subsidiary in the poet's treatment.

The first, i.e., the primary kind, is made beautiful by a spontaneous presentation of emotions like love. The second is rendered lovely by a description of the animals etc. in a way natural to their species.

The secondary sentient ones and non-sentient ones become sources of delight when they are so described that they promote the rise of sentiments.

Poets should note that such is the body of content brimming with beauty and serving the purpose of their descriptive art which they should strive to adopt into the work.

There is also another kind of poetic content which becomes the subject of the poet's art: it will be replete with the means for the attainment of the fourfold values of life; and is worthy of emulation by the people as befitting in their daily life.

'*Rasavat*' is not an ornament because there is nothing palpable apart from it which is adorned by it, and because the literal meaning of that word itself is contradicted.

Nor *preyas* (praise) adornment; for its opposite, viz., dispraise, also might be an adornment at that rate. And the use of accepted figures of speech (like the simile) along with 'praise' would have to be regarded as a case of two 'merged' or 'mixed' figures; and it should come to have an independent status too like other figures, even as instances not involving praise or eulogy.

In the same way, the characteristic of adornment is not found in *ūrjasvin* (lit., the high-spirited) and *udātta* (lit. the exalted), as well as the two-fold *samāhita* (lit., the abated).

When the subject matter is described in a way conducive to beauty by virtue of its own infinite natural charm and by means of exclusively artistic expression, we may take it as an instance of creative beauty relating to content.

There are two forms of poetic statement: One of them partially adds up to the beauty of the adorned; another suggests it primarily, remaining subservient itself and thus exhibiting itself as an adornment.

Now we shall set forth the nature of *rasavat* in such a way that it will become the life-essence of all adornments of figures of speech on the one hand and quintessence of poetry itself on the other.

That adornment of figure of speech, which functions like *rasa,* suffuses poetry with *rasa* is designated as *rasavat* inasmuch as it causes poetic appeal to connoisseurs.

Any object, which illuminates such aspects of the things described as are full of propriety undimmed, capable of delighting the connoisseurs and not contained in plain denotation of the word, should be considered as an 'illuminator' or *dīpaka.*

Dīpaka is two-fold: It may either be single or in a series. That is, one single object might illuminate many things, or many objects may illuminate many other things.

The second type (viz., *dīpaka* in a series) again is three-fold: 'several ones are illuminated by several', or 'one illuminates a second and that a third in a serial order' (or 'the illuminated ones will in their turn be illuminators').

Just as a verb referring simultaneously to more than one subject becomes appealing to the connoisseurs by reason of its adding beauty to the main theme described, so also an agent or subject (which has such a simultaneously multiple reference conducive to the beauty of the whole) should be deemed as a *dīpaka-alaṇkāra.*

That content which conveys similarity implicitly, by virtue of an essentially metaphorical usage of words, is termed 'metaphor' (*rūpaka*) since it involves a surrender of its own form in favour of another.

The similarity implied will be such that it will become a source of aesthetic charm in respect of poetic content. *Rūpaka* or metaphor is two-fold: (1) extended to each individual part and (2) restricted only to some aspect.

The soul adornment (or figure of speech) is held by the wise to be threefold:

1. explicitly stated, 2. implied by indicators and 3. suggested.

By virtue of their creative imagination, poets are seen transforming metaphor to yield the highest poetic effect in such novel ways that new shades of figures are brought into relief thereby.

When an extraneous word-meaning or sentence-meaning becomes the main theme of a description in so far as it lends charm to the proposed subject on hand;

By virtue of similarity or some other relation between the two, the figure of speech will be designated 'Praise of the inapposite' (*aprastutapraśaṇsā*).

When that which can be conveyed by quite a different sentence is conveyed by one sentence in such a way that it adds charm to the subject of description, the figure of speech involved is called 'euphemism' (*prayāyokti*).

Where we have outwardly dispraise stated in so many words but actually praise is suggested in such a way that it adds beauty to the subject primarily described, the figure of speech should be called 'Veiled Praise' (*vyāja-stuti*).

Either by way of fancying or by way of similarity or by way of both, when the poet desires to convey the extraordinary nature of the subject under description, and employs such indicative words as '*iva*' (= 'as though') or leaves them to be understood suggestively from the context of the several words and meanings which take either of the forms 'It is like this' or 'It is like itself'.

... and which involves thus a coordination of the well-conceived matter on hand with a purport quite apart from it, we have the figure of speech called *utprekṣā* or poetic fancy.

When, in respect of an action, agency is attributed to one though it be really inactive since it so appears in the eyes of the percipient, because of its extreme likelihood in view of its unique natural endowment, (we have another kind of *utprekṣā* or poetic fancy).

Atiśayokti or hyperbole is that which is the vital principle underlying all figures and in which the aesthetic qualities of the subject described are raised to a unique height of exquisiteness in a very artistic manner.

Sentiments, natural objects, and figures of speech—all of them reach their highest point of artistic beauty when their inherent brightness is so heightened by the element of hyperbole.

In order to invest rare beauty in the features of the subject described, if its similarity with another object, possessing the same features in a greater measure, is stated, we get the figure of speech, viz., simile.

Simile is illustrated in various ways such as explicit mention of the common feature, an implicit reference to it by the sentence as a whole, and a use of express words like *eva* (= as); but in all these the predicate is the element which makes the simile aesthetic.

Though there might be similarity present in the subject of poetic fancy also, its main purport lies elsewhere.

The figure called '*upameyopamā*' involving mutual similitude between the '*upamāna*' and '*upameya*' should also be regarded as coming under this *upamā* only because *upamā* exists therein also and there is no separate definition possible for it.

Association of equals or *tulyayogitā* (admitted by some) is really no separate figure. We have in it two or more similar objects brought together, each one of them claiming equal attention as subjects of description, since primacy is not affirmed of any one of them specifically. Only one should serve as the primary subject described; and when more than one claim to be primary, how could one say which is the adorned and which the adornment?

In case it is held that, in this figure, all subjects are equally important as things meant to be described, or that they are really similar to each other, then these very conditions force us to conclude that the figure is clearly *upamā* and nothing else.

The learned think that *ananvaya* is on par with *kalpitopamā* or 'invented simile'.

Pushing out one thing and bringing in of another in its place cannot be deemed as any figure of speech, because the exchange is the same as before.

When two separate meanings come to be conveyed by the same words, that special function of equivocation in words will be deemed as a figure of speech, viz., *śleṣa.*

The learned say that the indicator of *śleṣa* is a new entity other than the paranomistic word, as well as the suggestive function of the whole sentence and also the expression such as *iva* sometimes.

One and the same word will be denoting two meanings here; between the word and the two meanings so denoted as if they were identical, similarity will be found to be the ruling principle behind such unique technique of the poet.

By the remembrance of similar-sounding words, we get at the meaning, first of the one and next of the other. Since sound or word gets lost as soon as it is produced, remembrance (of past impressions of meaning) alone should be held as governing all such (equivocal) denotation.

When there is similarity in respect of meanings conveyed by the specific word, and when the similarity in features of the two is also present, still if the features of the one are shown as singularly distinct from those of the other, with a view to bring about the excellence of the subject on hand, we get the figure of speech called *Vyatireka*. It is of two kinds—(1) explicitly stated and (2) suggested.

When a subject is described without clearly intending the effect of other figures like *upamā* but intending to bring out its distinctive excellence over or superiority to the well known features associated with it in the world, we have another type of figure: *vyatireka*.

We have *virodha* or paradox when the (apparent) contradiction between two statements is overcome in an ingenious way and the final meaning is made to become reasonable.

Samāsokti ('condensed metaphor') as well as *sahokti* ('description of concurrent occurrences') is not regarded as a figure of speech; for it happens to possess the features of another figure on the one hand and is devoid of poetic beauty on the other.

When, in order to enrich the beauty of the subject described, two subjects are simultaneously described in one and the same sentence, the learned regard it as a figure called *sahokti* or description of concurrent occurrences.

When another idea is pointed to on the basis of its factual similarity (to the idea on hand) without explicit use of expression like *iva*, we have *dṛṣṭānta* or poetic analogy.

On the basis of similarity between two main sentence ideas or imports, when (along with the one on hand.) the other one is also describe, understood as the figure *arthāntaranyāsa* or 'corroboration' because it corroborates the first idea.

Suggestion, by way of a denial, for the sake of aesthetic emphasis of the main subject-matter is to be regarded as *ākṣepa* or paralipsis.

All these three figures beginning with *dṛṣṭānta* will have two types, namely (1) relating to an idea yet to be stated and (2) relating to an idea already stated depending upon the intention of the poet (and the middle one may contain explicit indicators of corroboration or may not contain them).

In order to enrich the beauty of the effect, when it is imagined to be produced uniquely in some way other than the usual cause whose agency is denied, we have the figure of speech known as *vibhāvanā* or 'inscrutable effect'.

When a feature fancied as something allows room for the rise of other fancies too in such a way as to result in aesthetic charm, the figure of speech is designated *sasandeha* or 'poetic doubt'.

With the object of endowing a unique form to the subject matter described, when its actual nature or form is suppressed or concealed, we get the figure of speech known as *apahnuti* or 'poetic concealment'.

Just like words which join in a group to form a sentence, when figures of speech come to be mutually associated with each other in the production of a total impression of beauty, it may be regarded as an instance of the 'mixed' figure of speech.

When all the different figures noticed above get merged inseparably, and strike us in a sentence in various ways, the designation of *saṅkara* is given to such an instance of figurative beauty.

The other figures left out here are really not separate figures because they are either non-different from the ones defined or they are lacking in aesthetic charm.

Though counted as a figure of speech by ancient theorists, *yathāsaṁkhya* (or 'enumeration in a respective order') is not accepted by us as an independent figure because of both the reasons mentioned.

Artful speech of a good poet appeals to one's heart even like one's beloved: Both the beloved and poetic speech share common attributes, namely possession of striking qualities like grace, alluring charm of word-usage or foot-steps appeal of elegant but sparse ornaments, abundance of tasteful sentiment and tender-heartedness and elegance of expression.

When we find the speakers giving vent to such expression as is replete with the beauty of unlimited enthusiasm and also capable of expressing their ideas powerfully; when the intended object at the end will remain inscrutable from the beginning (i.e., suspense remains constant till the denouement), the unique and boundless poetic skill underlying it all should be regarded as the poetic beauty of an episode.

When a poet is constructing a plot of his own, based though it might be on a well known source, if he succeeds in infusing even a small streak of originality, the beauty gained thereby will be singular;

Even as an episode too can shine forth as the vital essence of the work as a whole, brimful of sentiments reaching their utmost limit.

An organic unity which strikingly underlies the various incidents described in different parts of the work leading to the ultimate and intended, each bound to the other by a relation of mutual assistance, reveals the essence of creative originality which is most aesthetic only in the case of a very rare poetic genius who is endowed by nature with the gift of an extraordinary inventive imagination.

When even one and the same theme is again and again described in different places with a new touch of creative originality, and is made to radiate the glow of sentiments and figures of speech, it manifests a strikingly new mode of artistic beauty.

When integrated with the beauty of the plot, even the conventional themes, that come to be described in court-epics and so forth conforming to set patterns, attain a novel artistic beauty.

Another type of beauty in respect of Acts etc., is instanced when the beauty is so exclusive to an Act that it cannot be attained by any other Act, either preceding or following, in the play and the Act thus serves as a touchstone in its own way of the ruling sentiment in the play.

When the inventiveness of the poet in devising some other incident also ultimately contributes to add significance to the total plot, it should be regarded as another type of beauty of episode.

When actors, expert in the art of pleasing the audience, are seen to play the role of an audience themselves on the stage with other actors performing, such a play-episode within a play-episode may be regarded as illustrating a literary art which beautifies the entire drama exquisitely.

The art of the dramatic plot should be pleasing by the construction of delightful 'junctures' (*sandhis*); each of the parts should be organically related to other parts, the succeeding one following logically from the preceding one.

It should not be vitiated by any excessive craze for observing rules even when they are inopportune. Only in such cases, the episode will reveal a unique charm of originality.

When there is a departure from the enriched *rasas* of the source-book and a new delightful *rasa* is delineated by the poet at the conclusion of his work, so that the delight of the readers is ensured, we should regard it as beauty of a whole work.

When a good poet concludes his work with only such a select incident in his original source as promotes the singular prosperity of the hero depicted as an ideal character in all three worlds, with the idea of avoiding the distasteful culmination of the story in the original, it should be regarded as another appealing form of beauty relating to a whole work. Supposing the even flow of the main story has been broken and its sentiment impaired by the intrusion of some incident whose connection with the main story is almost indiscernible; the poet might give the incident such a turn that it will become inevitable for the conclusion of the main story and thus maintain the unbroken course of rasa and invest he whole work with a very unique novelty thereby.

Again, though the hero is concerned in achieving primarily a single goal, when he is seen to attain incidentally many other equally great fruits, which add up to make his glory shine very brilliantly, such an assemblage of his great achievements will contribute in another way to the beauty of a work as a whole.

Even if we let alone the artistic skill of the poet in devising original incidents or episodes, we find that he can display his unique art even in designating his main plot with a very significant title.

Even when great poets compose different literary works based on an identical theme, they are each seen to possess infinite individual beauty, each possessing distinctiveness from the others.

Whatever works might be composed by great poets who are able to instruct in new forms of political strategy, they may be taken as embodying literary beauty.

Kuntaka, from the Vakrokti-Jivita
translated by K. Krishnamoorthy

8

Abhinavagupta

With Bharatamuni and Ānandavardhana, Abhinavagupta (tenth to eleventh century, AD) is among the very greatest figures in Indian aesthetics. He has a further distinction, which the other two do not have—namely, he is also one of the most important Kashmir Shaivite philosophers. His work is comparable, to think in comparative terms, to that of Immanuel Kant in the Western tradition. P.V. Kane remarks about Abhinavagupta that he was one of the most remarkable personalities of medieval India. He was a man of very acute intellect and was an encyclopaedic scholar. He had taken all knowledge for his province.[1] Historically speaking too, Abhinavagupta stands at one of the most crucial moments of Indian history. He had completed his work by the end of the tenth century, and he retired into exile in a Kashmir cave about the same time as Mahmud of Ghazni began his raids on India. Thus, his life and philosophy represent the last great pinnacle of intellectual achievement in ancient India. 'In his eager search for knowledge, Abhinavagupta states that he resorted to teachers of *tarka* (*Nyāya* and *Vaiśeṣika* systems), and of Buddha, *Ārhata* and *Vaiṣṇava* doctrines. Abhinava was proficient in yogic practices, he believed that he had realized the Highest Reality (Siva).'[2]

The concept of *Śāntarasa* posited by Abhinavagupta, and defended with extraordinary logical rigour, reflects his visionary poetics. He argues: 'the eight *rasas* are like eight gods, and the *śānta* is like their highest centre, Siva.' But this insistence on transcendence as the highest value in literary aesthetics also

[1,2] P. V. Kane, *History of Sanskrit Poetics,* Motilal Banarsidass, Delhi, 1971, pp. 236 and 240, respectviely.

reflects Abhinava's realisation of the need to modify Bharata's formulation to suit the changing cultural ethos. Bharata's achievement in literary aesthetics is mainly of two types: 1) he synthesised the concept of poetry and the concept of drama, which were treated separately by his predecessors, and formed a common concept of literature; and 2) he combined theology, philosophy and criticism which his predecessors had kept distinct as such. He was thus great synthesiser.

The excerpt selected here is from J. L. Masson and M. V. Patwardhan on Abhinava's concept of *Śāntarasa* (*Śāntarasa and Abhinava's Philosophy,* The Oriental Institute, Pune, 1969, pages 120–143).

On *Śāntarasa*: Aesthetic Equipoise

The nature of *śānta* will now be explained according to those who follow the reading *nava rasāḥ* (nine *rasas*), instead of the reading *aṣṭau rasāḥ*. In this connection some say that *śama* is the *sthāyibhāva* of *śanta* and that it arises from *vibhāvas* such as ascetic practices, association with Yogins, etc. It can be represented on the stage by *anubhāvas* such as the absence of lust, anger, etc. Its *vyabhicāribhāvas* will be firmness, wisdom, etc. Others however do not accept this, because, they say, *śama* and *śānta* are synonyms. Nor do they wish to relinquish the figure of 49 *bhāvas* that was given by Bharata. Moreover, they say that it is proper for the *vibhāvas* such as the seasons, flowers, etc., to be connected with love, etc., which arise immediately after these *vibhāvas* are apprehended. But ascetic practices, Vedic recitation, etc., do not immediately give rise to *śānta*. Should one argue that ascetic practices, Vedic recitation, etc., are the immediate causes of the knowledge of the truth, then, since the knowledge of the truth which precedes *śānta* is their immediate effect, they cease to be the *vibhāvas* of *śānta*. Even the absence of lust, etc., cannot be the *anubhāva*, because it is not conclusive evidence of *śānta*, inasmuch as it is found to be present in *rasas* other than *śānta* as well, and because it cannot be combined with a stage-representation (*prayoga*). After all, it is not possible to display a cessation of activity. For example, even the *anubhāvas,* sleep, a swoon, etc., can be shown by actions like breathing in and out, falling down, lying on the ground, etc. As for *vyabhicāribhāvas*, how can firmness of mind, etc., which is accompanied by a desire for the attainment of objects, be appropriate to *śānta*? Those to be instructed cannot be taught how to attain the knowledge of truth by means of a state of complete inactivity. Those people whose minds are pained by the sufferings of other people have not yet reached a state of tranquillity characterised by correct perception of the highest truth, but rather they are still caught in the turmoil of worldly life. Therefore *śāntarasa* does not exist.

The reply is as follows: Just as in this world there is the trilogy of *dharma*, etc., so also, it is quite well-known that *mokṣa* too is one of the goals of life, and it is found to be taught predominantly in the *śāstras* and in the *smṛtis* and *itihāsas*, etc., by specifying the means leading to its attainment. Just as the states of mind that are proper to love, etc. and expressed by such words as sexual love (*rati*) etc., by being made capable of being relished through the activity of the poet and the actor, are brought to the status of *rasas* such as *śṛngāra*, etc., in relation to the spectators who are possessed of the proper sympathetic response; in the same way, we ask you to tell us why the state of mind which is appropriate to the highest goal of man known as *mokṣa* cannot be raised to the status of a *rasa*? That state of mind just described is indeed the *sthāyibhāva* of *śānta*. But one must consider what its name is. Some say that it is complete detachment (*nirveda*—world-weariness) that is born from a knowledge of truth. For this detachment is quite different from the detachment that arises from poverty, etc., because its cause, viz., knowledge of the truth, is different. It was for this very reason—i.e., because *nirveda* is the *sthāyibhāva* of *śānta*—that it has been mentioned by Bharata midway between the *sthāyibhāvas* and the *sancāribhāvas* (i.e., *vyabhicāribhāvas*). Otherwise, i.e., if *nirveda* had not been intended by Bharata as the *sthāyibhāva* of *śānta*, the sage who had great regard for uttering an auspicious word at the commencement of a section of his work (*māngalika*) would not have mentioned *nirveda* at that place ... he would not have put the inauspicious word *nirveda* at the head of the list of *vyabhicāribhāvas*. When Bharata forbade the use of disgust *(jugupsā)* as a *vyabhicāribhāva* of *śṛngara*, he sanctioned by implication the interchangeability of the characters of the *sthāyibhāvas*, the *sancāribhāvas*, the *sāttvikabhāvas*, and the *anubhāvas*, in the case of all the 49 *bhāvas* as demanded by the requirements of a particular situation and as presented by the power of words and their senses. *Nirveda* arises from knowledge of the truth and overwhelms the other *sthāyins*. For only that emotion which is more highly stable than any of the other *sthāyins* such as love etc. which can tolerate co-existence with a variety of emotions, that alone (namely *nirveda*), they say, can overwhelm other *sthāyins*.

They also raise the following objection: if *nirveda* which arises from knowledge of the truth, is said to be the *sthāyibhāva* of *śānta*, . . . in which case how could *vairāgya* (detachment) and similar other things (e.g., *samādhi*, which have been mentioned as *vibhāvas* of *nirveda*) be the *vibhāva* of nirveda? If one were to claim that detachment, etc., become the *vibhāva* of *nirveda* because they are the means of attaining to the knowledge of the truth, then it would mean that you are giving the name *vibhāva* to that which is the cause of another cause, and that would involve you in a great absurdity since *vibhāva* means the direct cause of a *sthāyibhāva* and not the distant or remote cause. Moreover *nirveda* is an attitude of rejecting everything, an attitude of not being attached to anything, and it would on the contrary be helpful to the emergence of the knowledge of the truth, far from being the effect of the knowledge of the truth, it would be a cause leading to it, because a detached person will strive in such a fashion that the knowledge of the truth arises in him. And *mokṣa* comes from a knowledge of the truth. It is not that one knows the truth, and then feels detached, and from that detachment *mokṣa* would arise. For Īśvarkṛṣṇa says:

'From detachment comes only *prakṛtilaya* (i.e., dissolution into the eight causes, *pradhana*, *buddhi*, *ahankāra* and the *pancatanmātras*, and not *mokṣa*)'.

Objection: Everywhere one sees a very great detachment on the part of those who know the truth. Even Patanjali has said:

Thereafter from that knowledge of the truth (*puruṣakhyāti*) arises an extreme aversion to the *guṇas* (detachment)'. That is true (*bhavatyevam*). But Patanjali himself has said: 'Such detachment is really the highest state (*kāṣṭhā*) of knowledge. Thus, then, knowledge of the truth (leading to aversion according to Yogasutra 1.16) means nothing but knowledge of the truth reinforcing itself from stage to stage. And so *nirveda* is not the *sthāyibhāva* of *śānta*. On the other hand, knowledge of the truth alone would be the *sthāyibhāva*. As for right perception, which will be mentioned (by Bharata) while describing *nirveda* as a *vyabhicāribhāva*, as a *vibhāva* of *nirveda*, and which leads to the dissipation of the attitude of acceptance, for attachment to unworthy objects, on the part of a person who has been deceived by a delusion of long standing, as exemplified in the following stanza:

> 'In vain, did I milk a bull mistaking it for a cow bending under the burden of her full udder; in vain did I embrace an ugly eunuch thinking him to be a young girl; in vain did I cherish a longing for a piece of glittering glass thinking it to be beryl. All this I did when bemused as I was, I bowed to you, a miser unable to appreciate merit.'

Well, that perception of truth has been mentioned as a *vibhāva* (cause of only the ordinary kind of *nirveda*) whose nature is sadness arising from a realization of one's stupidity in wasting energy in a worthless cause. We will speak of this perception of truth there (i.e., in the seventh chapter while commenting on the section on *nirveda*).

Objection: 'Attachment to the sense-objects is rooted in false knowledge. It will cease when knowledge of the truth arises. This is what the revered *Akṣapāda* has said in his *Sutra* beginning with the words *duḥkhajanma* etc., when he says that knowledge of the truth is caused by the removal of false knowledge and that it is further the cause of *vairāgya* which is of the nature of the removal of all faults (*doṣa*) such as attachment to worldly pleasures.' 'So *nirveda* is the *sthāyin* and *tattvajñāna* is a *vibhāva*).' Who says so? For *nirveda* is a certain state of mind which is characterised by a flow of sadness, whereas *vairāgya* is a higher form of detachment than is *nirveda*, for the latter is often used non-technically to mean simply 'weariness' or disgust'. Even granting that *vairāgya* and *nirveda* are identical, still Gautama placed it in the midst of several [other causes of *mokṣa*] and did not mention it as the immediate cause of *mokṣa* (for it is only the remote cause, and so it does not follow that according to Akṣapāda *nirveda* that is *vairāgya*, is the *sthāyibhāva* of *śānta*). Moreover to say that *nirveda* arising from *tattvajñāna* is the *sthāyibhāva* of *śānta* means that you are giving to *śama* the name *nirveda*. Reply: *śama* and *śānta* have been explained as synonyms like *hāsa* and *hāsya* (i.e., *sthāyibhāva* and rasa). But the synonymity in the case of *śānta* and *śama* is only apparent and not real. There is a real difference between *śānta* (the *rasa*) and *śama* (the *sthāyibhāva*), for *śama* is *siddha*, an accomplished fact, while *śanta* is *sādhya*, something to be accomplished; *śama* is *laukika*, worldly while *śānta* is *alaukika*, other-worldly; *śama* is *sādhārana*, ordinary, while *śānta* is *asādhārana*, extraordinary. Therefore, *nirveda* cannot be the *sthāyibhāva* of *śānta.*

Others believe that only eight mental states have been mentioned (by Bharata), such as love, etc. Those same mental states when depending on extraworldly *vibhāvas* such as *śruta* (study of scriptures and especially of the (*Upaniṣads*), which are different from the ordinary *(kathita) vibhāvas*, become indeed unusually lovely (*vicitra*). And from out of their midst one can become the *sthāyin* here, i.e., in the case of *śāntarasa*. Out of them (*tatra*), *rati* alone having for its object one's own Self consisting of undisturbed bliss, is the means of attaining *mokṣa*. And so, that *rati* itself is the *sthāyin* in *śānta*. For it has been said:

> 'That man whose love is centred in the Self, who is gratified in his Self and who takes all delight in the Self—for such a man there is nothing any longer to be accomplished.'

In the same way, any of the *sthāyibhāvas* beginning with *rati* and *hāsa* and ending with *vismaya* can be explained as the *sthāyibhāva* of *śānta*, because we find that a person attains to liberation if he realises the oddity of everything in the world (*hāsa*); if he sees that the whole world is lamentable (*śoka*); if he perceives the happenings in the world as harmful to his spiritual well-being, and angry with them, desires to conquer them (*krodha*); if he resorts to extraordinary energy dominated by the absence of delusion in order to overcome worldly temptations (*utsāha*); if he feels afraid of all the objects of the senses (*bhaya*); if he feels disgust for young women, etc., though they are desirable for all other people (*jugupsā*); if he feels astonished at his unprecedented realisation of his own self (*vismaya*). And Bharata agrees with this position. For while Bharata enumerates particular *bhāvas* by using words like *rati*, etc., and includes thereunder other varieties of the same by using the word *ca*, he does admit their ability to lead to liberation, provided that they are the result of extraordinary causes (i.e., *vibhāvas*) different from ordinary causes. But in the case of those people who hold this view (namely that any one of the *sthāyibhāvas* such as *rati*, etc., can be the *sthāyibhāva* of *śānta*), the different *sthāyibhāvas* would cancel each other out and so not even one of them could be regarded as the *sthāyibhāva* of *śānta*. If it is said that the different *sthāyibhāvas* can be the *sthāyibhāvas* of *śānta* because of the different approaches leading to it, that is as good as already refuted. Further, because of the different *sthāyibhāvas* of *śānta* depending on the approaches of the persons concerned, there would be an infinity of *śāntarasas*. If it is said that there would be only one *śāntarasa* and not countless *śāntarasas* because of its being the cause of one single result, namely *mokṣa*, then even *vīra* and *raudra* would have to be regarded as one rasa because both lead to one single result, namely destruction (of one's enemy). Others say that all the *sthāyibhāvas, rati*, etc., become merged together, just as different flavours merge together in a beverage, and when so merged they become the *sthāyibhāvas* of *śānta*. But because different states of mind cannot coexist at one time, and because some are mutually antagonistic, even this is not a very attractive thesis.

What then is the *sthāyibhāva* of *śānta*? The reply is as follows: knowledge of the truth alone is the means of attaining *mokṣa* and so it would be proper to regard that alone as the *sthāyibhāva* of *mokṣa*. Knowledge of the truth is just another name for knowledge of the Self. The knowledge of any object other than the Self is the knowledge of worldly objects. For anything that is different from the Self is nothing but non-self. Our teacher has dealt with this at great length. And we have gone into it in some detail elsewhere, and so at this moment there is no point in dilating. Therefore, the *ātman* alone possessed of such pure qualities as knowledge, bliss, etc., and devoid of enjoyment of imagined sense-objects, is the *sthāyibhāva* of *śānta*. Its status as a *sthāyibhāva* should not be explained in the same terms as the status, as a *sthāyibhāva*, in the case of other *sthāyibhāvas*; there is a great difference between the *ātman*'s status as a *sthāyibhāva* and the other *sthāyibhāvas*' status as *sthāyibhāvas*. For *rati*, etc., which arise and disappear due to the emergence and disappearance of their respective causes, are called *sthāyibhāvas* in so far as they attach themselves for some time to the canvas (wall) in the form of the *ātman* which is of an unchanging nature relative to them. But knowledge of the truth is the canvas behind all emotions, and so it is the most stable of all *sthāyibhāvas*. It transforms all the states of mind such as love, etc., into transitory feelings, and its status as a *sthāyibhāva*, having been established by its very nature, need not be specifically mentioned. And therefore it is not proper to count knowledge of the truth separately in addition to the eight *sthāyibhāvas*. Between a lame bull and a dehorned bull, bullness which is the generic property present in both the bulls is not considered a third thing. And so the number, viz. forty-nine, of the *bhāvas* is not disturbed. Should one demand to know why then knowledge of the truth is separately considered as a *sthāyibhāva* by me, Abhinavagupta, we reply that it is so because it can be separately enjoyed. For whereas *rati*, etc., can be the subject of ordinary perception in their pure form, without being mingled with anything else, the nature of the Self is of course not the subject of ordinary perception in its pure form without being mingled with anything else, the way *rati*, etc., are. But even though in its pure nature it is an indeterminate form, still when it is investigated at the time of the return from abstract meditation, it invariably appears as mingled with various mental states.

Or let it appear like that (i.e., let the nature of the Self appear as you say, soiled by the various mental states). Still you cannot consider as *sthāyibhāvas* all possible moods of the mind, for they are of no use so far as the eight *rasas* actually mentioned by Bharata are concerned. They rather deserve to be regarded as transitory feelings and not otherwise (i.e., not as *sthāyibhāvas*). And thus only can the statement (*praghaṭṭaka*) that there are in all forty nine *bhāvas* be justified. This nature of the Self cannot be said to be transitory because it would be impossible, unimaginative (*avaicitryāvaha*) and improper. *Śama* is the nature of the Self. Bharata has designated it (i.e., the nature of the Self) by the word *śama.* If that same nature of the Self is called *śama* or *nirveda,* there is no objection. Only note that *śama* is a different kind of state of mind altogether. And this special *nirveda* is only apparently similar to the *nirveda* that arises from other causes such as poverty, etc. Although their causes are different, nonetheless, because they are similar, they are both called *nirveda.* This is similar to what takes place in love, fear, etc. Therefore the nature of the Self is itself the knowledge of the Truth, and it is also tranquillity. Further (*tathā ca*) *rati*, etc., are only particular dark colorations (*kālusyoparāgaviśeṣāh*) of the Self (or of *śānta*?). Having by means of continued concentration realised its form as being pure, though connected with them (i.e., *rati*, etc.), there is even at the time of withdrawing from meditation (*vyuthāna*), complete tranquillity of the spiritual aspirant, the *sādhaka.* As has been said: *praśāntivāhita samskārāt.* This entire collection of ordinary and extra-ordinary states of mind can become the helper of the major emotion known as knowledge of the Truth. Its *anubhāvas* are *anubhāvas* helped by *yama*, *niyama*, etc., and also the *svabhāvābhinayas* which will be described in the three chapters beginning with *upāngābhinaya.* And so they (i.e., these *anubhāvas*) are concerned with *śāntarasa* itself. This itself is its nature (i.e., the nature of *śāntarasa*). The *vibhāvas* are the grace of God, etc. And love etc., which are soon to be completely destroyed, can be aesthetically enjoyed in *śānta* as subsidiary, momentary elements. Just as the *vyabhicāri* 'eagerness' appears as important in love during-separation or even love-during-union, as said in the phrase: 'love whose festivity never comes to an end', and just as *augrya*, a *vyabhicārin* appears as prominent in *raudra*; and just as *nirveda*, *dhrti* (firmness of mind), *trāsa* (fear) and *harṣa* (joy), though really *vyabhicāribhāvas*, appear as prominent in *karuṇa*, *vīra*, *bhayānaka* and *adbhuta;* so in *śāntarasa*, *jugupsā* (disgust), etc., appear predominantly, since they are completely opposed to love. For the *mahāvrata* (ceremony) one carries about a human skull (tr.n. obscure). At the time of begetting a son by a widow from her brother-in-law, anointment of one's own body with oil has been recommended with a view to creating a sense of disgust. For the man who has done all that must be done with regard to his Self (i.e., who has realised the true nature of his Self), his efforts are all for promoting the good of other people, and so his energy takes the form of an effort that is prompted by the wish to help others. This is a synonym for compassion, and it is very intimately connected with *śānta*. And so some people call *Śāntarasa*, *dayāvīra* (compassionate heroism) and some call it *dharmavīra* (religious heroism) because of the intensity of this energy (*utsāha*) which becomes its *vyabhicāribhāva*.

Objection: 'Energy is based on egoism as its essence, whereas *śānta* consists primarily in a loosening of egoism.' Reply: It is not improper for an opposing mood to be a *vyabhicāribhāva* (in *śānta*), for we find, for instance, *nirveda* as a *vyabhicāribhāva* in love. In the verse 'With the forest-ground overgrown with grass as my bed' and other similar stanzas, we find a high degree of *utsāha* in helping others. There is no state that is devoid of *utsāha*. For in the absence of desire and effort, one would be like a stone. And so because one has understood the higher Self and the lower Self, there is nothing left to do with regard to one's own Self, and therefore, for those whose hearts are tranquil, to give their all-in- all, i.e., to give their bodies, for the sake of helping another is not contrary to *śānta*. 'One should preserve one's self', and such similar advice is meant in the sense of guarding one's body and is meant for those who have not realised their Self, because ascetics are not concerned with guarding their bodies at all. For it has been said:

> 'The life-breaths (*prānah*) are the cause of *attaining dharma*, *artha*, *kama* and *mokṇa*. When they are destroyed what is not destroyed? When they are guarded, what is not guarded? (i.e., all is guarded).'

In this stanza the motive (*nidāna*) for the preservation of the body is shown to be its capacity to achieve the well-known four goals of life. In the case of the man who has realised his Self however, it is often heard, in the context of *sannyāsa* that he should throw his body into water, fire or a pit. Thus the idea is that since somehow the body is to be renounced sometime or other, if it be given up for the sake of another, what would not be achieved? (i.e., so much is thereby gained). Should one argue that Jimūtavāhana and others were not ascetics, we should ask how that matters to us? Certainly they had attained to knowledge of the Truth. For it would be inconceivable that those who consider their body as their soul should abandon for the sake of others the very body which is to them their all-in-all, for in their case there would be no urge for *dharma,* etc. In a battle, a warrior has no intention of abandoning his body for a religious cause, but rather he enters the battle only in order to conquer his enemy. In suicide by jumping off a cliff, etc., the main purpose is the desire to attain a more beautiful body in the life to come. Therefore whatever deeds, beginning with the imparting of spiritual advice and culminating in renunciation of one's body, are performed in order to achieve the benefit of others and without reference to one's own benefit, are certainly inconceivable in the case of people who have not attained to a knowledge of the true nature of *Ātman.* And they i.e., people who do these deeds are also knowers of the Truth. For those who know the Truth, there is liberation in all the (four) stages (*āśrama*) of life. This is what is taught in the *Smṛtis* and *Śrutis.* As has been said:

> A man who is attached to worship of the gods, who is grounded in the knowledge of the Truth, who is gracious to guests, who, having performed the ceremonial rites to his ancestors (*śrāddha*), gives out wealth, even though he be (only) a house-holder, (this man) is freed.'

However (*kevalam*) in the case of Bodhisattvas, etc., although they have known the truth, there is, because of their religious or righteous actions springing from a desire to do good to others and expected by them to result in the benefit of others, a reappearance of a body appropriate to that (i.e., to those actions that they have performed).

Even in the case of *rasas* which occupy a subsidiary position in a poetic work, the attainment of 'repose' (i.e., aesthetic enjoyment) is met with, because that is only appropriate to their nature as *rasas*. For instance, in the *Rāmāyaṇa*, in the case of Rāma when he obeys his father's orders and goes into exile, repose is met with in this, though the aesthetic repose is only subsidiary. The same should be understood in the case of *sṛngara* and other *rasas* when they occupy a subsidiary position in a poetic work. Hence although *śāntarasa* has come to stay in the *Nāgānanda,* it is not the major *rasa*, because in that play the achievement of the three goals of human life (*dharma, artha and kāma*), with special emphasis on helping others, is the final result in the case of Jimūtavāhana. With this thought in mind, Bharata will say while defining a *nāṭaka,* that 'it is possessed of qualities such as wealth, flirtatious ways, etc.' This means that a dramatist should introduce into the *nāṭaka* all kinds of actions in which opulence and flirtation are predominant and in which emphasis is placed on the two goals of life, *artha* and *kāma*, because such actions have the charming purpose of winning a sympathetic response from all people (i.e., because such actions have a universal appeal). We will describe this in that very section dealing with the definition of a *Nāṭaka*. With this in mind, Bharata will not prescribe any *jātyaṃśaka* in *śānta*. Hence the view of some that *śāntarasa* does not exist in as much as Bharata has not prescribed any *jātyaṃśaka* in its case, is refuted.

Others however say: 'Jimūtavāhana saved an old woman who needed protection, and who said: "Oh son, who will save you?" He had no power. He wanted to harm nobody.' We agree with this. Should it be further argued that there is no power … of Bodhisattvas (?). But the *śānta* does not teach by means of *kākatāliya* (*nyāya*) (?). Therefore it is proved: *utsāha* is principally intended in this play and therefore *vira* is the major *rasa*, and it is characterised by compassion. In the *Nāgānanda* other moods like love for Malayavati, detachment, etc., become subsidiaries according to the circumstances (*yathayogam*). As has been said:

tacchindreshu pratyayāntarāṇi saṃskārebhyāḥ

And so we have refuted the contention that *anubhāvas* cannot exist because of a complete absence of action in the case of a man who is *śānta*. When, however one has reached the culminating state of *śānta* and all *anubhāvas* are absent, this *śānta* cannot be represented. In love and sorrow, etc., also, in the culminating stages, it is correct that there is no possibility of representation.

Sympathetic identification however is possible for those who have planted in them the *saṃskáras* that are the seeds of such knowledge of the Truth. As Bharata will say:

'People devoid of passion take delight in *mokṣa*'.

After all not everybody is always sympathetic to everything. For instance, a man whose nature is heroic will not sympathetically identify with a character in *bhayānaka*. Objection: 'How can a heroic type of person take any delight in such a presentation?' The reply is: in a work where this (*śānta*) is presented, surely there is one or other of the other *rasas* such as *sṛngāra*, *vīra*, etc., since the work is intended to be useful to the goals of life other than liberation. Its aesthetic relish is grounded in *śānta* however. In *prahāsana*, etc., too, where *hāsya*, etc., are principal, the aesthetic relish is grounded in other *rasas* which in their wake (*anuniṣpādi*). According to some, the justification for exposition of the different drama-types is the intention to cater to aesthetic enjoyment in the case of different kinds of spectators (*adhikārin*). Therefore *śāntarasa* does exist. And so in old manuscripts, after the passage 'we will show how the *sythāyibhāvas* develop into the rasas', is read definition of *śānta* in the phrase 'What is called *śānta* has for its *sthāyibhāva śama*', etc. In this connection, the aesthetic enjoyment of all *rasas* is similar to that of *śānta*, because it (i.e., this aesthetic enjoyment) is turned away from actual sense-object contact. (Because we are particularly concerned with one *rasa*, except that it is mixed with other latent mental impressions (*vāsana*). In order to indicate that it (*śānta*) is at the root of all rasas, it was named at the beginning. In ordinary worldly dealings, one does not mention separately a thing common to all, and so its *sthāyin* was not separately given. But even a thing which is common to a number of other things deserves to be separately reckoned by the discriminating man, and so it (*śāntarasa*) has become separate as the object of cognition in the form of aesthetic enjoyment of the spectator who is admitted to be a discriminating reader. In the *Itihāsas*, the *Purāṇas*, doctrines, etc., we hear of nine *rasas* as well as in the revered *Siddhāntaśāstra*. Thus it is said:

> 'He should display the eight *rasas* in the places alloted to the eight gods. And in the centre he should display *śāntarasa* in the place of the supreme God (*Śiva*).'

Its *vibhāvas* are *vairāgya*, fear of *saṃsāra*, etc. *Śānta* is known through the portrayal of these. Its *anubhāvas* are thinking about *mokṣa*-texts, etc. Its *vyabhicāribhāvas* include world-weariness, wisdom, contentment (*dhṛti*), etc. And as *bhakti* and *śraddhā* which are directed towards meditation on God and which are reinforced by *smṛrti*, *mati*, *dhṛti*, are in any case (*anyathaiva*) helpful (to *śānta*), neither of them should be counted as a separate rasa. Here is a *sangrahakārikā* on this matter:

> '*Śānta* rasa is to be known as that which arises from a desire to secure the liberation of the Self, which leads to a knowledge of the Truth, and is connected with the property of highest happiness.'

By the three adjectives qualifying *śānta* in this verse, the *vibhāvas*, *sthāyibhāva* and *anubhāvas* are shown respectively.

> 'Various feelings, because of their particular respective causes arise from *śānta* (a state of mental calm). But when these causes disappear, they melt back into *śānta*.'

In this verse and others it has been summarily shown that *śānta* is the source of all other *rasas*.

As for the statement that will be made by Bharata to the effect that in the *Ḍima* type of drama there are six *rasas*, excluding both *hāsya* and *śṛngāra*, here is what is meant: by giving the definition: 'It is based on a composition with an exciting *rasa*', there can be no question at all of *śānta*, as it is opposed to *raudra* which is predominant in the *Ḍima*. So what is the point of separately excluding it? Since *śānta* is impossible and since *Ḍima* has its source (i.e., since it is based on) an exciting *rasa*, what else can be excluded (but *śānta*)? Had he only said that it can be associated with six *rasas*, excluding *śṛngāra* and *hāsya* (without adding the qualifying phrase *diptarasakāvyayonih*), *śānta* would not have been excluded. Objection: 'This quarter stanza (*diptarasakāvyayonih*) excludes *karuṇa*, *bibhatsa* and *bhayānaka* as predominant *rasas*.' This is not true, because when (he) says that the *Ḍima* is associated with the styles called *Sāttvatī* and *Ārabhatī*, they are automatically excluded since they belong to style *Kaiśiki*. But *śānta* uses only the *Sāttvatī* style, and therefore this qualification alone would not be enough to exclude it. And therefore the definition of the *Ḍima*, far from arguing against the existence of *śanta*, is evidence for its existence. *Śṛngāra* however would be possible in a *Ḍima* because demons make love in a violent manner. *Hāsya* is helpful to *śṛngāra* and therefore only their exclusion was specifically mentioned, because both are possible and only a possible thing can be excluded, but not an impossible thing such as *śānta*.

Because *śānta* is common to all *rasas*, it would be improper to name especially a colour or god that is appropriate to it, as one has done for the other *rasas*, but they have been invented by some. And so the reasonableness of *śānta* has been shown. Its true nature is *hāsya*. *Vira* and *bibhatsa* tend to lead towards it. Therefore there is in the case of *śānta* the advice about the practice of *yama*, *niyama*, meditation on God, etc. It stands to reason that it leads to a great result (i.e., *mokṣa*), as it eschews enjoyment of worldly objects (*anupabhogitayā*), that it is more important than any other *rasa*, and that it pervades the entire plot. And so enough of further elaboration.

What is the nature of its true relish? It is the following: The nature of the soul is tinged by *utsāha, rati*, etc., which are capable of imparting their peculiar tinges to it. It is like a very white thread that shines through the interstices of sparsely threaded jewels. It assumes the forms of all the various feelings like love, etc., which are superimposed on it, because all these things are capable of importing their tinges to it. Even then (*tathābhāvenāpi*) it shines out through them, according to the maxim that once this *Ātman* shines, it shines forever. It is devoid of the entire collection of miseries which consist in (i.e., which result from) turning away from the *Ātman*. It is identical with the consciousness of the realisation of the highest bliss. It takes its effect through the process of generalisation in poetry and drama. It makes such a heart (i.e., the heart of the sensitive spectator or reader) the receptacle of an other-worldly bliss by inducing a peculiar kind of introspection (*antarmukhāvasthābheda*).

There are only these nine *rasas,* because only they deserve to be taught, as they are useful to the four goals of life or are exceptionally pleasant. Therefore, what others say, namely that this restriction on numbers is because only these nine are well-known to enlightened literary critics, though other *rasas* are possible, has been refuted. This will be explained in the chapter on the *bhāvas*. It is wrong to say that affection, with a *sthāyibhāva* of being moved (*ārdratā*) can be a rasa, because affection is nothing other than attachment, and all attachment culminates in *rati, utsāha* or some other such accepted *sthāyibhāva* ... For instance, the love of a child for its mother and father terminates in (i.e., can be included under) 'fear'. The affection of a young man for his friends terminates in *rati*. The affection, as of Laksmana, etc., for his brother terminates in (i.e., can be included under) *dharmavīra.* The same is true of the affection of an old man for his son, etc. The so-called *rasa* 'cupidity' with the *sthāyibhāva* of 'greed' can be refuted in the same manner, because it will terminate in some other (*sthāyibhāva*) such as *hāsa or rati.* The same holds true of *bhakti*.

Abhinavagupta, from the Abhinavabhārati
translated by J. L. Masson and M. V. Patwardhan

9

Jñāneśvara

Jñāneśvara is to Marathi literature what Dante, his contemporary, is to modern Italian literature. He is considered by common consent to be the greatest poet, stylist and thinker in the seven-hundred-year tradition of Marathi poetry. His life and work are nothing short of a miracle. He is believed to have willed himself to death at the age of twenty after completing his great work, the *Bhāvārthadīpikā*, popularly known as the *Jñāneśvarī*. The poem is an elaborate commentary on the *Bhagavadgītā*, involving a verse-by-verse textual analysis, which Jñāneśvara composed as an offering to his teacher Nivṛttināth. Though it is not exactly the first Marathi poem, the *Dīpikā* founded the tradition of Marathi poetry and in the course of time acquired the status of the central canonical work in the Vārkari movement in Maharashtra.

At the time Jñāneśvara wrote it, writing a philosophical commentary on a Brahminical scripture in a new language like Marathi was an act of radical cultural departure. It was an important shot in the battle against the cultural hegemony of Sanskrit and high-caste Hinduism waged by the Bhakti poets all over India. As such, the *Jñāneśwari* is couched in political, social and linguistic attitudes which, for thirteenth-century India, are remarkably progressive.

The text of Jñāneśwara's commentary on the *Gītā* employs the device of invocation, both at the beginning of the poem as well as at the beginning of the individual sections. It is in these invocatory parts that we get the poet's philosophy of language, poetry, style and readership. The abundance of imagery that surrounds his explication shows the wealth of his imagination. Extracts from these parts are reproduced here to represent the direction in which non-Sanskrit literature in India was moving during the early centuries of the second millennium. The *Jñāneśvarī* deserves the credit of being the first critical text in modern Indian languages, though of course that is not its only and main achievement.

The *Dīpīkā* has been translated several times. The latest and the most readable translation is by Swami Kripānanda (State University of New York Press, 1989). It is infact a revised version of the translation published by Pradhan and Lambert, which in turn was a reworking of the translation by R. K. Bhagwat (in two parts, Part I with S. V. Pandit, and Part II with V. V. Dixit). The extracts reprinted here are from the original, i.e., the translation by R. K. Bhagwat (*Jñāneśvarī English Rendering*, Publishing Association, Poona, 1953). Though the diction and syntax of this rendering is quite archaic, it is very close to the original.

Note: Several terms in this extract have been transliterated for the reader's convenience.

Invocations

. . . Oh Om, the Primeval being, the very form of Supreme Self, the subject-matter of the Vedas, be bowed to, All glory to it. Oh you, the form of self who can be known from self experience alone, I hail you. Oh God, you yourself are, as I, the humble disciple of Nivṛttinath, propound, that Gaṇeśa who is the very light of the understanding power of all, and (Oh hearers) hear this attentively. This entire Vedic literature is, as it were your own beautiful image, and its body in the form of orthography is shining flawlessly. The *Smṛti* Scriptures are the very limbs of that image, while the stanzas of the poetry are the very movements of the limbs, and the eloquence of the meaning is the pose of their beauty. The eighteen *Purāṇas* (mythologies) are like the jewelled ornaments and the principles (and truths) are the gems, the phraseology being the sockets in which the gems are set. The gentle and beautiful poetic composition is a colourful yarn and its ground in the form of literature is substantial and bright. See further: if these poetic dramas are planned with taste they can constitute jingling bells (*ghungarē)* that create a jingling sound in the form of meaning. And the principles and truths arrived at, as the result of an analysis of these dramas, if subjected to skilful tests—the resultant factors (*padē*) constitute the gems set on jingling bells. The ideology of the poets, Vyās and others, constitutes the belt (round the waist) formed of a silken scarf, while the ends of its ornamental border glitter (above the jingling bells). The six different schools of (Hindu) philosophy that are called *ṣaḍdarshanē* (six points of view) are the six arms (of the image of *Gaṇeśa*) and for the same reason, the arms in the six hands differ from each other.

The logic (*tarkaśāstra*) is the battle axe: the *Nyāyaśāstra* (the doctrine of Social and Political Science) is *aṅkuśa* (elephant goad). The *Vedānta* is a sweet juicy pudding (*modak*). The broken tusk in one hand represents the mutilated doctrine of Buddhism, defeated as a result of the commentary by followers of the Nyāya philosophy. Proceeding in this order, it naturally follows that the logical debate that establishes Absolute Brahman is the bountiful hand (*varadahasta* of Gaṇeśa) and the establishment of religion is his hand stretched forth in reassurance or in token of favour (*abhayahasta*). Pure and right thinking is the straight (elephant) trunk helping to secure the Supreme unalloyed bliss of the Absolute. The talk that removes all differences (of opinion) is his complete (unbroken) and white tusk. *Unmeṣas* (the thrill of the lustre of knowledge) are the small glistening eyes of God Gaṇeśa—the remover of all obstacles. The introductory as well as the concluding portions of the *Mimāṅsa* (the Science of interpretation of Vedic texts) are the two ears on which hover the bees in the form of sages, taking the juicy honey (oozing from the temples). Duality and non-duality are the two temples glistening with corals in the form of philosophy and both these temples, being quite close to each other on the elephant head of Gaṇeśa appear as if equipoised and merged into one. Besides, the fragrant flowers in the form of the ten Upaniṣads, full of floral honey in the form of deepest and truest knowledge, appear beautiful on the crown. The syllable 'a' forms the two feet of Gaṇeśa, the syllable 'u', his big belly while the syllable 'm'—the grand crown of his head. The combination of these three syllables 'a, u, m' forming AUM (Om), covers up and comprehends all the truth revealed as Divine word or word Absolute, I therefore bow, through the grace of the good preceptor, the primary seed of the entire Universe. Now I bow to the world-attracting Śāradā (the Goddess of learning) who inspires the diverse and new expressions of literary beauty and who sustains and fulfils the desire for truth and beauty. Since the good Master who has taken me across to the other side of the ocean of the mundane existence is dwelling in my heart, I hold in high regard the quality of right thinking. Just as an application to the eyes of divine antimony confers on men the super-human power and enables them to see big underground treasures wherever they might cast their glance, or just as the possession of the gem 'Chintamani' fructifies all desires, in that way, I Jñāneśvara say, that I have, through the grace of Sri Nivṛttināth, become fully gratified in desires. Therefore a wise one should worship the preceptor and realise the status of one who has realised his highest duty. The watering of the roots makes the branches and leaves get fresh, or a dip in the ocean accomplishes the object of bathing in all the holy waters in the Universe, or the taking of nectar includes taking in all health-giving juices: in that way the preceptor who makes successful all my wishes—to that preceptor Nivṛttināth I bow again and again. Now hear the very grand and solemn tale. It is the very birth-place of all arts and enjoyments, or it is a garden of unique trees in the form of right thinking: or it is the very treasure of the Supreme truths which are the very roots of all happiness; or it is an ocean filled with the nectar of nine artistic sentiments (*navarasa*—nine classes of emotions or feelings)—all these are this tale. Or this tale is the very place of salvation or the original fountain spring of all learning (*vidyā*) or the abode of all groups of Scriptures; or this tale is the mother home of all religious thoughts, the very heart-cherished thing of the virtuous people; and the treasure house of beauty of Goddess Sarasvatī: or the very Goddess in the form of the faculty of speech has revealed her grandeur in the form of this tale through her inspiration to the genius of sage Vyāsa. For all these reasons this tale is the very queen amongst the great Epics and source of grandeur of all literary works and from this has been secured the sweetness of the *Navarasas* (Nine Rasas) including romance, etc. Do hear one more special feature of this work. The glory of word beauty has been rendered pure and refined through this tale and the tenderness of the highest wisdom of realisation of the Self has been enhanced. This tale has made talent wider or truth truer and the truth has become more tasteful and sweet, while the very consummation of happiness has been made more consummate. This has added sweetness to the sweet, beauty to romantic amours and supreme goodness to worthy things, thereby giving them more pleasing aspect. This tale has secured the essence of artistic perfection for arts, and unique glory to merit, and therefore the sins of king Janamejaya got easily washed out. Thinking a little longer it would appear that by this tale artistic patterns are made more artful and all qualities more lustrous. In short, just as the Universe appears more bright through the Sun's splendour, in that way the Universe has also got greatly illumined and adorned being pervaded by sage Vyāsa's genius, or just as seed sown in a fertile soil automatically grows extensively in that way all truths and subjects worth being known have come to fruitful perfection in the *Bhārata* Epic: or just as one living in a city naturally becomes well-informed, gentle, and refined in conduct, in that way the entire Universe has become bright and clear on account of Vyāsa's words: or just as the tenderness of beauty becomes specially visible in a woman in her early youth; or just as all trees and shrubs, big and small in the garden lands get abundance of growth at the advent of the spring season; or just as there appears nothing special in point of form in a molten lump of gold, but the real beauty comes in when it is converted into ornaments; in that way with the idea that the beauty of all varieties of patterns of one's liking could be expressed by studding them with ornaments in the form of Vyāsa's composition, all story writers have approached this tale, for inspiration and with the object of securing adequate position, all the mythologies have accepted even subordination, and have contributed in the form of sub-narratives to the great epic *Bhārata,* and therefore it is, that what is not contained in this epic, is not to be had anywhere else in the Universe, and this has led to the adage 'The entire world of literacy or universe of truth and beauty is rendered stale by being tasted by Vyāsa (*Vyāsocchiṣhta*).' In this way this eloquent tale has been told by sage Vaiśampāyan to the King Janamejaya—the narrative which is the very birth-place of the highest spirituality in the Universe. You should therefore hear this tale attentively—that tale which is unparalleled, supreme, full of great merit, unique, and the very home of Unity with the very essence of divinity. The portion named *Gītā* preached by Lord Kṛṣṇa to Arjuna is but a particle of the pollen dust of lotus flower in the form of the epic *Bhārata*; or this is the butter incomparable in quality in the form of *Gītā* that emerged through the churning process to which the talent of Sage Vyāsa subjected the ocean of truth. This butter by being successfully boiled in the fire of knowledge with careful thinking has been converted into flavoured ghee: that tale the spiritual vision of which the ascetics wish for, which is actually experienced by the saints and which is revered all over the three worlds, which transpired in due course in the *Bhīṣmaparva*, which is named *Bhagavadgītā*, which is praised both by God Brahmadeva and God Śaṅkara.

And which is taken in with great regard, by Sanat and others—the sweetness of such a story should be enjoyed with refined, equipoised mind by the hearers, in the way, the young ones of the bird *cakor* pick up with feeble mind the tender atoms of the nectar of the small phase of early moon in the '*Śarad*' season. The narrative is preached without words (uttered), is experienced even before the senses come to know of it; its subtle truths are grasped even before its words actually fall into the ears. Just as the black bees carry away the flower dust from the lotuses even before the lotuses come to know of it, in that way becomes the state of hearers. Only the *Kumudinī* (Lotus-plant) possesses the skill of embracing the rising moon and to experience his love without even leaving her own place; in that way only that seeker, whose heart is calm and steady on account of serious and solemn temper can understand the *Gītā* truth. Therefore such saints as are worthy of taking their place by the side of Arjuna on the occasion of hearing the *Gītā* teaching, should kindly pay attention to this story. I might perhaps be considered a bit impudent, over-bearing through familiarity in saying this, yet such is really not the case. Oh hearers, you possess solemn and generous hearts, and therefore I have made this humble request at your feet. It is the nature of parents that they should feel happy at the prattling of their child, in that way since you have once accepted me and called me your own favourite, it is for you now to put up with whatever shortcomings you may notice in me, without any such prayer coming from me: but I have committed another fault and it is of venturing to illumine, enlighten the meaning of the *Gītā* and I have therefore to pray you to hear attentively that illuminating comment. I have of my own accord made myself overbold, without weighing in my mind how difficult it is to carry successfully to its end this work. Could there stand any comparison between the brilliance of the Sun and that of the glow-worm? Or that I, an ignorant person, should embark upon the doing of such a thing, is like a lapwing trying to measure the depth of the ocean with her beak! Another thing: anyone thinking of holding in an embrace the entire sky, must himself be bigger than that sky: in that way the work I have undertaken is indeed simply beyond my scope. The grandeur of its meaning is well praised by God Śaṅkara who was once discoursing on the depth of the meaning of *Gītā*, to questions asked by Goddess Pārvatī who was dismayed and felt puzzled. God Śaṅkara then said 'Oh Bhavāni, the *Gītā* truth is as un-utterable and as perennially fresh as your own majestic appearance and beauty. This *Gītā* truth is the very word of the Almighty, whose very snoring of sleep threw up the Veda itself. How an insignificant, such a diminutive and a very dull thing as myself would fare in such a vast and limitless task (I have undertaken), in a region of profoundest mystery wherein even the Vedas lost themselves completely? How to bring within grasp such unbounded *Gītā* principles? And who could illumine this mighty flame of uncommon splendour? How can a small eye-fly hold in its fist the big sky? But even in this state I consider myself able enough, and the only authority on which I do so is the favour of good preceptor Nivṛttināth towards me, I, Jñāneśvara say. Without that support I am indeed—stupid and thoughtless: yet the lamp of the saint's kindness to me is brilliant and clear. Only in the *Parīs* lies the power by which iron is converted into gold; and so is the power of the ambrosia of bringing a dead person to life. If only the Goddess Sarasvatī is propitious, even a dumb one can command the faculty of speech: that way lies the power of certain things of bringing about certain results, and if these take place in that way there is no reason to feel any mystery of it. One who has got a mother like the desire-yielding cow (*Kāmadhenu*) could never be in want of anything and it is for this reason that I have prepared myself to compose this work. My request therefore to you is 'It is up to you to make good whatever is defective and to drop out whatever is excessive in my work.' Now therefore attend here. I shall be able to talk only if you could make me talk in the way the puppet's movements depend upon the movements of the strings on which they are worked. In that way I am a favoured one of the Saints and the righteous and the protegé of their kindness. I have entirely delivered myself up unto them and they should adorn me with ornaments as they like. Just at this, the preceptor said 'Suffice now: there is hardly any need for you to say all this: hasten up and turn your attention to the composition.' Jñānadeva felt extremely elated at the preceptor Nivṛttināth's words and he said 'Now hear with calm and patient attention.'

... Now, cleansing the heart and making it a boarded frame with feet (*cauraṅga*), let there be installed on it the preceptor's feet (foot-prints). Filling the cavity formed by putting the hands side by side hollowing the palms (*añjulī*) in the form of union, with partially blown flowers in the form of all of sense-centres, let the floral oblations be dedicated at the feet of the preceptor. Let the body of the preceptor be smeared with fragrant sandal paste in the form of single-pointed desire (to render service), cleansed with water in form of deep devotion Let the tender feet of the preceptor be adorned with jingling anklets prepared of gold in the form of unalloyed love. Let the preceptor's toes be adorned with rings in the form of deep and unswerving devotion. Let there be placed on the feet of the worthy preceptor, fully blown lotuses having eight petals constituted of the eight righteous feelings, laden with fragrance in the form of righteous joy. Let there be burnt before him incense in the form of conceit and let there be waved round him the lighted lamp (*niranjana*) in the form of the notion, 'I am myself Supreme Brahman'. Let the preceptor's feet be closely embraced with the feelings of complete identity. Let the feet of the preceptor wear the pair of wooden sandals in the form of my body and life and let enjoyment and liberation be waved around them. I should be eligible to render the service of the preceptor in such a way, that I should secure through such service all the qualifications for (attainment of) all the (four) objects of existence of man. The blaze of knowledge should go up straight to the abode of rest of Supreme Brahman in such a way that the faculty of speech is immediately transformed into the sea of nectar. Each letter (uttered) should have eloquence of such a type that crores of full-moons should be waved around it. When the East is dominated by the Sun it gives an empire of light to the entire universe; in that way the (faculty of) speech should be able to make a gift of Diwali-festival in the form of knowledge to the entire society of hearers. By offering service to the feet of the preceptor, the (faculty of) speech attains a unique luck—luck that brings out words from the mouth that make the divine resonance (*nādabrahma*) look small before them, and to whose level cannot come up even the dignity of the oneness of the Deity;—luck that makes the creeping plant of oration grow in abundance, so that the entire universe enjoys a lovely scenery of the spring season under its bower in the form of hearing;—luck that brings about the miracle of the words (oration) securing Supreme Brahman, which the mind along with speech were unable even to trace and they had to come back disappointed;—luck that makes it possible for the words to store in themselves the Supreme Spirit which is not intelligible to knowledge and also not securable by meditation that the speech (of the disciple) is invested with such infinite beauty is due to the grace of the pollen of the lotus in the form of the dust of the preceptor's foot. What more should be said; it (preceptor's love) is not securable anywhere else but in the 'mother', declared Jñānadeva. (He said further) 'I am only an infant while the preceptor is the mother with an only child, with the result that the flow of her affection turns solely towards me. Oh hearers, the preceptor has showered his kindness on me, in the way the cloud pours down all its waterstore for the sake of the bird *Cātak*. Therefore, even from the stray talk the unengaged mouth might indulge in, an eloquent discourse like that on the *Gītā*, emerges. When luck is favourable, even sand could be converted into gems, and when the longevity of life has not ended, even an assassin turns friendly. Were the master of the universe to be pleased and to give food for satisfying hunger, even small bits of stone turn into nectar (sweetened) rice when boiled. In that way when the good preceptor calls one his own, then even the mundane existence leads to liberation. Just see, did Lord Kṛṣṇa–the incarnation of Nārāyaṇa. The primeval man (*purāṇa puruṣa*—God) the one all-revered by the entire universe—did he permit the Pāndavas to be ever in want of anything? In that way, Śri Nivṛttināth brought up and exalted my ignorance to the same level with knowledge. But enough of this; I am overcome with feelings of affection while speaking. Whoever does possess knowledge to extol adequately the greatness of the preceptor? Now, through his grace, I am dedicating at the feet of you saints he interpretation of the *Gītā*. At the end of the Chapter XIV the Lord of the Union (of the individual soul with the Deity) declared, as an established truth that the man of knowledge is as much the master of deliverance as the God Indra is of the riches of the Heavens; or that one who performs religious duties enjoined to Brahmins (*Brahmakarma*) throughout a hundred births, alone becomes God Brahmadeva and none else; or that the bliss of emancipation goes to the lot of the man of knowledge alone, in the way the light of the Sun becomes available only to the one having a vision, and to none else. Looking (mentally) round for one who becomes qualified to attain such knowledge (the Lord) found only one such. The magical collyrium shows treasures hidden underground but the seer must be one born with feet foremost.

In that way there is no doubt that the mind must be very pure to enable knowledge to get deeply impressed on it. The lord has after careful consideration laid down as an established truth, that knowledge cannot be firmly impressed, unless there is asceticism. Lord Hari has further thought out how the mind can get asceticism. Should one come to know that food has been cooked mixed with poison, he walks away pushing aside (untouched) the plate (in which the food has been served). In that way, once the fact of the mundane existence being only transitory, is firmly impressed on the mind, asceticism, even though pushed away would closely follow you. The Lord is preaching in Chapter XV how it (mundane existence) is transitory, by giving it the form of *sham* tree. A (common) tree, if pulled out and re-planted with the roots upwards and the top downwards withers away; but this tree is not like that. With the aid of this simile (of a tree) the Lord has skilfully swept out clean the cycle of mundane existence. This Chapter XV is intended to prove the nullity of the mundane existence and to establish in one's self the truth of the proposition, viz., 'I am myself Supreme Brahman.' I am now going heartily to lay bare the secret of the Sacred Work (*Gītā*) and you do hear about it. The King of Dwāraka—the full moon, bringing into full tide the ocean of bliss—further said, 'Oh Son of Pāndu (there is) the semblance of the universe that obstructs the way leading to the abode of Supreme Self; this universe of vast expanse is not the mundane existence, this is the form of a giant tree, which is static. But is it not like other trees, that have their roots at the base and the branches upwards, and consequently it cannot normally be brought under control. However extensive the top, were an axe to be applied at the base or a fire applied there, the tree is cut at the base and topples down with its branches. But this tree cannot be easily felled down. Oh Arjuna, it is such a novel tale to narrate that all is extraordinary with this tree. The growth of this tree is all directed downwards. The Sun is at an immeasurable height, while his rays spread out downwards; in that way the growth of this tree is downwards in a very curious way. The floods of water occupy the entire cavity of the sky at the time of world dissolution; in that way every nook and corner of the universe is stuffed with this tree; or after sunset, the night gets fully stuffed with darkness; in that way the sky (space) is packed to its fullest capacity by this tree. It (the tree) bears neither any fruit that could be tasted nor any flower that could be smelt. What exists is this tree by itself all alone, Oh Son of Pāndu, it is top-rooted; yet is not (first) up-rooted and (then) placed in that (topsy-turvy) position; and consequently it is ever fresh and green. Even though truly called up-rooted, still, it has also got innumerable roots at the base. Owing to rank growth of grass (round about) there grow its branches in the tuft of its descending shoots (*pārambyā*). As in the case of *Pimpal*, *Vaṭa* and other trees, similarly, Oh Dhanañjaya, it is also not the case that it has got branches only at the base. There appear in abundance branches on the top-side also. It looks as if the very sky has become its (tree's) foliage or the wind has taken the tree-form or the three different states (namely creation, sustenance and end) have appeared in incarnation (in the form of this tree). Such a big (world-tree), with its upwending roots has come into existence. What is its top, what are the marks of the base, how and why it is down-spreading, and how are its branches, what are the roots at the base, what and how are the branches in the upper region, and why it is called 'Áśvattha'—all these queries have been answered by that self-knowing God. All this I would make clear in select and choice phraseology, so that you will be able fully to realize it. Hear you, Oh lucky one; this is a befitting occasion for you; so you hear it attentively, creating ears (to hear) all over your body!

... Summarising thus the purport of the entire *Bhārata*-Scripture in one single verse, Sañjaya delivered it into the hands of the Head of the Kurū Clan. The scope of fire is unlimited; yet in order to make up the want of the Sun (light) caused by sunset, it is utilized by simply kindling with it only one end of a cotton wick. In that way Brahman in the form of (articulate) sound is infinite in volume, it is transformed into (a finite volume and form of) one lakh and a quarter verses of *Bhārata*-Scripture. *Bhagavadgītā* made up of 700 verses, forms the quaint essence of the *Bhārata*-Scripture; and this last verse of the 700 verses, which represents the very perfection of Saṅjaya's dictum—Saṅjaya the disciple of Sage Vyāsa—it is an all-inclusive sum and substance of the entire *Gītā*-Scripture. One who holds fast this verse next to his heart will have conquered nescience, root and branch. These 700 verses constitute as it were so many foot-steps of the *Gītā* Scripture, and instead of calling them foot-steps, they might be taken as the ambrosia raining down from the sky in the form of *Gītā* -Scripture. Or, I rather feel that these verses are the very pillars of the Court (hall) of the King 'Supreme Self: or the *Gītā* might be likened to the Goddess described in the *Saptaśati* Scripture (*Saptaśati* – 700 verses)—the Goddess that got gladdened by giving absolution (by slaying him) to the demon named Mahiṣa—buffalo—in the form of infatuation. Therefore, one who becomes its devotee (servant) through mind, body and speech would be the sovereign King of the empire in the form of self-bliss: or these are the lustrous verses in the form of *Gītā*, that compete with and even excel the Sun in point of splendour, created by Lord Kṛṣṇa for fighting out the darkness in the form of nescience; or these verses constitute a bower of the vine (creeping plant), provided as a resting place for the weary travellers wending the path of wordly affairs; or this *Gītā* constitutes a lake in the form of Lord Kṛṣṇa's mouth, buzzing with black bees in the form of lucky saints that enjoy (honey in) the lotuses in the form of verses; or it appears to me that these (700) verses are none else but as many bards (*bandījan*) singing profusely the greatness of *Gītā*; or the *Gītā* is a town enclosed all-round by a (wall in the form of) 700 beautiful verses, wherein have come together to dwell all the Scriptures; or the verses are the outstretched arms of the devoted wife in the form of *Gītā*, coming to embrace her Lord—the Supreme Soul; or these (verses) are the black bees on the *Gītā*-lotus flower, or the waves on the ocean in the form of the *Gītā*, or the horses of the chariot in the form of the *Gītā* of Śri Hari; or these verses are an assemblage of (the floods of) all the holy waters come together into the holy Ganges, at the advent of the unique occasion (*parvaṭī*) of the planet Jupiter entering into the Zodiacal sign Leo (*Simhāstha*) in the form of Pārtha (*nar*); or instead of being a row of verses they are the rows of gem 'Cintāmani' capable of attracting even ascetics' minds, or, of the *Kalpataru* trees planted to win pure meditation. Who could be able to trace, each one separately, of these 700 verses, every one of which excels every other (in point of greatness). There could exist no such terminology as 'milk-yielding' or 'dry' (lit. a cow that has recently calved or calved one year back) in regard to '*Kāmadhenu*' (desire-yielding cow). It is meaningless to use these adjectives. 'In the front or in the rear' in regard to a lamp or 'younger or elder' in the case of the Sun, or 'deep and shallow' in the case of the sea of nectar: in that way *Gītā* verses should not be talked of as 'of the beginning' or 'of the end'. Could the *Pārijātaka* flowers be distinguished and classified as stale or as fresh? Where is the need of my maintaining that *Gītā* verses are all alike in point of greatness, none being more or less (great) than the other, since the *Gītā* knows no distinction such as its sense and its words—which convey the sense. It is generally known that in the *Gītā* Lord Kṛṣṇa is the 'sense' as well the 'word'. In the case of *Gītā* what is secured by understanding its import is also equally got by its verbal recital. With such bold dash this Scripture brings about complete identity between the sense and its vehicle the word, therefore now no topic is left on which I can expatiate and argue. In fact the *Gītā* is the literary and glorious image of Lord (Kṛṣṇa). Any other Scripture subsides within itself, i.e., loses its importance having exhausted its function, once it makes known its intended meaning. Such is not however the case with the *Gītā*. It is ever (without any wastage or destruction) Supreme Brahman in its entirety. Just see: how out of love for the entire universe the Lord made easily available to all, the Supreme Bliss of the Self, making Arjuna only the excuse. The Moon cools down the hearts of all three worlds, making the bird *Cakor* only the excuse; or Lord Śaṅkara brought down to the earth the Sacred Ganges, with the object of cooling down the fever (heat) caused by the advent of Iron Age, (*Kaḷi kāḷ*) making Sage Goutama only the excuse. In that way the cow in the form of Lord Kṛṣṇa has provided this milk in the form of *Gītā*, in sufficient quantity, to the entire universe, making Partha the calf. You will attain the Supreme state were you to concentrate on it (*Gītā*) heart and soul; not only that, but were you only to knead (i.e., set into motion repeatedly) your tongue with it, with the intent of reciting it, you would be strengthening your spiritual power all round, as soon as you hold to your lips the cup in the form of the recital of a quarter of the verse, just as the *parīs*, with a single dash (of its touch) converts iron into gold. Or were you to turn aside your face, without making the cup in the form of the recital to touch your lips, but simply turn your ears to it the mere falling of the *Gītā*-letters into your ears would also result in the same. In short, the *Gītā* gives nothing short of liberation, whosoever, either hears it, or recites it or comprehends its meaning in the way a generous donor never refuses (anything) to anyone. Therefore have recourse only to the *Gītā*, in the company (for help) of the learned: what will you gain by taking to other scriptures? The Subject (of the conversation) frankly carried on (discussed) separately (at different time and place) by Kṛṣṇa and Arjuna, has been rendered into such a simple form that anybody may understand it if he so wishes to. When a fond mother sits down to feed her child, she prepares the morsels of such size (so small) as could be easily swallowed by it: or just as the air which is infinite in extension and fitful, in its motion is brought under control and made serviceable by an ingenious man with the contrivance of a fan. In that way that which could not be secured (grasped) through (ordinary) words was converted into *Anuṣṭupa* metre and made so easy ... Were the pearls not to be created by rain drops of *Svātī nakṣatra* (the 15th Lunar asterism), how could they appear to advantage on the person of beautiful (ones)? How could the ears hear the sound were the musical instruments not to send out any? How could one have fragrant smell, were there created no flowers at all? How could the tongue have sweet taste, were the dainties not to be sweet or how could the eye see itself (its reflection) were there to be no mirror at all? How could he (the seer) worship the preceptor were he not to appear in a manifested form? In that way who could have been able to grasp the infinite, Supreme Brahman, had it not been encompassed within the measure of 700 verses? The clouds continue to draw water (by the process of evaporation) from the sea but the world looks to the clouds, not to the sea although it (the sea) is immeasurably wide! How could the ears and the mouth have been able to experience (enjoy) this theme, which is beyond the scope of the faculty of speech, had it not been composed into verses? That the sage Vyāsa has stored up in the form of (*Gītā)* Scripture, the talk of Lord Kṛṣṇa, has been a great favour done to the universe and that same Scripture I am now making available in the Marathi language after closely scrutinizing every word of Śri Vyāsa. I, an insignificant being, am simply prattling on a subject, on which the imagination and intellect even of a sage like Vyāsa, beset with uncertainty proceeds haltingly. *Gītā*-Deity is so affable (simple). If he has accepted the floral wreaths in the form of the preaching of sage Vyāsa surely he would not say 'Nay' to the simple (bent) grass leaves (*dūrvādaḷ*) from me! Herds of elephants go to rivers for water (to quench their thirst). Could the insignificant sand-flies be denied (the water there)? The young birds, getting new wings and not being able to fly efficiently (get fatigued in attempting to fly) and simply hover in that very sky (cavity), in which the mighty eagle speeds with magnificent sweeps. Because the swan walks so stately (on the earth), does it mean others should not walk in their own (crude) style? A pitcher, when dipped in a vast and deep lake etc., is filled with water according to its capacity; how can it prevent the mouth from holding a mouthful of water (*cuḷa*) according to its modest capacity? Because of its larger size a torch can shed a greater amount of light; does not the small wick also shed light according to its own (limited) power? The size of the reflection of sky on the sea-surface is in proportion to its (sea's) wide expanse; yet there is also its reflection on the surface of the small pond in proportion to its petty size. In that way, because the great talents like Sage Vyāsa and others deal with (move about in) this Scripture, I should forbear from stepping into it, does not stand to reason. Because aquatic animals of the size of the mountain Mandāra live in the sea, should not the other smaller fish, etc., even swim there? Aruna (the Sun's Charioteer) sees the Sun because of his close contact with the Sun; does not an ant living on the (distant) earth also see him? Therefore it cannot be said it is improper, that quite ordinary persons like us should compose *Gītā* in the people's dialect (*deśīkarē*). The father walks ahead while his child follows in his foot-steps (foot-marks); would not the latter reach the same place as the father reached? In that way, if I follow the track of Sage Vyāsa, enquiring of the commentators (Śaṅkara, Rāmānuja, etc.) about the (correct) way, where else can I go and how can I fail to reach the proper destination, even though I might not be personally competent? Besides he worthy preceptor—Nivṛttināth—that preceptor whose forbearance like that of the earth does not get sick of the quick and the still (movables and immovables)—whose ambrosia the Moon borrows and (therewith) cools down the universe—whose splendour is secured by the Sun for removing the darkness, and from whom the sea derives its supply of water, the water its sweetness, the sweetness its beauty, the wind its force, the sky its expanse, knowledge its bright and sovereign glory, the *Vedās* their eloquence and the happiness its fervor—in short, all things their (respective) forms and shapes—who places all under his obligations—that all powerful and worthy preceptor has entered into me and inspired me. What wonder is there then, that I should be enabled to preach in all its bearings the *Gītā* in Marathi idiom. That Hill-Koli (named) Ekalavya, who rendered service (i.e., worshipped) the very earthen idol on the hill-top in name of its preceptor (Droṇācārya) made all the three worlds applaud his skill in archery: Trees (whose roots are) associated with (those of) sandal trees also become fragrant like sandal: Sage Vaśiṣṭha spread out his ochre coloured sheet of cloth (*cchaṭi*) by way of challenge as a substitute for the Sun; what of myself then? (In contrast to the inanimate sheet of cloth) I am a living being endowed with a virile mind and possess a preceptor so powerful that with a single glance (of his) he can elevate his disciple and enable him (disciple) to occupy the same status as he enjoys. With a vision already perfectly fine (clear) and in addition backed up by the (light of the) Sun, what is there that could not be seen? There the daily act of my continuous respiration is capable of yielding perennially new compositions (literary masterpieces): given the grace of the preceptor, are there any miracles that cannot be wrought, says Jñānadeva.

For all these reasons I have preached the substance of the *Gītā*, through the medium of Marathi, in a style that would make all the people understand it. If one were to sing the Marathi version with great skill, there would not be found wanting an attraction in that singing. If therefore one were to sing it, it would be an adornment to his singing. Were one merely to read it (instead of singing it) in a simple way, even then, the *Gītā* would not be found any the less charming. An ornament even in an unworn state looks beautiful; would not its looking beautiful, in the state of being worn, be only in the fitness of things? The pearls if studded with gold lend it additional beauty; yet they do not look less beautiful by themselves even though not so studded: The fully blown flowers of the '*mogrā*' plant during the spring season are not deficient in fragrance whether (they are) unwoven (loose) or inwoven. In that way, I have composed in the 'Ovī' form of verses (*prabandha*) a type of metrical composition which when set to music appears to advantage and even without any musical element looks charming (if merely recited). In this 'ovī' form of composition, I have interwoven letters smelling the essence of Supreme Brahman, in a way that would make all including even children, understand it. It never becomes necessary to look up for any floral growth on a sandal tree for having fragrance; in that way, one gets into rapt concentration in spiritual meditation, as soon as he hears this versified composition (recited): What then if he hears a sermon on it? Will it not throw him into a state of ecstasy? While it is being recited, the erudition contained in it is invested with such a superb bloom that even a flow of nectar (if one be passing nearby) would not be able to attract towards itself the hearers' attention away from that (erudition)! This inborn poetic genius has become (as it were) the very abode of rest with the result that (mere) hearing (of the recital) conquers (i.e., proves more valuable spiritually than) constant study and meditation. Anyone will be able to secure the enjoyment of the select portion of the bliss of the self by hearing, which will nourish further the other sense-centres through auditory sense. The bird *Cakor* enjoys, through its inherent power, the Lunar rays—yet cannot any one (else) also avail himself of the Moonlight: In that way (although it is true that) only those that are fully qualified, can secure knowledge of the deep secret contained in this science of metaphysics, yet ordinary people even will enjoy happiness through this rhapsodical work. This is really all due to the glory of Sri Nivṛttināth. It is not (in fact) a composition, but is the glory of his favour. That secret which in immemorial times, the slayer of the demon Tripura (viz., Lord Śiva) whispered into the cavity of the ears of goddess Pārvatī, somewhere, where exactly we do not know, in the neighbourhood of the sea of milk—that very secret (knowledge) was secured by Machindranāth, while abiding secretly in the stomach of the alligator, living amidst the waves of the sea of milk. Machindranāth met Couranginā̄th, the limbless cripple, on the 'Sapta-Śṛngi' mountain; the latter got all his limbs restored to him as before as the result of Machindranāth's mere vision. Getting desirous of enjoying undisturbed, enrapt concentration in spiritual meditation (*samādhi*) Machindranāth gave over the profound mystery (*mudrā*) to Gorakhnāth—the very lake of lotus flowers in the form of the path of Yoga and the unique warrior capable of vanquishing the sense of objects, and installed him on his own spiritual throne, endowing him with all his powers. Gorakhnāth preached to revered Gaininā̄th the bliss of monism along with all its traditions, that had descended down from the very God Śri Śaṅkara. Gaininā̄th seeing that the 'Kali' age (*kaliyuga*) was swallowing up all beings, called on Nivṛttināth with a mandate, 'You do embrace the traditional lore (*sampradāya*) that has descended down to us through the chain of teacher and disciple from the Lord Śaṅkara—the love which I have fortunately received thus, and make haste (run fast) to protect all the beings that are being devoured by the Kali (strife personified).' Nivṛttināth, naturally kind and very tender-hearted, and having in addition got such a mandate from his preceptor, started like monsoon clouds to cool the universe. Then moved with compassion at the sight of the people in distress, he profusely showered on them the sentiment of tranquillity (note the pun on the expression *śāntarasa* which means: (i) a liquid that has the power to soothe and cool anything and (ii) the 9th poetic sentiment of tranquility), which, by generating aversion to mundane affairs, inclines a man to the path of salvation thus enabling him to shake off all worldly-cares and miseries under the pretext of putting together systematically the meaning of *Gītā*. The upshot of that activity is this book. On that occasion I stood before him, with a strong desire to take in (the *śāntarasa*), like the bird *Cakor* and that brought me the present (magnificent) success. In this way, the preceptor following the traditions imparted to me, through discourse on that subject, the treasure of (the knowledge of) enrapt concentration in spiritual meditation. Had it not been so, whence could I, who never recite nor read, nor yet know how to serve the preceptor properly, have secured such capacity? But remember that the preceptor, making me only a plea (an instrument) composed this work and protected the world. So whatever merits or flaws might have been penned (uttered) here as coming from a mere instrument (of the preceptor), should all be borne by you as would a mother. I hardly knew how to chisel a word most fittingly, how to broach and treat methodically a subject (problem), or what in fact the figures of speech are. In fact it was the good preceptor that did all the talk, making me only a mouthpiece, just as the dancing of a doll takes place according to the movements of the string or other mechanism on which it works. I am not quite particular about tendering an apology to you for any merits or demerits, since I was intended by the preceptor merely as a conveyance for carrying the composition. And any deficiency (in it) that might stand out in the conference of you saints—were such deficiency not to be made up (by you), I would be all wrath with you in a spirit of affection (being accustomed to your indulgence). (If the inferiority—base condition—of iron is not removed at the touch to it) of *parīs,* whose fault would it be? The only part that a stream has to play is to flow and mingle with the Ganges; if it does not then get one with the Ganges, whose fault would it be? Therefore, now that I have luckily approached the feet of you saints, what more do I want in the world? Oh sires, through the grace of my preceptor I have been favoured by the close friendship of saintly men like you who have fulfilled all the ambitions of my life perfectly. Just see, having secured a parental home (*māher)* like you, I was enabled to carry quite happily to its successful completion this book—my cherished desire. It might become possible to cast entirely of gold the earth-globe, or, to create the seven mountains (*kulācal*) of Chintamani gems; or it might be easy to fill up the seven seas with nectar, or it would not be difficult to convert all the (minor) stars into as many moons; or to lay out and plant pleasure-gardens of '*Kalpataru*' trees; but it would be very difficult to discover the hidden sense of *Gītā* by resolving its intricacies. Yet that 'I', a complete mute (dunce) has been enabled to expound the Scripture in the Marathi language in a way that could make all view (i.e., understand) it clearly; that I could swim across the vast sea in the form of this stupendous composition, and waved and paraded the banner of victory (in my hands) in the form of fame; that I could erect a temple in the form of the *Gītā* interpretations, the temple that looks like the mountain Meru with its enormous tops (*śikhara*) and therein install and worship the image of the preceptor: or that an infant that had missed its frank and guileless mother in the form of the *Gītā* teaching, and was wandering aimlessly, should be able to meet its mother again: The credit of all these acts of piety is due to you (the audience). I, Jñānadeva, proclaim to you all the saints that whatever I have said here is the net result of assimilating all your piety, and is not merely empty talk (i.e., a thing to be trifled with). What more should I say to (you) all? That I have been shown (enabled to see) the festival of the completion of this work, is, (as I take it) the fruition of my life. I feel extremely happy that you fulfilled all my expectations to the full extent I confidently hoped of you. O Sires, you have created for me another universe in the form of this work and that makes us simply laugh (out of ridicule) at the Sage Viśvamitra. Where was the greatness in his creating for, and his giving importance to 'Triśaṅku', a mortal world simply for belittling God Brahmadeva! God Śambhu created the ocean of milk, getting charmed with Upamanyu; but it (sea) is not also fit to be compared (with this work) since it contained poison (which was later on churned out). The sun comes in hot haste for delivering the universe from the demon in the form of darkness who has devoured it; yet while doing so, he makes the people suffer from the (tormenting) heat. The moon pours out to cool down the heat-stricken universe; but being herself contaminated, she too is not worthy of being used as a standard of comparison with regard to this work. Therefore, I say, there is no other thing (in the world) that can bear comparison to this work, which meritorious achievement you saints have caused to be created in the three worlds through my agency. Nay, that this religious sermon, kīrtana (praising God with the help of music and singing), has reached its (successful) termination, is all your doing, what remains as my role in it, being that of only a servant. [...]

Epilogue

Now the Supreme Self should get itself propitiated by this sacrifice in the form of a literary production and should grant me in charity the only boon (*prasāya*) that the evil vision of the vile and wicked should drop all its crookedness and sting and they should develop a love towards good actions, and further there should be created fellow-feeling (towards one other) amongst the beings. May the darkness in the form of sins get destroyed and may the entire universe (people) conduct itself in the light of the rising Sun in the form of one's own (religious) duty; and may each and every being (as a class) get the fulfilment of each and every wish of his. Let the concourse of saints that shower down all that is propitious on the universe, appear and visit perpetually the aggregate of beings on this earth. These saints are as it were the blossoms of the moving (walking) *Kalpataru* trees, or the inhabited places (towns) of sentient 'Chintamani' gems or the talking oceans of the nectar. May these saints who are uncontaminated Moons and heatless (cool) Suns be the constant kinsmen (*soyarē*) of all. In short, let all the three worlds be all happy and perfected (with the bliss of Monism), and let them render service eternally to the Primeval Male-Supreme Being. And especially those in this universe that (internally) live on (the constant study of) this work (*Gītā*)—may they have the perfect happiness both temporal as well as spiritual. Hearing this, the Lord of the Universe (in the form of the preceptor Nivṛttināth) said, 'This boon has been granted to you', at which Jñānadeva became very happy. There is in this 'Kali-age', the most holy in all the three worlds, and a very ancient place called 'Pancakrośa' (the modern town named 'Newāse'), on the southern bank of the river Godavari, in (the province of) Maharashtra (modern Deccan), where there dwells the deity named 'Mahālaya' (known as 'Mohanirājā' in modern times), the living thread (the root cause) of the universe. In this holy place rules most justly King Śri Rāmacandra, the crown gem in the Soma Dynasty of the Kṣatriya race, and the very abode of all the arts. At this place, Jñānadeva, the Disciple of Nivṛttināth, the follower of the traditional sect (School) of Mahesha (the Great God Śiva), gave the *Gītā* the garb of Marathi (language). I, Jñānadeva, the disciple of Nivṛttināth, declare that this 18th Chapter is the pinnacle (*śhikhar*) of the beautiful dialogue named *Gītā* that took place between Lord Kṛṣṇa and Arjuna (and is described) in the celebrated 'Bhīṣma' Parva (part) of the Great epic '*Mahā-Bhārata*', and which is the very essence of the 'Upaniṣads' and also the parental home of all the Scriptures, and in which (*Gītā* lake) the Supreme Swans—the Yogins—take resort, in the way do the swans in the lake (known as 'Manasa'). May the aggregate of beings derive complete happiness day by day from the wealth, in the form of the holy Scriptures. Jñānadeva composed (edited) this commentary (on the *Gītā*), in the year *śaké* (saka) 1212 and 'Sacidānandabābā', with great reverence became its writer (copyist).

Jñāneśvara, from the Bhāvārthadīpikā
translated by R.K. Bhagwat

10

Amīr Khusrau

Amīr Khusrau (1253–1325 AD) was of Turkish origin; his ancestors had migrated to India a generation or two before his birth. Though a soldier by profession, he made a name for himself at an early age as a scholar and a poet. Appreciation came to him so early in life that the famous saint at Delhi, Sheikh Nizamu'd-Din Auliya, took him under his spiritual care while Khusrau was still a boy. Khusrau served the Delhi court and had a long, though occasionally perturbed, career. He was prolific as a poet and composer. His contribution to Indian music and Persian and Hindi poetry is remembered by the common people in India even today. It is somewhat curious that though he was familiar with Sanskrit, and with Sanskrit literature on poetics, and though he was himself a poet of excellence, he did not translate any of the Sanskrit theoretical documents about poetry and literature. The fact that he wrote poetry in two languages, Persian and Hindi, and was familiar with several of the living languages of India of his times, shows that he believed literature to be a matter of creation in languages that are spoken and understood. His brief comments on India's multilingualism, learning and cultural excellence reveal a profound catholicity of taste. They also show his respect for bilingual literary practice and literary translations. Khusrau can be claimed as an exponent of what we today call comparative literature. The extracts included here are from his composition, *Nuh-Siphir* (1318) translated into English by R. Nath and Faiyaz 'Gwaliari' under the title *India As Seen by Amir Khusrau in 1318 AD.* (Historical Research Documentation Programme, Jaipur, 1981). The verses included are from Nath and Faiyaz's Chapter IV: 15–17, 47–65, 78–93, 94–104; Chapter V: 1–3, 64–76, 82 (pp. 53–76).

Multilingual Literary Culture

... The Brahmans of India have greater wealth of philosophical thought than what Rumi had revealed to the World.

As nobody has tried to learn from the Brahmans, their learning has not been revealed to the world.

I have done a bit of research in this matter and, after winning their confidence, I have gained some insight into their secrets of learning.

... In order that you may not have an iota of doubt, I shall put up ten arguments (in support of my preference to Indian Wisdom and Learning). My first point is there is inestimable learning ('Ilm') in every nook and corner of India.

It is unfortunate that people outside India are not aware of its arts and sciences.

My second point is that the people of India speak different languages. But the people outside India cannot speak in Indian dialects.

The people of Khita (Chinese Turkistan), Mongols, Turks and Arabs are unable to speak Indian languages.

But we can speak any language of the world as fluently and effectively as a shepherd tends his sheep.

Our mastery over the languages is as assertive as is our capacity to conquer other lands.

But, no country has the courage to look at us aggressively.

My third argument is based on Wisdom. It is irrefutable and wise men will accept it.

Scholars come to India from all over the world, to learn its arts and sciences.

But the Brahman never went out of India to acquire knowledge. He did not consider it necessary to go out to improve upon his worth of learning or to seek judgement on it.

It is well known that a great scholar like Abu Ma'asir visited India. He was like a star from the Heavens and there was none comparable to him on Earth.

He came to India and resided in the ancient city of Banaras for ten years to acquire knowledge from the Brahmans.

He learnt Astrology so proficiently that he excelled all others. I believe, there is nobody who could have acquired so much knowledge as he did, though other scholars have also tried it at length.

Whatever he has written, it is with the ink of India. That is, it is all due to the knowledge he acquired in India.

Now I shall put up my fifth argument to convince those who challenge me. In the *Dimnā-Khalīlā* (*Pancatantra*), which is also an ancient work of India, there is only conversation of animals and birds.

Had there not been an excellent flight of imagination in this work, the world would not have acknowledged its merit.

Because it is such a marvellous and meaningful work, it has been translated into Persian, Turkish, Arabic and Dari.

This book was written in India and other languages have only borrowed it, in their own way.

Can there be a better Book of Wisdom than the *Dimnā-Khalīlā*? The scholars of the world derive inspiration from it.

My eighth argument is that Indian Music is overwhelmingly moving. We put fire of our heart and soul in it.

It is known to everybody in the world that there is nothing like Indian Music (it is par excellence).

Truly, musicians have come to India and they introduced some new features to it.

They learnt Indian Music and lent tempo to it.

In fact, they became proficient in this Art and made their own contribution to it.

But this was possible only after they stayed in India for more than 30 or 40 years.

However, the foreigners could not add anything to the basic principles of Indian Music.

My ninth argument is that our Music is so sweet that it captivates the wild deer and attracts it even in the face of the hunter's arrow.

When (the) wild deer hears the sound of sweet music, it stands hypnotized by its effect.

When the Hindu musician finds the deer standing helplessly hypnotized, out of compassion he bids it to move away.

But the deer is struck by the charm of Music and is so completely lost that it cannot move.

My tenth argument is that no wizard in the art of poetry like Khusrau (himself) exists under the Sun.

I have established India's superiority in the sphere of Knowledge and Learning. Now I will proceed to describe the beauty of Indian languages. These languages are such that I have also learnt and gained something from the common languages of the peasants of India.

I know it, I understand it, I can speak it and on inquiry I have been, to some extent, enlightened by it.

. . . one feature is common to all languages, that is, each one has a taste of its own.

Somebody claims his language to be the best, while the other thinks his own to be better than others.

Everybody is proud of his own language and does not admit superiority of any other one.

It shall be improper on my part to talk of Persian, Turkish and Arabic and beguile myself of their virtues.

One should talk of his own country. As I belong to India, it is only befitting that I also talk of the things Indian.

There is a different language in every corner of this land with its own system and technique.

Sindhī, Lāhorī, Kashmīrī, Kubrī, Dhur-Samundrī, Tilangī, Gūjar, Ma'abrī, Ghourī, Bengali, Oudhi, Delhī and around it, within the boundaries of this land are the languages of India.

All these are Hindwī languages, languages of India since olden times and they are spoken by the people at large.

There is yet another language which is the best of all. It is the language of the Brahmans.

It is known as the Sanskrit since ancient times. Common people do not know its usage.

Only the Brahmans know this language. But every Brahman cannot claim to have mastered it.

Like the Arabic, the Sanskrit also has its grammar, definitions, system, technique and rules, and literature.

This language is a pearl among pearls.

Amīr Khusrau, from Nuh-Siphir
translated by R. Nath and Faiyaz 'Gwaliari'

11

Keshavadāsa

Keshavadāsa (1555–1617) is a major poet of the Hindi tradition of poetry. Of the various works ascribed to him, *Kāvyapriyā*, *Rasikapriyā* and *Rāmacandrikā* were definitely written by him. The *Rasikapriyā* was written for the benefit of literary scholars. It offers a catalogue of poetic conventions and aesthetic assumptions accepted by the literary community of Keshavadāsa's time. It is, therefore, more a text of historical interest rather than of original theoretical interest. However, in its orientation it becomes representative of the sixteenth century Indian literary taste, and by implication, of the prevalent theoretical beliefs. At the same time, the *Rasikapriyā* follows a certain methodological discipline which has its roots in the Bhakti tradition of poetry and philosophy. Though Keshavadāsa's text offers definitions and descriptions of the conventional aesthetic categories such as '*nāyaka*' and '*nāyikā*' or *śṛṇgārā* and *viraha*, he treats all *nāyakas* as forms of Kṛṣṇa and all *nāyikās* as forms of Rādhā. All *śṛṇgārā* is seen as an expression of love between Kṛṣṇa and Rādhā, a kind of cosmic affair. It is often believed that the medieval Indian aesthetics had posited a new theoretical category of Bhakti *rasa*. When we follow Keshavadāsa's text carefully, it becomes clear that bhakti was not an additional *rasa*, a new sentiment not known to Bharata, but that bhakti is an aspect of all sentiments described by Bharata and Abhinavagupta. Bhakti *rasa* is, in Keshavadāsa's meticulous rendering of it, a category of literary convention, loaded with metaphysics and folklore which overlaps with all other aesthetic sentiments, *rasas*.

The translation of the *Rasikapriyā* used here is by K. P. Bahadur (*The Rasikapriya of Keshavadasa: Translated into Verse*, Motilal Banarsidass, 1972, pp. 239–247). In the translation, as it would happen with any other translation of poetry, the musical quality of the original is lost. However, the extracts reproduced here may indicate the quality and concerns of Indian literary theory during the sixteenth century.

Kinds of Poetry

Says Keshavadāsa all poetry
Is of four kinds, as poets do know,
Kaushiki, *Bhārati*, *Arabhati*,
And *Sāttviki*, which is the fourth.

Says Keshavadāsa: where merriment
And love and tenderness combine,
Of simple words and happy sense.
That's poetry of *Kaushiki* kind.

(Example of poetry of the *Kaushiki* kind)

Some women to meet him essay,
Through go-betweens, and some enjoy
In their minds the bliss of sport: some take
Many a vow in sacred sports,
So that they may some converse make
With him, and hear his winning speech:
Some who as goddesses are, always
Do run to see him, and appease
All day the gods with gifts, I fear
Oh! bosom friend, that he's so dark.
What can I do? No sooner she hears—
She, my Kṛṣṇa's name, this woman laughs.

Says Keshavadāsa: that verse in which
The sentiment heroic is,
And wonder too, and merriment;
Appealing to the mind whose sense—
That soul delighting poetry
is of the kind called '*Bhārati*'.

(Example of poetry of the *Bhārati* kind)

The ear-rings of gold which she wears
Are verily the chariot's wheels,
The pendants which are glittering there
The banner which does greatly please:
Head ornament the charioteer.
The saffron lines on forehead laid
As though spokes are, and the nose-pearl
Is as it were the hub well made.
Her one glance does Śri Kṛṣṇa purchase!
Big eyes she has: and a gem shines
On her forehead, as if Kāmadeva
On fishes' chariot were reclined!

Says Keshavadāsa: that verse in which
The violent sentiment, and dread,
And loathing are, in which there is
Alliteration, and words have
Meaning diverse: such poetry
Should be considered '*Arabhati*'.

(Example of poetry of the *Arabhati* kind)

Dense and dreadful clouds, rain-filled,
Whose splendour is of black and white,
Do thunder on the first and fifth
Of Sāvan's lunar days: the sky
They roam, these hideous messengers
Massive as elephants: all around
The lightning strikes! Braja women are
With awe filled by the fearful sound
Now that Śri Kṛṣṇa is far away
Grim horror stalks all people thus.
It seems as though all night and day
Death dances on the land of Braja.

Where wonder, valour, evenness,
All the three sentiments do merge

In equal measure, and the sense
Is understood as soon as heard,
That is considered by all men
To be the pure *Sāttviki* verse.

(Example of poetry of the *Sāttviki* kind)

The bosom companion says to another *nāyika*:
'Oh! foolish girl, burn and destroy
Your million cravings and desires,
Oh! kindle not within your heart
A blaze that burns like Holi's fire!
The love of Radha and Śri Kṛṣṇa
Consider of the highest kind,
Kāmadeva's and Rati's love even
Inferior to theirs I find,
Bhavāniji too cannot sow
Discord between them: not to speak
Of others: Sarasvati's glow
Before them too does little seem;
Though simple she considered is,
One are their souls, and thoughts, and minds,
Though separate are their bodies, still
Through ardent eyes the two are joined!'

Says Keshavadāsa: thus I've portrayed
The sentiments of poetry, nine,
Now of their four faults I'll relate
But unto these give not your mind.

Defects of Poetry

Conflict, dryness, and nauseousness,
Contrariness, and the unwise,
Says Keshavadāsa, these lack goodness,
So these the poets don't describe.

Where contrary sentiments, like love
And loathing, and awe, are described,
And violence too, and tenderness,
Are by poets mentioned side by side—
There the conflicting sentiment
is by all men known to arise.

(Example of a verse with conflicting sentiment)

When laughing I converse, then all
Do laugh; when shorn of shame I see,
With loathing are they filled, and fall
Away from me; if words I speak
I am reproached, and if I long
For something, passion in me wakes—
So your advice to love him not
I kept in mind, Oh! friend, always
Knowing that love will my heart not win,
And for a moment if my gaze
I chance to throw upon Śri Kṛṣṇa
To censure me men will not stay.

Where outwardly the lovers speak
With loving words, but in hearts hid
Their lies, deceit and duplicity,
That is the sentiment insipid.

(Example of insipidity in verse)

Whose mind in cunning is so steeped
On seeing this world, her do you tell
Love's riddle; Oh! so sad it is,
And laughable! ne'er have I heard
A co-wife could be thought a friend,
As with my eyes today I see!
So woman vain! I understand
With your heart you love not, but with speech!

Says Keshavadāsa: where a poet tells
Of pleasures of sex in the midst of grief,
With relish; there is known to dwell
The sentiment which disgusting is.

(Example of the disgusting sentiment in verse)

The bosom companion says to the *nāyaka*.
To bathe, to give alms unto all,
To eat, drink, and with song console,
All this the *nāyika* has forgot:
Her wisdom has fled, and her soul
Hard as a stool's top has been made!
Oh! lover fond, consider not
No sooner she on you will gaze
All pleasures she will leave unsought!
Thus anxious, dull your letter proved
Sweet words her please not—she who turns
From love, how will she laugh and look
When in her grief's furnace burns?'

Says Keshava where good and bad mix,
'Tis sentiment of opposites.

(Example of sentiment of contrariness in verse)

When Śri Kṛṣṇa said, 'Give me some milk,'
The cowherd girl thus made reply,
'I will not give it on credit,
If you should need it, friend, then buy
And you will get!' Then he exclaimed,'
'I am used to free milk, why should I?'
The cowherd maid said, 'tis the same
If I give or give not, for nigh
My home is where I soon will be!'
Śri Kṛṣṇa then said, 'Why do you fight?'
'When was there love 'twixt you and me?
I love to fight!' the maid replied:
Śri Kṛṣṇa then said, 'Will fighting make

Your milk sell?' And the girl said, 'if
It does not sell, I'll myself take
The milk, but you I'll never give!'

Where thoughtlessly those very things
Imagined are, and by poets described,
Which far from understanding lie,
That sentiment unseemly is.

(Example of impropriety in verse)

A danger of deception bright,
A casket of romantic love,
And beneficial to all life
As holy Ganga water, pure,
The treasure selfishness does hold,
The sources of good to others—like
The story of love's god in gold
Entangled—and outspreading wide
As stream of nectar: giving joy
To wise man: shaming Guara quite,
And Gira—which the hermits foil,
And creatures of the world, unwise—
A voice such as these, know my queen,
Is poisonous: thus do I well ween.

(The opposing sentiments)

Know tenderness, and merriment,
Love, loathing, valour, awe, to be,
Says Keshavadāsa, such sentiments
As are opposing mutually.
So do I say: from the hateful
Is fear born, from love merriment:
From valour is the wonderful,
From horror follows compassion.
Says Keshavadāsa, so I with care,
Have various sentiments described,

And lack of sentiment, and where
I've erred, may poets set it right.

(The significance of *Rasikapriyā*)

As lovers miserable appear
Without their loved ones, even so
Poets of the language are, I fear,
The *Rasikapriyā*—who do not know.
More knows he of love, who has read
The Rasikapriyā, and knowledge gains
Of sentiments, and practices,
And joy and salvation attains.

Keshavadāsa, from the Rasikapriyā
translated by K. P. Bahadur

12

Al Badāonī

(Abdul-'l-Quādir Ibn-i-Mulukshāh)

It is generally believed that Indian critics learnt the discourse of literary history from Western criticism. However, that assumption needs to be properly qualified. There indeed were forms of literary history practised in medieval India; and several histories of literature were written in Persian from the fourteenth century to the end of the eighteenth century. The most accurate in factual details and the most readable in its style is Badāonī's *Tawārīkh*, a history of Persian poetry composed in India during the sixteenth century. Badāonī wrote it as a sequel to his general history of the reign of Akbar.

Badāonī's achievement is impressive for several reasons. First, he was clear about the aims of his history. Then, he is consistent in methodology employed to analyse poets and poems. And, finally, his standards of evaluation are uniform throughout the massive work. The three extracts presented here form, respectively, the 'Introduction', a fairly detailed analysis of the contribution of the poet Faizī, and the 'Conclusion'. The first and the final sections throw light on his historiography, the middle one on his method of practical criticism. The English translation used is by Sir Wolseley Haig (Asiatic Society of Bengal, Calcutta, 1925). Haig was an outstanding scholar of Arabic and Persian, and was a Professor of Arabic, Persian and Hindustani at the Trinity College, Dublin. The translator's notes have been retained here as they form material of value for understanding Badāonī's work and times.

Excerpts from the *Tawārīkh*

I will state at the outset[1] that as the author of the *Tārikh-ī-Niẓāmī*[2] has given an account of the nobles of the realm immediately after his history of the empire, and as most of them are now dead, and gone to perdition,[3]

[In no one have I seen fidelity,
If thou hast found one who possesses it convey to him my blessing.]

I will refrain from polluting the nib of my pen with a description of such worthless wretches, and will commence with the enumeration of some of the holy men of the age, for an account of noble men who have chosen the way of God is in every way to be preferred to an account of scoundrels and debauchees. And so will I not be a mark for threats and combinations.[4] ('Throw dust on the faces of those who praise without stint,' and again, 'may God protect us from the wickedness of tyrants.'[5]) An account of the base acts of the followers (of the Divine Faith),[6] with whose unclean existence the age is polluted may be thus described:

Their letters do not spell sense,[7]
Nor do their thoughts tend in the direction of sense;
Think meanly of the base, and of those whose faith is weak,
Form the same estimate of the latter as of the former.
When one can call to mind one's friends,
And so make the heart a garden of sweet memories,
Pity were it to mention one's enemies
For that were to quit the sweet garden for the midden.[8]

The holy men by whose noble existence the reign of Akbār Shāh was adorned have now, for the most part, withdrawn, as the '*anqā*'[9] retires to the mountains of Qāf, to the neighbourhood of the Great God. It is as though they had all conspired together to roll up and remove the baggage of life from this dwelling of care and deceit and to take up their abode in the home of joy and bliss. And now of that caravan not one remains to encourage stragglers.

'The mansions are deserted, temporary and permanent dwelling alike,'
'Nothing remains but owls and rubbish.'[10]

I shall begin with that class of men who were regularly employed in the Imperial service until[11] their fame reached such a pitch that it was as manifest as the sun at midday.

2. Shaikh Faiẓī, the Poet Laureate[12]

In many separate branches of knowledge, such as poetry, the composition of enigmas, prosody, rhyme, history, philology, medicine, and prose composition Shaikh Faiẓī had no equal in his time. At first he used to write under his well-known poetical name of Faiẓī, but later, imitating the title of his younger brother, whom the Emperor describes in writing as 'Allāmī,[13] and in order to glorify himself, he chose a political name in the same measure, viz. Fayyāẓī,[14] but it did not suit him, and one or two months later, having packed up the baggage of this life, he took it from the world with the most bitter regret. He was a master[15] of malevolent activity, idle jests, conceit, pride and malice, and one epitome of hypocrisy, baseness, dissimulation, love of pomp, arrogance and ostentation. All Jews, Christians, Hindūs and fire-worshippers, not to speak of Nizārīs and Sabāḥīs held him in the very highest honour for his heresy, his enmity to the followers of Islām, his reviling of the very fundamental doctrines of our faith, his contemptuous abuse of the noble companions (of the Prophet) and those who came after them, and of holy Shaikhs, both dead and living, and of his unmannerly and contemptuous behaviour towards all learned, pious, and excellent men, both in secret and openly, and both by day and by night. Not content with this he used, despite the sacred faith of Muhammad (may God Bless and assoil him and his family) to regard all forbidden things as lawful, and all the injunctions of the sacred law as unlawful, and, with a view to washing away the stain of his ill-repute, which the waters of a hundred oceans (poured over it) till the day of judgement will not wash away, he used, in the height of his drunkenness, and while he was ceremonially impure,[16] to write a commentary[17] on the *Qur'ān* written entirely in words which contained no dotted letter, and his dogs[18] used to trample on it in all directions. At last, after all his denial of the truth, his obstinacy, his pride and his heresy, he hastened to the place to which he belonged, and went in such sort that I pray that nobody may see or hear of the like. When the Emperor went to visit him when he was at his last gasp, Faiẓī barked like a dog in his face, and the Emperor used to relate this story in open *darbār*, his face was swollen and his lips had become black, so that the Emperor asked Shaikh Abū-1-Faẓl what caused this blackness of the lips and suggested that Faiẓī had rubbed *misī*[19] on his teeth, as the people of India use to do, but Abū-1-Faẓl replied that this was not so, and that the blackness was caused by the blood which Faiẓī had been vomiting. But, without a doubt, the sufferings which he had already endured were very little considered with reference to his vice, his abuse of the faith, and his revilings of his holiness the last of the Prophets (may God bless him and his family, all of them). Many abusive chronograms were discovered for the date of his death. One was as follows:

> 'When Faiẓī the atheist died an eloquent man uttered (as the date of his death) the words,
>
> "A dog has gone from the world in an abominable state."'[20]

Another said:

> 'The date of the death of that carrion Faiẓī is fixed by the words "The four religions of fire."'[21]

Another found the following chronogram:

> 'Faiẓī the inauspicious, the enemy of the Prophet,[22]
> Went, bearing on him the brand of curses,
> He was a miserable and hellish dog, and hence
> The words "what dog-worshipper has died" give the date of his death.'

In the same strain was the chronogram:

> 'The laws of apostasy have been overthrown.'[23]

And another wrote: 'Faiẓi was an apostate.' [24]
And to the same effect is the following:

> 'Since he could not choose but go, there is no help but that
> The date of his death shall be found in the words, "He is for ever in fire."'[25]

He wrote poetry for a period of exactly forty years, but it was all imperfect. He could set up the skeleton of verse well, but the bones had no marrow in them, and the salt[26] of his poetry was entirely without savour. His taste in lewd raving, in boastful verse,[27] and in infidel scribblings, is well known, but he was entirely devoid of any experience of the love of truth, of the knowledge of God, and of any idea of a painful longing for God, and 'a favourable reception is the lot of enemies.' Although his *divān* and *maṣṇavī* contain more than twenty thousand couplets there is not among them one couplet that is not as much without fire as his withered genius, and they are despised and rejected to such an extent that no one, even in lewdness, studies his verse, as they do those of other base poets.

'Verse which is wholly devoid of pith
Remains, for all time, a rough draft.'

And this is stranger still, that although he has spent the whole revenue of his *jāgīrs* in having his misleading lies written and copied, and has sent copies of them to all his friends, both far and near, nobody has ever taken a copy in his hand a second time.

Thy poetry has doubtless taken a lesson from the dignity of the veil,
... For it displays no desire to come out of its private corner in the house.

The following few couplets are taken from his selected poems which he wrote as memorials of himself, and entrusted to Mirẓā Niẓāmu-d-dīn Ahmad and others:

'Cover not thy eyelashes[28] when thy eyes travel, like feet, (the road of love)
For stout wayfarers march with naked feet.'

'Why dost thou cut my hand, thou sword of love? If justice is to be done Cut out the tongue of the slanderer of Zulaikhā.'

'When we cast our bounteous glance on those who sit in the dust
We distribute even to ants brains like those of Solomon.'

'The flood of my tears will hardly turn thy heart of stone;
To turn this mill-stone the flood of Noah is required.'

'O love, overthrow not the *Ka'bah*, for there, for a moment,
Those exhausted in the faith of love sometimes take rest.'
'O love, have I leave to remove from the shoulder of the sky
To my own shoulder the banner of thy power?'
'How long shall I stake my heart on the blandishments of the fair?
I will burn this heart and obtain a new heart.
Faiẓī, my hand is empty and the road of courtship is before me,
Perhaps I shall be able to pledge my *dīvān* for this world and the next.'

The following is the opening couplet of a boastful ode, of which he was very proud:

'Thanks be to God that the love of beautiful ones is my guide.
I am of the religion of Brahmans and of the faith of the fire-worshippers.'

The following couplet is also by him:

'In this land there is a sugar-lipped multitude
Who have mixed salt with their wine and are drunk indeed.'
(Poet) say thyself in what part of his poetry there is any savour.

The following couplets are from the *Maṣṇavi Markaz-i-Adwār* which he wrote in imitation of the *Makhzan-i-Khiyāla*[29] and which did not turn out fortunately for him:[30]

'To beg[31] for what aid I come to this door,
That I have become richer in heart and hand?
I asked for little, but my stock increased
Then, though I sat down, my footsteps advanced.'

The following couplets are from his projected[32] *maṣṇavī, Bilqīs-u-Sulaimān*:

I set myself again to place
The slit of my pen opposite to the window of my heart:
There comes from that window and enters this window[33]
That very light which serves as a guide to the soul,

Although from this court of injustice
The throne of the Sulaimān of my words[34] has gone on the breeze,
Yet it occurred to me to consider a plan
Whereby by means of spells, I might bind the demons in chains,[35]
Bind them, by what means I have, to the throne of my rhetoric,
And adorn that (throne) from the treasures of my mind."

The following is an enigma which he composed on the name of *Qādirī*:[36]

'I will leave the mark from love's brand
Since it is a memorial in my heart, and is the only scar there.'

When he was absent as an envoy in the Dakan I sent him two letters from the lower slopes of the Kashmir mountains, informing him of the Emperor's disfavour towards me and of his refusal to admit me to his presence in order that I might pay my respects. In the petition which Faiẓi sent to court he recommended me to the Emperor's favour and Shaikh Abū-1-Faẓl was ordered to embody that petition in the *Akbarnāma* in order that it might be read as an example of what such documents should be. The following is a copy of that petition, which was dated on the 10th day of the month *Jamādi u-l-Awwal*, A. H. 1000 (February 23, 1592), and despatched from Ahmadnagar to Lāhor:

'Refuge of the world! There lately came to me from Badāon two relatives of Mullā 'Abdu-1-Qādir, in a very disturbed state of mind, weeping, weeping and tortured by anxiety. They told me that Mullā 'Abdu-l Qādir had for some time been sick, and had been unable to keep his promise to attend at court, that some of the Emperor's officers had carried him off with force and violence,[37] and that they did not know what the end of the matter would be. They also said that the long duration of his sickness had not been reported to your majesty. Cherisher of the broken spirited! Mullā 'Abdu-l Qādir has much aptitude, and he has studied what the Mullās of Hindustan usually study in the ordinary branches of learning. He acquired accomplishments under my honoured father, and I, your slave, have known him for nearly thirty-eight years. In addition to his acquirements in learning he has some skill in poetry, and good taste in prose composition, both Arabic and Persian. He has also acquired some knowledge of Indian astrology, and of accounts, in all their branches. He is acquainted with Indian and foreign music, and by no means ignorant of chess, both the two-handed and four-handed game,[38] and has some practice in playing the *bīn*.[39] In spite of all these acquirements he is endued with many virtues. He is not avaricious, has a contented mind, is not vacillating, is truthful, straightforward, respectful, unambitious, humble-spirited, meek, moderate in his requests, almost entirely devoid of the dissimulation so common at court, and entirely faithful and devoted to the Imperial Court. When the imperial forces were sent against Kūmbhulmer,[40] he, having requested permission to accompany them, went thither in the hope of offering his life to your majesty, and was in action and was wounded, and when the fact was reported he received a reward. Jalāl Khān Qūrci[41] first presented him at court, and said, when presenting him: "I have discovered for your majesty an *Imām*[42] with whom you will be well pleased. Mīr Fathu-'llah[43] also acquainted your sacred majesty, to some extent, with his affairs, and my respected brother[44] is also aware of his circumstances; but it is well known that 'a grain of luck is better than a load of merit.'

Since your majesty's court is the court of the just, your slave, acting as though he were present in person at the foot of the august throne, when he saw a helpless man suffering persecution, has represented the case to your majesty. Had he not represented it at this time he would, in a manner, have been guilty of insincerity and want of proper regard for the truth. May God (who is praised) deign to keep the slaves of your majesty's court constant in the path of truth, justice, and righteous dealing under the heavenly shadow of your majesty, their Emperor; and may He long maintain your majesty as their shelter, the cherisher of the miserable, the bestower of favours, the coverer of faults, with boundless wealth, glory, greatness and majesty, by the honour of the pure ones who dwell in the courts of God and the enlightened ones who rise betimes to praise him. Amen. Amen.

If any should ask me what rules of humanity and faithfulness I observe in so harshly reviling one who had so much goodwill for me and so much sincere friendship, and especially how it is that I, forgetful of the command, 'Mention not your dead but in connection with good,' have thus written of a man after his death, and have become one of those who disregard their obligations, I reply, 'All this is true, but what could I do? 'The claims of the faith and the safeguarding of one's compact with God are above all other claims, and 'Love is God's and hatred is God's' is an established precept. Although I was for full forty years in the company of Faiẓī, yet after the gradual change in views, the corruption of his nature, and the disordering of his disposition and especially in his mortal sickness, our relations were changed, and as our association together became mere hypocrisy we were freed each of the other. All of us have our faces set towards that court where all disputes shall be decided. 'On that day the intimate friends shall be enemies to one another, except the pious.'[45]

Among the property left by Faiẓī were four thousand six hundred valuable bound books, all corrected, of which it might have been said with but little exaggeration that most of them were either in the handwriting of the authors or had been written in the authors' time. These became the property of the Emperor, and when they were presented before him he caused them to be catalogued in three sections, giving the first place to books of verse, medicine, astrology, and music; the middle place to works on philosophy, religious mysticism,[46] astronomy, and geometry; and the lowest place to commentaries, the traditions,[47] books on theology, and on all other subjects connected with the sacred law.[48]

Faiẓī wrote a hundred and one books, the *Nal-u-Daman*[49] and others, which he used to reckon. When he was near death he wrote, at the earnest solicitation of some of his friends, some couplets in praise of the Prophet (may God bless and assoil him), and of his ascent,[50] and incorporated them in the *Nal-u-Daman*.

The following couplets are taken from the conclusion of that work:

'O King of Kings,[51] who seekest after wisdom,
Wealthy as the sea and glorious as the sky,
The world is a banquet linked with joy,
The reign is the wine, which stupefies the heavens;
I am the minstrel singing melodies drawn from the veins of my heart,[52]
My pen is the sounding organ.
If from this banquet, in which thy conversation is the cup-bearer
I arise, my song will still remain.
The drinkers circulate the tale
That there is no[53] singer, and yet the assembly is full of song.
To-day, with my honey-sweet music
I am Bārbud, thou the Khusrav of the age.[54]
Though I have polished my pen on the heavens
I am standing before thee on one leg.[55]
Look now on the arrangement of my mystical characters
And now on my long years spent in thy service.
This poem, which bears on its tongue the name of love
Takes thy name[56] to heaven.
I am the inebriating wine of true wisdom,
If I ferment no blame is mine.
I am the bell of thy caravan
And must surely be excused if I give forth sounds.
The reward of my handiwork is this (appreciative) eye,
Which I reckon among the gifts of God.
A hundred nightingales, drunk with love, have arisen, singing
That the rose of Persia has blossomed in India.
I have arrayed in splendour virgin thoughts
In the Ganja of my genius and the Dihlī of my mind.[57]
Before this, when my poems were all the current coin I had
Faiẓī was the name written on my signet;
Now that I am chastened by (spiritual) love
I am Fayyāẓī[58] of the ocean of superabundance.[59]

In thy reign, incomparable King,
Have I plucked from the bush of time the rose of good fortune.
The breeze of my genius has diffused the odour of roses over my banquet,
My cup has been filled to overflowing with the wine of delight;
I have sat laughing, like a cup of sparkling wine,
While the cupbearer, like the bottle, stood behind me
Drinking deeper draughts than either I or my good fortune,
My days have been good, but my means of spending them better.
My gardener has been happy, like thy reign,
For my basil plant has grown freely.
These four thousand jewels of pure water,[60]
Which I have stirred up with the water which is like fire,
Accept, for the lustre of the gems is all thine,
They were produced that they might be scattered round thy crown;
If I have scattered more than I have said
I have then reckoned my harvest without any deficiency.
From this ocean which, in its turmoil, rears its head to the highest heaven
Gems bubble forth on the crest of each wave.
Thus employed, in the art of arranging mystic sayings,
My speech has set itself to no mean employment.
Every pithy phrase with which my pen has charged itself
Has been brought by my heart from distant recesses.
My pen points out to me the road to inscrutable mysteries
Where a mountain of meaning best appears,
Hidden under phrases slight as a blade of grass.
This book is illuminated with my heart's blood.
Its allegories are filled to overflowing with true wisdom.
If its melodies be chanted in the mountains
Their sound will dance among the grains of flowing sand.[61]
I have woven from my swiftly travelling breath
Sacred threads for the Brahmans of the nine monasteries.
My thought, which stirs up mystic truths,
Is an ocean which produces gems from its waters.

This writing, which brings to the light the essence of all things,
Is but half the shadow of my pen.
Every truth contained in it is as water in the stream,
Every knotty saying is as the curl in lovely hair.
This poem is a pearl of which the price may be fixed
For it shows forth the felicity of both worlds;
This lovely idol from the workshop of Āẕar[62] received
Its adornment in the month of Āẕar[63]
In the thirty-ninth year of the Imperial reign,
In the new Divine Era,[64]
When I reckoned up the years of the *Hijrī* era
I computed them to be a thousand and three *alifs*.[65]
This garden, which is full of thy perfume
Is but one rose of the plant of thy boundless wealth.
I have the prospect of the joy of another cup
In laying out four gardens more.[66]
If love thus consumes me entirely,
I shall make moonlight shine from my ashes.
The transparent glass of my heart is melted,
And I will give it, as a mirror, into the hands of the assembly.
The story-tellers of the market-place base their stories on their dreams;
But I have awoken from such stories.
This is the arena of those who have traversed the heavens
And in it valiant heroes are to be descried;
Scribes whose very breath breathes magic, with the points of their pens
Have completed the adornment of this epic.
I also, for the sake of making a name in the world,
Have with my skill in words made a talisman.
I melted down both my heart and my tongue
In displaying this picture to the world.
When my genius scattered its wit into pen,
The pen poured the water of life into the inkstand;
The Messiah saw musk in a moist bladder
And dried it with His breath.

Is this an inkstand filled with ambergris,
Or a censer emitting smoke of ambergris?
When this lofty dome (the sky) became my cradle
The year was 954 (A.D. 1547).[67]
Now that I have spent forty-nine years in this monastery
I have passed through the seventy-two sects (of Islām)
My meeting-place has been in the idol-temples of India,
The fire-temples of Persia have been in my heart.
With a hundred incantations and magical devices
Have I cleaned from the mirror of the king's heart the scum of rust.[68]
This day, among the great tribe of the ages
The sky beat the *naubat* for me on the roof;[69]
Eloquence, that king who has been my surety,
Has enthroned himself on my tongue.
I have become both the equal of the *amīrs*
And the prince of poets.
In every direction I go, uttering my wise words,
The ranks of mystic significations bow the knee to me.
Since love entered into my mind
I have become the adorner of the diadem which is over the
nine thrones of the heavens.
The valiant swordsmen of the kingdom of rhetoric,
The archers of the battle of pretensions,
When they cast their eyes on my forces,
Cast down their shields in the field before me.
My pen, on account of my great fame
Writes as my autograph, 'He who is mighty in speech';
'The pride of the philosophers' is the writing on my forehead
'The greatest[70] of the poets' is the device on my seal.
The heavenly key has opened
To my thoughts the door of mystic significations.
When my breath gave birth to this poem
Khiẕr[71] came, and bestowed on me his length of days.
If the door has been opened before me
My poems have also been endued with long life.

If I reckon up all that both worlds can give
I find it to be but dust from the stour[72] which I have raised.
This pen, which has traversed the whole of my poem,
Drives its splinters under the nails of bad penmanship.[73]
See now the drift of this book, which shall last for ever,
See boundless wisdom concealed in (boundless) love.
Those who are not dumb before this splendour
Are men who are not admitted to the privy chamber of imagination.
As for him whose business is with words,
Let the age endow him with justice.
It is the practice of those of meagre wit
Ever to gibe at their contemporaries:
What of those who have fallen asleep, wrapped in the sheet of the earth?
Knowest thou what they said of the men of their time?
And those who shall obscure my light with smoke
Will I afflict in their eyes (with their smoke).[74]
Moreover, a time will come when I shall be no more,
And shall no longer be the nightingale of this garden;
Then those who struck a thorn into my rose
Shall sigh for sorrow over my shrine.
O thou who hast poured the lees of the draught into my pure wine
Pluck but a rose of the spring of justice,
Or else take my goods at my valuation;
Look to their worth and consider yourself fortunate in me
In the morning, when I sing in this meadow
My melodies shed a hundred gardens of flowers.
I am humble as dust in the path of true appraisers
Who this day, despite the ungrateful,
When they opened this treasure from my stock.
Cast on it a glance which justly estimated it
And looked (with pity) on other unfortunates.
They, like the ocean, teemed with gems
And the diver who brought the gems to the surface
delighted in their commendation.
Art is intensely jealous of love

For I have compounded this poem with love's magic.
This pen is the source of great wonder
That from a dry reed such moist sweetness should flow.
This breath of mine is a monument to love,
For it is vapour which arises from my inward fervour.
Fayyāẓī on this incantation of thine
How long will thou dilate?
It is best that thou should'st bring thy tale to a close
Before thou becomest, thyself, no more than a tale.
O thou consumed with love restrain thy breath;
Have done with love's tale, have done!'

Conclusion

This is the account of some of those poets, most of whom were contemporary with the author and were writing during the time in which he was writing, and whose *dīvans* are current in this age and are circulated as examples. As for those who have leapt from the net of this memoir and are here neither described nor indicated by casual mention, I make them over to those who shall hereafter set foot in the plain of existence, for this series (of poets) is as endless as the *Burhán- i-Taṭḇīq*,[75] and to comprehend them all within the limits of one age, or one short space of time is beyond the limits (of any capacity) and beyond the extremity (of its powers).

A maṣṉavī.

'Two couplets one day scared my heart,
As the singer was chanting them to his guitar
Many Junes, Decembers, and Aprils
Will come after we have become dust and bricks,
While those who are now invisible to me
Will come and pass over my dust.'

Praise be to God! My pen, in its atrabiliousness, has like a madman, dealt drily and coolly with everybody, and has poured out from the cup of its heart every drop of black bile which it had in its spot of original sin[76] and given forth from the columns[77] of its fingers all that came to its tongue, so that (I am not sure) what those who come after we will say when, in their search for treasure[78] they have hastened[79] in the tracks of the crows' feet of this impudent (pen),[80] or what answer I shall give in respect of all my idle gossip. I fear that in accordance with the saying, 'Thou shalt be treated as thou hast treated others' they will deal with me as I have dealt with these poets.

> 'Thou hast called me a promise-breaker, but I fear
> That this accusation will be laid to thy charge on the day of resurrections.'

But there is here a subtle distinction if the discriminating neglect it not, and it is this, that I have apportioned eulogy and execration according to the canon of the unmistakable sacred law and have bestowed praise and blame in accordance with my zeal for the faith, and my case is similar to that of the boor who entered a company seated at table and began to eat without any regard to the others, and collected all the dishes round himself. One of the company said, 'Sir, who are you, and why do you thus intrude upon us?' He replied, 'I am a Turk, and I am servant of the *dārogha*,[81] and I am hungry.' But if others, besides myself, should be jealous for the faith I shall not resent their criticism; nay, rather, my life is a sacrifice for those people who shall apprise me of my faults. But if they be not jealous for the faith let them hang their heads and hold their peace; for in truth the bird of my pen, with its sharp bill and its sublime flight, is in the position of that beast[82] which shall come forth as the first sign of the Judgment Day, for it stamps on the foreheads of the circumstances of the folk of this last age the words 'this one is a Muslim,' or 'this one is an infidel,' exalting some to God's mercy and setting apart others as accursed, and the saying of the prophet (may God bless and assoil him) is clear on this point, 'O God, I have not blessed, and I have not cursed in my cursings any but him whom Thou hast cursed.' It is related that that chief of the prophets (may God bless and assoil him while the sun and the moon shall rise) invoked curses on the polytheistic 'Arabs and on the chiefs of the Quraish, and particularly on one mentioned by name, for a whole month after he had been slandered[83] by the wicked, and said, 'O God, curse the infidels, who stray from Thy way, who make Thy prophet a liar, and who slay Thy saints. Thou art Lord of this world and the next. O God, preserve me in safety, and join me to the pious!' And, since the end is but a return to the beginning, there is, in these days when the faith is exiled (for 'the faith appears as a stranger, and verily, it has become as it appears') every occasion for the constant recital of the following prayer, 'O God, assist him who assists the religion of Muhammad and forsake him who forsakes the faith of Muhammad!'

The author of the *Mirṣādu-l-'Ibād*[84] four hundred years ago uttered his complaint and said:

'O kings of the earth, hasten, all of you,
That you may catch the perfume which is all that is left of the faith!
Islam has gone from your hands, and ye heed it not;
Infidelity has captured the world, and ye sleep!'

Forsaking the custom of authors, who have in respect of each of their works, of whatever sort, a hundred hopes of favour from the age and from the people of the age, and, having dedicated a work to somebody, make it a means of being admitted to the intimacy of kings, of begging for rewards, and of attaining their objects I, without desire or expectation (of material gain but) seeking aid from God, trusting in Him, and firmly laying hold of the skirt of his universal favour and his bounty well-known in bygone times, have placed these, my first fruits, on the dish of speech merely for the sake of virtuosos among those to come, who may be desirous of, and anxious for, information regarding our times, that haply its flavour may please the palates of souls, and also that some relish from the morsels on the table of their favour may become the lot of the palate of the compiler of the work, who is, as it were, their gardener.

'If thou drink wine, pour a draught out on the ground,
Fear not that sin which carries some gain to others.'[85]

I shall now explain what it was that originally led me to collect these fragments.[86] Since a complete revolution, both in legislation and in manners, greater than any of which there is any record for the past thousand years, has taken place in these days, and every writer who has had the ability to record events and to write two connected sentences has, for the sake of flattering the people of this age, or for fear of them, or by reason of his ignorance of matters of faith, or of his distance from court, or for his own selfish ends, concealed the truth, and having bartered his faith for worldly profit, and right guidance for error, has adorned falsehood with the semblance of truth, and distorted and embellished infidelity and pernicious trash until they have appeared to be laudable, confirming the truth of the verse, 'These are they who have purchased error at the price of true direction: but their traffic hath not been gainful,'[87] I am convinced that the people of succeeding generations who shall see their false fables and all their unprofitable prolixity will, in accordance with the saying, 'he who hears dispenses with the solution of his difficulties,' with another class of men, regretful not in the least, be perplexed, and will expect and await (something else), and therefore, that the veil may be drawn aside, it is incumbent on me, who am acquainted with some, at least, of the affairs narrated, and have even been intimately connected with these transactions, to place on record what I have seen and what I have heard, for my evidence regarding these things is that of any eye-witness who is certain of what he relates, and does not spring from mere supposition and guesswork ('and when can that which is heard resemble that which is seen?') in order that, on the one hand, my record may be an expiation of the writings,[88] past and present, which I have been compelled and directed to undertake, and, on the other, right may be proved to be on the side of the Muslims and mercy may be shown to me.

'Perchance some pious man may one day put up a prayer for mercy for this poor wretch.'

And when I examine the matter well I perceive that this rough draft, and other rough drafts like it, have all the merits of fair copies, for, in conformity with the couplet.

'Reduce a word at once to writing.
For words slip suddenly for one's memory.'

Something, at least, of what the author knows whether by having seen occurrences or by having heard of them, is (at once) entered in them and reduced to writing. At the same time to define such scribbling as literary compositions can, to do no more than justice, be nothing but mere boasting and vaunting, which are repugnant to refined natures, and so far am I from vain-glory and pride in this matter that I am ashamed of them, and if I should attempt any lofty flights regarding them this base coin of mine, this worthless and contemptible merchandise, my faulty and inappreciated style, is sufficient to refute and falsify my claim.

In these matters nobody knows me as well as I know myself.

A story by way of Moral

A fox said to a camel, 'O uncle,
Tell me truly whence you come.'
The camel replied, 'Lo, I come from the bath
Where I have bathed my limbs in water hot and cold.'
The fox said, 'You have fine proof of what you say,
For both your forelegs and your hindlegs are very dirty.'

It is now high time for me to raise the hand of supplication to the court of that Providence who lacks nothing and who cherishes his servants, and to ask of Him that which shall be most expedient for me, although His glorious majesty is fettered by no expediency. I shall therefore conclude with the following supplications, which are free from all spaciousness and elaboration, and are (therefore) not far from the assurance of a favourable answer.

Supplications

O King, look upon us with the eye of acceptance and mercy! O Lord of all things visible and invisible, compose us in the seeking of Thy will, and remove from our way, and from the way of all Muslims, all disunion, disquiet, and perplexity! Bestow Thy pardon and forgiveness on us in our time. Let Thy gracious favour and guidance both impel and lead us. Deliver us not up into the hands of our own disunion and leave us not to ourselves, neither entrust us with ourselves, but preserve us from our own wickedness, and bring our affairs and those of all Muslims to a happy conclusion in Thy pardon and acceptances. Pardon what we have done in the past and preserve us from what we would do in the future.

Whatever Thou bestowest on Thy servant, bestow on him faith.
Bestow on him adherence to Thy will.

Forsake us not in Thy wrath; let us not be occupied with any but Thee. Displace us not from Thy remembrance. If Thou shouldst question us we have no answer ready, if Thou art angry we have no strength to abide it. From Thy servant proceed faults and lapses, and from Thee all pardon and mercy. O Ancient of Days that changest not, and Glorious one without peer! O Hidden and Omniscient God, Thou that hearest and seest, that hast no need of description or explanation, our faults are many, and Thou knowest and seest us; grant unto us a good end, let us die Muslims, and join us to the pious; and bless and assoil Muḥammad and the race of Muḥ ammad, and all Thy prophets and apostles.

Look on me as though I were entirely free from disobedience,
Consider not mine offences, consider Thy mercy.
Ward off from me all the evils of the age,
Keep me afar from every evil that there is,
So direct for me all worldly affairs and religious matters,
That I may be free from want in both worlds.
By Thy favour Thou keepest me in safety
From the calamities and tumults of these latter days.
Thou accomplishest the desires of Thy poor servant,
Thou makest me a partaker of worldly and spiritual blessings.
Deliver me not helpless into the hands of mine own lusts,
But grant me protection from my dominant lusts.

Send me not as a beggar before any one,
My begging is at Thy door and no other.
Give me a portion of lawful gain,
Give me a corner apart from the worldly.
Pardon and veil my sin,
For it is Thou that veilest and pardonest sins.
Grant me knowledge of Thine eternal bounty.
Free me from ignorance and error.
Preserve me from companionship with the unworthy.
Cause me to meet with a pious and sympathetic friend.
Set my face on the road towards Thee,
Free me from all else but Thee.
Accomplish not my desire in any object
The end of which will bring me shame.
No one but Thee knows what is for my good.
Thou knowest my loss and my profit.
Enrich me with the treasure of contentment.
Give me ease in the joy of serving Thee.
Incline me not to objects of this world,
Make my heart cold to such desires.
So accustom me to thoughts of Thee
That I may think on no other but Thee.
Open before me the door of knowledge of Thee
And in that privy chamber impart Thy secrets to me.
Give me a cup from the flagon of love
And grant me, from that wine, a new intoxication
So fashion my inclinations to the world to come
That I may no more desire the things of this world.
Though death shall rend my upper garment
Let not the dust of this world settle on my lower garment.
When the sword of death cleaves my life,
When 'Azāzil[89] shall resolve to accept the faith,
Of Thy mercy cast one glance towards me,
Open in my face the door of Thy favour,
Declare to me the glad tidings of Thy gracious forgiveness.

That I may have rest in the sleep of death.
Grant unto me such power that, in that perplexity,
My cross-examination[90] may be easy to me.
When the people of this world set their faces towards the resurrection.
And raise their heads in bewilderment from the dust.
Captured, by their evil fate, in disobedience
Their faces blackened with shame for their sins,
When, in that confusion, in the heat of the Resurrection Day,
The rocks shall become water from the fierceness of the sun's rays,
When there shall not be, in all that plain full of grief
Any refuge but the shadow of the Most High
Of Thy bounty, O Creator, Lord of many claims,
Cast the shadow of Thy favour on my head!
When the balance of justice is brought into the midst
And the deficiency and excess of all shall be made apparent,
When I shall have in my company mountains of sin,
Beside which the mountains shall seem no larger than a blade of grass,
It is not impossible to Thine illimitable mercy
To weight down the scale of my obedience:
In that place of fear and confusion
When the records of each one's acts shall fly open
And my record shall be so black
That it will be impossible to enter any fresh sin therein,
Wash my record with the cloud of Thy clemency,
And, by that washing, raise me to honour:
When the fire of hell shall leap forth as a banner
To draw to itself all the people of the world
Pour, of Thy grace, some water on my fire
And bring me forth purified from that fire.
When over hell the narrow bridge[91] shall appear
And the people shall raise a shout for joy,[92]
That bridge, long as the dark nights of separation,
Soul-melting as the sighs from lovers' hearts,
Narrower than a hair,

Darker than the smoke of the night of separation,
Sharper than a sharp cutting sword,
Shooting forth tongues of flame like hell fire
If Thou take me not by the hand, woe is me,
For the nethermost pit of hell will be my place!
I bring no goods with me but hope,
O God, make me not hopeless of forgiveness!

Praise be to God, and thanks, that after all this smearing of myself with the smoke of the midnight lamp and all this fever of the brain I have gained freedom from this hasty work. Ah, how much distraction have I not suffered at the hands of these troubled times, before this valuable coin of time (to complete my work) and this priceless jewel (the work itself) was obtained.

Please God this work will, for a while, be preserved from the treachery of lack of preservation,[93] of faithlessness, or of evil guardianship, and will thus be safeguarded from the picking and stealing of the ignorant cutpurses of this age, and, being constantly hidden under the protection of God's guardianship, will receive the ornament of acceptance, and no damage will reach it from the evil eyes of squinting (rogues) of varying degrees,[94] the hands of impotent (foes) will fail to reach the skirt of the beauty of this creature of my wit, and whoever is not admitted to the knowledge of its secret will remain disappointed.

A thousand thanks to the God of the world.
For that I have entrusted my jewel to one who can appraise jewels.

It was the intention of my languid and secretive[95] heart and my wearied mind to gather together the *Key to the History of Kashmīr*,[96] and the histories of the Kings of Gujarāt, Bengal and Sind, with an account of the wonders of India, and to have them bound together in one volume with this, but that stuff did not match this, for silk must be joined with silk. Therefore, on Friday, the twenty-third of the month Jamādī'u-ṣ-Sānī A. H. 1004 (March 5, A.D. 1595) I shortened the rope of prolixity and contented myself with writing this much. I composed the following verses with the object of giving, in an enigma, the data of its completion:

Thanks be to God, by whose clemency this Selection[97] has arrived at completion.

When I sought the date of it from my heart (my heart) replied.

(It is) a selection which has no second.

Praise be to God whose assistance has enabled me to complete it, and blessings and peace be on the best of mankind, our lord Muḥammad, and on his family, and on his great companions, till the Day of Resurrection.

Al Badāonī, from the Muntakhabu-t-Tawārīkh
translated by Sir Wolseley Haig

Translator's Notes

1. *Makhti-na-mānad:* literally, 'let it not be concealed,' a common form of commencing a history.
2. *Niẓāmu-'d-Din Aḥmad, vide Āīn-i-Akbarī passim.* His history is generally known as the *Ṭabaqāt-i-Akbari.*
3. Such expressions as this explain Badāonī's reason for keeping this history secret. The literal translation is 'and have not been pardoned.'
4. *l.c.*, 'were I to mention these men at all I could only mention them in such a manner as would lead to my being persecuted, for I will not give praise where it is not due. I will therefore keep silence regarding them.'
5. Two pious ejaculations in Arabic, the former, which is one of the *aḥādis*, or traditional sayings of Muḥammad, denouncing flatterers, while the latter prays for protection from tyrants.
6. These are evidently the persons intended by the word *Ṭalbat.* Badāonī as a good Muslim was much scandalized by the strange freaks of the followers of this new religion of Akbar's.
7. The reference to the idiomatic use of the word *ḥarf* 'a letter of the alphabet' as in the phrase *ḥarfzadan*, 'to talk,' is hard to reproduce in a translation. The meaning of the line is: 'The letters (or sounds) of which their talk is composed do not spell (or make) sense.'
8. *Gulkhan*: lit., 'dustbin,' otherwise 'the furnace used for heating a bath.' The unsavouriness of the latter would be due to the nature of the fuel used.

9. A fabulous bird, described as being 'known as to name, but unknown as to body.' Its abode is in Qāf, a mountain encircling the world, which may be described in much the same terms as is the bird. In practical, as opposed to mythical geography, the name is given to the Caucasus.
10. This Arabic couplet is clearly a parody on the opening couplet of the fourth *qaṣidah* of the *sab'amo'alleqāt*. In the second hemistich the word *ṣum* appears in the text, and also in MSS (A) and (B). This does not make sense. I prefer to read *ṣum*.
11. *Bā* in the text, despite the clear meaning of the passage and the authority of both MSS.
12. Literally *Malik-al-sh'orā* (Poet laureate) 'King of poets', the official title given to him by Akbar in A.H. 997 (A.D. 1580).

    Shaikh Abu'l Faiẓ Faiẓī, one of the most learned men of Akbar's court, was the eldest son of Shaikh Mubārak of Nāgor, and elder brother of the famous Abū-l-Faẓl. He was born at Āgra in A.H. 954 (A.D. 1547). His acquirements in Arabic literature, the art of poetry, and medicine were very extensive, and he used to treat poor people gratis. As a young man he was regarded with suspicion and ill-treated by the orthodox in Āgra on account of his *Shi'ah* proclivities, and when he was summoned to court the orthodox believed, or affected to believe, that he was to be called to account for his heterodoxy, and carried him to court by force. He was however, very favourably received by Akbar, and in a short time became his constant companion and friend. He was instrumental, in A.H. 986 (A.D. 1578–79), in bringing about the downfall of Shaikh 'Abdu-n-Nabi the Ṣadr, who had been one of his persecutors. It is said that Faiẓī wrote a hundred and one books. In 1586 he planned a *Khamsah*, or collection of five epics, in imitation of the *Khamsah* of Nizāmi. The first, *Markazu-l-Adwār*, was to consist of 3000 verses, and was to be an imitation of *Nizāmi's Makhzanu-l-Asrār*. The *Sulaimān-u-Bilqis* and the *Nal-u-Daman* were to consist of 4000 verses each and were to be imitations of *Khusrav-u-Shirin* and the *Lailā-u-Majnūn*; and the *Haft Kishwar* and the *Akbarnāmā*, each of 5000 verses, were to correspond with the *Haft Paikar* and the *Sikandarnāmā*. This great undertaking was never completed. Portions were written, and in 1594–95 Faiẓi, encouraged by Akbar, completed the *Nal-u-Daman* and presented a copy to the Emperor. The *Markazu l-Adwār* appears also to have been completed. Faiẓī translated from the Sanskṛt the *Līlavatī*, a work on arithmetic, and the *Bhagavad Gītā*. Faiẓī was sometimes employed as tutor to the Princes, and sometimes acted as an ambassador. He suffered from asthma and died on Safar 10, A.H. 1004 (Oct. 15, 1595). He was a member of Akbar's 'divine faith.' *Vide Āīn-i-Akbarī*, i, 490 *et passim* and Badāonī, vol. ii. text pp. 260, 309, 365, *et passim*.

A long description of Faiẓī as a poet is given in the *Āīn* (i, 549) from which I give the following extracts: 'He was a man of cheerful disposition, liberal, active, an early riser. He was a disciple of the Emperor, and was thus at peace with the whole world.** He wrote for nearly forty years under the name of Faiẓī, which he afterwards, under divine inspiration, changed to Fayyāẓī.** His excellent manners and habits cast a lustre on his genius.** He composed many works in Persian and Arabic. Among others he wrote the *Sawāṭi 'u-l Ilhām* (vide p. 194 n. f)** Genius as he was, he did not care for poetry, and did not frequent the society of wits. He was profound in philosophy.** The gems of thought in his poems will never be forgotten. In the *Ṭabaqāt* he is thus described, "He is one of the greatest of learned men and S͟haik͟hs and is much respected for his resignation to the Divine will and for his habits of solitary meditation. He has grown to maturity in the Emperor's service and has been honoured with the title of *Maliku-s͟h-S͟h'arā*. In the art of poetry he is a prodigy, and he has written a work on ethics, entitled *Mawāridu-l-Kilam*, which contains no dotted letters, and he has also written a commentary on the word of God, which contains no dotted letters. It is known as the *Sawāṭi-u-'l-Ilham*. His *dīvān* contains over 15,000 verses and he has written some *maṣnavis*. In poetry he is the chief of all poets of the age, and in prose composition he is alone and unapproachable. In branches of knowledge foreign to the Arabic, and in philosophy, medicine and many other sciences he has much skill. In universality of knowledge he has no equal. I have enjoyed intimate friendship with this most learned man of the time from my childhood up. His gentle disposition is equalled by his cheerfulness. His angelic nature imposes an obligation on all his contemporaries."'

13. *'Allāmī* 'my very learned man,' a title bestowed on S͟haik͟h Abū-l-Faẓl by Akbar.
14. *Faiyyāẓī–Faiẓī* signifies 'abundance'; with the *yā-yi-nisbatī* added to it, as usual in a *tak͟hallus*, it becomes Faiẓī. Faiyyāẓ is an intensive adjective formed in the same measure as *'Allām*, from the same root, and signifies 'profusely generous.' *The yā-yi-nīsbatī* converts it into a *tak͟hallus*. The letter *yā* in Allāmī is, on the other hand, the sign of the first (singular) possessive pronoun in Arabic.
15. *K͟hayulā*. The word has perplexed the editor of the text, who says, in a plaintive footnote. *Sic*, in all three MSS.
16. *Janābat* 'Vir de quo egreditur semen coitus, lavabit aquâ omne corpus suum; et immundus crit usque ad vesperum.' Lev xv. The Muḥammadan law on

this point was the same as the Mosaic. The obligation was contemptuously set aside by the 'divine faith'; *vide* Badāonī, ii, text p. 305.

17. The *Sawāṭi-'u-1-Ilham*, vide *supra* p. 194 and note 412.
18. Faiẓī was very fond of dogs.
19. A dentifrice used in India for blackening the teeth.
20. *Makkī az jahān raft ba ḥāl-e-qabīḥ*. 60 + 20 + 10 + 1 + 7+ 3 + 5 + 1 + 50 + 200 + 80 + 400 + 5 + 2 + 8 + 1 + 30 + 100 + 2 + 10 + 8 = 1003. One year short.
21. *Bachār maẓhabnār*. 2 + 3 + 1 + 200 + 40 + 700 + 5+ 2 + 50 + 1 + 200 = 1204. This chronogram gives two hundred years in excess. Badāonī perhaps thought that any stick was good enough to beat a dog with. The 'four religions of fire' were probably Judaism, Christianity, Hinduism, and Zoroastrianism, the 'divine faith' of Akbar being, perhaps, substituted for one of these.
22. *Cheh sag parastī murd*. 3 + 5 + 60 + 20 + 2 + 200 + 60 + 400 + 10 + 40 + 200 + 4 =1004.
23. *Qāedah ilhad shikast*. 100 + 1 + 70+ 4+ 5+ 1 + 30 + 8 + 1 + 4 + 300 + 20 + 60 + 400 = 1004.
24. *Būd Faiẓī mulḥidī*. 2 + 6 + 4 + 80 + 10 + 800 + 10 + 40 + 30 + 8 + 4 + 10 = 1004.
25. *Khālid fil-nār*. 600 + 1 + 30 + 4 + 80 + 10 + 1 + 30 + 50 + 1 + 200 = 1007. Three years in excess.
26. *Maṣaliḥ*. 'Spices,' 'flavouring materials'
27. *Fakhriyyāt*. Verses boasting of their own accomplishments in poetry are a favourite form of composition among Persian poets, and especially among Indian poets writing in Persian.
28. i.e., 'Veil not thyself.'
29. This is a mistake. The *Markazu-'l-Adwār* was written in imitation of Niẓ āmi's *Makhzanu 'l. asrār*, *vide supra* p. 412 n.1
30. By this expression Badāonī appears to mean merely that he did not live to finish it.
31. *Darvīzah* in the text. The MSS. have *Daryūzah*. The difference affects neither the meaning nor the scansion.
32. *Mauhūm* 'imaginary.' The meaning may perhaps be that the poem was the work of Faiẓī's imagination, but I believe my translation to be correct. The poem was never finished. *Vide* p. 412 n.1.
33. i.e., the light is conveyed from the window of the poet's heart to the nibs of his pen, the slit between which is compared to another window.
34. i.e., the poet's words of wisdom.
35. As Sulaimān is said to have done.

36. The meaning of the passage may be, 'an enigma which he addressed to Qādirī'. I have not been able to solve the enigma.
37. *Bi shiddat i tamām.* MS (A) substitutes *sharārat* (malice) for *shiddat.*
38. Akbar himself played both games. *Vide Aīn-i-Akbarī,* i, 308.
39. The bīn is a stringed instrument consisting of a narrow strip of wood connecting, and placed over the openings of, two dried gourds, spherical, or nearly so, in shape. Along the wooden bridge are stretched five or seven steel strings, which are played with a plectrum.
40. This place, the name of which is variously spelt by Badāonī, is Kūmbhalgarh, a fortress on the western border of the Udaipur State in Rajputāna, about 40 miles north of Udaipur city. *Vide* text, vol. ii. pp. 227, 266. It was in April 1576 that Badāoni asked for and obtained leave to accompany this expedition.
41. *Jalāl Khān Qūrcī* was a commander of five hundred. He distinguished himself in the field and Akbar was much attached to him. He was murdered, in mistake for Shimāl Khān, early in 1576. *Vide Aīn-i-Akbarī* i, 475.
42. The reader and leader of prayers in the *musjid.*
43. *Vide* p. 216.
44. Shaikh Abū-1-Fazl.
45. *Ala khilāyaomaēzinb'aza humb'az aduvun illal-muttaqin Qur'ān*, c. xliii. The text A has *muttaqūn.*
46. *Tasavvuf* the doctrines of the Ṣūfis.
47. *Ḥadis* (*ḥadith*). the sayings of Muḥammad.
48. The classification indicates Akbar's contempt for orthodoxy, and evidently much shocked Badāoni's prejudices.
49. The text is corrupt here, and reads as though there were a hundred and one books of the *Nal-u-Daman*, which was not the case. From other sources, e.g., the *Miratu-l-'Ālam*, we know that *Faiẓī* was credited with the authorship of a hundred and one books in all. The *Nal-u-Daman* is the story of the loves of Nala, King of Nishada or Mālwa, and Damayanti, daughter of the king of Vīdarbha, or Berar. Faiẓī's source of inspiration was the *Mahābhārata*, where the story is given at length.
50. *M'erāj (mi'rāj)*. According to the belief of Musalmāns Muḥammad was caught up one night from Jerusalem to heaven, his means of conveyance being *Buzāq*, an animal smaller than a mule and larger than a ass. While in heaven he held 90,000 conversations with God, but on his return found his bed yet warm. This belief was one of those selected for ridicule by Akbar and the followers of the 'divine faith,' *vide* text, vol. ii, p. 316.

If Faiẓī's recantation were genuine it must be regarded as, in some sort, a triumph for orthodoxy.

51. Akbar.
52. Literally 'bloody melodies' (*pardahā-yi-khūnī*). I believe the meaning to be that which I have given.
53. The text has, wrongly, 'thou art not (a singer)'. From the scansion it is clear that the simple negative (not) is the correct reading.
54. A celebrated musician at the court of Khusrav.
55. The attitude, in India, of a supplicant, or penitent.
56. *Ṭugrā* (*ṭughrā*). Literally, 'thy royal sign manual.'
57. The reference is to the two great poets Niẓāmī of Ganja (in imitation of whose *Lailā-u-Majnūn* this poem was written) and Amir Khusrav of Dihlī. Faiẓī means to say that he has conceived poetical ideas which neither Niẓāmī nor Amir Khusrav ever conceived.
58. *Vide* p. 43. n. 2.
59. Mr. Blochmann (*Āīn-i-Akbarī*, i, 549) charitably supposes 'the Ocean of Superabundance' to mean 'God's love,' as, indeed, it may; but it is just as likely to signify Abkar's generosity, or spiritual gifts.
60. i.e., the verses of the *Nal-u-Daman*.
61. *Rēg-e-ravān (rīg-i-ravān)* commonly means quicksand. I take it to mean here the sands of mountain streams, as quicksands are not commonly found in the mountains.
62. The father of Abraham, said by the Musalmāns to have been a sculptor of idols.
63. The ninth month of the Persian solar year.
64. The era instituted by Akbar, beginning with the first year of his reign (A.H. 963 = A.D. 1556). In this era the years were solar, and the old Persian solar months were used. The era was instituted in 1582; *vide* vol. ii, text, p.306.
65. i.e., A.H.. 1003 (A.D. 1594–95), the numerical value of the letter *alif* being one. There is a play on the words *alf* 'a thousand.' and *alif*, the letter *alif*.
66. *Scil.* the *Markazu l-Adwār*, the *Sulaimān-u-Bilqīs*, the *Haft Kishwar*, and the *Akbarnāma*.
67. Faiẓī refers to his own birth in that year. *Vide* p. 411, n. 1. The next verse fixes the date of the completion of this poem.
68. It is obvious that this 'conclusion' of the *Nal-u-Daman* does not consist of the couplets written in praise of the prophet and on his ascent, mentioned on p. 422. Here Faiẓī, after boasting of his electicism mentions with

pride his part in weaning Akbar from orthodoxy. The whole extract consists of the glorification of Akbar and the poet, chiefly the latter.

69. The *naubat* was the daily music played at stated hours over the gate houses of the emperor and some of the chief grandees.
70. Literally, 'the seal,' i.e. the last and greatest.
71. The guardian of the water of life.
72. 'Dust in motion.' I know of no *English* word by which to translate *gubār* (*g͟hubār*) 'dust in motion' as opposed to *gard* 'dust at rest'.
73. Faiẓī here praises his penmanship. Driving splinters under the nails is a well-known torture. The meaning of the verse is that other penmen will be tortured by envy owing to the excellence of his handwriting.
74. This verse may also mean, 'I will hold them excused, owing to (the badness of) their eyesight.'
75. I take this to be the name of a book. The words mean 'the demonstration of comparison.'
76. *Suvaēdā* (*suwaidā*) the black spot of original sin which the Musalmāns believe to be in every heart.
77. Jadāval: 'ruled columns.'
78. The text has *kajkāō* and MS (A) has *kanjkā* of neither of which can I make sense. *Kanjkāo*, the reading of MS (B), given as a variant in the text, is correct.
79. The text has *wadīdah*. The variant *dawīdah* given in the text on the authority of MS. (B) is correct.
80. *Zāgpāē kajkulā*. The letter h at the end of *kulah* is not in the text.
81. Prefect of a town or village. In India, a police officer.
82. *Dabbatul arz,* the beast which, according to the Musalmāns, is to come forth as the first sign of the coming Judgment Day, touching the believers with the staff of Moses and marking the faces of the infidels with the seal of Solomon.
83. The text has *qunwal.* MS (A) has *qutwat.* Which appears to be the correct reading.
84. I regret that I have been unable to find mention of this book, or of the name of its author. The meaning of the title is a highway for (God's) servants.'
85. i.e. 'pour a draught on the ground that those who are dead and turned to dust may benefit by it.' The conceit is a favourite one among Persian poets and occurs in the 'tomb-song' Hāfiẓ (ode 439, Jarrett's edition), and frequently in the quatrains of *'Umar-i-K͟hayyām.*
86. Literally 'potsherds.'
87. *Ūlāikal lazina ashtarū-aẓ zalālat bil hudā famā rabiḥat tijaratahum, Qur'ān,* ii, 15.

88. Badāonī here refers to the works undertaken by him under the orders of Akbar, viz.: the translation of the *Mahābhārata* and the compilation of parts of the *Tārikh-i-Altī,* (*vide Āin-i Akbarī,* i, 104, 199, and Badāonī, in text), 320, 399.
89. Satan.
90. After a corpse is laid in the grave it is visited by Munkir and Nakīr, two black livid angels, of a terrible appearance, who order the dead person to sit upright and examine him as to his faith. If he answer rightly they suffer the body to rest in peace and it is refreshed by the air of Paradise, but if not they beat him on the temples with iron maces. They then press the earth on the corpse, which is tormented till the day of resurrection.
91. *Alṣirāt* (*as-ṣirāt*) the bridge over the midst of hell, which is here graphically described, must be passed by all after the Judgment. Muhammad and his Muslims will, with God's aid, pass rapidly over its path, narrower and sharper than the edge of a knife, but the unbelievers, following them, will lose their footing, and fall through the briars, which hedge it in on either side, into the flames of hell.
92. *Nishāṭ*. Joy does not, at first sight, appear to be an emotion suitable to the occasion. The meaning may be either that men will be overjoyed to see that hell is bridged at all, or that the devils in hell will rejoice to see that the bridge is so perilous.
93. Badāonī here declares his intention of keeping this work, the *Muntakhabu-t-Tawārīkh*, a secret. His anxiety that it should not become known during his life-time will be easily understood by anybody who has read it. He designed it to be a counterblast, in the interests of Islām, to the writings of Abū-1-Fazl and his elder brother Faiẓī, who had borne the chief part in leading Akbar into the paths of religious speculation and had so far succeeded in leading him away from orthodoxy as almost to persuade him that he was God. According to a statement in the *Mir'ātu l-Ālam* the book was made public during the reign of Jahāngir, who showed his displeasure by disbelieving the statement of Badāonī's children that they had not known of its existence. Badāonī's work was certainly not known in A.H. 1025 (A.D. 1616), the tenth year of Jahāngir's reign, in which year the *Ma'āsir-i-Raḥīmī* was written, whose author complains of the want of a history besides the *Ṭabaqāt* and the *Akbarnāma.*
94. Badāonī here does not hesitate to attack the highest
95. The text here has sāṭir 'a butcher,' or 'butcherly,' which makes no sense. MS. (A) has *sātir* which I have translated. Badāonī apparently refers again to his intention of keeping his book a secret.

96. This was, apparently, the History of Ka<u>sh</u>mīr, based on that of Mullā <u>Sh</u>āh Muhammad of <u>Sh</u>āhābād, which Badāonī, by Akbar's order, compiled in A.D. 1591. *Vide* vol. ii, text, p. 374.
97. The letters of the word *inte<u>k</u>ḥāb* ('selection') have the following values, 1 + 50 + 400 + 600 + 1 + 2 = 1054. If we subtract the value of the second letter, 50, we obtain the date 1004.

13

Mirzā Asadullāh Khān Ghālib

Mirzā Ghālib (1797–1869), who wrote poetry of extraordinary beauty both in Persian and Urdu, is probably as widely known an Indian literary figure as Kalidasa or Tagore. He was a legend in his own lifetime, whose fame had spread from Delhi to Calcutta. He lived during the period of decline of the Mughal empire, and though born in a prosperous family, he lived a life of ever-multiplying penury. He was a witness to the fall and destruction of his beloved city, Delhi, in 1857. Though he never compiled his poems, or even preserved them carefully, his influence on the poets of his generation and subsequent generations has been so pervasive that Ghālib at once stands out as the symbol of India's creativity during the period of cultural decline in the nineteenth century. His comments, like Keats's, on poetry and poets come to us through his letters, which have now been translated (*Ghalib and His Poetry*, by Sardar Jafri & Qurratulain Hyder, Popular Prakashan, Bombay, 1970) The letters included here are from pages 30, 32, 38, 40 and 41, respectively. These letters bring out the social background to literature during Ghalib's times more effectively than any other document of the century does; but more than that they establish an attitude to creativity and literature, an attitude of healthy appreciation but not carried to any excess. The desolation of the social scene which characterises Ghalib's period also shows, by contrast, his abiding faith in poetry as a way of life, and poetry as ultimate freedom.

Poetry as Freedom

To 'Tufta'

... Why seek my permission to send me your poems? Do send them along although I am no longer a practising poet, like an aged wrestler can only teach the tricks of the trade. Don't think I am exaggerating. Can't write verse any more. I am amazed at my earlier work and wonder how I had composed all that.

April 12, 1858

To Mirzā Hātim Ali Beg 'Mehr'

... I have never kept my poems with me. Nawab Ziauddin Khan and Nawab Hussain Mirzā used to collect whatever I composed. Their houses were sacked, and their libraries destroyed. Now I yearn for my own poems. The other day a beggar, who has a good voice, got hold of a *ghazal* of mine from somewhere. When he showed me that piece of paper I wanted to cry ...

1858.

To 'Mehr'

... Among the poets Firdausi, among the mystics Hasan Basri and among the lovers Majnun ... they crown the lists in these fine arts. The pinnacle is reached when a poet becomes Firdausi, the faqir Hasan Basri and the lover Majnun ... Laila had died before him. You have survived your beloved ... The sons of the Mughals are incorrigible. When they love, they love with a vengeance and destroy the object of their passion ...

To Shiv Narain 'Aram'

... I am glad that *Dastambo*[1] has been sold. Who bought the copies—Englishmen or Indians? Bhai, the light has gone out of India. The land is lampless. Lakhs have died and among the survivors hundreds are in jail. Those outside cannot afford to buy books. I think the English must have bought its copies and it must have been sent to the Punjab. Fewer copies must have been sold in the Purab.

April 19, 1857

---

[1] *Dastambo*: Ghalib's account of the Mutiny, 1857.

To 'Tufta'

... I find both Avicenna and Naziri to be futile. To live one's life one requires just a little happiness; philosophy, empires, poetry are all nonsense. If the Hindus had their avatars and the Muslims their prophets, so what? If you lived as a famous man or as a non-entity, what of it? One should have some means of reasonable livelihood, and good health. The rest is all illusion ... Soon this illusion may end too. My means of livelihood and my health may vanish and I may reach the state of Void. In this Silence in which I find myself now, I am not aware either of myself or of this world or the Hereafter. I duly answer questions, continue my dealings with others, but know that all this is delusion, not a river, but a mirage, not life but vainglory. Both you and I are fairly good poets. Agreed that some day we might become renowned like Saadi and Hafiz. But what did they gain that we would?

1859

To 'Majrooh'

Mir Nehdi, aren't you ashamed of yourself when you say in your couplet: 'Mian, this is the language of Delhi'. From the Jama Masjid to Rajghat Gate is all wasteland. If the debris were removed the place would look haunted ... And the people are still proud of Delhi's language! What a laugh. Where is Delhi? It is now a military camp.

1860

Ghālib, from his letters
translated by Sardar Jafri and Qurratulain Hyder

14

Rabindranath Tagore

Tagore (1861–1941) belongs to World literature and Indian literature, as much as he belongs to Bangla literature. Being the only Indian recipient of the Nobel Prize for Literature (1913) (which he later returned in protest against the Jallianwalla Bagh incident), a charismatic nationalist, and a member of the distinguished Tagore family, he is one of the few internationally known Indians. Along with Bankimchandra Chatterjee, Tagore ushered Bangla literature into the twentieth century by contributing copiously to all forms of writing: poetry, novel, story, drama, essay and criticism. In addition to being a first-rate writer, he was also a painter, a composer and an educationist.

Tagore's uncommon popularity among the reading public is reflected in the fact that to this day he is the most frequently translated Indian writer. As with other Indian Romantics of his time, Tagore's standing as a writer has been questioned by every succeeding generation, and is yet to be settled.

All that he wrote was in Bangla, except the translations of his own works he made into English, and some of his critical essays. The essays were in fact his lectures delivered at Oxford and in the U.S.A. during his tours. The essay selected for inclusion here is one such lecture, which is reproduced from the collection. *Personality: Lectures Delivered in America* (1917). Tagore's educational philosophy and his literary philosophy had an integral link, namely, his theory of personality. He believed that art is created out of a surplus of emotions. A close reading of the essay reveals that Tagore had his own brand of phenomenology, very well thought out and lucidly presented.

What Is Art?

We are face to face with this great world and our relations to it are manifold. One of these is the necessity to have to live, to till the soil, to gather food, to clothe ourselves, to get materials from nature. We are always making things that will satisfy our needs. Thus we are always in touch with this great world through hunger and thirst and all our physical needs.

Then we have our mind; and mind seeks its own food. Mind has its necessity also. It must find out reason in things. It is faced with a multiplicity of facts, and is bewildered when it cannot find one unifying principle which simplifies heterogeneity of things. Man's constitution is such that he must not only find facts, but also some laws which will lighten the burden of mere number and quantity.

There is yet another man in me, not the physical, but the personal man; which has its likes and dislikes, and wants to find something to fulfil its needs of love. This personal man is found in the region where we are free from all necessity,—above the needs, both of body and mind,—above the expedient of the useful. It is the highest in man,—this personal man. And it has personal relations of its own with the great world, and comes to it for something to satisfy personality.

The world of science is not a world of reality, it is an abstract world of force. We can use it by the help of our personality. It is like a swarm of mechanics who though producing things for ourselves as personal beings, are mere shadows to us.

But there is another world which is real to us. We see it, feel it; we deal with it with all our emotions. Its mystery is endless because we cannot analyse it or measure it. We can but say, 'Here you are.'

This is the world from which Science turns away, and in which Art takes its place. And if we can answer the question as to what art is, we shall know what this world is with which art has such intimate relationship.

It is not an important question as it stands. For Art, like life itself, has grown by its own impulse, and man has taken his pleasure in it without definitely knowing what it is. And we could safely leave it there, in the subsoil of consciousness, where things that are of life are nourished in the dark.

But we live in an age when our world is turned inside out and when whatever lies at the bottom is dragged to the surface. Our very process of living, which is an unconscious process, we must bring under the scrutiny of our knowledge,—even though to know is to kill our object of research and to make it a museum specimen.

The question has been asked, 'What is Art?' and answers have been given by various persons. Such discussions introduce elements of conscious purpose into the region where both our faculties of creation and enjoyment have been spontaneous and half-conscious. They aim at supplying us with very definite standards by which to guide our judgement of art productions. Therefore we have heard judges in the modern times giving verdict, according to some special rules of their own making, for the dethronement of immortals whose supremacy has been unchallenged for centuries.

This meteorological disturbance in the atmosphere of art criticism, whose origin is in the West, has crossed over to our own shores in Bengal, bringing mist and clouds in its wake, where there was a clear sky. We have begun to ask ourselves whether creations of art should not be judged either according to their fitness to be universally understood, or their philosophical interpretation of life, or their usefulness for solving the problems of the day, or their giving expression to something which is peculiar to the genius of the people to which the artist belongs. Therefore when men are seriously engaged in fixing the standard of value in art by something which is not intended in it,—or, in other words, when the excellence of the river is going to be judged by the point of view of a canal, we cannot leave the question to its fate, but must take our part in the deliberations.

Should we begin with a definition? But definition of a thing which has a life growth is really limiting one's own vision in order to be able to see clearly. And clearness is not necessarily the only, or the most important aspect of a truth. A bull's-eye lantern view is a clear view, but not a complete view. If we are to know a wheel in motion, we need not mind if all its spokes cannot be counted. When not merely the accuracy of shape, but velocity of motion, is important, we have to be content with a somewhat imperfect definition of the wheel. Living things have far-reaching relationships with their surroundings, some of which are invisible and go deep down into the soil. In our zeal for definition we may lop off branches and roots of a tree to turn it into a log, which is easier to roll about from classroom to classroom, and therefore suitable for a textbook. But because it allows a nakedly clear view of itself, it cannot be said that a log gives a truer view of a tree as a whole.

Therefore I shall not define Arts, but question myself about the reason of its existence, and try to find out whether it owes its origin to some social purpose, or to the need of catering for our aesthetic enjoyment, or whether it has come out of some impulse of expression, which is the impulse of our being itself.

A fight has been going on for a long time round the saying, 'Art for Art's sake', which seems to have fallen into disrepute among a section of Western critics. It is a sign of the recurrence of the ascetic ideal of the Puritanic age, when enjoyment as an end in itself was held to be sinful. But all puritanism is a reaction. It does not represent truth in its normal aspect. When enjoyment loses its direct touch with life, growing fastidious and fantastic in its world of elaborate conventions, then comes the call for renunciation which rejects happiness itself as a snare. I am not going into the history of your modern art, which I am not at all competent to discuss; yet I can assert, as a general truth, that when a man tries to thwart himself in his desire for delight, converting it merely into his desire to know, or to do good, then the cause must be that his power of feeling delight has lost its natural bloom and healthiness. The rhetoricians in old India had no hesitation in saying, that enjoyment is the soul of literature,—the enjoyment which is disinterested. But the word 'enjoyment' has to be used with caution. When analysed, its spectrum shows an endless series of rays of different colours and intensity throughout its different worlds of stars. The art world contains elements which are distinctly its own and which emit lights that have their special range and property. It is our duty to distinguish them and arrive at their origin and growth.

The most important distinction between the animal and man is this, that the animal is very nearly bound within the limits of its necessities, the greater part of its activities being necessary for its self-preservation and the preservation of race. Like a retail shopkeeper, it has no large profit from its trade of life; the bulk of its earnings must be spent in paying back the interest to its bank. Most of its resources are employed in the mere endeavour to live. But man, in life's commerce, is a big merchant. He earns a great deal more than he is absolutely compelled to spend. Therefore there is a vast excess of wealth in man's life, which gives him the freedom to be useless and irresponsible to a great measure. There are large outlying tracts, surrounding his necessities, where he has objects that are ends in themselves.

The animals must have knowledge, so that their knowledge can be employed for useful purposes of their life. But there they stop. They must know their surroundings in order to be able to take their shelter and seek their food, some properties of things in order to build their dwellings, some signs of the different seasons to be able to get ready to adapt themselves to the changes. Man also must know because he must live. But man has a surplus where he can proudly assert that knowledge is for the sake of knowledge. There he has the pure enjoyment of his knowledge, because there knowledge is freedom. Upon this fund of surplus his science and philosophy thrive.

There again, there is a certain amount of altruism in the animal. It is the altruism of parenthood, the altruism of the herd and the hive. This altruism is absolutely necessary for race preservation. But in man there is a great deal more than this. Though he also has to be good, because goodness is necessary for his race, yet he goes far beyond that. His goodness is not a small pittance, barely sufficient for a hand-to-mouth moral existence. He can amply afford to say that goodness is for the sake of goodness. And upon this wealth of goodness,—where honesty is not valued for being the best policy, but because it can afford to go against all policies,—man's ethics are founded.

The idea of 'Art for Art's sake' also has its origin in this region of the superfluous. Let us, therefore, try to ascertain what activity it is, whose exuberance leads to the production of Art.

For man, as well as for animals, it is necessary to give expression to feelings of pleasure and displeasure, fear, anger and love. In animals, these emotional expressions have gone little beyond their bounds of usefulness. But in man, though they still have roots in their original purposes, they have spread their branches far and wide in the infinite sky high above their soil. Man has a fund of emotional energy which is not all occupied with his self-preservation. This surplus seeks its outlet in the creation of Art, for man's civilisation is built upon his surplus.

A warrior is not merely content with fighting, which is needful, but, by the aid of music and decorations, he must give expression to the heightened consciousness of the warrior in him, which is not only unnecessary, but in some cases suicidal. The man who has a strong religious feeling not only worships his deity with all care, but his religious personality craves, for its expression, the splendour of the temple, the rich ceremonials of worship.

When a feeling is aroused in our hearts which is far in excess of the amount that can be completely absorbed by the object which has produced it, it comes back to us and makes us conscious of ourselves by its return waves. When we are in poverty, all our attention is fixed outside us,—upon the objects which we must acquire for our need. But when our wealth greatly surpasses our needs, its light is reflected back upon us, and we have the exultation of feeling that we are rich persons. This is the reason why, of all creatures, only man knows himself, because his impulse of knowledge comes back to him in excess. He feels his personality more intensely than other creatures, because his power of feeling is more than can be exhausted by his objects. This efflux of the consciousness of his personality requires an outlet of expression. Therefore, in Art, man reveals himself and not his objects. His objects have their place in books of information and science, where he has completely to conceal himself.

I know I shall not be allowed to pass unchallenged when I use the word 'personality', which has such an amplitude of meaning. These loose words can be made to fit ideas which have not only different dimensions, but shapes also. They are like raincoats, hanging in the hall, which can be taken away by absent minded individuals who have no claim on them.

Man, as a knower, is not fully himself,—his mere information does not reveal him. But, as a person, he is the organic man, who has the inherent power to select things from his surroundings in order to make them his own. He has his forces of attraction and repulsion by which he not merely piles up things outside him, but creates himself. The principal creative forces, which transmute things into our living structure, are emotional forces. A man, where he is religious, is a person, but not where he is a mere theologian. His feeling for the divine is creative. But his mere knowledge of the divine cannot be formed into his own essence because of this lack of the emotional fire.

Let us here consider what are the contents of this personality and how it is related to the outer world. This world appears to us as an individual, and not merely as a bundle of invisible forces. For this, as everybody knows, it is greatly indebted to our senses and our mind. This apparent world is man's world. It has taken its special features of shape, colour and movement from the peculiar range and qualities of our perception. It is what our sense limits have specially acquired and built for us and walled up. Not only the physical and chemical forces, but man's perceptual forces, are its potent factors,—because it is man's world, and not an abstract world of physics or metaphysics.

This world, which takes its form in the mould of man's perception, still remains only as the partial world of his senses and mind. It is like a guest and not like a kinsman. It becomes completely our own when it comes within the range of our emotions. With our love and hatred, pleasure and pain, fear and wonder, continually working upon it, this world becomes a part of our personality. It grows with our growth, it changes with our changes. We are great or small, according to the magnitude and littleness of this assimilation, according to the quality of its sum total. If this world were taken away, our personality would lose all its content.

Our emotions are the gastric juices which transform this world of appearance into the more intimate world of sentiments. On the other hand, this outer world has its own juices, having their various qualities which excite our emotional activities. This is called in our Sanskrit rhetoric *rasa*, which signifies outer juices having their response in the inner juices of our emotions. And a poem, according to it, is a sentence or sentences containing juices, which stimulate the juices of emotion. It brings to us ideas, vitalised by feelings, ready to be made into the life-stuff of our nature.

Bare information on facts is not literature, because it gives us merely the facts which are independent of ourselves. Repetition of the facts that the sun is round, water is liquid, fire is hot, would be intolerable. But a description of the beauty of the sunrise has its eternal interest for us,—because there, it is not the fact of the sunrise, but its relation to ourselves, which is the object of perennial interest.

It is said in the *Upanishads*, that 'Wealth is dear to us, not because we desire the fact of the wealth itself, but because we desire ourselves.' This means that we feel ourselves in our wealth,—and therefore we love it. The things which arouse our emotions arouse our own self-feeling. It is like our touch upon the harp-string: if it is too feeble, then we are merely aware of the touch, but if it is strong, then our touch comes back to us in tunes and our consciousness is intensified.

There is the world of science, from which the elements of personality have been carefully removed. We must not touch it with our feelings. But there is also the vast world, which is personal to us. We must not merely know it, and then put it aside, but we must feel it,—because, by feeling it, we feel ourselves.

But how can we express our personality, which we only know by feeling? A scientist can make known what he has learned by analysis and experiment. But what an artist has to say, he cannot express by merely informing and explaining. The plainest language is needed when I have to say what I know about a rose, but to say what I feel about a rose is different. There it has nothing to do with facts, or with laws,—it deals with taste, which can be realised only by tasting. Therefore the Sanskrit rhetoricians say, in poetry we have to use words which have got their proper taste,—which do not merely talk, but conjure up pictures and sing. For pictures and songs are not merely facts,—they are personal facts. They are not only themselves, but ourselves also. They defy analysis and they have immediate access to our hearts.

It has to be conceded, that man cannot help revealing his personality, also, in the world of use. But there self-expression is not his primary object. In everyday life, when we are mostly moved by our habits, we are economical in our expression; for then our soul-consciousness is at its low level,—it has just volume enough to glide on in accustomed grooves. But when our heart is fully awakened in love, or in other great emotions, our personality is in its flood-tide. Then it feels the longing to express itself for the very sake of expression. Then comes Art, and we forget the claims of necessity, the thrift of usefulness,—the spires of our temples try to kiss the stars and the notes of our music to fathom the depth of the ineffable.

Man's energies, running on two parallel lines,—that of utility and self-expression—tend to meet and mingle. By constant human associations sentiments gather around our things of use and invite the help of art to reveal themselves,—as we see the warrior's pride and love revealed in the ornamental sword-blade, and the comradeship of festive gatherings in the wine goblet.

The lawyer's office, as a rule, is not a thing of beauty, and the reason is obvious. But in a city, where men are proud of their citizenship, public buildings must in their structure express this love for the city. When the British capital was removed from Calcutta to Delhi, there was discussion about the style of architecture which should be followed in the new buildings. Some advocated the

Indian style of the Moghal period,—the style which was the joint production of the Moghal and the Indian genius. The fact that they lost sight of was that all true art has its origin in sentiment. Moghal Delhi and Moghal Agra show their human personality in their buildings. Moghal emperors were men, they were not administrators. They lived and died in India, they loved and fought. The memorials of their reigns do not persist in the ruins of offices and factories, but in immortal works of art,—not only in great buildings, but in pictures and music and workmanship in stone and metal, in cotton and wool fabrics. But the British government in India is not personal. It is official and therefore an abstraction. It has nothing to express in the true language of art. For law, efficiency and exploitation cannot sing themselves into epic stones. Lord Lytton, who unfortunately was gifted with more imagination than was necessary for an Indian Viceroy, tried to copy one of the state functions of the Moghals,—the Durbar ceremony. But state ceremonials are works of art. They naturally spring from the reciprocity of personal relationship between the people and their monarch. When they are copies, they show all the signs of the spurious.

How utility and sentiment take different lines in their expression can be seen in the dress of a man compared with that of a woman. A man's dress, as a rule, shuns all that is unnecessary and merely decorative. But a woman has naturally selected the decorative, not only in her dress, but in her manners. She has to be picturesque and musical to make manifest what she truly is,—because, in her position in the world, woman is more concrete and personal than man. She is not to be judged merely by her usefulness, but by her delightfulness. Therefore she takes infinite care in expressing, not her profession, but her personality.

The principal object of art, also, being the expression of personality, and not that which is abstract and analytical, it necessarily uses the language of picture and music. This has led to a confusion in our thought that the object of art is the production of beauty; whereas beauty in art has been the mere instrument and not its complete and ultimate significance.

As a consequence of this, we have often heard it argued whether manner, rather than matter, is the essential element in art. Such arguments become endless, like pouring water into a vessel whose bottom has been taken away. These discussions owe their origin to the idea that beauty is the object of art, and, because mere matter cannot have the property of beauty, it becomes a question whether manner is not the principal factor in art.

But the truth is, analytical treatment will not help us in discovering what is the vital point in art. For the true principle of art is the principle of unity. When we want to know the food-value of certain of our diets, we find it in their component parts; but its taste-value is in its unity, which cannot be analysed. Matter taken by itself, is an abstraction which can be dealt with by science; while manner, which is merely manner, is an abstraction which comes under the laws of rhetoric. But when they are indissolubly one, then they find their harmonies in our personality, which is an organic complex of matter and manner, thoughts and things, motives and actions.

Therefore we find all abstract ideas are out of place in true art, where, in order to gain admission, they must come under the disguise of personification. This is the reason why poetry tries to select words that have vital qualities,—words that are not for mere information, but have become naturalised in our hearts and have not been worn out of their shapes by too constant use in the market. For instance, the English word 'consciousness' has not yet outgrown the cocoon stage of its scholastic inertia, therefore it is seldom used in poetry; whereas its Indian synonym '*chetana*' is a vital word and is of constant poetical use. On the other hand the English word 'feeling' is fluid with life, but its Bengali synonym '*anubhuti*' is refused in poetry, because it merely has a meaning and no flavour. And likewise there are some truths, coming from science and philosophy, which have acquired life's colour and taste, and some which have not. Until they have done this, they are, for art, like uncooked vegetables, unfit to be served at a feast. History, so long as it copies science and deals with abstractions, remains outside the domain of literature. But, as a narrative of facts, it takes its place by the side of the epic poem. For narration of historical facts imparts to the time to which they belong a taste of personality. Those periods become human to us, we feel their living heart beats.

The world and the personal man are face to face, like friends who question one another and exchange their inner secrets. The world asks the inner man,—'Friend, have you seen me? Do you love me?—not as one who provides you with foods and fruits, not as one whose laws you have found out, but as one who is personal, individual?'

The artist's answer is, 'Yes, I have seen you, I have loved and known you,—not that I have any need of you, not that I have taken you and used your laws for my own purpose of power. I know the forces that act and drive and lead to power, but it is not that. I see you, where you are, what I am.'

But how do you know that the artist has known, has seen, has come face to face with this personality?

When I first meet anyone who is not yet my friend, I observe all the numberless unessential things which attract the attention at first sight: and in the wilderness of that diversity of facts the friend who is to be my friend is lost.

When our steamer reached the coast of Japan, one of our passengers, a Japanese, was coming back home from Rangoon; we on the other hand were reaching the shore for the first time in our life. There was a great difference in our outlook. We noted every little peculiarity, and innumerable small things occupied our attention. But the Japanese passenger dived at once into the personality, the soul of the land, where his own soul found satisfaction. He saw fewer things, we saw more things; but what he saw was the soul of Japan. It could not be gauged by any quantity or number, but by something invisible and deep. It could not be said, that because we saw those innumerable things, we saw Japan better, but rather the reverse.

If you ask me to draw some particular tree, and I am no artist, I try to copy every detail, lest I should otherwise lose the peculiarity of the tree, forgetting that the peculiarity is not the personality.

But when the true artist comes, he overlooks all details and gets into the essential characterisation.

Our rational man also seeks to simplify things into their inner principle; to get rid of the details; to get to the heart of things where things are One. But the difference is this: the scientist seeks an impersonal principle of unification which can be applied to all things. For instance he destroys the human body which is personal in order to find out psychology, which is impersonal and general.

But the artist finds out the unique, the individual, which yet is in the heart of the universal. When he looks on a tree, he looks on that tree as unique, not as the botanist who generalises and classifies. It is the function of the artist to particularise that one tree. How does he do it? Not through the peculiarity which is the discord of the unique, but through the personality which is harmony. Therefore he has to find out the inner concordance of that one thing with its outer surroundings of all things.

The greatness and beauty of Oriental art, especially in Japan and China, consists in this, that there the artists have seen this soul of things and they believe in it. The West may believe in the soul of Man, but she does not really believe that the universe has a soul. Yet this is the belief of the East, and the whole mental contribution of the East to mankind is filled with this idea. So, we, in the East, need not go into details and emphasise them; for the most important thing is this universal soul, for which the Eastern sages have sat in meditation, and Eastern artists have joined them in artistic realisation.

Because we have faith in this universal soul, we in the East know that Truth, Power, Beauty, lie in Simplicity,—where it is transparent, where things do not obstruct the inner vision. Therefore, all our sages have tried to make their lives simple and pure, because thus they have the realisation of a positive Truth, which, though invisible, is more real than the gross and the numerous.

When we say that art only deals with those truths that are personal, we do not exclude philosophical ideas which are apparently abstract. They are quite common in our Indian literature, because they have been woven with the fibres of our personal nature. I give here an instance which will make my point clear. The following is a translation of an Indian poem written by a woman poet of medieval India,—its subject is Life.

I salute the Life which is like a sprouting seed,
With its one arm upraised in the air, and the other down in the soil;
The Life which is one in its outer form and its inner sap;
The Life that ever appears, yet ever eludes.
The Life that comes I salute, and the Life that goes;
I salute the Life that is revealed and that is hidden;
I salute the Life in suspense, standing still like a mountain,
And the Life of the surging sea of fire;
The Life that is tender like a lotus, and hard like a thunderbolt.
I salute the Life which is of the mind, with its one side in the dark and the other in the light.
I salute the Life in the house and the Life abroad in the unknown,
The Life full of joy and the Life weary with its pains,
The Life eternally moving, rocking the world into stillness,
The Life deep and silent, breaking out into roaring waves.

This idea of life is not a mere logical deduction; it is as real to the poetess as the air to the bird who feels it at every beat of its wings. Woman has realised the mystery of life in her child more intimately than man has done. This woman's nature in the poet has felt the deep stir of life in all the world. She has known it to be infinite,—not through any reasoning process, but through the illumination of her feeling. Therefore the same idea, which is a mere abstraction to one whose sense of the reality is limited, becomes luminously real to another whose sensibility has a wider range. We have often heard the Indian mind described by Western critics as metaphysical, because it is ready to soar in the infinite. But it has to be noted that the infinite is not a mere matter of philosophical speculation to India; it is as real to her as the sunlight. She must see it, make use of it in her life. Therefore it has come out so profusely in her symbolism of worship, in her literature. The poet of the *Upanishad* has said that the slightest movement of life would be impossible if the sky were not filled with infinite joy. This universal presence was as much of a reality to him as the earth under his feet, nay, even more. The realisation of this has broken out in a song of an Indian poet who was born in the fifteenth century:

> There falls the rhythmic beat of life and death:
> Rapture wells forth, and all space is radiant with light.
> There the unstruck music is sounded; it is the love music of three worlds.
> There millions of lamps of sun and moon are burning;
> There the drum beats and the lover swings in play.
> There love songs resound, and light rains in showers.

In India, the greater part of our literature is religious, because God with us is not a distant God; He belongs to our homes, as well as to our temples. We feel His nearness to us in all the human relationship of love and affection, and in our festivities He is the chief guest whom we honour. In seasons of flowers and fruits, in the coming of the rain, in the fullness of the autumn, we see the hem of His mantle and hear His footsteps. We worship Him in all the true objects of our worship and love Him wherever our love is true. In the woman who is good we feel Him, in the man who is true we know Him, in our children He is born again and again, the Eternal Child. Therefore religious songs are our love songs, and our domestic occurrences, such as the birth of a son, or the coming of the daughter from her husband's house to her parents and her departure again, are woven in our literature as a drama whose counterpart is in the divine.

It is thus that the domain of literature has extended into the region which seems hidden in the depth of mystery and made it human and speaking. It is growing, not only into history, science and philosophy, but, with our expanding sympathy, into our social consciousness. The classical literature of the ancient time was only peopled by saints and kings and heroes. It threw no light upon men who loved and suffered in obscurity. But as the illumination of man's personality throws its light upon a wider space, penetrating into hidden corners, the world of art also crosses its frontiers and extends its boundaries into unexplored regions. Thus art is signalling man's conquest of the world by its symbols of beauty, springing up in spots which were barren of all voice and colours. It is supplying man with his banners, under which he marches to fight against the inane and the inert proving his claims far and wide in God's creation. Even the spirit of the desert has owned its kinship with him, and the lonely pyramids are there as memorials of the meeting of Nature's silence with the silence of the human spirit. The darkness of the caves has yielded its stillness to man's soul, and in exchange has secretly been crowned with the wreath of art. Bells are ringing in temples, in villages and populous towns to proclaim that the infinite is not a mere emptiness to man. This encroachment of man's personality has no limit, and even the markets and the factories of the present age, even the schools where children of man are imprisoned and jails where are the criminals, will be mellowed with the touch of art, and lose their distinction of rigid discordance with life. For the one effort of man's personality is to transform everything with which he has any true concern into the human. And art is like the spread of vegetation, to show how far man has reclaimed the desert of his own.

We have said before that where there is an element of the superfluous in our heart's relationship with the world, Art has its birth. In other words, where our personality feels its wealth it breaks out in display. What we devour for ourselves is totally spent. What overflows our need becomes articulate. The stage of pure utility is like the state of heat which is dark. When it surpasses itself, it becomes white heat and then it is expressive.

Take, for instance, our delight in eating. It is soon exhausted, it gives no indication of the infinite. Therefore, though in its extensiveness it is more universal than any other passion, it is rejected by art. It is like an immigrant coming to these Atlantic shores, who can show no cash balance in his favour.

In our life we have one side which is finite, where we exhaust ourselves at every step, and we have another side, where our aspiration, enjoyment and sacrifice are infinite. This infinite side of man must have its revealments in some symbols which have the elements of immortality. There it naturally seeks perfection.

Therefore it refuses all that is flimsy and feeble and incongruous. It builds for its dwelling a paradise, where only those materials are used that have transcended the earth's mortality.

For men are the children of light. Whenever they fully realise themselves, they feel their immortality. And, as they feel it, they extend their realm of the immortal into every region of human life.

This building of man's true world,—the living world of truth and beauty,—is the function of Art.

Man is true, where he feels his infinity, where he is divine, and the divine is the creator in him. Therefore with the attainment of his truth he creates. For he can truly live in his own creation and make out of God's world his own world. This is indeed his own heaven, the heaven of ideas shaped into perfect forms, with which he surrounds himself; where his children are born, where they learn how to live and die, how to love and to fight, where they know that the real is not that which is merely seen and wealth is not that which is stored. If man could only listen to the voice that rises from the heart of his own creation, he would hear the same message that came from the Indian sage of the ancient time:

'Hearken to me, ye children of the Immortal, dwellers of the heavenly worlds, I have known the Supreme Person who comes as light from the dark beyond.'

Yes, it is that Supreme Person, who has made himself known to man and made this universe so deeply personal to him. Therefore, in India, our places of pilgrimage are there, where in the confluence of the river and the sea, in the eternal snow of the mountain peak, in the lonely seashore, some aspect of the infinite is revealed which has its great voice for our heart, and there man has left in his images and temples, in his carvings of stone, these words,—'Hearken to me, I have known the Supreme Person.' In the mere substance and law of this world we do not meet the person, but where the sky is blue, and the grass is green, where the flower has its beauty and fruit its taste, where there is not only perpetuation of race, but joy of living and love of fellow creatures, sympathy and self-sacrifice, there is revealed to us the Person who is infinite. There, not merely are facts pelted down our heads, but we feel the bonds of the personal relationship binding our hearts with this world through all time. And this is Reality, which is truth made our own,—truth that has its eternal relation with the Supreme Person. This world, whose soul seems to be aching for expression in its endless rhythm of lines and colours, music and movements, hints and whispers, and all the suggestion of the inexpressible, finds its harmony in the ceaseless longing of the human heart to make the Person manifest in its own creations.

The desire for the manifestation of this Person makes us lavish with all our resources. When we accumulate wealth, we have to account for every penny; we reason accurately and we act with care. But when we set about to express our wealthiness, we seem to lose sight of all lines of limit. In fact, none of us has wealth enough fully to express what we mean by wealthiness. When we try to save our life from an enemy's attack, we are cautious in our movements. But when we feel impelled to express our personal bravery, we willingly take risks and go to the length of losing our lives. We are careful of expenditure in our everyday life, but on festive occasions, when we express our joy, we are thriftless even to the extent of going beyond our means. For when we are intensely conscious of our own personality, we are apt to ignore the tyranny of facts. We are temperate in our dealings with the man with whom our relation is the relationship of prudence. But we feel we have not got enough for those whom we love. The poet says of the beloved:

'It seems to me that I have gazed at your beauty from the beginning of my existence, that I have kept you in my arms for countless ages, yet it has not been enough for me.'

He says, 'Stones would melt in tenderness, if touched by the breeze of your mantle.'

He feels that his 'eyes long to fly like birds to see his beloved.'

Judged from the standpoint of reason these are exaggerations, but from that of the heart, freed from limits of facts, they are true.

Is it not the same in God's creation? There, forces and matters are alike mere facts—they have their strict accounts kept and they can be accurately weighed and measured. Only beauty is not a mere fact; it cannot be accounted for, it cannot be surveyed and mapped.

It is an expression. Facts are like wine-cups that carry it, they are hidden by it, it overflows them. It is infinite in its suggestion, it is extravagant in its words. It is personal, therefore, beyond science. It sings as does the poet, It seems to me that I have gazed at you from the beginning of my existence, that I have kept you in my arms for countless ages, yet it has not been enough for me.'

So we find that our world of expression does not accurately coincide with the world of facts, because personality surpasses facts on every side. It is conscious of its infinity and creates from its abundance; and because, in art, things are challenged from the standpoint of the immortal Person, those which are important in our customary life of facts become unreal when placed on the pedestal of art. A newspaper account of some domestic incident in the life of a commercial magnate may create agitation in Society, yet would lose all its significance if placed by the side of great works of art. We can well imagine how it would hide its face in shame, if by some cruel accident it found itself in the neighbourhood of Keats's 'Ode on a Grecian Urn.'

Yet the very same incident, if treated deeply, divested of its conventional superficiality, might have a better claim in art than the negotiation for raising a big loan for China, or the defeat of British diplomacy in Turkey. A mere household event of a husband's jealousy of his wife, as depicted in one of Shakespeare's tragedies, has greater value in the realm of art than the code of caste regulations in Manu's scripture or the law prohibiting inhabitants of one part of the world from receiving human treatment in another. For when facts are looked upon as mere facts, having their chain of consequences in the world of facts, they are rejected by art.

When, however, such laws and regulations as I have mentioned are viewed in their application to some human individual, in all their injustice, insult and pain, then they are seen in their complete truth and they become subjects for art. The disposition of a great battle may be a great fact, but it is useless for the purpose of art. But what that battle has caused to a single individual soldier, separated from his loved ones and maimed for life, has a vital value for art which deals with reality.

Man's social world is like some nebulous system of stars, consisting largely of a mist of abstractions, with such names as society, state, nation, commerce, politics and war. In their dense amorphousness man is hidden and truth is blurred. The one vague idea of war covers from our sight a multitude of miseries, and obscures our sense of reality. The idea of the nation is responsible for crimes that would be appalling, if the mist could be removed for a moment. The idea of society has created forms of slavery without number, which we tolerate simply because it has deadened our consciousness of the reality of the personal man. In the name of religion deeds have been done that would exhaust all the resources of hell itself for punishment, because with its creeds and dogmas it has applied an extensive plaster of anaesthetic over a large surface of feeling humanity. Everywhere in man's world the Supreme Person is suffering from the killing of the human reality by the imposition of the abstract. In our schools the idea of the class hides the reality of the school children; they become students and not individuals. Therefore it does not hurt us to see children's lives crushed, in their classes, like flowers pressed between book leaves. In government, the bureaucracy deals with generalisations and not with men. And therefore it costs it nothing to indulge in wholesale cruelties. Once we accept as truth such a scientific maxim as 'Survival of the Fittest' it immediately transforms the whole world of human personality into a monotonous desert of abstraction, where things become dreadfully simple because robbed of their mystery of life.

In these large tracts of nebulousness, Art is creating its stars,—stars that are definite in their forms but infinite in their personality. Art is calling us the 'children of the immortal,' and proclaiming our right to dwell in the heavenly worlds.

What is it in man that asserts its immortality in spite of the obvious fact of death? It is not his physical body or his mental organisation. It is that deeper unity, that ultimate mystery in him, which, from the centre of his world, radiates towards its circumference; which is in his body, yet transcends his body; which is in his mind, yet grows beyond his mind; which, through the things belonging to him, expresses something that is not in them; which, while occupying his present, overflows its banks of the past and the future. It is the personality of man, conscious of its inexhaustible abundance; it has the paradox in it that it is more than itself; it is more than as it is seen, as it is known, as it is used. And this consciousness of the infinite, in the personal man, ever strives to make its expressions immortal and to make the whole world its own. In Art the person in us is sending its answers to the Supreme Person, who reveals Himself to us in a world of endless beauty across the lightless world of facts.

Rabindranath Tagore, from Personality

15

Sri Aurobindo

Poet, philosopher, mystic, political activist and nationalist, Sri Aurobindo (1872–1950) is an enigmatic and misunderstood figure of the modern Indian renaissance. He was educated from his early childhood in England, and when he returned to India at the age of twenty-one, he had to learn his mother tongue, Bengali, from a tutor employed for the purpose. In no time, however, Aurobindo had acquired mastery over Bengali, Sanskrit, Gujarati as he had done with respect to English, French and Italian earlier. The knowledge of so many languages, and his untiring zeal for reading, gave Sri Aurobindo familiarity with a vast body of world literature, such as perhaps only Goethe had before him. As such, he developed an extremely receptive attitude to literary forms and experiments, and acquired a catholicity of literary taste. This literary background, his anti-British political programme, and the visionary mysticism combined to produce Sri Aurobindo's curious critical masterpiece, *Future Poetry.* It is curious, for half of it is a synoptic history of English poetry, and the other half is a manifesto of mystical poetry. But the literary wisdom and critical insight pervading the volume have rarely been matched by any other critic or critical work in modern India.

Future Poetry is, a serious book of literary criticism, though it has not had the reception it deserved. It is a book of criticism by a poet involved in writing a highly experimental kind of poetry. Besides, the ideas in it are not derived either from the West or from ancient India. They are Sri Aurobindo's own creation. The ideas present in Sri Aurobindo's criticism represent, generally speaking, the romantic mood in Indian literature of the early twentieth century. Two of his essays are included here. 'The Sources of Poetry' was written by him when he was barely twenty-five, when he had not yet turned a mystic. 'The Essence of Poetry' is a chapter, a crucial one, from *Future Poetry.* Both of these were originally written in English, which also seems to have become the major language of twentieth-century Indian literary criticism.

The Sources of Poetry

The swiftness of the muse has been embodied in the image of Pegasus, the heavenly horse of Greek legend; it was from the rapid beat of his hoofs on the rock that Hippocrene flowed. The waters of Poetry flow in a current or a torrent; where there is a pause or a denial, it is a sign of obstruction in the stream or of imperfection in the mind which the waters have chosen for their bed and continent. In India we have the same idea; Saraswati is for us the goddess of poetry, and her name means the stream or 'she who has flowing motion'. But even Saraswati is only an intermediary. Ganga is the real mother of inspiration, she who flows impetuously down from the head of Mahadev, God high-seated, over the Himalaya of the mind to the homes and cities of men. All poetry is an inspiration, a thing breathed into the thinking organ from above; it is recorded in the mind, but is born in the higher principle of direct knowledge or ideal vision which surpasses mind. It is in reality a revelation. The prophetic or revealing power sees the substance; the inspiration perceives the right expression. Neither is manufactured; nor is poetry really a *poiesis* or composition, nor even a creation, but rather the revelation of something that eternally exists. The ancients knew this truth and used the same word for poet and prophet, creator and seer, *sophos, vates, kavi.*

But there are differences in the manifestation. The greatest motion of poetry comes when the mind is still and the ideal principle works above and outside the brain, above even the hundred-petalled lotus of the ideal mind, in its proper empire, for then it is Veda that is revealed, the perfect substance and expression of eternal truth. The higher ideation transcends genius just as genius transcends ordinary intellect and perception. But that great faculty is still beyond the normal level of our evolution. Usually we see the action of the revelation and inspiration reproduced by a secondary, diluted and uncertain process in the mind. But even this secondary and inferior action is so great that it can give us Shakespeare, Homer and Valmiki. There is also a tertiary and yet more common action of the inspiration. For of our three mental instruments of knowledge,—the heart or emotionally realising mind, the observing and reasoning intellect with its aids, fancy and memory, and the intuitive intellect,—it is into the last and highest that the ideal principle transmits its inspirations when the greatest poetry writes itself out through the medium of the poet. But if the intuitive intellect is not strong enough to act habitually, it is better for the poetry to descend into the heart and return to the intellect suffused and coloured with passion and emotion than to be formed directly in the observing intellect.

Poetry written from the reasoning intellect is apt to be full of ingenious conceits, logic, argumentation, rhetorical turns, ornamental fancies, echoes learned and imitative rather than uplifted and transformed. This is what is sometimes called classical poetry, the vigorous and excellent but unemotional and unuplifted poetry of Pope and Dryden. It has its inspiration, its truth and value; it is admirable in its way, but it is only great when it is lifted out of itself into intuitive writing or else invaded by the heart. For everything that needs fire rather than Light, driving-force rather than clearness, enthusiasm rather than correctness, the heart is obviously the more potent instrument. Now, poetry to be great must have either enthusiasm or ecstasy.

Yet the poetry that rises up from the heart is usually a turbid stream; our own restless ideas and imaginations mix with the pure inrush from above, and turbulent uprush from below, our excited emotions seek an exaggerated expression, our aesthetic habits and predilections busy themselves to demand a satisfaction greatly beyond their due. Such poetry may be inspired, but it is not always suitable or inevitable. There is often a double inspiration, the higher or ecstatic and the lower or emotional, and the lower disturbs and drags down the higher. This is the birth of romantic or excessively exuberant poetry, too rich in expression, too abundant and redundant in substance. The best poetry coming straight from the right centres may be bare and strong, unadorned and lofty, or it may be rich and splendid; it may be at will romantic or classical; but it will always be felt to be the right thing for its purpose; it is always nobly or rapturously inevitable.

But even in the higher centres of the intuitive intellect there may be defects in the inspiration. There is a kind of false fluency which misses the true language of poetry from dullness of perception. Under the impression that it is true and inspired writing it flows with an imperturbable flatness, saying the thing that should be said but not in the way that it should be said, without force and felicity. This is the *tamasic* or clouded stimulus, active, but full of unenlightenment and self-ignorance. The thing seen is right and good; accompanied with the inspired expression it would make very noble poetry. Instead, it becomes prose rendered unnatural and difficult to tolerate by being cut up into lengths. Wordsworth is the most characteristic and interesting victim of *tamasic* stimulus. Other great poets fall a prey to it, but that superb and imperturbable self-satisfaction under the infliction is his alone. There is another species of *tamasic* stimulus which transmits an inspired and faultless expression, but the substance is neither interesting to man nor pleasing to the gods. A good deal of Milton comes under this category. In both cases what has happened is that either the inspiration or the revelation has been active, but its companion activity has refused to associate itself in the work.

It is when the mind works at the form and substance of poetry without either the revelation or the inspiration from above that respectable or minor poetry is produced. Judgement, memory and imagination may work, command of language may be there, but without that secondary action of a higher than intellectual force, it is labour wasted, work that earns respect but not immortality. Doggerel and bastard poetry take their rise not even in the observing intellect but from the sensational mind or the passive memory guided only by the mere physical pleasure of sound and emotion. It is bold, blatant, external, imitative, vulgar; its range of intellectuality and imaginativeness cannot go beyond the vital impulse and the vital delight. But even in the sensational mind there is the possibility of a remote action from the ideal self; for even to the animals who think sensationally only, God has given revelations and inspirations which we call instincts. Under such circumstances even bastard poetry may have a kind of worth, a kind of inevitability. The poet in the sensational man may be entirely satisfied and delighted, and even in the more developed human being the sensational element may find a poetical satisfaction not of the highest. The best ballad poetry and Macaulay's lays are instances in point. Scott is a sort of link between sensational and intellectual poetry. While there are men mainly sensational, secondarily intellectual and not at all ideal, he will always be admired.

Another kind of false inspiration is the *rajasic* or fiery stimulus. It is not flat and unprofitable like the *tamasic,* but hasty, impatient and vain. It is eager to avoid labour by catching at the second-best expression or the incomplete vision of the idea, insufficiently jealous to secure the best form, the most satisfying substance. *Rajasic* poets, even when they feel the defect in what they have written, hesitate to sacrifice it because they also feel and are attached either to what in it is valuable or to the memory of their delight when it was first written. If they get a better expression or a fuller sight, they often prefer to reiterate rather than strike out inferior stuff with which they are in love. Sometimes, drifting or struggling helplessly along that shallow and vehement current, they vary one idea or harp on the same imagination without any final success in expressing it inevitably. Examples of the *rajasic* stimulus are commonest in Shelley and Spenser, but few English poets are free from it. This is the *rajasic* fault in expression. But the fiery stimulus also perverts or hampers the substance. An absence of self-restraint, an unwillingness to restrict and limit the ideas and imagination is a sure sign of a *rajasic* ideality. There is an attempt to exhaust all the possibilities of the subject, to expand and multiply thoughts and imaginative visions beyond the bounds of the right and permissible. Or else the true idea is rejected or fatally anticipated by another which is or seems to be more catching and boldly effective. Keats is the principal exemplar of the first tendency, the Elizabethans of the second. The earlier work of Shakespeare abounds with classical instances. As distinguished from the Greek, English is pronouncedly *rajasic* literature and, though there is much in it that is more splendid than almost anything done by the Greeks,—more splendid, not better—a great deal even of its admired portions are rather rich or meretricious than great and true.

The perfect inspiration in the intuitive intellect is the *sattwic* or luminous inspiration, which is disinterested, self-contained, yet at will noble, rich or vigorous, having its eye only on the right thing to be said and the right way to say it. It does not allow its perfection to be interfered with by emotion or eagerness but this does not shut it out from ecstasy and exaltation. On the contrary, its delight of self enjoyment is a purer and more exquisite enthusiasm than that which attends any other inspiration. It commands and uses emotion without enslaving itself to it. There is indeed a *sattwic* stimulus which is attached to its own luminosity, limpidity and steadiness, and avoids richness, force or emotion of poignant character even when these are needed and appropriate. The poetry of Matthew Arnold is often, though not always, of this character. But this is a limited inspiration. *Sattwic* as well as *rajasic* poetry may be written from the uninspired intellect, but the sensational mind never gives birth to *sattwic* poetry.

One thing has to be added. A poet need not be a reflective critic; he need not have the reasoning and analysing intellect and dissect his own poetry. But two things he must have in some measure to be perfect, the intuitive judgement which shows him at a glance whether he has got the best or the second-best idea, the perfect or the imperfect expression and rhythm, and the intuitive reason which shows him without analysis why or wherein it is best or second-best, perfect or imperfect. These four faculties, revelation or prophecy, inspiration, intuitive judgement and intuitive reason, are the perfect equipment of genius doing the works of interpretative and creative knowledge.

Sri Aurobindo, The Harmony of Virtue

The Essence of Poetry

In order to get a firm clue which we can follow fruitfully in retrospect and prospect we have proposed to ourselves, it will not be amiss to enquire what is the highest power we demand from poetry; or—let us put it more largely and get nearer the roots of the matter,—what may be the nature of poetry, its essential law, and how out of that arises the possibility of its use as the *mantra* of the Real. Not that we need spend a vain effort in labouring to define anything so profound, elusive and indefinable as the breath of poetic creation; to take the myriad-stringed harp of Sạraswati to pieces for the purpose of scientific analysis must always be a narrow and rather barren amusement. But we do stand in need of some guiding intuitions, some helpful descriptions which will serve to enlighten our search; and to fix in that way, not by definition, but by description, the essential things in poetry is neither an impossible, nor an unprofitable endeavour.

We meet here two common enough errors, to one of which the ordinary uninstructed mind is most liable, to the other the too instructed critic or the too intellectually conscientious artist or craftsman. To the ordinary mind, judging poetry without really entering it, it looks as if it were nothing more than an aesthetic pleasure of the imagination, the intellect and the ear, a sort of elevated pastime. If that were all, we need not have wasted time in seeking for its spirit, its inner aim, its deeper law. Anything pretty, pleasant and melodious with a beautiful idea in it would serve our turn; a song of Anacreon or a plaint of Mimnermus would be as good as the *Oedipus, Agamemnon or Odyssey*, for from this point of view they might well strike us as equally and even, one might contend, more perfect in their light, but exquisite unity and brevity. Pleasure, certainly, we expect from poetry as from all art; but the external sensible and even the inner imaginative pleasure are only first elements; refined in order to meet the highest requirements of the intelligence, the imagination and the ear, they have to be still farther heightened and in their nature raised beyond even their own noblest levels.

For neither the intelligence, the imagination nor the ear are the true recipients of the poetic delight, even as they are not its true creators; they are only its channels and instruments; the true creator, the true hearer is the soul. The more rapidly and transparently the rest do their work of transmission, the less they make of their separate claim to satisfaction, the more directly the word reaches and sinks deep into the soul, the greater the poetry. Therefore poetry has not really done its work, at least its highest work, until it has raised the pleasure of the instrument and transmuted it into the deeper delight of the soul. A divine *Ānanda*, a delight interpretative, creative, revealing, formative—one might almost say, an inverse reflection of the joy which the universal Soul has felt in its great release of energy when it ranges out into the rhythmic forms of the universe the spiritual truth, the large interpretative idea, the life, the power, the emotion of things packed into its original creative vision—such spiritual joy is that which the soul of the poet feels and which, when he can conquer the human difficulties of his task, he succeeds in pouring also into all those who are prepared to receive it. And this delight is not merely a godlike pastime; it is a great formative and illuminative power.

The critic—of a certain type—or the intellectually conscientious artist will, on the other hand, often talk as if poetry were mainly a matter of a faultlessly correct or at the most an exquisite technique. Certainly, in all art good technique is the first step towards perfection; but there are so many other steps; there is a whole world beyond before you can get near to what you seek; so much so that even a deficient correctness of execution will not prevent an intense and gifted soul from creating great poetry which keeps its hold on the centuries. Moreover, technique, however indispensable, occupies a smaller field perhaps in poetry than in any other art,—first, because its instrument, the rhythmic word, is full of subtle and immaterial elements; then because, the most complex, flexible, variously suggestive of all the instruments of the artistic creator, it has more infinite possibilities in many directions than any other. The rhythmic word has a subtly sensible element, its sound value, a quite immaterial element, its significance or thought value, and both of these again, its sound and its sense, have separately and together a soul value, a direct spiritual power, which is infinitely the most important thing about them. And though this comes to birth with a small element subject to the laws of technique, yet almost immediately, almost at the beginning of its flight, its power soars up beyond the province of any laws of mechanical construction.

Rather it determines itself its own form. The poet least of all artists needs to create with his eye fixed anxiously on the technique of his art. He has to possess it, no doubt; but in the heat of creation the intellectual sense of it becomes a subordinate action or even a mere undertone in his mind, and in his best moments he is permitted, in a way, to forget it altogether. For then the perfection of his sound-movement and style comes entirely as the spontaneous form of his soul: that utters itself in an inspired rhythm and an innate, a revealed word, even as the universal Soul created the harmonies of the universe out of the power of the word secret and eternal within him, leaving the mechanical work to be done in a surge of hidden spiritual excitement by the subconscient part of his Nature. It is this highest speech which is the supreme poetic utterance, the immortal element in his poetry, and a little of it is enough to save the rest of his work from oblivion. *Svalpam apyasya dharmasya!*

This power makes the rhythmic word of the poet the highest form of speech available to man for the expression whether of his self-vision or of his world-vision. It is noticeable that even the highest experience, the pure spiritual which enters into the things that can never be wholly expressed, still, when it does try to express them and not merely to explain them intellectually, tends instinctively to use, often the rhythmic forms, almost always the manner of speech characteristic of poetry. But poetry attempts to extend this manner of vision and utterance to all experience, even the most objective, and therefore it has a natural urge towards the expression of something in the object beyond its mere appearances, even when these seem outwardly to be all that it is enjoying.

We may usefully cast a glance, not at the last inexpressible secret, but at the first elements of this heightening and intensity peculiar to poetic utterance. Ordinary speech uses language mostly for a limited practical utility of communication; it uses it for life and for the expression of ideas and feelings necessary or useful to life. In doing so, we treat words as conventional signs for ideas with nothing but a perfunctory attention to their natural force, much as we use any kind of common machine or simple implement; we treat them as if, though useful for life, they were themselves without life. When we wish to put a more vital power into them, we have to lend it to them out of ourselves, by marked intonations of the voice, by the emotional force or vital energy we throw into the sound so as to infuse into the conventional word-sign something which is not inherent in itself. But if we go back earlier in the history of language and still more if we look into its origins, we shall, I think, find that it was not always so with human speech. Words had not only a real and vivid life of their own, but the speaker was more conscious of it than we can possibly be with our mechanised and sophisticated intellects. This arose from the primitive nature of language which, probably, in its first movement was not intended,—or shall we say, did not intend,—so much to stand for distinct ideas of the intelligence as for feelings, sensations, broad indefinite mental impressions with minute shades of quality in them which we do not now care to pursue. The intellectual sense in its precision must have been a secondary element which grew more dominant as language evolved.

The reason why sound came to express fixed ideas, lies not in any natural and inherent equivalence between the sound and its intellectual sense, for there is none,—intellectually any sound might express any sense, if men were agreed on a conventional equivalence between them; it started from an indefinable quality or property in the sound to raise certain vibrations in the life-soul of the human creature, in his sensational, his emotional, his crude mental being. An example may indicate more clearly what I mean. The word 'wolf', the origin of which is no longer present to our minds, denotes to our intelligence a certain living object and that is all, the rest we have to do for ourselves: the Sanskrit word *vṛka,* 'tearer', came in the end to do the same thing, but originally it expressed the sensational relation between the wolf and man which most affected the man's life, and it did so by a certain quality in the sound which readily associated it with the sensation of tearing. This must have given early language a powerful life, a concrete vigour, in one direction a natural poetic force which it has lost, however greatly it has gained in precision, clarity, utility.

Now, poetry goes back in a way and recovers, though in another fashion, as much as it can of this original element. It does this partly by a stress on the image replacing the old sensational concreteness, partly by a greater attention to the suggestive force of the sound, its life, its power, the mental impression it carries. It associates this with the definitive thought value contributed by the intelligence and increases both by each other. In that way it succeeds at the same time in carrying up the power of speech to the direct expression of a higher reach of experience than the intellectual or vital. For it brings out not only the definitive intellectual value of the word, not only its power of emotion and sensation, its vital suggestion, but through and beyond these its soul-suggestion, its spirit. So poetry arrives at the indication of infinite meanings beyond the finite intellectual meaning the word carries. It expresses not only the life-soul of man as did the primitive word, not only the ideas of his intelligence for which speech now usually serves, but the experience, the vision, the ideas, as we may say, of the higher and wider soul in him. Making them real to our life-soul as well as present to our intellect, it opens to us by the word the doors of the Spirit.

Prose style carries speech to a much higher power than its ordinary use, but it differs from poetry in not making this yet greater attempt. For it takes its stand firmly on the intellectual value of the word. It uses rhythms which ordinary speech neglects, and aims at a general fluid harmony of movement. It seeks to associate words agreeably and luminously so as at once to please and to clarify the intelligence. It strives after a more accurate, subtle, flexible and satisfying expression than the rough methods of ordinary speech care to compass. A higher adequacy of speech is its first object. Beyond this adequacy it may aim at a greater forcefulness and effectiveness by various devices of speech which are so many rhetorical means for heightening its force of intellectual appeal. Passing beyond this first limit, this just or strong, but always restraining measure, it may admit a more emphatic rhythm, more directly and powerfully stimulate the emotion, appeal to a more vivid aesthetic sense. It may even make such a free or rich use of images as to suggest an outward approximation to the manner of poetry; but it employs them decoratively, as ornaments, *alamkāra,* or for their effective value in giving a stronger intellectual vision of the thing or the thought it describes or defines; it does not use the image for that profounder and more living vision for which the poet is always seeking. And always it has its eye on its chief hearer and judge, the intelligence, and calls in other powers only as important aids to capture his suffrage. Reason and taste, two powers of the intelligence, are rightly the supreme gods of the prose stylist, while to the poet they are only minor deities.

If it goes beyond these limits, approaches in its measures a more striking rhythmic balance, uses images for sheer vision, opens itself to mightier breath of speech, prose style passes beyond its province and approaches or even enters the confines of poetry. It becomes poetical prose or even poetry itself using the apparent forms of prose as a disguise or a loose apparel. A high or a fine adequacy, effectivity, intellectual illuminativeness and a carefully tempered aesthetic satisfaction are the natural and normal powers of its speech. But the privilege of the poet is to go beyond and discover that more intense illumination of speech, that inspired word and supreme inevitable utterance, in which there meets the unity of a divine rhythmic movement with a depth of sense and a power of infinite suggestion welling up directly from the fountain-heads of the spirit within us. He may not always or often find it, but to seek for it is the law of his utterance, and when he can not only find it, but cast into it some deeply revealed truth of the spirit itself, he utters the *mantra.*

But always, whether in the search or the finding, the whole style and rhythm of poetry are the expression and movement which come from us out of a certain spiritual excitement caused by a vision in the soul of which it is eager to deliver itself. The vision may be of anything in Nature or God or man or the life of creatures or the life of things; it may be a vision of force and action, or of sensible beauty, or of truth of thought, or of emotion and pleasure and pain, of this life or the life beyond. It is sufficient that it is the soul which sees and the eye, sense, heart and thought-mind become the passive instruments of the soul. Then we get the real, the high poetry. But if it is too much an excitement of the intellect, the imagination, the emotions, the vital activities seeking rhythmical and forceful expression which acts, without enough of the greater spiritual excitement embracing them, if all these are not sufficiently sunk into the soul, steeped in it, fused in it and the expression does not come out purified and uplifted by a sort of spiritual transmutation, then we fall to lower levels of poetry, and get work of a much more doubtful immortality. And when the appeal is altogether to the lower things in us, the mere mind, we arrive outside the true domain of poetry; we approach the confines of prose or get prose itself masking in the apparent forms of poetry, and the work is distinguished from prose style only or mainly by its mechanical elements, a good verse form and perhaps a more compact, catching or energetic expression than the prose writer will ordinarily permit to the easier and looser balance of his speech. That is to say, it will not have at all or not sufficiently the true essence of poetry.

For in all things that speech can express there are two elements, the outward or instrumental and the real or spiritual. In thought, for instance, there is the intellectual idea, that which the intelligence makes precise and definite to us, and the soul-idea, that which exceeds the intellectual and brings us into nearness or identity with the whole reality of the thing expressed. Equally in emotion, it is not the mere emotion itself the poet seeks, but the soul of the emotion, that in it for the delight of which the soul in us and the world desires or accepts emotional experience. So too with the poetical sense of objects, the poet's attempt to embody in his speech truth of life or truth of Nature. It is this greater truth and its delight and beauty and therefore a joy for ever, because it brings us the delight of the soul in the discovery of its own deeper realities. This greater element the more timid and temperate speech of prose can sometimes shadow out to us, but the heightened and tearless style of poetry makes it close and living and the higher cadences of poetry carry in on their wings what the style by itself could not bring. This is the source of that intensity which is the stamp of poetical speech and of the poetical movement. It comes from the stress of the soul-vision behind the word; it is the spiritual excitement of a rhythmic voyage of self-discovery among the magic islands of form and name in these inner and outer worlds.

Sri Aurobindo, from Future Poetry

16

B. S. Mardhekar

Mardhekar (1909–1951) is acknowledged as the most significant Marathi poet of the twentieth century, and as one of the pioneers of Indian modernism. He wrote some experimental fiction, in the stream of consciousness mode; but his reputation rests mainly on his contribution to the fields of aesthetics and literary criticism.

He wrote criticism in Marathi as well as in English. His major critical works were collected under the title *Arts and Man* and published posthumously. The essay reproduced here is from that collection. Mardhekar's criticism shows a keen interest in philosophy, logic and linguistics. In formulating his ideas, he followed the leading Western thinkers of his generation, mainly Croce, Collingwood and I. A. Richards. But, in spite of this influence, Mardhekar's theory of 'rhythm, contrast, balance' is his own. The Mardhekar Law of Beauty has haunted Marathi criticism for half a century; and almost all theoretical discussion in Marathi about literary beauty focuses on Mardhekar's views. If Marathi is one of the very few Indian languages in which the branch of philosophy known as Aesthetics has made any development, it is thanks to Mardhekar's pioneering of that branch. The essay by R. B. Patankar included in the second part of the present anthology, 'Aesthetics: Some Important Problems', offers a searching critique of Mardhekar's theory.

Though Western literary influence, and the English type of education, had influenced the Indian critical climate in the early part of this century, it was not until Mardhekar accepted it that an unhesitating acceptance of the Western lead in literary criticism became acceptable. Mardhekar is thus India's first 'modernising' critic. Hence his writing is important historically too.

Poetry and Aesthetic Theory

No one who ponders over the various problems of the aesthetic science and tries to seek light upon them from the writings of art critics and aesthetic philosophers will fail to be struck by the amount of confusion that has been imported into aesthetic theory by the fact that poetry has been treated as being on a par with the other fine arts. Such a conception, and the consequent temptation to treat the *Ars Poetica* as a representative art in the analysis, discussion and illustration of aesthetic problems, arise from causes which are not difficult to discern.

Poetry deals in words as carriers of emotional meanings. The intimate apprehension of emotional meanings is a biological necessity. Without the prompt apprehension of such meanings and the quick and proper reaction to them, the sentient being will not be able to maintain itself in the constant struggle for existence, nor succeed in perpetuating its species. The attraction of poetry, which helps the above process, is, therefore, quite natural, and its interest for human beings both widespread and perennial. Art critics and aesthetic philosophers, sharing this interest and moved by this attraction like the vast majority of human beings, with leanings primarily humanistic, tend almost invariably to resort to poetry while illustrating their analyses of aesthetic problems. Secondly, all discussion, and therefore, aesthetic discussion, must be carried on in words. Those, therefore, who have a special facility in handling and manipulating linguistic symbols, by the volume of their voice, their repetitions and the charm of their verbal expression, come finally to saturate men's minds with their opinions, and induce a sort of mental hypnosis in which these opinions are accepted without challenge.

The chief traffickers in this kind of soporific aesthetics are the poets. Either by explicit aesthetic formulation or by recording their own reactions before a work of non-literary art, both of which could not but be in terms of poetic (that is to say, non-aesthetic-emotional) experiences, they have brought the assurance of an apparently authentic certainty to what was before merely a tempting surmise, namely, the assumption that poetry is a fine art on the same level as painting, music, sculpture, dancing, etc.

This all too human prejudice in favour of poetry, and the natural inclination to regard poetry as a typical fine art instead of recognising that there is a hierarchy of order among the fine arts, have received their most powerful philosophical sanction from the intuitional aesthetics of Benedetto Croce. It is a significant indication of the 'pattern of criticism', to use a happy phrase of Mr. Eliot, which the Crocean aesthetics has set, that Croce's article on Aesthetics in the latest edition of the *Encyclopaedia Britannica* begins with the examination of a poem, a piece from Virgil, and that the first sentence of the second paragraph reads as follows:

'What has been said of "poetry" applies to all other "arts" commonly enumerated; painting, sculpture, architecture, music.'

As a reaction against the 'compartmental' and unrelated criticism of his predecessors, the setting up of the abstract Crocean conception of Art, as against the various individual fine arts and transcending them, might have been both necessary and opportune; but unless the exact content of this conception is determined by a rigorous logical analysis, its value as what Dr. Richards would call 'a speculative instrument' for the investigation of aesthetic problems is of the most dubious kind. Once transfer it from the purpose for which it is relevant to other issues, and you will immediately land yourself in a complete aesthetic mess. It will then seem to you to follow with an absurdly evident necessity that, for the purposes of aesthetic theory and the elucidation of aesthetic problems in all their manifold aspects, one art is as good as another; that poetry is no worse than painting and music no better than either. What is, however, denied here is not that there is nothing common to the various fine arts, but that an abstraction—made for a certain purpose and with certain metaphysical or otherwise subjective predilection—can be rightfully held valid for the whole field of aesthetic science and be elevated to the position of a supreme principle from which any inference is legitimate without much further ado. *L'estetica dell' una parola*, as we might describe the Crocean aesthetics without irreverence, even as Gentile has described the Crocean philosophy, *la filosofia delle Quattro parole*, has, I humbly submit, sinned in this latter way.

The tendency to think of human life as of the highest value and the emotions which directly administer to its prolongation by ensuring its smooth and even flow as of paramount significance, reinforced by poetic utterances and justified by a philosophy, making of poetry the *Ars Artis*, has led to some unfortunate results in aesthetic theory. Since everyone understands, or thinks he understands, poetry, more or less, because its counters are his counter, and because the poet's experience differs from his experiences only in being more integral, less attenuated, and not essentially; and since there is a prima facie similarity between poetry and the other fine arts as both are in a strictly limited sense useless, the temptation is as obvious as it is compelling, to interpret all artistic creation and every aesthetic process in terms of those involved in literary production. The familiar facility with which such an interpretation can be given and the spurious, effortless and cheap joy which it is supposed to impart, soon turns what was once a temptation into a settled habit of mind.

Now in so far as poetry is a fine art (and it is not denied that it is a fine art, the contention merely being that it is not of the same order as the other fine arts), that is in so far as it yields an enjoyment that is aesthetic as opposed to the poetic or non-aesthetic-emotional (which means involving emotions that are in the last analysis either immediately or remotely instrumental), its products and processes must necessarily partake of the character of works of art and aesthetic processes. There is, therefore, nothing inherently absurd or illegitimate in the interpretation of the latter in terms of the former. Before, however, an interpretation of this type is essayed, it is absolutely essential that the literary processes and their products should be subjected to a stringent analysis and the nature of their terms adequately ascertained.

The next step is to equate these terms to exactly corresponding terms in similar aesthetic products and processes. Error may creep in either in the first or in the second step. Either the preliminary analysis is defective, or else there is a slight shifting in the placing of the terms of the one process against those of the other so that they do not really correspond. More often both these causes have combined to produce much false speculation and wrong aesthetic interpretation. Poetry thus conceived in ambiguous terms and poetical interpretation thus illegitimately extended have become a curse to aesthetic theory and a standing obstacle to the proper and full enjoyment of the other fine arts.

In order to detect where the ambiguity of the current analysis of the literary process and its products resides, and to realise the nature of the shift that has taken place in equating their terms to those of the aesthetic process, we cannot do better than examine the character of the middle term in those processes, that is of the 'medium' of poetry. For in poetry, as in every other fine art, a clear understanding of the nature of its medium is the beginning of appreciation. It is the prerequisite of any aesthetic which aspires to be scientific. To grasp the precise nature of the medium of any fine art is to furnish oneself with a speculative instrument of the utmost value, which can at once reveal what is relevant, and differentiate between what is not, like grain and chaff, when one undertakes criticism of that art.

Most of the errors, conflicts and confusion which are visible in the various aesthetic theories will be found ultimately to spring from a failure to define the concept of medium of art. Once you boggle over this concept, and fail to perceive the medium of any particular art, you will commit all the current fallacies. You will appreciate one thing in the comfortable delusion that you are appreciating something else. You will indulge in perorational aesthetics and believe that you have written a magnificent piece of acute art criticism. Fine phrases, although they cannot butter parsnips, are yet able to cover an incredible amount of faulty analysis, counterfeit enjoyment and mistaken enthusiasm.

Perhaps in the foregoing paragraph, while accusing others of a certain fault, I might appear to some to remain self-condemned for one very like it. Still more likely it is that I might appear to be making much ado about nothing. For no great philosopher is required to enlighten us on the question, what is the medium of poetry. The answer is perfectly simple: Words; though not, fortunately, 'Words, Words, Words!'

But the matter is not so simple and it is advisable to cite a philosopher. As seasoned a scientific thinker and as acutely clear-headed a psychologist as Prof Spearman has the following sentence on page 88 of his book, *The Creative Mind:*

> 'And as the former (painter) employs for this purpose (representation of the physical world outside him) the medium of pigments, so the latter (the literary artist) uses words and phrases.'

Immediately on the same we happen to read in the next paragraph:

> 'The beauty sought by the painter is, in the main, that of his medium' the obvious implication being that the aims of the painter and the literary artist are different. No more comment is needed than the mere juxtaposition of these two statements. Such a juxtaposition at once reveals how great a source of misunderstanding a half-hearted, perfunctory and superficial analysis can become even in the hands of one who is nothing if not severely analytical. If Prof Spearman had gone sufficiently deep into the analysis of the medium of painting as well as that of the literary art, he would have come nearer to the truth in aesthetic theory and realised that the artistic aim of all the arts, painting and poetry included, is the same, namely, the revelation of the beauty of their several mediums. The differences between the various arts are the differences of their mediums. It is not that while painters seek the beauty of their medium, poets seek the beauty of something else.

That is a fairly recent book. But take one still more recent. Commenting on Prof Abercrombie's critical position that 'The inspiration is the poem; something self-contained and self-sufficient, a complete and entire whole', Prof Dewey in a footnote of his book, *Art as Experience,* asks significantly, presumably believing the question to be disarming, 'if it is already self-sufficient and self-contained, why does it seek and find words as a medium of expression?' Now here again, it the nature of the medium, that is, of words, had been duly taken into account, it would have become apparent that the question posed is as meaningless as a similar question about paper, pen and ink would be. It is, however, needless to multiply illustrations of this point.

Let us then examine the nature of the medium of poetry, that is, of words, as briefly as possible. A word has primarily two aspects: (a) Sensational and (b) Intentional. In the first instance, it is a phenomenon of sound, a complex of auditory sensations, a group of vowels and consonants. In language, however, these sounds are not significant in themselves but only as they serve as symbols for something else. They are in short subsidiary to the second aspect, the Intentional. The intentional aspect is the sole justification of the existence of that particular combination of vowels and consonants. Language arises out of the necessity of communication and immensely facilitates it. It is fashioned by man for the more efficient carriage of human intercourse, and answers to the incessant demand of ever increasing thought contents for easier handling.

The evolution of meaning is a process of constructive thought, which thought is essentially a function of a limited consciousness. It is the product of the interaction of the circumscribed consciousness with that within which it finds itself so circumscribed, and meaning has relevance and value for such a consciousness only. But the more frequent these interactions grow, the more various, the more complex they become, the less certain becomes the grasp of the circumscribed consciousness upon the meanings that emerge out of them, the more awkward, the more precarious its handling of them. A limited consciousness in its primary, least developed stages might perhaps be able to manipulate meanings themselves bodily but it has very soon to face the necessity of finding some convenient shorthand, abbreviated method of storing them for social currency. It is only when incipient thought gathers weight and volume and craves for definition that it crystallises itself into words.

The sensation or sound aspect of a word is symbolical of the intentional, and is only used as a manageable vehicle for it. The combination of the two aspects in a word is at once a boon to, and a bane of every limited consciousness. In a world where partial or divided consciousness, as of the human being, did not exist there would be no meanings at all. To a consciousness that is universal, everything would be its own meaning, every thing its own symbol. The division and combination of symbol and significance would be both impossible and unnecessary then. As we shall see presently, the necessity and nature of this division and this combination has not been sufficiently constantly nor sufficiently clearly kept in mind when equating the aesthetic to the literary process.

Now the intentional aspect of words or language can itself be further analysed into two aspects. Meaning, as a fact of mental life, has the two facets: (a) Cognitive and (b) Affective. It is, of course, a commonplace of psychology that there is no clear-cut division between the two, and it is only when someone fails to find some more original argument that he thinks it worthwhile reminding others of it. Yet the distinction between an experience that is predominantly intellectual and one that is predominantly emotional is not difficult to perceive. There are intellectual ideas, theoretical meaning and emotions, or emotional meaning. We need remark here this easily observable though not sharply marked difference.

Next we have to recognise two subdivisions of the affective aspects or two categories of emotions. The first category we may call that of *pure* or *absolute* emotions, and group the second under the heading of *contingent* emotions. Pure or absolute emotions are the immediate accompaniments of the perception of the quality of any sensation, or of a pattern, a *Gestalt,* an organisation of relations. They are the necessary concomitants of any experience that is sensuous or formal, and do not derive from any 'experience of this world', as that expression is understood when we say that old men are more experienced than the young. I have used the word emotions, but strictly speaking the word should be in the singular. We may call this emotion 'aesthetic' and so distinguish it from the other group of contingent emotions which are 'poetic'. They are contingent because they depend upon a specific human world order. They are contingent upon the existence and persistence of a particular demand of the environment.

It is, as I stated above, only in so far as they facilitate human reactions to the existing environment and ensure survival, that they are of any value. If the environment changes so that certain reactions are found to be no longer necessary, then the emotions which had formerly served these reactions tend to disappear, gradually suffering and ultimately vanishing altogether. Those emotions, for example, which accompanied the relations of the two sexes in the old days of chivalry have lost their *raison d'être* in our times. For in a world where there is municipal peace, and physical culture is no longer the exclusive prerogative of only a section of mankind, the sentiment of chivalry is superfluous, except in so far as it is demanded by the requirements of social etiquette or a sense of decorum—that is to say, by the intrinsic grace of the conduct in which it displays itself, or except in so far as it is helpful to sublimate the sexual impulse. That emotion of love which governs the relations between parents and children would tend to disappear in a state organised on the Soviet model, in which a Government department looks after old parents and little babies, because in such a state that emotion would lose its sole relevance. That the prospect of such a disappearance is instantly resented and seldom fails to rouse profound indignation is only a reflection of the way in which the self-protective mechanism in man works, and confirms the view of the contingent nature of this kind of emotions. And nothing can indicate more clearly how men are willing to deceive themselves into faulty intellectual positions in the interests of poetry than all the flowers of language and rhetoric, all the glowing paeans of praise and admiration bestowed upon the nobility of filial piety and dutifulness, in terms of which their resentment and their indignation usually manifest themselves.

We may call the contingent emotions 'interested' also, since they are indulged in simply because they are biologically significant and useful, whereas the aesthetic emotion is 'disinterested', and subserves no biological plan. Again the contingent emotions are merely 'instrumental': they promote ends that are outside the situations which realise the said emotions. In contrast, the aesthetic emotion is an end in itself; the end is fulfilled in the very moment in which the emotion is realised. It is thus significant on its own account.

To summarise the result of the foregoing discussion schematically:

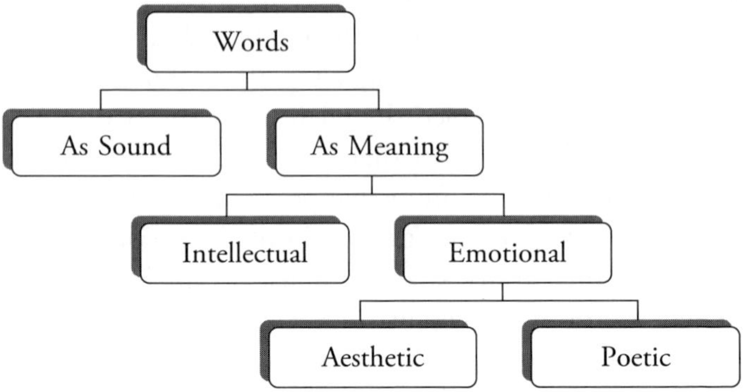

With the aid of the above analysis, I wish to maintain the proposition that words, as implying both sound and meaning, are not the medium of poetry. Words can be said to be the medium of poetry only if we understand by words 'emotional meanings of the poetic type'. A less ambiguous way of stating the position would be to say that emotional meanings are the medium of poetry. It is these meanings that the poet works with and that he manipulates, and neither sound nor intellectual ideas as ideas. To speak roundly of words being the medium of poetry is to smuggle in sound and ideas as mere cognitive facts, and that works havoc—as will be seen in the next paragraph—in aesthetic theory. Poets who are second-rate are so, either because they employ the medium of one art while fashioning a work of another art, and thus, aspiring to become musicians when they ought to think of remaining poets, fall between two stools; or else because intellectual ideas have not in them been turned into fuel for an emotional blaze. The latter of these points I shall not labour at all, since very few would be disposed to dispute it.

'Meditate often on these truths, that some time or other they may become your feelings'. And Sir Walter Raleigh, in his Wordsworth monograph, has spoken of the true mystic poet making thought the food of his emotions rather than emotions the food of his thoughts.

But despite the patent turns in the fortunes of Tennyson and Swinburne on the one hand, and of Browning on the other, the proposition that sound is irrelevant in poetry will be contested. Now I wish to state categorically that sound as sound has absolutely no place in poetry at all. That is the province of music. This proposition must be firmly grasped and never lost hold of. Sounds have only symbolic value in poetry, as carriers of emotional meanings, and not intrinsic value as in music.

Only in so far as it develops, adds to, or emphasises the meaning for which it conventionally stands is the sound of a word either of significant or relevant in poetry. The besetting sin of second-rate poets and third-rate literary criticism is to consider this quite irrelevant element as in some sense a legitimate factor in poetic effects, to praise verse that is at least musical. Justifying Shelley to his students, Sir Arthur Quiller-Couch said: 'As students of poetry and its technique again, we shall have something to say; but not so as to convey that he was *vox et praeterea nihil*: which is, for all their polemics, the impression which Arnold and Swinburne agree in conveying with their combined dispraise and praise.' The whole essay is indeed illuminating and shows how fatally mischievous (because essentially accidental, conventional and obviously irrelevant) the element of sound can become in literary appreciation and critical judgment.

The fact is that there is no inherent necessity that a particular combination of sounds must express a particular meaning. The same meaning is expressed by different combinations of sounds in different languages, and sometimes even in the same language (as witness some of the synonyms, if not all). Conversely, the same combination of sounds may express different meanings in different languages or even in the same language.

The sound of the word 'murmur' is relevant in '—murmur of flies on summer eves,' because of its associations in an English mind; that is, because of purely accidental circumstances. There is nothing in the mere vowels and consonants which make up that word that necessitates either the meaning or the associations. The same combination of vowels and consonants will convey an altogether different meaning to a Maratha man. The sound sensations of the word 'wail' will in a similar way mean different experiences in English and in the Indian language Marathi. The same view of the function of sounds in language can be illustrated by the following pairs: French 'Paris' and Italian 'pari'; Italian 'para' and Marathi sound equivalent to the same; French pronunciation of 'bien' and a similar utterance in Marathi. Readers can easily supply more examples of this as well as of the other proposition that the same sounds may express different meanings in the same language, from any book on Phonetics.

This division between sound and meaning and the relevance of the latter alone in poetry is the core of the precept about the agreement of sound and sense in poetry. The misunderstanding of the nature of the medium of poetry is the cause of the ephemeral character of the commonly boosted 'sound poetry' of our day; for whenever an artist, and therefore a poet, allows himself to be seduced by an irrelevant or secondarily relevant aspect of that with which he works into playing false to his medium, he inevitably condemns himself to speedy oblivion. To go a step further, not only are sounds irrelevant in poetry and outside its scope, but even the recognition of a sound effect, if sufficiently subtle, is dependent upon and conditioned by the prior realisation of the pattern of its emotional meanings. The protocols to the sixth poem in Dr Richards's book, *Practical Criticism,* and the analyses they embody and the prosodic conclusions to be derived from them would be sufficient to convince the reader of the truth of the above assertion. Particularly illuminating in this respect are the comments on the delicate rhyming of the first two lines:

'Margaret! are you grieving
For golden grove unleafing?'

Unless then the beauty of sounds is transmuted into the beauty of emotional meaning by the mechanism of associations or otherwise, poetry can take no cognisance of it. The quality of sound *qua* sound has no place in poetry. Many a rhymester could dribble out more melodious verse than that of even Shakespeare or Dante! And epic poets are greater than writers of lyrics not because they are more musical but because they achieve larger, more complex and withal more coherent organised wholes of emotional meanings. It is indeed a curious irony that in music, where sounds and sound patterns alone are significant, men will hunt after emotional meanings, while in poetry, which offers them emotional meanings, they will not rest until they have squeezed what little drop of music they can out of it.

The foregoing analysis is not original except for the thoroughness, emphasis and categorical way with which it discards the calm of pure sound in poetry. The most important thing is the next step: to demonstrate, and correct if we can, in the light of the above analysis, the shift that has taken place in relating the aesthetic process to the literary. We might write the aesthetic process schematically thus:

ARTIST : MEDIUM : BEAUTY

Now we proceed to substitute the specific determinants of particular arts. First, let us take painting:

ARTIST : MEDIUM : BEAUTY

PAINTER : VISUAL ASPECT OF WORLD : BEAUTY
(colour, line, mass, etc.)

Then poetry:

POET : EMOTIONAL MEANINGS : BEAUTY

The beauty of the medium is revealed by organising it, by using it in accordance with formal principles. Now to remember our Spearman. One is led to treat painting and poetry as having different ends only when one has no clear conception of the medium of either. If you say pigments are the medium of poetry, then you pave the way to unending ambiguity and confusion; for once you start including irrelevant factors in the middle term, why and on what principle would you stop at one point rather than at another? You attempt to write your painting process thus:

PAINTER : PIGMENTS : BEAUTY

and then proceed to write your literary process. Your first two terms are:

POET : WORDS

and you put MEANING as your third term, forgetting that this is already included in the second term in a way in which BEAUTY is not included in PIGMENTS. Another way of saying the same thing is this: taking the literary process first, you roughly analyse it in this way:

POET : WORDS : MEANING

Then the corresponding aesthetic process is supposed to be somewhat like this:

PAINTING : PIGMENTS : MEANING

The fallacy here lies, as can be easily seen, in the middle term. Pigments in the second process really correspond to the second and third terms put together in the first process. If you break up a term into two in the first process, you are logically bound to do likewise in the second. You must formulate your two processes thus:

POET : WORDS : MEANING : BEAUTY
PAINTER : PIGMENTS : COLOURS : BEAUTY

The common mistake is to seek the meaning of colours in pictures as you seek the meaning of words in poetry. But as words are meant for meanings, so pigments are meant for colours and not colours for meanings. Colours are not fashioned by men to signify something. No meanings, no words: but not no meanings, no colours in any intelligible sense of the terms. The word 'green' means green colour. If there had been no sensation of green that you wanted to communicate, there would never have come into being that particular combination of sounds to signify that fact. But greenness, the colour green, does not *mean,* in its own primary right, anything: it is just that colour. We come to associate certain ideas with greenness undoubtedly, but these are accretions: the green colour would still be green even if we forgot or eliminated all these associative factors. But if we forgot all the meaning of the word 'green', that combination of vowels and consonants would not exist in our vocabulary.

So, whereas meaning is subsidiary, associative phenomena merely in the case of colours, sound is subsidiary, associative phenomena merely in the case of meanings (of words). The real correspondence is not this:

MEANING : WORD : MEANING : COLOUR

but rather this:

MEANING : WORD : COLOUR : PIGMENT

You can ask what is the meaning of colour, only if you ask what is the meaning of meaning also:

PAINTER : PIGMENTS : COLOURS : MEANING

POET : WORDS : MEANINGS : MEANING
(of meaning)

This is perfectly legitimate, but then the question becomes not of meaning in the popular sense, but one of philosophical analysis, and in that case one has to refer to any book on the psychology of sensations and to Ogden and Richards's book, *The Meaning of Meaning.*

To summarise:

MEANING + CARRIERS OF MEANING—WORD

Or, thus:

COLOUR + CARRIERS OF COLOUR—PIGMENT

To grasp that the sensation aspect—that is, the sound aspect of words—is purely symbolica, is a vehicle for meaning even as oil or water paint is a vehicle for colour; that sound in the one case and oil or water paint in the other are in plain fact merely instrumental, and although indispensable without doubt as instruments, are not on that account essentially relevant to the nature of the creative process involved, is at once to detect the shift and understand its vitiating character. What has been discussed here in relation to painting applies to all the other fine arts in terms of their several mediums.

And if you can guard yourself against this shift, then there is no harm in treating the creative process deduced from poetry as typical of all arts. Thus you will save yourself from falling into the pitfall of the representational versus abstract art controversy. Nor will you then misconceive the aesthetic process, because you have initially yielded to the emotional potency of poetry and tried to construe the former in terms of that underlying the latter.

Such an unambiguous treatment of poetry together with an analysis of the mediums of the various fine arts will bring a systematic unity in aesthetic theory, and yield principles which will hold valid for the entire field of artistic creation without exception. Upon the foundations of such an analysis alone can you erect securely the science of aesthetics and rid critical judgments of their bewildering and conflicting diversity. The supposed gap between the appreciation of literature and of the other fine arts will be bridged not by a sleight of the philosopher's hand, but by discovering the identity of the underlying formal processes But this can happen, and poetry cease to be a curse to aesthetics, only when we realise the doubly emotional character of poetry, that is, only when we learn to distinguish between emotions which are the medium of poetry and that specific *sui generis* aesthetic emotion to which poetry (or those mediumal emotions as organised) like all other arts gives rise; which aesthetic emotion is evoked by beauty, that is, by the perception of formal organisations, simply in virtue of their character of being formal organisations, instead of mere chaotic conglomerations.

B. S. Mardhekar, from Arts and Man

17

G. N. Devy

G. N. Devy, known as Chief Editor of the 'People's Linguistic Survey of India' and a cultural activist, spent several years working with Adivasis and other nomadic communities in India. Before working alongside Adivasis, he was Professor of English at the Maharaja Sayajirao University of Baroda. Some of his important works in the area of literary criticism are *After Amnesia* (1992/2017), *Of Many Heroes* (1997/2017) and a long philosophical essay 'The Being of Bhasha', first published as part of *The G. N. Devy Reader* (2008) and then extended to a full-length book under the same title, *The Being of Bhasha* (2014). He brings the interconnectedness of culture and literature to the centre of literary criticism and views literature as a creation of the 'people' who give it the status of literature rather than the miraculous creation of an individual. Devy writes in English, Gujarati and Marathi. The text reproduced here is from *Of Many Heroes: An Indian Essay in Literary Historiography.*

Para-literature

'In every literary epoch there is,' according to Russian Formalism, 'not one but several literary schools. They exist in literature simultaneously, but one of them represents the canonised crest. The others are not canonised and exist obscurely. . . .'[1] The Formalistic historiography allows an element of arbitrariness in canon formation, which it describes as 'automatization perceptibility.' Once allowance is made for the mysterious arbitrariness in how some literary trends get to become the canonised crest and others exist obscurely, the creation, existence and decline of the non-canonised other trends becomes a foreclosed question. However, the question of obscure traditions, marginal styles and non-canonised texts is of utmost importance to literatures with multilingual historical contexts. The question has a great political urgency in societies that have experienced colonial domination and gender discrimination.

Let us try to conceptualise the 'other, obscure, suppressed or sub-cultural' literary phenomena by using the epithet 'para'.[2] This prefix has travelled from its Greek origin through Latin, and Middle French to Middle English, retaining most of its original sense, and it now means: 'by the side of, beside, alongside of, by past, and beyond.' Para-literature would, therefore, include all such activities as are normally considered socially parallel, linguistically parasitical, psychologically paranoid and historically parenthetical. What is common to all forms of para-literature is that they are literatures without interlocutors, taboo to literary history.

Para-literature as creative activity is analogous to Comparative Literature as a method of literary study in one important respect. In the initial stages of its development, European scholars of Comparative Literature divided the entire field of literary study into National Literature, Comparative Literature, and General Literature.[3] Whereas National Literature and General Literature were defined with relatively greater precision, Comparative Literature, being neither, was given the nebulous and vast middle space between the two. Similarly, Para-literature occupies the middle space between literature and nonliterature. It is not literature, because it is not accepted in literary canons. It is also not non-literature, because it has the formal attributes of literature. Para-literature is, thus, the middle-space literature.

The middle space is densely populated. It contains a bewildering range of forms of linguistic creativity such as science and crime fiction, magazine stories, film and television scripts, street-plays, biographies, autobiographies, memoirs, travelogues, philosophic writings, religious discourses, popular and folk songs, folklore, proverbs, mantra, tantra and liturgical verses, lullabies, oral narratives, archaic literature, works in slang and dialect, children's literature, performed poetry (as in *mushairas*), pornography, graffiti, comics, advertisements, jokes, cartoons, translations, adaptations, abuse terms and letters. Of course this is a random list of middle space literary forms. It can accommodate other forms not listed above provided they are literary and overlooked by histories of literature.

The middle-space literature can be differentiated from non-literature by virtue of its context, style and performance. For instance, abuse terms, graffiti, pornography, popular romances and love-letters have in common the theme of sex-relations; yet each of these has its proper style, context and performance. We cannot interchange the style, context and performance of any of these genres without risking disastrous consequences. In other words, the middle-space literature is not without its aesthetic form, unlike non-literature. All forms of middle-space literature involve a certain linguistic skill and aesthetic sensibility. They have their own distinctive discourses and conventions, standards of excellence and criteria of achievement. They all have their cultural uses. Any language would be much the poorer without these or similar forms of linguistic creativity.

It is the differentiation between literature and the middle-space literature that is the more problematic. One may hastily assume that para-literature or the middle space literature is 'low-brow' literature. But that is not the case. It cuts across all social classes. Who does not require, at one time or another in their lives, abuse words, graffiti, detective or pulp fiction, oral narratives, popular poetry, love-letters and religious recitations? Can we say that liturgical verses or national anthems are low brow?

One may argue that the creative imagination called in operation by para-literature is inferior to the imagination employed by the writers of classics. This claim needs to be investigated by psychologists. However, there are countless writers who work as journalists, commercial copywriters, film and television writers. For instance, one of the most creative of India's contemporary poets, Arun Kolatkar, works in the field of advertising. He writes very good poetry in two languages: Marathi and English. Can the imagination that writes poetry in Marathi be different from the imagination that writes Kolatkar's poetry in English and the 'poetic' imagination different again from the imagination that writes advertisement copy?[4] To put this in another way, not all good poets can be good prose writers, or good journalists or commercial artists. Each kind of writing requires a specific kind of linguistic orientation, and none of these orientations is superior or inferior. The notion that poetic imagination is closer to Truth, and therefore superior to other forms of imagination, is a belief left over to us by the nineteenth century European conflict between reason and imagination, which created exaggerated and romantic claims in favour of imagination. On the other hand, if poets were traditionally expected to be prophets in India, they were also expected to quieten their mental activity, including that of imagination, in order to be able to receive large visions of life. The idea that literature employs imagination which is superior to the kind of imagination used in para-literature reflects the equation of power between the two types of literature rather than any valid aesthetic perception.

The question of power immediately brings in the question of institutionalisation of literature. Rather than saying that para-literature is non-literature, it would be more appropriate to say that it is non-classroom literature, that as literature it is neither taught nor learnt. Para-literature is all literature which is excluded from literary history; and if seen grudgingly as a document it is never given the status of a monument. The difference between literature and para-literature has to be sought, therefore, with reference to the causes behind institutionalised literature teaching. Two questions need to be asked here: why do we teach literature? and, why do we not teach all manifestations of literary creativity?

Literature teaching is a unique invention in human history. It does not pass on knowledge in the same way as the teaching of sciences and technology do. Sciences and technology face the danger of extinction if they are not transmitted through some form of teaching. Literature faces no such danger, for literature as a creative activity does not depend on the teaching of literature. Literature teaching does not aim at shaping future writers as the classroom work in fine arts aims at shaping artists. While other human sciences deal with human reality, literature teaching deals with a level of reality created by human beings.

Closest to it come the teaching of linguistics and philosophy which handle a secondary level of reality, namely, language and thought. But they rarely glorify the aesthetic and emotive aspect of their subject to the extent literature teaching does. To generalise, literature teaching has the following two characteristics: it is a non-useful activity, and the thought content it seeks to transmit is irrational.

Perhaps the above generalisation can be restated by saying that the greatest use of literature teaching is that by using ambivalent literary signs for the construction of its pedagogic narratives, it allows the irrational elements in a culture a respectable articulation. If scientific thinking keeps a society moving forward, signs of irrational impulses keep it integrated. Literature is such a system of signs. It is, in other words, a totemic system. It is a system embodied in verbal signs which continue to persist in their meaning over long periods of time, signs which are totems that articulate for successive generations of people the irrational content of their own personalities. Literature, this system of totems, keeps successive generations bound by a sense of historic flow of time, by a sense of being a community. All communities are bound together by the literary signs they value. No literature is *objectively* beautiful or useful in itself. Literatures are vested with these qualities by the communities that are bound together by those linguistic totems. Literature is taught as a valuable discipline because it helps us to identify the most persistent and irrational images of our ancestors in the verbal icons created by them. Totems do not possess any inherent significance. They acquire it by virtue of their situation in a given community.

It may be possible to understand the universal urge to impart literary teaching to younger generations in any given society in the light of the above comments. The reason why all kinds of literature do not receive an institutional status is that totems always create, and almost inevitably depend on, a contrary system of taboos.[5] If, literature is understood as a system of totems, para-literature can be seen as a system of taboos, which is not allowed to enter the sacred portals of a classroom. In fact, collectively and irrationally agreed upon, taboos too keep communities bound together. Totems and taboos, respectively, represent a community's desires in their sublimated or repressed forms. The relationship between the two is the relationship between the sacred and the profane. This relationship depends on how a given community distributes its cultural space. In terms of the material substance of which they are composed, their structural organisations, and their expressivity, totems and taboos may be identical; but their status in terms of the sacred and the profane may vary radically. For instance, pornography and romance, or abuse terms and proverbs, may have identical substance, structure and complexity; yet the irrational needle of a community's compass mapping the range of the sacred and the profane will show the forms in these pairs as distinct as the east and the west, or the north and the south. It may be deduced from these anthropological observations about the nature of canon formation in literary studies that the distinction between literature and para-literature, even if explained in terms of a science of literary criticism, is really guided by the systems of totems and taboos of the society that creates and preserves a given literary tradition. Exclusions of authors, texts, styles in a given history of literature, or inclusion of certain other authors, texts, forms and styles, are matters which, in the first instance, are determined by extra-literary considerations. It is not because the critical consensus about an author or a technique is initially wrong that after a time that author or technique is given legitimacy. These fluctuations occur because taboos can turn into totems in course of time. For example, travelling across the seas was taboo in India till the early part of this century. Today it has a totemic importance. Neither totems nor taboos have permanence of status. They may interchange their positions with appropriate shifts in the cultural history of a community. This exchange is an essential aspect of literary history, though unfortunately it has remained generally neglected.

When new literary traditions emerge, or branch off from an established literary tradition, the new literatures are initially treated as taboo/para-literatures. The history of literature in the modern

Indian languages tells us that in the initial period of development of these new traditions, the period of transition from Sanskrit to these new languages was seen as a gradual vulgarisation. A similar attitude was displayed in Europe towards the literatures and languages branching out of Latin in medieval times. In the early phases of English literary writing outside England and Scotland, in countries like Ireland, America and Australia, the British attitude to such literature was invariably patronising. On the other hand, when a literary tradition acquires substance, the preceding literary trends or traditions lose their acquired status. Though it is true that not all obsolete literature gets relegated to the category of para-literature, literary history does keep agitating against literary obsolescence.

However, not all para-literature is a product of literary history's amnesia, nor is all of it the result of hesitation on the part of literary criticism to assimilate new modes of writing. Much of para-literature is downgraded to that status due to contemporary repressions guided by the hierarchic stratification within a community. In most communities a lower 'aesthetic' value is attached to literature produced by and for women and children in literary criticism and history controlled by the men and adults of those communities. Children and women form two major repressed segments of most communities. Their literary requirements, and aesthetic sensibilities are taken less seriously than they deserve. Para-literature therefore accurately reflects the patterns of social repression. In addition to these, there is one more conventional method of repression in India. The subcontinental and poly-linguistic country always has had a common mainstream literary tradition, whether in Sanskrit, Pali, Persian, Hindi or English. The regional literary traditions in India have to encounter the imperialism of the mainstream traditions. At present, this is the condition of about eighty-five tribal and minority languages and literary forms in these languages. Each of these languages is spoken by more than 10,000 people but not listed as languages of administration in the eighth Schedule of the Indian Constitution.[6] The literary aesthetics of these languages is never given even the minimum passing consideration in Indian literary discourse. Their situation is like that of literatures in Indian languages in relation to the contemporary world canon of literature. Para-literature is thus the literature of linguistic communities on the periphery of political orders.

The psychological desire to castrate one's adversary often takes linguistic expression. The linguistic creativity of politically subjugated sections is then made a victim of this desire by the dominating language groups. During the nineteenth century, European anthropologists turned perfectly normal literary activity in Africa into para-literature. Orientalism did that for the Asian nations. Para-literature, in which it is the usual practice to include oral narratives and folk forms, is perceived to be closer to the region of the unconscious. If one were to follow psychoanalytic criticism with persistence, it would seem to provide an explanation of the phenomenon. However, the unconscious itself is not a category free of political conditioning, as argued by Kumkum Sangari.[7] In a thought-provoking essay, she shows how Freud's discovery of the unconscious was an inevitable result of the political history of European colonialism during the nineteenth century:

> A significant facet of the history of designating the unconscious in Europe consists of the histories of primitivization. In the late nineteenth century the primitivization of certain categories becomes quite strident: most notably of sexuality and of women who, along with non-western societies are placed on the scale of evolution.
>
> The scientization of the primitive is carried out side by side with its aesthetization through a series of 'revaluations'. The 'primitive' ranges from the external and measurable to the internal and immeasurable... Conversely, the 'primitive' can either be equated with or contained in the unconscious.[8]

The primitive in society, the unconscious in the psyche, and the 'para' in literature may have intrinsic attributes in a given period, but these are not absolute categories. Their attributes in a given period are gradually determined over a preceding long period through processes of repression. Therefore, what is civilised can come to be considered primitive, what belongs to accessible areas of consciousness can be relegated to the territory and terror of the unconscious, and what is literature can invite description as para-literature. Movements in the opposite direction too are possible. These movements are of crucial formative importance in the history of literature, both as a system of totems and taboos and as dynamic cultural practices.

Since there is essentially no difference between literature and para-literature, the boundaries between the two are not permanently sealed, and there is a constant mutual exchange. This exchange proceeds along certain established lines. To articulate the nature of this exchange should be one of the primary objectives of literary history. As in the history of language, so too in the history of literature, the trends and styles initially developed on the margins tend to gravitate towards the centre. Removed from the original context, sometimes the para-styles change their intended performance in the changed literary context. Conventions of comic literature often originate in the not-so-comic dialects of the socially less privileged classes. Conventions of the tragic, epic and canonical originate in the well-formed registers of the socially privileged classes. Once formulated, these languages and literatures become socially usable systems. Thus, the marginal (or *desi*: regional) and the dominant (or *mārga*: mainstream) literary traditions keep alternating their positions.[9] This continuous and inevitable mobility of literary conventions is what the term 'evolution' of literature should rightly imply.

Literature, as a social and cultural activity, is a continuous reordering of the total field of meaning available to a society through language, a continuous restructuring of various levels of received language. Literature, in order to be socially meaningful, has to reappropriate the sources of language so as to invest the language system with new possibilities of consciousness. Hence, the linguistic activity on the margins of a language community, the para-literary activity, has an important role to play in the literary enrichment of that language. For this reason it deserves attention as literary history.

It may be said that the distinction between literature and para-literature is not a distinction between two different fields, but a distinction within a single field, as the one between totems and taboos within a single culture, or as between the self and the non-self within a single field of consciousness. The political dispossession of linguistic and social margins is the root cause of the creation of such categories. The relationship between literature and para-literature is closely comparable to that between the psychologically masculine and the psychologically feminine other. It is a relationship in which the female other is seen as being closer to the unconscious, the primitive, the marginal, and yet indispensable. Ultimately, it is the need for this dialectics of self-cognition of literature that creates the category of para-literature.

If the dialectical relationship between the dominant trends and marginal trends is considered a process forming the backbone of the history of literature, it would still be necessary to specify the nature of this dialectics in a given culture, for it may vary from culture to culture. In other words, canon formation may be a common experience for all literatures in the world, but the processes through which canons are formed in a given literary culture are likely to be peculiar to that particular literary tradition. For instance, the canons of English literature have been shaped generally speaking by the conservative forces in British society. The canons of post-Sanskrit Indian literatures have, on the other hand, been formed by socially heterodox tendencies. It is not enough for literary history to describe the canons; it is also necessary, and even more important, to explain the culture specific processes of canon formation so as to make literature a socially integrated sub-system of culture. Therefore, if the relationship between literature and para-literature is of vital importance to the self-cognition of literary canons, it would be essential for any perspicuous literary history to take into account the nature of a society's narcissistic structure.

Swa and *Para*: Self and the Other

It is at this stage that we have to introduce another term to help us conceptualise the narcissistic structure of Indian society, as understood in Indian traditions. The term we can use is *para*, which is accepted by a large majority of modern Indian languages as the term for 'other'. The original Sanskrit term, replete with meanings, indicates: 'distant, further, enemy, afterwards, beyond, other, far off, etc.' Its superlative form, *param* however moves into a more idealistic plane by generating sacred terms such as *parameshwar* and *parabrahman*, terms related to the discourse of the other world. The term is shared by Dravidian languages too, with revealing deviations. Tamil uses *parai* as the term for drums played by outcaste drummers of the *paraiyan* community, which, incidentally, is also the origin of a similar English term, 'pariah'. One is not sure if the Greek *para* and the Sanskrit *para* have a forgotten common source; but it is possible to deduce from the linguistic evidence we have, that in all languages in which the Greek and the Sanskrit term *para* has been assimilated, the term is used to indicate 'otherness' as a psychological phenomenon as well as a spatial term, as if the psychological space is revealed through this term as a geographical metaphor. Thus modern English has 'parish' and 'parochial' indicating restricted psychological and geographical spaces. In Indian languages the term *paradesh* is used to indicate foreign or alien land. Such peculiar usage of the term for describing space as well as otherness, indicating unarticulated wisdom inherent in human languages, is properly theorised in Lacan's formulation:

> The notion of the role of spatial symmetry in man's narcissistic structure is essential in the establishment of the basis of a psychological analysis of space.... Let us consider that animal psychology has shown us that the individual's relation to a particular spatial field is, in certain species mapped socially, in a way that raises it to the category of subjective membership. I would say that it is the subjective possibility of the mirror projection of such a field into the field of the other that gives human space its originally 'geometric' structure, a structure that I would be happy to call kaleidoscopic.... Such, at least, is the space in which the imagery of the ego develops, and which rejoins the objective space of reality.[10]

Indian epistemology too admits the kaleidoscopic structure within the ego-space. But the kaleidoscoping it visualises is not between the field of the self and the field of the non-self. It is rather between the field of the self and the field of the greater-self. It is a theology-bound epistemology. The *Katha Upanishad* is eloquent on this issue:

> The tree of eternity has its roots in heaven above and its branches reach down to earth. It is Brahman ... Brahman is seen in a pure soul as in a mirror clear, and also in the Creator's heaven as clear as light; but in the land of shades as reflections in trembling water. When the wise man knows that the material senses come not from the Spirit, and their waking and sleeping belong to their own nature, then he grieves no more. Beyond the senses is the Spirit of man, and beyond this is the Spirit of the universe, and evolver of all. And beyond is Purusha, all pervading, beyond definitions.[11]

Here too, as in Lacan, the key terms are 'mirror' and 'reflection' which complete the grand circle of human consciousness by inductive leaps. But the mapping of the narcissistic structure is different. Indian texts, whether emerging from the *Vedas*, the *Upanishads*, or secular literature, see the self and the non-self as reflections of *Purusha*, the greater-self, as mere passing images of a reality beyond human perception. In that sense, the dichotomy between the self and non-self has not been conceptualised in radical terms. Buddhist psychology too did not visualize any such opposition between the self and the non-self. In fact, the entire spectrum of human existence is seen in Indian thought in terms of a complex continuum. To introduce concepts of polarities in it is considered by Indian thought as tantamount to a profoundly ignorant act of consciousness.

How can one reconcile this concept of the ego-space with the rational and sensory perceptions, which form the physical basis for the recognition of the non-self? Traditional Indian epistemology circumvents this difficulty by introducing a taxonomy of knowledge. Indian tradition divided knowledge into false knowledge, *avidyā*, and authentic knowledge, *vidyā*. The two are not radically different, but they can be recognised as such in terms of a polarity in the spectrum of knowledge. *Avidyā* is the knowledge flowing from the senses to the soul. *Vidyā*, on the contrary, is the knowledge flowing from the soul to the senses. The knower of *vidyā* is a *guru*, a spiritual guide. These categories were neatly separated from those related to systematised perception of material phenomena, for which the terms *jñāna* and *vijñāna* (approximately corresponding to modern humanities and science, respectively) were employed. The knower of the latter was known as *ācharya*, a teacher, a scholar. An experience of *para*, the foreign or alien, thus brings into play the knowledge of the other, which, when it is guided by *vidyā* (spiritual knowledge) obscures the duality between the self and the non-self, leading to a recognition of the self within the non-self.

Sudhir Kakar, who has presented highly engaging theses on Indian psychoanalysis, comments on the sense of the self in Hindu tradition at length in his study, *The Inner World*. His observations as a professional scholar of psychology would be of immense use to us in defining the priorities of Indian literary history. Discussing the concepts of 'I', 'Ego' and 'Self ', he writes:

> The distinction between *vidya* and *avidya*—true and false consciousness—between reality and *maya*, illustrates a fundamental difference between Hindu and Western world images, as well as a discrepancy in the modes of thought and perception, which even the best intentioned movements of cultural ecumenism cannot hope to bridge satisfactorily. The maintenance of ego boundaries, between 'inside' and 'outside', and between 'I' and 'others', and the sensory experiences of social relations based on these separations, is the stuff of reality in Western thought and yet *maya* to the Hindus, The optimal discrimination of this reality of separateness, expressed in terms of heightened ego functions such as reality sense, reality testing and adaptation to reality, is the stated goal of most Western psychotherapies, but of paltry importance in the Hindu ways of liberation. A good reality sense, according to psychoanalysis, shows itself in the absence of a conscious feeling of the self or the various selves. This, however, is precisely the situation which the Hindu ways of liberation would seek to reverse. And if in the course of development, the child learns to differentiate between himself and what is not a part of him, between 'me' and 'not-me'—a process in which the individual's sense of space, time, causality and

> individuality are formed, and ego boundaries are constituted—then in a certain sense the Hindu ways of liberation ... seek to undo this process of ego development.[12]

If, as modern psychoanalysis tells us, the tendency of the dominant Indian psychological type is towards establishing the non-duality of self and non-self in the narcissistic field, the tendency in the altruistic field must, therefore, be that of allowing a free interplay between the central and *para* cultural elements.

It would, however, be inaccurate to think that the Aryan epistemology of the self-other relationship remained unchanged in the long history of India. Hinduism has been an amorphous mass of ideas and practices, within which an amazing variety of dissenting viewpoints emerged and eventually merged. Besides, for about a thousand years India has produced a powerful and complex tradition of Indian Islam, and for two centuries created hybrid cultural practices out of the encounter with the modern West. Yet, the amazing capacity to assimilate alien cultural, linguistic, and literary elements is a unique and essential feature of Indian history. Though the Western countries too have been exposed to a very large number of alien cultures during the last two hundred years, their assimilation of alien cultural traits has been relatively restricted in correspondence with their relationship of otherness with the foreign cultures.

It is of course not true that the metaphysics of non-duality between the self and the non-self did not create social stratification in India. All the evidence in Indian history goes directly against such an assumption. No other society in the world is, has been, perhaps more fragmented, stratified and torn with strife as Indian society. It is divided linguistically, regionally, in terms of caste, income, faith, and profession. What is true, perhaps, is that the tendency of dissension is counterbalanced by the political and social organization based on consensus. It is for this reason that a careful study of the exchanges between literature and para-literature becomes all the more vital to a proper understanding of India's literary past, and through it the literary present.

Tradition and Transactions

European literary historiography uses the paradigm of a single dominant literary tradition. There is very little debate about the central canons of British literature. Occasional debates about particular preferences of styles and periods do take place, such as the one created by T. S. Eliot's preference for the Metaphysicals over the Romantics, but the overall range of the canon has never been in doubt. At no stage in the tradition of English literary criticism was any allowance made for the inclusion of a non-British writer in the British canon,[13] even when some very good works were produced in the language of the British isles outside, in other continents. On the other hand, in India a writer of Greek ancestry like Ashvaghosha, or of Irish nationality like Nivedita, or with Caribbean background like Naipaul or with Arabic training like Ibn Battuta, have been accepted as *Indian* writers. Languages such as Persian, Arabic, English, French, and Portuguese have been accepted in India as languages of *Indian* literature. The English canons have never thought of any translation as a great work of literature, the emphasis of Anglo-poetics being on the original (though perhaps aesthetically the most intricate work in English is the King James' version of the Bible, a translation). In India some of the most respected literary classics have originated in attempts to translate: the *Jñāneśvarī* in Marathi, Kamban's *Rāmāyana* in Tamil, Tulsi's *Rāmāyana* in Hindi, Tagore's *Gitanjali* in English are some examples. Again, Indian literature has in it the peculiar phenomenon of bilingual writers. The number of bilingual writers in India is so large, and the longevity of this practice is so substantial that bilingual literature is more a norm than an exception in India. Considering these major differences between literary practices in India and Western countries, it is obvious that the concept of a single dominant literary tradition, a single and fairly well-defined literary canon and historical criticism couched in a unidirectional philology will not prove adequate to interpret the history of literature in any Indian language.

This particular problem for literary historiography can get a useful lead from developments in general historiography in India in recent years. Specifically useful in this respect is Romila Thapar's important essay on tradition in *Cultural Transaction and Early India: Tradition and Patronage*.[14] In this essay Thapar discusses the Indian views of tradition, more particularly the historical reconstruction of tradition. Through several convincing examples, she makes it clear that at any given time there may be a normative code of tradition, but at the same time there exist numerous deviations from the norm. It is therefore possible, as Thapar argues, to project a variety of traditions as dominant in Indian history and culture, none of which is more or less authentic than the rest. One of the more striking examples she selects to put her view across is that of the *Mahābhārata*. The story of Shakuntala used by Kālidāsa existed in *Mahābhārata* previous to his rendering. The two versions have different philosophical and ideological orientations. After Kālidāsa's use of the story, the two versions co-existed in Indian culture. Thapar asks: Which of the two is more authentic? Her answer is that authenticity of tradition arises out of subjective reading by historians:

> For such a diverse community to create a uniform cultural tradition for itself can become an exercise in juggling with history. Traditions are not self-created: they are consciously chosen, and the choice from the past is enormous.... If we are to understand the role of religion in the Indian society of earlier times we may have to be moved away from the paradigm of Hinduism and the other religions in India as projected in the colonial period.... Complex societies have competing value systems and attempts are made by the more established to delete ideologies of protest or of divergent values...[15]

What is true of the national history of India is also, and far more pertinently, true of its literary history, given the multilingual literary context. Western historiography of literature is based on literary histories which do not have multiple parallel traditions. The term 'parallel' can be applied to popular or folk traditions in European contexts. In India the parallel traditions are really alternative traditions rather than 'low' value traditions.

When Pānini wrote his grammar in the pre-Christian centuries, he spoke of two discourses in Sanskrit, one used by the common people and another that was grammatically correct. When Bharata composed his treatise on drama, he spoke of two types of theatre, one catering to the public and the other based on dramatic conventions. Both Pānini and Bharata speak of the popular and the doctrinaire as insiders, not in terms of the self and the other. Daṇḍin, the seventh century Sanskrit theoretician, describes several competing literary styles from different regions of India. They were all styles of Sanskrit poetry; in describing these, Daṇḍin does not arrange them in an aesthetic or sociological hierarchy. In the eleventh century, Rājashekhara could write plays in Maharashtri as well as in Sanskrit. Jayadeva in the twelfth century wrote poetry in Bengali as well as in Sanskrit. Hemachandra, in the thirteenth century, wrote in Gujarati and in Sanskrit. Nāmadeva wrote poems in Hindi and in Punjabi too, in addition to writing in Marathi. Thyāgarāja, writing in Telugu had no hesitation in learning the diction and metre of Gujarati poetry. Ekanātha prepared a scholarly edition of Jñānadeva's *Bhāvārthadīpikā*, using writing as the medium, and 'published' most of his own poems using the oral medium of singing. There are innumerable writers who write in Urdu and Hindi, Hindi and Punjabi, Oriya and Bangla, Gujarati and Marathi, English and some Indian language. None of them show signs of any unusual anxiety of being torn or split between traditions. An average Indian reader, if he or she is reasonably well educated, reads works in his or her own language, in one or two other Indian languages, in English translation from other languages; and yet does not feel anxiety or guilt for the loss of his linguistic, literary or cultural identity. The Indian tradition has given to every sensitive Indian the ability to internalise a multiplicity of traditions.

In India, the folk traditions can be as erudite as the dominant lexical traditions; and apparently outmoded styles and diction can find unexpected revivals. Thus it would be improper to classify the traditions either into clearly demarcated periods, or into categories with clearly demarcated class origins of literature. It would be inappropriate even to speak of literary traditions in terms of a tradition of texts in a single given language. A more appropriate approach would be to think of literary history in terms of a constant exclusion of para-literatures from the cultural centres creating a constant assimilation of *para* literatures into the centres of culture, creating a complex pattern of conflict and collaboration of many minor traditions. It may have been purely a linguistic coincidence that the term for tradition in Indian languages, *parampara*, implies the historiographic view proposed by Romila Thapar, for the term is formed by combining *param* (superlative of *para*) and *para*.[16] We may interpret the term to mean, in the light of the foregoing discussion, 'consideration of all literary margins'. Such a view of *parampara*, tradition, will not be very far from the spirit of the term *sāhitya*, meaning togetherness or co-existence, employed for the literary arts.

The term *sāhitya*,[17] one of the several Indian terms for literature, has implicit in it a vitally important insight for literary historiography. There are other terms in Indian languages which are synonyms for *sāhitya* such as *vāngmaya*, *saraswata*, *kāvya*, *lekhan*, etc. While *vāngmaya* and *saraswata* indicate the literary or poetic quality of writing, *lekhan* refers to the act of writing. None of these has superseded *sāhitya* so far because it accurately reflects the historical fact that all literary traditions and movements in India resulted from a togetherness, *sāhitya*, of multiple traditions.

The idea of a pure state of authentic existence at the point of origin is not appropriate to view Indian literary history; probably it is not appropriate to view any literary history at all, except that of proto-Indo-European literature, if it existed at all, for at that point of history we have with us nothing but a sense of mystery and myth. So far, Western literary historiography has not come to terms with the basic fact about literary history that all traditions of literature originate in the act of translation. An act of translation holds together two, or sometimes more, different traditions momentarily, for a cross fertilisation, and in that sense all translations are *sāhitya*.

Translation as Origin

'Translation is the wandering existence in a perpetual exile,' says J. Hillis Miller.[18] The statement obviously alludes to the Christian myth of the Fall, exile and wandering. In Western metaphysics translation is an exile, a fall from the origin; and the mythical exile is a metaphorical translation—a post-Babel crisis. Given this metaphysical precondition of Western aesthetics, it is not surprising that literary translations are not accorded the same status as original works. Western literary criticism provides for the guilt of translations for coming into being after the original; the temporal subsequentiality is held as a proof of diminution of literary authenticity of translations. The strong sense of being an individual, given to Western individuals through systematic philosophy and the logic of social history makes them view translation as an intrusion of 'the other'. This intrusion is desirable to the extent it helps define one's own identity; but not beyond that point. It is, of course, natural for the monolingual European cultures to be acutely conscious of the act of translation. The philosophy of individualism and the metaphysics of guilt, however, render European literary historiography incapable of grasping the origins of literary traditions.

One of the most revolutionary events in the history of English style has been the authorised translated version of the Bible. It was also the literary expression of Protestant Christianity. The recovery of the original spirit of Christianity was thus sought by Protestant England through an act of translation. It is well known that Chaucer was translating the style of Boccacio into English when he created his Canterbury Tales. When Dryden and Pope wanted to recover a sense of order, they used the tool of translation.[19] Similar attempts were made in other European languages such as German and French.

During the last two centuries the role of translation in communicating literary movements across linguistic borders has become very important. The tradition that has given us writers like Shaw, Yeats, Joyce, Beckett, Heaney in a single century—the tradition of Anglo-Irish literature—branched out of the practice of translating Irish works into English initiated by Macpherson towards the end of the eighteenth century.[20] Indian English literature too has gathered its conventions of writing from the Indological activity of translation during the late eighteenth century and the nineteenth century. Many of the Anglo-Irish and Indian English writers have been able translators themselves. Similarly, the settler colonies such as Australia, Canada, New Zealand have impressive modern traditions of literature, which have resulted from the 'translation' of the settlers from their homeland to alien locations. Post-colonial writing in the former Spanish colonies in South America, the former colonies in Africa, and in other parts of the world have experienced the importance of translation as one of the crucial conditions for creativity. In fact modernism and post-modernism as international movements would never have come into existence without the mediation of repeated acts of translation. Those who study Theory today know that if they did not have translations of theorists from a dozen different cultures, it would be impossible to think of a revolution in literary thought at all. Thus origins of literary movements and literary traditions can be traced back to various acts of translation.

Considering the fact that most literary traditions originate in translation, and gain substance through repeated acts of translation, it would be useful for a theory of literary history to seek support from a theory of literary translation. However, since translations are conventionally perceived as unoriginal, not much thought has been devoted to the aesthetics of translation. Most of the primary issues too have not been settled in relation to translation: issues related to the 'form' and 'meaning' of translation. No major critic has taken any well-defined positions about the exact placement of translations in literary history. Do they belong to the history of target languages, or do they belong to the history of source languages?

Or do they form an independent tradition all by themselves? This ontological uncertainty which haunts translations has rendered translation study a haphazard activity which devotes too much energy to discussing the problems of the original meaning and the meaning of the altered structure.[21]

Unfortunately for translation the various developments about the interdependence between meaning and structure in the field of linguistics have been based on monolingual data and situations. Even the sophisticated and revolutionary theoretical formulation proposed by Structural linguistics are not sufficient to unravel the intricacies of translation activity.

Structural linguistics considers language a system of signs, arbitrarily developed, that tries to cover the entire range of significance available to the culture of that language. The signs do not mean anything by or in themselves, they acquire significance by virtue of their relation to the entire system to which they belong. This theory naturally looks down upon translation which is an attempt to rescue/abstract significance from one system of signs and to wed it to another such system. But language is an open system. It keeps admitting new signs as well as new significance in its fold. It is also open, in the sociolinguistic sense that it allows an individual speaker or writer to use as much of it as he can or likes to do. If this is the case, then how 'open' is a particular system of verbal signs when a bilingual user, such as a translator, rends it open? Assuming that, for an individual, language resides within his consciousness, we can ask whether the two systems within his consciousness can be shown as materially different, whether they retain their individual identities within the sphere of his consciousness?

Or do such systems become a single, open and extended system? If translation is defined as some kind of communication of significance, and if we accept the structuralist principle that communication becomes possible because of the nature of signs and their entire system, it follows that translation is a merger of sign systems. Such a merger is possible because systems of signs are open and vulnerable. The 'translating consciousness' exploits the potential openness of language systems; and as it shifts significance from a given verbal form to a corresponding but different verbal form it also brings closer the materially different sign systems.

If we take the lead from Phenomenology and conceptualise a whole community of 'translating consciousness', it should be possible to develop a theory of inter-lingual synonymy as well as a more perceptive literary historiography. The concept of 'translating consciousness', and of communities of people possessing it, are no mere notions. In most Third World countries, where a dominating colonial language has acquired a privileged place, such communities do exist. In India several languages are simultaneously used by language communities as if these languages formed a continuous spectrum of significance. To conceptualize this situation is beyond European linguistics, which is based mostly on a monolingual view of language. The use of two or more different languages in translation activity cannot be understood properly through studies of foreign language acquisition. Such theories work round the premise that there is inevitably a chronological gap, an order or a priority scale in language learning situations. The field is stratified in terms of value-based indicators LI and L2, though in reality language learning activity may seem very natural in a country like India. In Chomsky's linguistics the concept of semantic universals plays an important role. However, his level of abstraction marks the farthest limits to which the monolingual Saussurean linguistic materialism can be stretched. In actual practice, even in Europe, the translating consciousness treats the Source Language and Target Language as parts of a larger and continuous spectrum of various intersecting systems of verbal signs.

The privileged discourse of general linguistics today is closely interlinked with developments in anthropology, particularly after Durkheim and Levi-Strauss. Colonial Europe had distributed various fields of humanistic knowledge into a three-fold hierarchy: Comparative studies for Europe, Orientalism for the Orient, and Anthropology for the rest of the world. In its various phases of development modern Western linguistics has connections with all these. After the discovery of Sanskrit by Sir William Jones, historical linguistics in Europe depended heavily on Orientalism.

For a long time afterwards linguisticians followed the path of comparative philology. And after Saussure and Levi-Strauss, linguistics started treating language with an anthropological curiosity. When linguistics branched off to its monolingual structuralist path, Comparative Literature still persisted in its faith in the translatability of literary texts.

Comparative Literature accepts that between two related languages there are areas of significance that are shared just as there may be areas of significance that can never be shared. Translation can be seen as an attempt to bring a given language system in its entirety as close as possible to the areas of significance that it shares with other given language or languages. All translations operate within this shared area of significance. Such a notion may help us distinguish synonymy within one language and the shared significance between two related languages.

The translation problem is not just a linguistic problem. It is an aesthetic and ideological problem which has a significant bearing on the question of literary history. Literary translation is not just a replication of a text in another verbal system of signs. It is replication of an ordered sub-system of signs within a given language into another corresponding ordered sub-system of signs within a related language. Translation is not a transposition of significance or signs. After the act of translation is over, the original work still remains in its original position. Translation is rather an attempted revitalisation of the original in another verbal space and temporal span. Like literary texts that continue to belong to their original periods and styles and also continue to exist through successive chronological periods, translation at once approximates to the original and transcends it. The problems in translation study are, therefore, very much like those in literary history. They are the problems of the relationship between origins and subsequentiality. And as in translation study, so in literary history the problem of origin has not been tackled satisfactorily. The point that needs to be made is that probably the question of origins of literary traditions will have to be viewed differently by multilingual literary communities possessing a 'translating consciousness'.

Notes

1. M. M. Bakhtin and P. N. Medvedev, *The Formal Method in Literary Scholarship: A Critical Introduction to Sociological Poetics*, trans. Albert J. Wehrle, The Goucher College Series (Baltimore and London: The Johns Hopkins University Press, 1978), p. 160.
2. G. N. Devy, "Para-Literature" in *Approaches to Para-Literature*, ed. Amiya Dev (Calcutta: Jadavpur University, 1992), pp. 50–57.
3. See Rene Wellek, "The Name and Nature of Comparative Literature", in *Discriminations: Further Concept of Criticism* (New Haven and London: Yale University Press, 1970); Henry H. H. Remak, "Comparative Literature at the Crossroads: Diagnosis, Theory and Prognosis", in *Yearbook of Comparative and General Literature*, Vol. I, IX, 1960; S. S. Prawer, *Comparative Literary Studies* (London: Duckworth, 1973).
4. For a provocative discussion of Kolatkar's bilingualism, see B. V. Nemade, "Arun Kolatkar and Bilingual Poetry" in *Indian Readings in Commonwealth Literature*, ed. G. S. Amur, V. R. N. Prasad, B. V. Nemade and N. K. Nihalani (Delhi : Sterling, 1985) pp. 71–86.
5. See Claude Levi-Strauss, "Social Structure", in *Structural Anthropology*, translated from the French by Claire Jacobson and Brooke Grundfest Schoepf, (Harmondsworth: Penguin, 1963 and 1979), pp. 277–323.
6. The Eighth Schedule lists the following languages; Assamiya, Bangla, Dogri, Gujarati, Hindi, Kashmiri, Kannada, Konkani, Manipuri, Maithili, Malayalam, Marathi, Nepali, Oriya, Punjabi, Tamil, Telugu, Sindhi, Urdu.
7. Kumkum Sangari, "Figures for the Unconscious", *Journal of Arts and Ideas*, March 1991, Nos. 20–21, pp. 67–84.
8. Ibid., p.75.
9. For a historical account of the two categories, *desi* and *mārga* see G. N. Devy, *After Amnesia: Tradition and Change in Indian Literary Criticism* (Bombay: Orient Longman, 1992), pp. 78–82.
10. Jacques Lacan, *Ecrits* (London: Tavistock, 1977), p. 27.
11. *Upanishads*, Penguin Classics, 1965, p. 65.
12. Sudhir Kakar, *The Inner World: A Psychoanalytic Study of Childhood and Society in India* (New Delhi: Oxford University Press, 1981), pp. 20–21. See the critique of Kakar by D. Venkata Rao, "The Stunting Lebensraum: Sudhir Kakar and the Subject of Psycho-coloniality", *Journal of Contemporary Thought*, No. 1, 1991, pp. 111–124.
13. Examples of writers of non-British origin in the history of English literature that can be cited as exceptions are Henry James, T. S. Eliot, Joseph Conrad, Arthur Koestler, etc. However, each of these had to

make efforts to project himself as a conformist to English cultural values in order to be accepted. W. B. Yeats, who did not follow the trend, continued to be treated as Irish.

14. Romila Thapar, *Cultural Transaction and Early India: Tradition and Patronage* (New Delhi: Oxford University Press, 1987), pp. 7–22.
15. Ibid., p. 23.
16. For a discussion of the difference between 'tradition' and 'parampara' see G. N. Devy, *After Amnesia*, pp. l6–20.
17. Though the term 'Sahitya' was highlighted by Viswanatha in the fourteenth century, it was in use in the discourse of Sanskrit poetics for many centuries preceding him. For a discussion of the concept see K. Krishnamoorthy's introduction to Sanskrit Literary Criticism in *Comparative Indian Literature*, ed. K. M. George, (Madras: Macmillan, 1984–86).
18. I have quoted from my notes of a lecture given by Prof. J. Hillis Miller at the ninth centenary celebration symposium at the University of Bologna, Italy, in October 1988.
19. Susan Bassnett-McGuire, *Translation Studies* (London: Methuen, 1980), pp. 58–64.
20. Robert Welch, "Language and Tradition", in *Changing States: Transformation in Modern Irish Writing* (London and New York: Routledge, 1993), pp. 11–34.
21. J. C. Catford, *A Linguistic Theory of Translation* (London: Oxford University Press, 1965).

Part II

Interpretation

18

K. Krishnamoorthy

Professor Krishnamoorthy has been a doyen of Sanskrit studies in India for the last five decades. He has published innumerable essays and books devoted to the discussion, interpretation and elaboration of critical concepts in Sanskrit poetics. Among his better-known works are his editions with commentaries of Kuntaka's *Vakrokti-jivita* and Ānandavardhana's *Dhvanyāloka.* Both have been used in this anthology. Professor Krishnamoorthy has also done a comparative study of Western and Indian aesthetics, and has commented on T. S. Eliot's criticism. His kind of scholarship, which is mainly interested in editorial finesse, is becoming extinct in contemporary Sanskrit studies. In this respect, he represents a whole generation of scholars such as S. K. De and P. V. Kane, of which he is the ablest example. The following pages form his entry to the encyclopaedic work edited by K. M. George, *Comparative Indian Literature* (Macmillan, Madras, 1984–86, pp. 1109–1126), and is used in the original as an exhaustive introduction to the section on Sanskrit literary criticism. This long essay is included here as a definitive commentary on the range and complexity of critical concerns in Sanskrit poetics. His bibliography should be of particular interest to students who wish to pursue the subject in greater detail.

Sanskrit Poetics: an Overview

INTRODUCTION

Sanskrit is not only the oldest of the Indo-Aryan languages, but also the repository of one of the most ancient literary records in the world, namely, the *Vedas* (2000 BC). One of the traditional names for this vast body of religious literature is *chandas* or 'pleasing metre', which underscores its pre-eminently poetic verse-form meant for recitation or chanting, preserving the original accents. *Ṛgveda* means the *Veda* of hymns; and the Vedic poets (*kavis*) were also seers (*ṛṣis*). We get references therein to speech (*vāk* or *sarasvatī*), personified as a goddess, who inspires the poet into a *furor poeticus*. The Vedic seers speak of their art often as a verbal craft 'like that of a carpenter fashioning out a chariot'. It is not unlikely that they had their own 'rules' (*śāstra*) of poetic composition; but they are not extant. In the Vedic age (c. 2000–800 BC), metres were invested with magical power and lauded as leading the chanter to heaven. We have also words like *kāvya*, *alaṃkṛti* and *rasa* in Vedic literature which became the key-terms of Sanskrit literary criticism in a later age; but they hardly have any critical significance in the Vedic texts.

Though modern scholars regard Vedic hymns as poetry, Indian tradition is reluctant to do so, because it accords the highest place of divine scripture (*śruti*) exclusively to the Veda while poetry (*kāvya*), by definition, is secular and of human authorship.

The next period (c. 800–200 BC) witnessed the rise of several intellectual disciplines (*śāstras*) to aid the understanding of the *Vedas*. Etymology (*inrukta*) and grammar (*vyākaraṇa*) among them contain some incidental references to poetic devices like the simile (*upamā*), besides a few citations from folk ballads or lyrics. Patanjali (150 BC) testifies to the aesthetic significance of the term *rasa* when he speaks of the actor in a drama as *rasika*, and also names a few folk-tales (*ākhyāyikās*) popular in his time such as *Vāsavadattā* and *Sumanottarā*. The Buddhist canonical work *Kavi-sutta* in Pāli speaks about four types of poets: (i) meditative (*cintakavi*), (ii) scholarly (*sattakavi*), (iii) inspired (*pratibhanakavi*) and (iv) missionary (*atthakavi*). The treatment of prosody by Piṅgala as well as Bharata reveals numerous classical measures, based on quantity as well as stress. Inscriptions in the classical *kāvya* style are found as early as the Christian era; one of them (AD 150) expressly mentions prose (*gadya*) and poetry (*padya*), besides literary excellences such as clarity (*sphuṭatā*) and sweetness (*mādhurya*), as well as figures of speech (*alaṇkāra*). All this evidence indicates that the cultivation of different genres of poetry and drama went hand in hand with speculations on literary criticism round about the Christian era, though none of those early attempts is available to us today.

The two great epics of India, namely the *Ramayana* and the *Mahabharata*, are again ascribed by Indian tradition to poet-sages and are regarded not as models of pure poetry but as repositories embodying legendary history (*itihasā*) as well as ideal ethical precept (*dharma*). Hence ancient Indian poetics (*alaṃkāraśāstra*) generally leaves them out of account; if they are alluded to once in a way, it is only to derive support from their example and not from their precept on literary theory.

NĀṬYAŚĀSTRA

However, the earliest treatise available to us is the *Nāṭyaśāstra* ascribed to sage Bharata (c. AD 200). It is a kind of encyclopaedia on dramaturgy, histrionics, dance, music, etc., and its concern with poetry proper is very cursory indeed. Yet, it gives us almost all the pivotal concepts of Sanskrit criticism which were to engage the attention of some of the best poet-critics and scholars of India for well over sixteen centuries. These are: *rasa-bhāva, aucitya, guṇa, doṣa, alaṃkāra, vṛtti* and the literary genres. In the domain of drama, however, its treatment is most exhaustive; and its norms regarding plot, characters, sentiments and style in as many as ten types of plays, have remained basically unaltered even after the lapse of so many centuries.

THE NAMES AND NATURE OF SANSKRIT POETICS

Usually, all early writers on the subject—*Bhāmaha* (c. 600), Daṇḍin (c. 700), Vāmana (c. 750), Udbhaṭa and Rudraṭa (c. 800)—call their treatises by the name *Kāvyālaṇkāra* or *Kāvyalakṣaṇa*, i.e., 'the embellishment or hallmark of poetry'. Some earlier names which are known only by references are *Kriyākalpa* and *Kriyāvidhi* which mean 'rules of the poetic art'. The designation *sāhitya-vidyā*, 'theory of literature', is a later one (c. 900). It emphasizes the perfect concord of sound (*śabda*) and sense (*artha*) as the *sine qua non* of literature. But the latest and most commonly used name is *Alaṃkāra-Śāstra*, 'science of beauty', because the word *alaṃkāra* in Sanskrit means not only a means of beautification but also beauty itself. This usage became current when poetics adopted the scientific methodology and terminology of allied disciplines like grammar, prosody, dramaturgy, erotics, logic and philosophy in the discussion of its basic concepts, especially after Ānandavardhana (c. 850), who was a philosopher of the first rank besides being a masterly poet-critic and who, for the first time, gave in his aesthetic theory of *dhvani* (implied or suggested meaning) an equal status to drama and poetry, and who blazed the trail for applied or practical criticism of not only select literary pieces but also whole works. The formal and normative approach to poetry is replaced here by an aesthetic perspective, and he represents the dividing line between old (*prācina*) and new (*navya*) poetics. His original insights and illuminating observations paved the way for an age of systematization which includes celebrated names like Kuntaka (1000), Mammaṭa (1150), Vidyānātha (1300), Viśvanātha (1350) and Jagannātha (1650).

The systematised classics of these authors were studied throughout India and there are dozens of commentaries on them, almost from every province, which restate the discussions often in the light of new considerations.

LITERARY GENRES

The major literary genres or *kāvya*-forms mentioned by Bhāmaha are: (1) art-epic in several cantos (*mahākāvya*), (2) drama (*abhinayārtha*), (3) prose-chronicle (*ākhyāyikā*), (4) romantic tale (*kathā*), and (5) smaller verse-units or single self-contained verses (*anibaddha*). To these should be added *campū* or mixed composition in ornate prose and verse on an exalted theme first mentioned by Daṇḍin. From time to time further subdivisions came to be noted, especially under the categories (4) and (5).

Kathā (tale)

1. *Upākhyāna*: an episodic story in a larger work.

2. *Ākhyāna*: an episodic story, sung and enacted by a bard.
3. *Nidarśana*: didactic bird-and-beast fable.
4. *Pravalhikā:* a story in dialogue form.
5. *Matallikā*: a story satirizing society.
6. *Maṇikulyā*: a story involving an initial puzzle.
7. *Parikathā*: a tale narrating several adventures.
8. *Khaṇḍakathā*: a partially narrated well-known story.
9. *Sakalakathā*: a complete story of a hero's life.
10. *Upakathā*: an incidentally recounted story.
11. *Bṛhatkathā*: a vast repository of tales.

Anibaddha (small verse units)

1. *Muktaka*: a self-contained stanza.
2. *Sandānitaka*: two run-on stanzas.
3. *Viśeṣaka*: three run-on stanzas.
4. *Kalāpaka*: four run-on stanzas.
5. *Kulaka*: four to fourteen run-on stanzas.
6. *Kośa*: anthology of independent verses composed by oneself and/or others.
   Śataka (century), *Pancāśikā* (fifty)
7. *Samghāta*: a short poem by a poet on a single subject consisting of several stanzas.
8. *Saṁhitā*: a collection of poems on different subjects.

Again, we have a number of divisions under the head of light literature (*Kṣudraprabandha*) in later works:

1. *Udāharaṇa*: alliterative and rhythmic prose paragraph with a metrical beginning and end.
2. *Cakravāla*: rhythmic prose-paragraph (following an initial verse), each component being a vocative and embodying the device of making the last word in a compound identical with the initial word of the next.
3. *Bhogāvali*: prose sections of eight or four uniformly structured sentences, beginning and ending with a stanza

and containing the vocative form *deva* at the head of each unit, and describing beauties in Nature.

4. *Birudāvali*: eulogy, a bombastic parade of royal titles to serve as content in the form of *bhogavali* above.
5. *Tārāvali*: a poem in twenty-seven stanzas.
6. *Karambhaka*: a poem containing stanzas in Sanskrit as well as other languages.
7. *Ratnāvali:* a poem in nine stanzas.

So also, drama (*rūpaka*) has a number of types and subtypes which can be conveniently classified in tabular form.

It should be noted that Sanskrit literary criticism is primarily schematic and formal; and a critic is expected to judge a given work by first determining the genre to which it belongs and whether it successfully fulfils all the classical norms governing it. The basic principles underlying the tabulated norms of the different literary genres are indeed broad and simple. These relate to common elements which any literary analysis or appreciation of given works should perforce include:

(1) plot, (2) characters, (3) *rasa* (sentiment) and *bhāva* (emotional state), (4) style: (i) *guṇas* and (ii) *alaṃkāras*, (5) judgement of literature-defects (*anaucitya* or *doṣa*), (6) gradations of beauty in literature, (7) *dhvani* (suggested meaning), (8) *pratibhā* (creative imagination), (9) *sahṛdaya* (critic with literary taste), (10) defence of poetry and criticism, (11) *vakrokti* (oblique expression), and (12) specimens of practical criticism.

But these involve in-depth studies in such varied, yet related, branches of learning as linguistics, semantics, psychology, grammar, aesthetics, logic and philosophy and raise even the eclectic discipline of poetics (*Alaṃkāraśāstra*) to a prestigious and independent status in the scheme of Sanskrit studies. Incidentally, a treatment under these broad heads will meaningfully include all the important concepts of the discipline such as *alarṃkāra*, *guṇa*, *rīti*, *rasa-bhāva*, *dhvani*, *vakrokti* and *aucitya-cum-anaucitya* and will help avoidance of needless repetition.

THEME AND TECHNIQUE OF PLOT-CONSTRUCTION (*VASTU-SAMVIDHĀNA*)

Whatever the literary genre, the theme serves as its very body or backbone. In the highest forms of poetry and drama, namely, *Mahākāvya* (art-epic in several cantos) and *Nāṭaka* (play extending to several acts), it is not so much an invented story which matters, but a plot structured in a well-ordered form. The more familiar to the audience, the better it serves to catch their aesthetic attention because they can concentrate more pointedly on the author's technique or masterly art in the arrangement of various incidents or scenes. The five noticeable divisions (*sandhis*) in a good plot are: (1) opening (*mukha*), (2) progress (*pratimukha*), (3) complication (*garbha*), (4) disentanglement (*vimarśa*), and (5) happy conclusion (*nirvāhana*). It will be seen that this kind of constructive skill endows an otherwise uninteresting story with suspense, surprise and artistic appeal. The action (*kārya*) does not move along a predictable line; its progress is deliberately made uneven and crisscross till the climax, when there is a sudden turn of events which removes the obstacles and eventually brings about the intended happy end. Corresponding to the uneven progress of the incidents, there will be uneven stages (*avasthās*) in the endeavours of the hero before he succeeds, and these are termed: (i) commencement (*ārambha*), (ii) effort (*prayatna*), (iii) possibility of gaining the end (*prāptyāśā*), (iv) certainty of reward (*niyatāpti*), and (v) successful attainment (*phalāgama*). Metaphorically, the main theme may be said to correspond to the seed (*bīja*), the water-drop (*bindu*) that nourishes it, and the fruit (*phala*) with two intervening accessories of sub-plot, namely, parallel incident (*patākā*) and episode (*prakarī*). Thus in the story of Rāma, if Rāma's coronation is regarded as the end, we first find incidents in favour of it, then unforeseen obstacles leading to complications, with possibilities of hope with the alliance of Sugrīva, certainty with the feats of Hanumān and happy conclusion after Rāvaṇa is slain. A good plot then involves a conflict, external or internal.

CHARACTERS

Much of the human interest in literature is due to characters created by writers.

A mechanical analysis of these can yield only the broad types we actually find in the masterpieces and they need not be construed as normative. High (*uttama*), middling (*madhyama*) and low (*nīca*) characters; each of them has a place if they are judiciously brought in where they belong according to the demands made by the genres. A villain, a rake, a jester and a courtesan fit in best in a low comedy like *Prahāsana*; but would be out of place in a serious play or art-epic whose loftiness demands semi-divine heroes and heroines. Realism has little scope in the rarefied atmosphere of these great and idealistic literary forms. Similarly, love-lyrics are so varied in range that they demand a great diversity of maidens in love. The broad types of 'heroes' and 'heroines' are indicated in *Alaṃkāraśāstra* to provide guidelines to poets and critics.

Heroes

(i) General characteristics:
good manners, sweet temper, generosity, capability, lively speech, popularity, eloquence, noble birth, steadiness, youthfulness, sharp intellect, dynamism, accomplishment in the arts, heroism in battle, firmness, radiance, learning and religiousness.

(ii) Four broad types:
  (1) exalted hero (*dhīrodātta*), e.g., Rāma.
  (2) bumptious hero (*dhīroddhaṭa*), e.g., Bhīma.
  (3) sportive hero (*dhiralalita*), e.g., Vatsarāja.
  (4) calm hero (*dhīra-śānta*), e.g., Cārudatta.

(iii) Different stages of love in the above heroes:
  (1) Courteous (*dakśiṇa*): one who feigns sincere love to his first wife when he is really in love with another woman, e.g., Agnimitra.
  (2) Discourteous (*śaṭha*): one who does not care for the feelings of the first woman, e.g., love in Amaru's love-poem *Amaruśataka*, (c. AD 800) verse 109.

(3) Callous (*dhṛṣṭa*): one who does not care even to hide his tell-tale indications of guilt, e.g., the lover in *Amaruśataka*, verse 60.

(4) Devoted (*anukūla*): one who is completely devoted to one woman (i.e., wife) only, e.g., Rāma.

(iv) Associates of heroes:

(1) Hero of sub-plot (*pīṭhamarda*), e.g., Sugriva.

(2) Cavalier (*vita*), e.g., Śekharaka in *Nāgānanda*.

(3) Jester (*vidūṣaka*), e.g., Vasantaka in *Svapnavāsavadatta*.

(v) Hero's rival:

(1) Anti-hero (*pratināyaka*), e.g., Rāvaṇa.

Heroines

(i) Three types:

(1) Wedded wife (*svīyā*), e.g., Sita for Rāma.

(2) Another (*anyā*), e.g., Sita for Rāvaṇa.

(3) Courtesan (*sādhāraṇa-stri*), e.g., Vasantasenā.

(ii) Sub-types of wedded wife:

(1) Guileless (*mugdhā*), e.g., Pārvati in *Kumārasambhava*, VIII, 2.

(2) Youthfully excited (*madhyā*), e.g., *Śiṣupālavadha*, VI, 19.

(3) Love-mad (*pragalbhā*), e.g., *Amaruśataka*, verse 64.

(iii) Further classes of the last two:

(1) Bold (*dhīrā*).

(2) Timid (*adhīrā*).

(3) Partly bold and partly timid (*dhīrādhīrā*).

(iv) These six kinds, again two-fold (6 × 2 = 12):

(1) First wife (*jyeṣṭhā*) e.g., Vāsavadattā.

(2) Second wife (*kaniṣṭhā*) e.g., Ratnāvalī.

(v) Two types of 'another':

(1) Virgin.

(2) Married woman.

Extra marital love in the main plot is strictly prohibited. However, there is no such restriction about love relating to a virgin.

(vi) Eight stages of love common to all types of heroines:

(1) One whose husband is under her control (*svādhinapatikā*).
(2) One who puts on her best show while receiving the lover (*vāsaka-sajjā*).
(3) One who suffers the pangs of separation (*virahotkanṭ hitā*).
(4) One who is jealous of her husband's extra marital love (*khaṇṇitā*).
(5) One who regrets her spurning the lover in a flurry (*kalahāntaritā*).
(6) One who has been deceived by her lover who misses his promised assignation (*vipralabdhā*).
(7) One whose lover is far away (*proṣita-priyā*).
(8) One who sallies forth on her own to meet her lover (*abhisārikā*).

(vii) Retinue of heroines:
maid-servants, friends, washerwomen, half-sisters, nuns, artists, etc.

Such detailed classifications indicate not only a minute literary analysis of a vast range of good literary works on the part of the theorists, but also their keenness in offering practical guidelines to new writers by posing before them the technical points which they should keep in mind while exercising their choice. Had they not gone so minutely into details, poets might have thought that blind conformity to broad types of characters would be enough to produce a standard play or poem. But the numerous subdivisions made in the types of heroes and heroines from several angles cannot but convince the poets that what is expected of them is highly individualised or 'round' characters and not 'flat' types. New permutations and combinations possible throw a challenge to genius instead of curbing originality. Like the rules of grammar and of prosody, rules of poetics too serve ultimately an aesthetic purpose, though apparently tedious and boring. Here again, the principle of propriety (*aucitya*) comes to play an important part in determining the choice of particular heroes, heroines and their companions in keeping with the kind of plot on hand and sentiment (*rasa*) intended. They held *rasa* by serving as the very foundation (*ālambanavibhāva*) for the rise of emotions. Further, the proper psychological and physical responses of characters to the stimuli provided in the plot become aesthetic to the spectator as these responses shed their raw implications on life; because literature is not a copy but a stylised shadow *sui generis*. These responses then come to be termed *anubhāvas* or aesthetically distanced ensuants of *rasa* or sentiment.

RASA AND *BHĀVA*

Perhaps these are the two key-terms in Sanskrit literary criticism which have led to endless controversy among scholars, ancient and modern. In fact, they challenge precise translation into another language because some regard them as objectively present in the poem or play, while others regard them as aspects of the subjective experience of the reader or spectator, and most philosophers raise *rasa* to a transcendental and spiritual level in their attempt to solve the difficulties which arise when it is viewed as an empirical experience.

Rasa is the very essence of all literature. It vitally animates all the constitutive elements of literature from within; and even like life in a living body, its existence cannot be gainsaid though it eludes our sense-perception. *Rasa* means 'sap', 'juice', 'taste', 'supreme joy', 'mental feeling' and 'aesthetic enjoyment'. All these shades of meaning somehow get fused in its ultimate connotation. So understood, it is the *ultima thule* (ultimate end) of all literature, the highest aesthetic value which is an end in itself. It can be attained only by a few gifted souls with hearts akin to the poets' (*sahṛdayas* or *rasikas*) because it is highly imaginative on the one hand and spiritual on the other. It is a state far from one's personal likes and dislikes, loves and hates. It is a disinterested, impersonal, contemplative state of ecstasy, *sui generis*.

Even granting all this, the critic cannot disown his responsibility of logically accounting for his enjoyment of literature in terms of its constituent elements. He will have to declare the reasons why he deems one work a success and another a failure. This intellectual activity on his part may presumably be post-ecstatic. But at this level he can convincingly show how each of the basic elements of the given literary work—plot, character and style—is endowed with an organic unity by the genius of the creative artist. This unity is conditioned by one *aṅgi-rasa* or ruling sentiment in the midst of other seven or eight subordinate ones, when the given work is an art-epic or a play or a romantic tale. In self-complete stanzas which breathe but a passing mood, we surely have no scope for fully delineated *rasas*. Therefore we should talk of their vital essence as *bhāva* and not *rasa*. Thus from the ineffable heights of spiritual rasa (in the singular) we come down to the level of diverse *rasas* and *bhāvas* which partake somehow of both subjectivity and objectivity. Yet these are not life emotions; they are only emotions embodied in literature or literary emotions. In life all emotions and mental states (*cittavṛttis*) are fleeting; but in literature at least some emotions can be delineated in a way more abiding and lasting and hence the term *sthāyibhāvas*. They are just nine and their corresponding aesthetic counterparts are the nine *rasas*:

Sthāyibhāvas	*Rasas*
(1) Love of sexes (*rati*)	the erotic (śṛṇgāra)
(2) Laughter (*hāsa*)	the comic (*hāsya*)
(3) Sorrow (*śoka*)	the pathetic (*karuṇa*)
(4) Heroic energy (*utsāha*)	the heroic (*vīra*)
(5) Fear (*bhaya*)	the frightful (*bhayānaka*)
(6) Anger (*krodha*)	the furious (*raudra*)
(7) Disgust (*jugupsā*)	the odious (*bībhatsa*)
(8) Wonderment (*vismaya*)	the marvellous (*adbhuta*)
(9) Dispassion (*śama*)	the tranquil (*śānta*)

It will be observed that while the names of *sthāyibhāvas* are nouns, those of *rasas* are adjectives. That is because they accompany the aesthetic experience of the connoisseur, the common denominator of all the emotional states or *bhāvas* delineated at length in the literary work outside as located in characters and, at the same time, rooted within the connoisseur's heart as primordial instincts. Only the above eight or nine mental states can permit of such elaborate delineation in literature, as they represent the most universal emotions in man. Other fleeting moods and feelings (listed as 33) group themselves with one or the other of these abiding states when delineated in literature. So while *bhāva* is a name commonly applicable to all mental states, they denote only passing moods when used alongside of the term *rasa* because it is none other than *sthāyibhāva* itself raised to a delectable and aesthetic level. Hence technically *bhāva* is tantamount to *vyabhicāri-bhāva*.

Vyabhicāri-bhāvas (33)

(1) Revulsion (*nirveda*)
(2) Anguish (*glāni*)
(3) Suspicion (*śaṇkā*)
(4) Jealousy (*asūya*)
(5) Arrogance (*mada*)
(6) Fatigue (*śrama*)
(7) Lassitude (*ālasya*)
(8) Wretchedness (*dainya*)
(9) Worry (*cintā*)
(10) Stupefaction (*moha*)
(11) Remembrance (*smṛti*)
(12) Steadfastness (*dhṛti*)
(13) Shame (*vriḍā*)
(14) Fickleness (*capalatā*)
(15) Joy (*harṣa*)
(16) Agitation (*āvega*)
(17) Foolishness (*jaḍatā*)
(18) Pride (*garva*)
(19) Despair (*viṣāda*)
(20) Eagerness (*autsukya*)
(21) Sleep (*nidrā*)
(22) Forgetfulness (*apasmāra*)
(23) Dreaminess (*supti*)
(24) Wakefulness (*vibodha*)

(25) Indignation (*amarṣa*)
(26) Dissimulation (*avahittha*)
(27) Ferocity (*ugratā*)
(28) Decision (*mati*)
(29) Sickness (*vyādhi*)
(30) Madness (*unmāda*)
(31) Death (*maraṇa*)
(32) Terror (*trāsa*)
(33) Doubt (*vitarka*)

In life all these and many more are merely 'mental states with their attendant pleasures and pains'. But when delineated in literary characters they become aesthetic, exclusively enjoyable, and are called by the technical term *bhāva* (short form of *vyabhicāri-bhāva*). In short lyric poems, by and large, these find independent expression and become no less enjoyable than the dominant emotions (which are termed *rasas*) delineated in art-epics and major plays. Hence when the emotions are to be referred to at the aesthetic level often they are termed *rasa-bhāvas* or *rasādis*. The latter expression *rasādi* includes, besides *rasas* and *bhavas*, their semblances (*ābhāsas*), their germination (*udaya*) and cessation (*śānti*) as well as commingling (*śabalatā*) with other mental states.

With this background, we are now in a position to understand the significance of Bharata's *locus classicus*, namely the *rasa-sutra*. It crisply states: '*rasa* results when there is a harmonious fusion of the three elements in drama, namely, *vibhāvas*, *anubhāvas* and *vyabhicāri-bhāvas*'. In the language of analytical theorists, all these elements and *rasa* come under the broad category of *artha* or content of literature, as distinguished from *sabda* or its linguistic form. Thus one can speak of *rasa* as the *kāvyārtha* or poetic content par excellence. Even tragic and odious emotions presented in literature become as aesthetic as pleasurable emotions because of the very nature of art-experience which is supra-mundane (*lokottara*) by definition.

STYLE

While the above findings are applicable in their entirety to drama which is a composite art made up of several elements like music, dance, painting and histrionics, a more formal structural analysis is required as a supplement to give us a complete idea of the art of poetry. The whole and sole medium of literature is language, and its natural qualities deserve exploitation to serve poetic ends, and new artistic patterns of expressive thought and language merit a close analysis. All these come under the broad category of style, which is indeed unique to every poet depending on his innate temperament, genius, talent and practice; yet we can distinguish some broad types of style in literature. Indeed, in this field too, Indians have shown an astoundingly remarkable flair for formal analysis. This may be set out as follows:

Poet's *rasāveśa* > *Kāvya*	end: *rasa* of reader
1. Simple (*vaidarbhi*)	2. Ornate (*gaudi*)

Techniques: Stylistic arrangement (*rīti*, *mārga*, *bandha*, *racana*, *saṃghaṭanā, vṛtti*) including use of *samāsas*

of sound-form (*sabda*)	and of sense-content (*artha*)	
figurative (*alaṃkāra*)	qualitative (*guṇa*) and	figurative (*alaṃkāra*)
1. Alliteration (*anuprāsa*)	1. Vigour (*ojas*)	1. Simile (*upamā*)
2. Chime (*yamaka*)	2. Sweetness (*mādhurya*)	2. Metaphor (*rūpaka*)
3. Pun (*śleṣa*), etc.	3. Lucidity (*prasāda*), etc.	3. Hyperbole (*atiśayokti*)
		4. Paradox (*virodha*), etc.

(i) *Gunas* (Literary Attributes)

It should be noted that genuine poetry springs from the poet's afflatus of *rasa* and culminates in the *rasa* of the reader. But this is achieved by a conscious and deft technique involving selection and arrangement into a rhythmic pattern of syllables, short and long compounded words, sentences, etc., with an eye to their sweetness or harshness, lucidity or pedantry, not only in respect of sound-effect but also sense-effect, in conformity with the overall *rasa* or *bhāva* in, question. These qualitative considerations are significantly termed *gunas* (of *śabda* and *artha*). Their number is usually given as three; but some theorists mention as many as 10. Some take them as rooted in sound and sense only (e.g., Daṇḍin); others opine that they belong to style (e.g., Vāmana). A few hold that they are really properties of *rasa* though they appear to be of sound and sense (e.g., Ānandavardhana); still others find them inherent in the nature of the creative poet (e.g., Kuntaka). But all are agreed on the point that they form the most significant and conspicuous ingredients of style, accounting for its clearly discernible variations like the delicate and the ornate, though each might be appealing in its own way. Originally, the two styles were named after regions, namely, the North (*Gauḍī*) and the South (*Vaidarbhī*); but later they were renamed the Delicate (*Sukumāra*) and the Ornate (*Vicitra*). A happy mixture of the two was recognised as a third known as *Pāncālī* or the 'Middle' (*Madhyama*). In critical judgement, the former was usually held to be the more natural and spontaneous and hence more appealing than the latter achieved by great labour. The words *mārga, bandha, saṃghaṭana, vṛtti, racanā*, etc., are more or less synonyms of *rīti* interpreted broadly as stylistic arrangement.

(ii) *Alaṃkāras* (Figures of Speech)

To the Indian analytical mind, discovery of new figures of speech was indeed the most favourite preoccupation for several centuries. They are devices for avoiding the obvious and achieving aesthetic form in respect of sound as well as sense, by turns of expression as well as poetic conceits. The underlying principle of all figures is therefore described as *vakrokti* or oblique expression. It is universally accepted that it is an activity of the exclusively poetic imagination, involving original turns of thought and language. It sees likenesses in things different (simile), talks of one as another (metaphor), fancies non-existent comparisons (*utprekṣā*) and indulges freely in exaggeration (*atiśayokti*). It means two or more things simultaneously (*śleṣa*) and revels in paradox (*virodha*). It notices strange and minute aspects of everything in nature (*svabhāvokti*); it overturns logic and reverses the roles of cause and effect (*vibhāvanā*) and makes impossible things possible (*asaṃgati*). It adduces parallels between remote objects (*dṛṣṭānta*), gives telling illustrations (*nidarsana*) and indulges in strange generalisations (*arthāntaranyāsa*). Doubt (*sandeha*), remembrance (*smaraṇa*) and even illusion (*bhrānti*) become delectable. It juxtaposes incompatibles (*viṣama*) and applauds by censuring (*vyajāstuti*). It overtly speaks of irrelevant subjects like birds and beasts when it covertly means something else most relevant (*anyokti*). It uses epithets with special significance (*parikara*) and even adopts word patterns like chain (*śṛnkhala*), iteration (*mālā*), respective reference (*yathāsaṃkhya*), and so forth.

These and many more are all happy devices of thought invented by a creative mind as the natural medium for poetry, however remote they may be from routine ways of expression in life. Since they all serve to beautify the thought, they are regarded as *arthālaṃkāras*. As many as a hundred of them have been defined and illustrated in the classical texts, and each one of them is subjected to further subdivisions, sometimes as many as thirty.

On the other hand, there are sound patterns too, artistically devised by the poet, such as alliteration (*anuprāsa*), chime (*yamaka*) and play upon words (*śleṣa*). These come under the head *śabdālaṃkāras* or figures of sound.

The importance of *guṇas vis-à-vis alaṃkāras* is self-evident. The *guṇas* are more intrinsic to poetry because they are intimately bound up with *rasas* while *alaṃkāras* are like external ornaments. Hence while the imagery of *alaṃkāras* is extremely desirable in poetry so long as they appear as spontaneous effusions of a creative genius suffused with rasa, they become sources of revulsion when indulged in excess because their artificiality is then obvious, and they mar *rasa*. There can be good poetry even without an obvious figure of speech; but not without poetic quality or style.

The formalist approach of the early theorists accommodated even *rasa-bhāvas* under a class of *alaṃkāras* or *guṇas*, in the field of poetry. In the opinion of later thinkers, this indicates a lack of philosophical judgement on their part. If virtually all figures are variations of the referential use of language, how can *rasa-bhāvas*—which, by definition, are undenotable but only suggestible—ever be classed on a par with simile and metaphor? This defect is remedied by the *dhvani* theorists, by regarding *rasa* as the soul of poetry, while figures are ornaments of its body.

JUDGEMENT OF LITERATURE

(i) Defects (*anaucitya* or *doṣa*)

In the classical tradition of Indian literary criticism, 'Defects' constitute an important concept, because all the rules of the discipline are concerned with an ideal literary work, absolutely free from blemishes of every kind. There is no writer who is silent over them. Though they are sometimes mentioned as negations of *guṇas* or literary merits, the most common view is that they are positive blemishes of poetic beauty and obstacles that block aesthetic experience. What deserves to be noted is that there are no absolute defects (*nitya-doṣas*) in poetry as in grammar, since impropriety of any kind is relative to the context. Even a merit so-called may turn into a defect if it rings as inappropriate in a given context. Hence, determination of *doṣas* demands a high degree of literary sensibility from the critic, and poetry cannot be judged mechanically.

Usually, defects are brought under five heads: 1. word, 2. part of a word, 3. sentence, 4. subjects and 5. *rasa*.

Dissonance (*duḥśrāvatva*), obscenity (*aślīla*), improper denotation (*anucitārtha*), archaism (*aprayukta*), vulgarity (*grāmya*), lack of full significance (apratīta), ambiguity (*saṃdigdha*), far-fetched meaning (*neyārtha*), distorted meaning (*nihatārtha*), wrong meaning (*avācaka*), forced meaning (*kliṣṭa*), opposite meaning (*viruddhamatikṛt*), reversal of the roles of subject and predicate (*avimṛṣṭavidheya*) are listed as common defects of word, word-part and sentence.

Harsh syllables (*pratikāla-varṇa*), *visarga*(*h*) deleted or changed (*lupta-hata-visarga*), excess or shortage in words required and repetition (*adhika-nyāna-kathita-pada*), gradual decline in emphasis (*patat-prakarṣa*), hiatus or obscenity and loss of euphony (*viśleṣa-aślīla-kaṣṭatā*) in word-combination (*saṃdhi*), wrong order in the placement of words and in the use of clauses, unintended equivocation, omission of required words, wrong constructions of compound words, wrong pauses in composition, etc., are said to be other defects that might vitiate sentences.

Absence of significance (*apuṣṭa*), disorder (*duṣkrama*), vulgarity (*grāmya*), self-contradiction (*vyāhata*), obscenity (*aślīla*), obscurity (*kaṣṭa*), monotony (*anavīkṛta*), illogicality (*nirhetu*), opposite sense (*viruddha*), ambiguity (*saṁdigdha*) repetition (*punarukta*), misrepresentation of well-known facts in various fields of knowledge (*khyāti-viruddha* and *vidyāviruddha*), incompleteness (*sākāṇkśatā*), incompatibility (*sahacārabhinnatā*), reversal of order (*asthānayuktatā*), erroneous presentation of particular as general and vice-versa (*aviṣeśe viṣeśa*), etc., are listed as defects tainting meaning (*artha*).

It will be observed that these flaws mostly relate to errors in grammar, syntax and composition and arise from an inadequate equipment in general knowledge, rules of logic and commonsense on the part of the poet. They are all classed as defects because Sanskrit composition, in its very nature, is expected to represent the highest classical standard attainable in all respects. Want of genius on a poet's part may be pardoned, but not lack of learning.

But overriding all these is the aesthetic standard of propriety dictated by *rasa*. While the defects earlier mentioned might mar only individual parts of a poem, impropriety in the delineation of *rasa* or *bhāva* mars the work as a whole. Briefly, these shortcomings are:

(1) Stating the intended *rasa*, etc., by name instead of suggesting it in the proper way.
(2) Elaborating the accessories of a *rasa* which is opposed to the one on hand.
(3) Rendering the comprehension of *vibhāvas*, etc., difficult by excessive attention to figures of speech, etc.
(4) Untimely elaboration or attenuation of *rasa*.
(5) Treatment of the same *rasa* over and over again.
(6) Lack of sufficient attention to the dominant *rasa*.
(7) Inordinately excessive treatment of secondary *rasas*.
(8) Violation of the canons governing different types of characters.
(9) Attribution of wrong traits to the subject.

These flaws as well as the ones noted earlier, it should not be forgotten, are never absolute, but relative and functional in character.

With proper discretion, a poet can not only remove their repulsiveness, but can actually turn them into positive merits. Thus a mad man is best described when his talk is rambling, incoherent and vulgar. A person in a fit of fury should use harsh language to be effective. An obscene hint sounds quite proper in the mouth of a prostitute. Once in a way, a learned speaker may allow himself difficult and technical language. When a character is swayed by sudden bursts of passion or wonder, he can flout the rules of propriety, and so forth.

Nor is it all; poets are indeed encouraged to adopt freely in their works certain poetic conventions though they flout the norms of commonsense.

(ii) Poetic conventions (*kavisāmayas*).

These may be briefly indicated here under convenient heads, particularly those relating to our earth, ignoring the ones about heaven and the netherworld.

(a) *Describing non-existent things as existing.* Lotuses bloom in all rivers; swans reside in all waters; mountains contain gems; cobras contain gems in their heads, etc.

(b) *Existing things described as non-existent.* Mālati flowers do not bloom in spring; sandal trees do not have flower and fruit; Aśoka trees have no fruit.

(c) *Restricting the existence of things to certain localities.* Pearls are found only in the river Tāmraparṇī; sandal trees are found only in Malaya mountain.

(d) *Abstract ones treated as concrete.* Darkness can be pierced by a needle; moonlight can be filled in a jug.

(e) *Inventions of fancy.* The *cakora* bird subsists only on moonbeams; the *cakravāka* gets separated from its mate at night; fame is white and infamy dark; anger and love are red; the god of love bears a sugarcane bow furnished with five flowery arrows and strung with a string of bees; women have a line of hair above the navel, etc.

These conventions, taken along with the legends and myths provided by the puranas, lend an atmosphere of unique grandeur to classical Sanskrit poetry; and they have become cliches of all Indian literature.

GRADATIONS OF BEAUTY IN LITERATURE

As explained above, poetic beauty (*saundarya*) is a total complex made up of several elements, some relating to form, some to content, many to style and quite a few to traditional conventions. Several manifestations of beauty in its synthetic aspect are noticed by poets, etc.:

(1) Sensuous beauty of sublimity perceived in the objects of Nature (*prakr̥ti-saundarya*).
(2) Beauty of sublimity (as of heroes and heroines) in man's emotions and actions as embodied in characters (*aśraya-saunḋarya*).
(3) Beauty inherently present in the poet's raw material, i.e., sound or sense (*sahaja*).
(4) Beauty in the technique adopted by a poet (*āhārya*).
(5) Beauty in the creative imagination of a poet (*bhāvikatva*).

Bhāsa (AD 200) quotes a maxim that 'beauty is that which pleases all'—while Kālidāsa (AD 350) and Bhāravi (AD 550) agree that inherent beauty needs no decoration. Kālidāsa also adds significantly that beauty in outer objects may not delight always, because it is also dependent on the mood of the beholder. When the mood is attuned properly, even a light distortion of a beautiful object may prove appealing. Thus we come to Magha's (AD 680) final description of beauty as that which retains its freshness of charm every time it is viewed.

DHVANI

These insights of poets lack logical precision. It was Ānandavardhana (AD 850), the doyen of Indian theorists, who remedied this defect by taking the analogy of a beautiful damsel. There are no doubt charming features in each of her flawless limbs, but what enchants an onlooker is her overall grace of personality (*lāvanya*) which is quite distinct from the perfection of parts. This overall beauty in literature is defined by him as *dhvani* or suggested meaning.

Dhvani is a higher kind of beauty because it is grasped at the highest level of sensitivity on the part of the connoisseur, after he has ceased attending to beauties of form and content for their own sake. The ordinary functions of language, namely primary denotation (*abhidhā*), secondary implication (*lakśaṣa*) and even purport (*tātparya*) of a sentence as a whole after constructing the words properly, become only means to serve the ultimate end of manifesting *dhvani*. Since *dhvani* is the sole meaning intended by the poet at one end and realized by the man of taste at the other, it deserves to be regarded as the very soul or vital essence that gives life to all the other aspects of literary beauty. In short, *dhvani* is what is beautified by all the other elements analysed by specialists of poetry—be it *guṇa*, *rīti*, *alaṃkāra* or *vṛtti*.

The range of *dhvani* is so vast that it not only covers all aspects of beauty noticed earlier, but goes far beyond them. If the entire world of nature and human thought can be described as *vastu* (subject), the *vastu* suggested in poetry is but one branch of *dhvani*. In all artistic or imaginative turns of expression can be termed *alaṃkāra* (embellishment), suggestion of associated imagery forms the second broad division of *dhvani*. But the imperial throne in the palace of *dhvani* is reserved for *rasa* because it is *dhvani* par excellence. Emotions and feelings can never be evoked in any way other than suggestion. This is true only when *rasa* reigns supreme in a given work. Such *dhvani-kāvya* will be automatically judged as a poem of the best grade, because it is an unmistakable and irrefutable index of a poet's creative art at its highest watermark. The credit for having provided room, in their wide aesthetic analysis of *rasa*, not only for the beautiful (*śṛṇgāra*), but also the sublime (*adbhuta*), the grand (*dhirodātta's vīra*), the comic (*hāsya*), the ugly (*bībhatsa*) and the pathetic (*karuṇa*) cannot be denied to Sanskrit theorists. Everything is grist to the poet's mill and even the ugly and the repulsive can be transformed by the art of poetry into aesthetic experience.

The whole gamut of aesthetic experience is thus very sensitively traversed, the crown being reserved for spiritual ecstasy or *śānta* which may be described paradoxically as passionless passion or boundless calm. No wonder that the great mystic that he was, Abhinavagupta (c. AD 1000) went to the extent of recognising *śānta* as the mainspring of all other *rasas*. Bhavabhuti (c. AD 700) seems to suggest that pathos deserves that pride of place; Bhoja declares that the all-embracing subjective ego's self-regard (*abhimāna*) comes to be technically termed *śṛṇgāra* and hence it should be regarded as the source of all other *rasas*. These divergent opinions do not affect the soundness of the dictum that the best order of poetry is constituted by *rasadhvani*; and even ordinary *vastu* and *alaṃkāras* come to be invested with a new halo of charm when they are suggested instead of being plainly stated, a charm that entitles them to rank on a par with *rasadhvani* itself. On deeper analysis, the latter too will open up their secret alliance with *rasa*, since nothing in the world can enter the realm of poetry without becoming a partner in *rasa*, at least as an indirect *vibhāva*.

It would be a mistake if one thinks that enjoyment of suggested rasa is a long-drawn-out process of reflective thinking. In fact, it flashes forth across the mind of the critic so quickly that he cannot notice any time-sequence intervening between his comprehension of the plain meaning and the suggested meaning. What *dhvani* demands from the critic is poetic sensibility and nothing else.

In the best or first-grade poetry discussed above, though we have stressed the dominance of *rasa* as vital, the invariable accompaniment of suitable *guṇas* and *alaṃkāras* therein should not be belittled; for, if *rasa* is the soul, *guṇas* and *alaṃkāras* constitute the very 'body' of poetry. How can there be a soul without a body? But the body should not distract attention from the soul. This is *aucitya* or propriety. All elements of structural beauty must become subordinate in order to let the aesthetic *rasa* have free play.

In actual practice, however, this ideal is not often realised. The structural elements often outshine the *rasa* and other forms of *dhvani*. In rare instances, even a suggested *vastu* might outshine a suggested *rasa*. Then the latter loses perforce its claim for the highest honour.

To accommodate all such border instances, *dhvani* theorists speak of another class of poetry called 'poetry of subordinated suggestion' (*guṇībhūtavyaṇgya*). In the world of literature, this class is no less wide than the first; and the critic enjoys it too, not as the next best, but as good poetry for a different reason. A reader might even prefer this kind to the earlier, according to his taste.

Though the literary masterpieces in Sanskrit can all be brought under the first or the second of the classes of poetry, there would still remain a vast body of literary work unaccommodated under them. These laborious lucubrations of boring 'experts' teeming with tedious verbal exercises and riddles would, strictly speaking, fall outside the purview of poetry. But for courtesy's sake they may be given the lowest place called *citra* (colourful portrait) when ancient; but this does not entitle a modernist to be recognized as a poet.

Thus an adoption of the theory of *dhvani* will enable one to grade literary works and attempt applied criticism by providing him a workable yardstick, not only for evaluating short poems, but even whole epics and plays. The connoisseur trained in the dialectics of *dhvani* will unerringly lay his finger on the poet's major lapses, if any, and will also convincingly demonstrate the plus points to the poet's credit, basing his judgement not so much on the poet's blind conformity to 'rules' but on his lively innovations in theme as well as technique.

PRATIBHĀ (CREATIVE IMAGINATION)

It follows from the above considerations that Indian criticism makes heavy demands on the poet's creative originality, however trite his borrowed theme be. In the making of a poet, *pratibhā* or creative imagination is always given the highest importance; it is said to be an innate gift with which one is born. No amount of learning or assiduous practice can succeed if this primary requirement is not present. On the nature of *pratibhā* the observations made by Abhinavagupta's teacher, Bhaṭṭa Tauta (c. 950) have become classical:

> It has been remarked that no non-sage can be deservingly called poet; a sage will be worth his name only by virtue of his vision. By vision

we mean that insight into Truth about all the manifold objects in the world and their varying states. One can win the distinction of a being a 'poet in the sciences' if he possesses this vision of Truth. But in common usage the world accords that title exclusively to one who possesses both vision and imaginative expression. Thus though Valmiki was highly gifted with an abiding clear vision, he was not hailed as a poet by people until he embodied it in an epic.

SAHṚDAYA (CRITIC WITH LITERARY TASTE)

In order to be receptive enough to such rare creations of poetic *pratibhā*, it goes without saying that an equally rare gift of sensibility or good taste is expected in the critic also. That is why Ānandavardhana insists on reminding us time and again that his doctrine of *dhvani* is a document based on the felt aesthetic experience of *sahṛdayas* or critics with good taste. Abhinavagupta goes a step further and declares the essential identity in the natures of the gifted poet and the gifted critic. Literally, *sahṛdaya* means 'one with a kindred heart'; but Abhinavagupta would prefer to think that the spirits of the ideal poet and the ideal literary critic are one and the same, not just similar. The names are two; but the spirit is one. Hence mere grammarians, dry logicians and science specialists have no right to attempt literary criticism. In the nature of things, it is the task of more gifted souls who have an aesthetic taste.

DEFENCE OF POETRY AND CRITICISM

Poetry in Sanskrit originated as a handmaid of religion, to judge from our premier epics. The *Rāmāyana* and the *Mahābhārata* were valued highly as popular and pleasing re-presentations of the ethical codes laid down in law-books. But soon secular poetry grew, adding a new sensuous dimension which proved more popular, and this aroused serious protests from orthodox philosophers. Rājasekhara (980) sums up their objections in his *Kāvyamimāmsā*: Poetry should not be taught because (1) it teaches untruth, (2) it teaches immorality and (3) it abounds in obscenity. His line of defence, however, is far from convincing because he merely refers to the point that even the Vedic scriptures are tainted with these very blemishes.

But Bhaṭa Tauta gives an effective rejoinder. He states:

> Surely, there is no real existence of sense-objects at all in the world of poetry because it is an imaginary one. How, then, can you complain that passions are profoundly excited by poetry?
>
> Should you urge that the dominant emotion delineated in poetry is c itself the object, well, your position contradicts the nature of aesthetic experience wherein the emotion is not felt as objective.
>
> If you should say that 'aesthetic experience' itself is passion, you fail to distinguish once again between aesthetic emotion and sexual passion. If you persist in holding that the vicious effect proves the viciousness of the cause, we have only to ask you back how a character like Sita can ever be an object for the love of two or more persons.
>
> Hence our stand is this: just as dust is used to clean up a dusty mirror, passion is utilized to remove passion in the critic.

In addition to this claim that immediate aesthetic joy or *rasa* is an end or value in itself, standard theorists are seen stating that literature indirectly serves to help people in realizing all the four recognised values of life, namely, morality (*dharma*), material prosperity (*artha*), worldly pleasures (*kāma*) and spiritual emancipation (*mokṣa*). Unlike the ordinances of the law-books in regard to these which might repel the student by their dryness, literature sugar-coats the bitter, pill of instruction by way of alluring *rasas* and is thus eventually more effective. Such pleasing instruction in literature is compared to the sweet and winsome influence of a beloved (*kāntāsammita*). To these are added the prospects of (everlasting fame, wealth and religious merit that a poet might well aspire for. In fact, religious theists of a later age (1250–1850) regarded multifaceted *bhakti* itself as the 'overall *rasa*'.

VAKROKTI

Deriving inspiration from the *dhvani* theory, Kuntaka (c. AD 980) developed his theory of *vakrokti*, oblique expression', to serve as an aid to practical criticism. His approach is eminently practical and he cannot accept the self-contradictory assertions of Ānandavardhana that *rasa* may be sometimes dominant when it is termed *dhvani* and sometimes auxiliary when it is called an *alaṃkāra*. If *rasa* is the soul and *alaṃkāra* is the body of poetry, strict logic demands that the soul must perforce be always dominant and can never brook any subordination. Again, Ānandavardhana had admitted two types of beauty in poetry in his scheme—the stated (*vācya*) and the suggested (*vyangya*) and recognized two classes of poetry depending on the relative preponderance of one over the other. But Kuntaka cannot accept such gradations of beauty in poetry, accepted as good by discerning critics. The only distinction logically possible in aesthetics is that of poetry from non-poetry. And there might be innumerable ways open to the poet for endowing his expression with beauty. So according to Kuṇtaka, the broadest principle which can do justice to all the categories of literary theory including *dhvani* (in all its varieties) is only *vakrokti* which might admit of innumerable varieties. A poem may be beautiful for more reasons than one; and it should be the task of the critic to be on the lookout for all the diverse elements that contribute to the poem's beauty as a whole. Except for these differences in principle, there is complete agreement between *rasa-dhvani* and *vakrokti* theorists who pioneered practical criticism of literature in Sanskrit.

PRACTICAL CRITICISM

The earlier writers on the subject had mostly contented themselves with illustrating their rules by their own made-to-order examples. Even the few who took the trouble of selecting right examples from accepted masterpieces of literature did not attempt literary assessment of whole works. Nor did celebrated commentators on particular poems like Mallinātha (1300) deem it their concern to attempt such literary criticism in detail. Hence the pioneering efforts in this neglected but most important field of applied criticism by Ānandavardhana and Kuṇtaka deserve more than a passing notice here.

TWO SPECIMENS

(i) Ānandavardhana on the *Rāmāyana* and the *Mahābhārata*. 'In the *Rāmāyana* indeed, Vālmiki has embodied the dominant sentiment of pathos as is evidenced by his own declaration "sorrow has taken the form of a stanza"'. It has indeed been maintained as predominant till the very end of the work because the poem closes at the point of the irreparable loss of Sita.

In the *Māhābhārata* too, which combines both the elements, instruction and poetry, it will be seen that its conclusion on a note of despair consequent on the miserable deaths of Vṛṣṇis as well as the Pāndavas, devised by the great sage Vyāsa, reveals his primary intention of preaching the moral of renunciation through his work and throws light upon the fact that he intended final emancipation as the foremost of human values, and calm (*śānta*) as the most predominant sentiment in the work as a whole.

(ii) Kuntaka on Kālidāsa's '*śākuntalā*'. 'In a whole literary work too, an attainment of aesthetic effect owing its origin to the inventive power of the poet will present a new shade of charm even like a new touch-up given by a painter to an old faded portrait.'

For example, in the play *Abhijñāna-śākuntalā*, we see in the hero so faint a recollection of the sweet impression of Śakuntalā's matchless beauty in her exquisite youth as soon as he sees her (in Act V) when she removes her veil that it does not rule out the possibility of his rejecting her as a wife of another person. Śakuntalā does everything to revive his memory by relating intimate incidents of their first honeymoon when both were filled with deep love for each other, incidents which are at once so intimate and delicate that they are bound to infuse confidence. The reason why Dushyanta is unable to recognize her even after listening to it is a mystery left unexplained in the original *Mahābhārata*. For explaining it adequately with a cogent reason, the poet has invented the episode of the curse of sage Durvāsas. Durvāsas is a sage blind to all soft feeling and highly irate by temperament, one who flies into a rage even at the slightest lapse. In that episode of Durvāsas, it is seen that Śakuntalā is completely overwhelmed by the excruciating pangs of her first separation from her lover; and as she is lying in her cottage in such a state, there comes this great sage to her doorstep, and flies into a fit of anger at being unnoticed and pronounces a curse:

> He whom you are thinking of with such raptness
> That you cannot see even me, a sage arrived,
> Let him not recall you, though reminded,
> Like one drunk who cannot, a statement his own (tr. IV. I)

Such is the curse flung upon Śakuntalā. And at once the sage starts moving out. Yet when he is appealed to by the two friends of Śakuntalā, the great sage yields to the extent of limiting the duration of his curse to the sight of the signet ring given to Śakuntalā by the king. And when Śakuntalā is on her way to meet her spouse, the ring adorning her tender shoot-like finger slips down without her notice and falls into the waters of a stream which she had entered for bathing. Mistaking the glittering glow of the ruby set in the ring for a fresh lump of flesh, a fish swallows it. In course of time, the fish gets killed by a fisherman who catches it and the ring recovered by him is at last presented to the king himself. Such an art of plot-construction may surely be regarded as the best medium for delineating literary sentiment. Thanks to it, the entire play has acquired a unique beauty.

Again, in due time, we have the incident of the song outwardly reviling the bee, whose inner significance is caught by the king, though his memory has been blacked out by the curse of the sage; deep down in his mind we notice that traces are still left of the old love on account of which he is very much upset.

> Seeing things lovely and hearing sounds sweet,
> If a happy man should get perturbed,
> It means his mind is recalling unawares
> The deep impressions of a former birth, (tr. V.2)

Here such a recollection of his beloved (so deep down in the subconscious), at once guileless and charming, appeals very much to the hearts of connoisseurs. What is more, she is turned down later; her story about the ring is dismissed as false; the account of her marriage with him and pregnancy, given by Sage Kanva's disciple, is discredited, and the king is seen in a fit of anger. Then, even transgressing the limits of natural shyness, Śakuntalā's veil is removed from her face suddenly. Yet the king is under the illusion that she is another's wife. Though her bubbling youthful charm, superior to that of all the women seen by him so far, impresses him highly, and though her narration, sweet like the notes from a lyre, of intimate incidents of their mutual love—like their pleasurable excursions in the penance grove—arouses his appreciation, still he shows the rudeness of rejecting her. Such rudeness too becomes understandable only by the intensity of his later repentance at the termination of the curse, a repentance which is indicative of the depth of his unmitigated love for her in his heart, and it is most appealing to the connoisseurs, and in devising the end of the curse, the poet prefaces it with a description of the intense wretchedness of the mental state of the king, who is now frenzied with the pangs of unbearable separation from his beloved Śakuntalā, after the slow return of his memory of the forgotten incidents. Synchronising with it comes the recovery of the lost ring too which again delights the readers very much. The chamberlain of the king observes: 'Gone are all his personal decorations'. (VI. 6–7).

All these epithets given to the king in suffering are full of artistic beauty. There is artistic beauty of 'number' in the word *gotreṣu* (where the plural is aesthetically used to refer to the name of a single rival in love). They all add to the aesthetic appeal of the situation. When the king, looking at the picture of his beloved drawn by himself, speaks gallantly of the sweet recollection of his love, his words bear the deep impress of his darling:

> O bee, if you dare to touch any more
> My darling's lip as red as 'bimba' fruit,
> .... I shall jail you in a lotus bud. (tr. VI. 20)

the speech finds a ready echo in our hearts.

If the exquisite episode invented by the genius of the poet were not there in the play, the unbearable fact of the king's forgetting his wife without any reason would become a blemish as much in the play as in the original story of the Mahabharata itself.

From Comparative Indian Literature

Bibliography

SANSKRIT

1. Abhinavagupta, *Abhinavabhārati*, vol.I, Oriental Institute, Baroda, Baroda, 1956.
2. ———, *Dhvanyāloka-locanā*, Chowkhamba, Banaras, 1940.
3. Ānandavardhana, *Dhvanyāloka*, Karnataka University, Dharwar, 1974.
4. Bhamaha, *Kāvyālankāra*, Wallace Printing House, Tanjore, 1927.
5. Bharata, *Nāṭyaśāstra*, vols. I IV, Oriental Institute, Baroda, vol. I, 2nd ed 1956; Vol II 1954; Vol. III, 1954; Vol. IV, 1964.
6. Daṇḍin, *Kāvyādarṭa*, Bhandarkar Oriental Research Institute, Poona, 1970.
7. Dhananjaya, *Daśarūpaka*, Adyar Library, Madras, 1969.
8. Hemachandra, *Kāvyānuśāsana*, Nirnayasagar Press, Bombay, 1934.
9. Jagannath, *Rasagaṇgādhara*, Nirnayasagar Press, Bombay, 1888.
10. Kuntaka, *Vakroktijivita*, Karnataka University, Dharwar, 1977.
11. Mammata, *Kāvyaprakāśa*, vols. I–II, Calcutta Sanskrit College series vol. I 1958; vol. II, 1961.
12. Rājasekhara, *Kāvyamimāmsā*, Oriental Institute, Baroda, 1924.
13. Rudrata, *Kāvyālankāra*, Nirnayasagar Press, Bombay, 1886.
14. Udbhata, *Kāvyālankārasārasaṇgraha*, Bombay Sanskrit Series, Poona 1925.
15. Vāmana, *Kāvyāiankārasūtravṛtti*, Nirnayasagar Press, Bombay, 1953.
16 Vidyanātha, *Pratāparudrīya*, Sanskrit Education Society, Madras, 1970.
17. Viśvanātha, *Sāhityadarpaṇa*, Chowkhamba, Banaras, 1947.

ENGLISH

1. De, S.K., *History of Sanskrit Poetics*, Firma K.L.Mukhopadhyaya, Calcutta, 1960.
2. ———, *Some Problems of Sanskrit Poetics*, Firma K.L.Mukhopadhyaya, Calcutta, 1959.
3. Gerow, Edwin, *Indian Poetics*, 2nd ed., Otto Harrassowitz, Wiesbaden, 1977.

4. Kane, P.V., *History of Sanskrit Poetics*, Motilal Banarsidass, Delhi, 1961.
5. Krishnamoorthy, K., *The Dhvanyāloka and its Critics*, Kavyalaya, Mysore, 1969.
6. ———, *Essays in Sanskrit Criticism*, Karnataka University. Dharwar, 1964.
7. ———, *Studies in Indian Aesthetics and Criticism*, D.V.K. Murthy, Mysore, 1979.
8. Kuppuswamy Sastri, M., *Highways and Byways of Literary Criticism in Sanskrit*, KSRI Madras, 1945.
9. Raghavan, V., *Some Concepts of Alaṇkāraśāstra*, Adyar Library, Madras, 1942.
10. ———, *Bhoja 's Ṣṛṇgāra-Prakāśa*, Punarvasu, Madras, 1963.
11. ———, *The Number of Rasas*, 2nd ed., Adyar Library, Madras, 1967.
12. Raghavan, V. and Nagendra, *An Introduction to Indian Poetics*, Macmillan Madras, 1 970.
13. Vijayavardhana, G., *Outlines of Sanskrit Poetics*, Choukhamba, Varanasi, 1970.
14. Warder, A.K., *Indian Kāvya Literature*, Motilal Banarsidass, Delhi, 1972.

PERIODICALS

1. Chaudhury, P. J., 'The Theory of Rasa', *Journal of Aesthetics and Art Criticism*, vol. XXIV, 1945, pp. 145–149.
2. Choudhury, I. N., 'Indian Poetics: A Study in Perfection', *Indian Horizons*, vol. XXIV, 1975, p. 6.
3. Gerow, E. and Aklujkar, A., 'On Śāntarasa in Sanskrit Poetics', *Journal of the American Oriental Society*, vol. 92, p. 80.
4. Honeywell, J. A., 'The Poetic Theory of Visvanatha', *Journal of Aesthetics and Arts Criticism*, vol. XXVII, no. 2, 1968–69.
5. Jhanji, Rekha, 'Bharata on Aesthetic Emotions', *British Journal of Aesthetics*, vol. XVIII, 1978, p. 66.
6. Krishnamoorthy, K., 'The Canon of Angi-rasa', *Indological Studies* (University of Delhi), vol. Ill, no. 2, 1975, pp. 101–9.
7. Kulkarni, V. M., 'The Conception of Sandhis in the Sanskrit Drama', *Journal of the Oriental Institute, Baroda*, vol. V, 1955–56, pp. 369–402.
8. Mukherjee, R., 'Rasa as a Spring of Art', *Journal of Aesthetics and Art Criticism*, vol. XXIV, 1965, pp. 91–96.
9. Pandey, K. C., 'A Bird's-eye View of Indian Aesthetics', *Journal of Aesthetics and Art Criticism*, vol. XXIV, 1965, pp. 59–73.

10. Ruth Katz and Arvind Sharma, 'The Aesthetics of Abhinavagupta', British Journal of Aesthetics, vol. XVII, 1977, p. 258.
11. *Subrahmaniam*, K., 'A note on the concept of a Critic in Sanskrit Poetics', *British Journal of Aesthetics*, vol. XXVIII, no. 4, 1978, pp. 368–69.
12. Thampi, G. B. M., 'Rasa as Aesthetic Experience', vol. XXIV, 1965, pp. 75–80.

19

A. K. Ramanujan

A. K. Ramanujan (1929–1993) is better known as a poet in English and Kannada, and a translator from Kannada and Tamil, than as an anthropologist, linguist and critic. His more important literary criticism has come to us through his memorable prefaces and afterwords to his remarkably well-wrought translations. Before moving to Chicago in 1963, Ramanujan taught English at Belgaum and Baroda. He was Professor of Dravidian Linguistics at Chicago, when he died in July 1993. The commentary on *Tholkāppiyam* included here is culled from his introduction to translations of Tamil poetry, *Poems of Love and War* (Oxford University Press, Delhi, 1985, pp. 235–68).

It is marked by a rare lucidity and understanding of the subject. It is also included to indicate the significance of *Tholkāppiyam* in the theoretical canon of Indian literature, and to disabuse the student of the commonly held idea that Sanskrit poetics was all that there was in ancient India.

Indian literary criticism is a story woven through many languages, and the Tamil strand in it is of as much importance as the Sanskrit one, since Tamil is the mother of three other literary languages: Kannada, Telugu and Malayalam. Hence *Tholkāppiyam* has a special place in the history of Indian literary theory. Ramanujan's commentary on it has done great service to the cause of modern interpretation of ancient Tamil poetics.

On Ancient Tamil Poetics

AKAM AND *PUṞAM*

Akam and *puṟam* are ancient, complex words. To understand them is to enter Tamil poetics, and much that is crucial to Tamil culture. According to *A Dravidian Etymological Dictionary*, they are also current in all the South Dravidian languages and in Telugu and Tulu. In classical poetry, as we have seen, *akam* poems are love poems; *puṛam* are all other kinds of poems, usually about war, values, community; it is the 'public' poetry of the ancient Tamils, celebrating the ferocity and glory of kings, lamenting the death of heroes, the poverty of poets. Elegies, panegyrics, invectives, poems on wars and tragic events are *puṟam* poems.

The *Tolkāppiyam* distinguishes *akam* and *puṟam* as follows:

> In (the five phases of) *akam* no names of persons should be mentioned. Particular names are appropriate only in *puṟam* poetry. (*Tol.* 57)

The dramatis personae for *akam* are types, such as men and women in love, foster-mothers, girl-friends, etc., rather than historical persons. Similarly, landscapes are more important than particular places. The reason for such absence of individuals is implicit in the word *akam*: the 'interior' world is archetypal, it has no history, and no names of persons and places, except, now and then, in its metaphors. Love in all its variety (with important exceptions)—love in separation and in union, before and after marriage, in chastity and in betrayal—is the theme of *akam*.

> There are seven types of love, of which the first is *kaikkiḷai* or unrequited love, and the last is *peruntiḷai* or mismatched love. (*Tol.* 1)

Peruntiṇai, or the 'major type' (as the *Tolkāppiyam* somewhat cynically calls it), of man–woman relationship is the forced loveless relationship: a man and a woman, mismatched in age, coming together for duty, convenience, or lust. At the other extreme is *kaikkiḷ ai* (literally, the 'base relationship'), the one-sided affair, unrequited love, or desire indicted on an immature girl who does not understand it. Neither of these extremes is the proper subject of *akam* poetry. They are common, abnormal, undignified, fit only for servants.

> Servants and workmen are outside the five *akam* types (of true love), for they do not have the necessary strength of character. (*Tol.* 25–26)

Most of the *akam* anthologies contain no poems of unrequited or mismatched love; only *Kalittokai* (e.g., "The Hunchback and the Dwarf", discussed below) has examples of both types. They follow none of the formal constraints on theme and structure that are characteristics of the *akam* poems.

Of the seven types, only the middle five are the subject of true love poetry. The hero and heroine should be 'well-matched in ten points' such as beauty, wealth, age, virtue, rank, etc. Only such a pair is capable of the range of love: union and separation, anxiety, patience, betrayal, forgiveness. The couple must be cultured; for the uncultured will be rash, ignorant, self-centred, and therefore unfit for *akam* poetry.

THE FIVE LANDSCAPES

The *Tolkāppiyam* opens its outline of *akam* poetics with a statement about the world of the poems:

> When we examine the materials of a poem, only three things appear to be important: *mutal* (the "first things", i.e., time and place), *karu* (the "native elements"), and *uri* (the "human feelings" appropriately set in *mutal* and karu) (*Tol.* 3)

'Place' is first divided into four kinds of regions, which are constituted by combinations of the five elements, earth, water, air, fire, sky (or space). Each region is presided over by a deity and named after a characteristic flower or tree:

> *mullai*, a variety of jasmine, represents the forests overseen by *Māyōn*, "the Dark One", the dark-bodied god of herdsmen (*Viṣṇu*);
>
> *kuṛiñci*, a mountain (lower, stands for the mountains overseen by *Ceyon*, the Red One, *Murukaṉ*, the red-speared god of war, youth and beauty;
>
> *marutam*, a tree with red flowers growing near the water, for the pastoral region overseen by *Vēntaṉ*, "King", identified with the rain god (*Indra*);
>
> *neytal*, a water flower, for the sandy seashore overseen by *Varuṇan*, the wind god. (*Tol.* 5)

A rather special fifth region, *pālai* or desert waste, is overseen by *Koṟṟavai*, a demonic goddess of war, according to later writers.

Pālai is supposedly a green desert tree that is unaffected by drought. *Pālai* has no specific location, for it is thought that any mountain or forest may be parched to a wasteland in the heat of summer.[3]

Time is divided into day, month and year. The year is divided into six 'large time units', the six seasons: the rains (August–September), the cool season (October–November), the season of evening dew (December–January) the season of morning dew (February–March), early summer (April–May), and late summer (June–July). The day is divided into five 'small time units': morning, midday, evening, nightfall, the dead of night. Some would add a sixth, dawn.

Particular 'large time units' and 'small time units' are associated by convention with particular regions.

> *Mullai* country is associated with the rainy season and evening;
> *kuṟiñci*, with the season of evening dew and midnight;
> *marutam,* with the later part of night and the dawn;
> *neytal* with the twilight or evening;
> *pālai* with summer, the season of morning dew, and midday.
> (*Tol.* 6–12)

Each of the five regions or landscapes is associated further with an appropriate *uri* or phase of love. (The phases of war are discussed below.)

> Lovers union is associated with *kuṟiñci*, the mountain;
> separation with *pālai*, the desert;
> patient waiting, with *mullai*, the forests;
> anxious waiting, with *neytal*, the seashore;
> the lover's infidelity and the beloved's resentment, with
> *marutam*, the cultivated agricultural region or lowland. (*Tol.* 16)

Of these five, the first is clandestine (*kaḷavu*), before marriage; the fifth occurs after marriage. The other three could be either before or after marriage. *Pālai*, separation, includes not only the hardships of the lover away from his love, his search for wealth, fame, and learning, but also the elopement of the couple, their hardships on the way, and their separation from their parents.

We may note a few features of the native categories of the Tamil system. First things (time and place) and native elements are distinguished from *uri* (appropriate human feelings and experience); the systematic symbology depends on the association between these two sets. They are distinct, yet co-present. They require each other; together they make the world. *Mutal* and *karu*, first things and native elements, are seen as the 'objective correlatives', or rather the correlative objects,[4] of human experience. It is also significant that in this Tamil system, though gods are mentioned, they are only part of the scene; they preside, but as natives of the landscape.[5] There seems to be no creator-creature relation in the early anthologies.

In the *karu*, 'things born into, or native to, a region', no dear distinction is made between nature and culture; among the native elements of a landscape are listed flora, fauna, tribes as well as arts, styles, instruments. Furthermore, the *Tolkāppiyam* (582 ff.) considers all native elements, especially all animate beings, as part of a continuous series[6] graded by degrees of sentience:

Things without any sentience: stones, water, etc.
Beings with one sense (touch): grass, trees, creepers
Beings with two senses (touch and taste): snails, shellfish
Beings with three senses (touch, taste, smell): termites, ants
Beings with four senses (touch, taste, smell, vision): crabs, lobsters, beetles, bees
Beings with five senses (touch, taste, smell, vision, hearing): birds, beasts, and uncultured people
Beings with six senses (touch, taste, smell, vision, hearing, mind): human beings and gods.

In poetry, says the *Tolkāppiyam*, the above categories are both used and crossed, say, in figures like metaphor and personification. Time may become a winged bird, a bird may be seen as a messenger of love, and love may be felt as a river in flood. As some philosophers would say, a metaphor is a 'category mistake'. A special figure (called *bhrāntimadalaṅkāra* in Sanskrit) depends on one thing being mistaken for another. George Hart (1975: 275–77) discusses this figure and points out that, historically speaking, it occurs first in Tamil and later in Sanskrit poetry. Here is a Tamil example:

What Her Girl Friend Said to Her

These fat cassia trees
are gullible:
the season of rains
that he spoke of
when he went through the stones
of the desert
is not yet here
though these trees
mistaking the untimely rains
have put out
long arrangements of flowers
on their twigs
as if for a proper monsoon.

Kōvatattaṉ,
Kuṛuntokai 66

The heroine is waiting for her lover's return; he has promised to return by the first rains. Cassia trees usually flower at that time and signal the season of rains. Here the girl friend is asking the heroine to be patient—not to be mindless and deluded like the cassia trees. Trees have only one sense (touch) and mistake an untimely sprinkle for the real monsoon. The woman should use her other senses, not make the same mistake.

Such a figure always involves animals (which lack mind, the sixth sense), or plants (which have only one sense) as in the above poem. This way of thinking prevents the use of some well-known figures of speech. For instance, the kind of 'pathetic fallacy' that directly attributes mind of animals and objects is quite rare in Tamil poetry (except in ironic contexts, or where the speaker is overwhelmed by feeling). However, animal behaviour may suggest witnesses; for only human beings have the sixth sense to see such parallels, their poetry, and their irony.

According to both the Indian and the Western traditions, every sign is a union of signifier and signified (e.g., Saussure 1959: 65–67). In the Tamil system of correspondences, a whole language of signs is created by relating the landscapes as signifers to the *uri* or appropriate human feelings.

In this world of correspondences between times, places things born in them, and human experiences, a word like *Kuriñci* has several concentric circles of meaning: a flower, the mountain landscape, lovers' union, a type of poem about all these, and musical modes for these poems. But its concrete meaning, 'a mountain flower' is never quite forgotten.

A conventional design thus provides a live vocabulary of symbols; the actual objective landscapes of Tamil country become the interior landscapes of Tamil poetry. Chart 1 tabulates some of these features. It would be useful, initially at least, to refer to the list of symbols when reading the poems.

The *Tolkāppiyam* takes care to add that 'birds and beasts of one landscape may sometimes appear in others': artful poets may work with an 'overlap of genres' (*tiṇaimayakkam*); they may even bring in war imagery to heighten the effects of an *akam* poem. The *Tolkāppiyam* further states that the above genres are not rigidly separated; the time and place appropriate to one genre may be fused with the time and place appropriate to another:

> Anything other than *uri* or the appropriate mood may be fused or transformed. (*Tol.* 15)

The following poem is a good example of this mixture of landscapes.

What She Said

The bare root of the bean is pink
like the leg of a jungle hen,
and herds of deer attack its overripe pods.
For the harshness
Of this season of morning dew

there is no cure
but the breast of my man.

Allūr Nanmullai
Kuṛuntokai 68

The season is morning dew (*kuṟiñci*), but the bird mentioned is a jungle hen (*mullai*), the beast is a deer (*mullai*). The mixture of *kuṟiñci* (lovers' union) and *mullai* (patient waiting) brings out effectively the exact nuance of the girl's mood, 'mixing memory and desire' in a kind of montage.

Thus, for poetry, the hierarchy of components is inverted; the human elements (*uri*), the native elements (*karu*), and the first elements (*mutal*) are in a descending order of importance for a poet. Mere nature description or imagism in poetry would be uninteresting to classical Tamil poets and critics, for it could not 'signify'; it would be a signifier without a signified, a landscape (*mutal* and *karu*) without an *uri*, an appropriate human mood.

POETIC DESIGN

The conventions make for many kinds of economy in poetic design. Consider the following poem:

What She Said

Bigger than earth, certainly,
higher than the sky,
more unfathomable than the waters
is this love for this man
    of the mountain slopes
    where bees make rich honey
    from the flowers of the *kuṛiñci*
    that has such black stalks.

Tevakulattar
Kuṛuntokai 3

The *Kuṛiñci* flower and the mountain scene clearly mark this as a *kuṛiñci* poem about lovers' union. The union is not described or talked about; it is enacted by the 'inset' scene of the bees making

Chart 1. Some Features of the Five Landscapes

	Lovers' Union	*Patient Waiting, Domesticity*	*Lover's Unfaithfulness, 'Sulking Scenes'*	*Anxiety in Separation*	*Elopement, Separation from Lover or Parents*
Characteristic flower (name of region and poetic genre)	*kuṟiñci*	*mullai* (jasmine)	marutam (queen's-flower)	*neytal* (blue lily)	*pālai* (desert tree)
Landscape	mountains	forest, pasture	countryside, agricultural lowland	seashore	wasteland (mountain or forest parched by summer)
Time	night	late evening	morning	nightfall	midday
Season	cool season, season of morning dew	rainy season	all seasons	all seasons	season of evening dew, summer
Bird	peacock, parrot	sparrow, jungle hen	stork, heron	seagull	dove, eagle
Beast (including fish, reptile, etc.)	monkey, elephant, horse, bull	deer	buffalo freshwater fish	crocodile shark	fatigued elephant, tiger or wolf lizard
Tree or plant	jackfruit, bamboo, *vēṅkai* (kino)	*koṉṟai* (cassia)	mango	*puṉṉai* (laurel)	*ōmai* (toothbrush tree) cactus
Water	waterfall	rivers	pool	wells	waterless wells, stagnant water
Occupation or people	hill tribes, guarding millet harvest, gathering honey	plowman	pastoral occupations	selling fish and salt, fisherfolk	wayfarers, bandits

This is not an exhaustive list; only a few of the elements that appear frequently in the poems are given here. The Tamil names or goal heroes, clans, musical instruments, and kinds of food have been omitted.

This chart first appeared in the *The Interior Landscape* (Ramanujan 1967). For a more complete table, see Singaravelu (1966: 22) or Zvelebil (1973: 100).

honey from the flowers of the *kuṛiñci*. The lover is not only the lord of the mountain; he is like the mountain he owns. Describing the scene describes his passion. The *kuṛiñci*, being a plant that takes about twelve years to come to flower, carries a suggestion assimilating the tree to the young tropical heroine who speaks the poem. The *Tolkāppiyam* calls this technique of using the scene to describe act or agent, *uḷḷuṛai uvamam*, hidden or implicit metaphor.

Furthermore, the poem opens with large abstractions about her love: her love is bigger than earth and higher than the sky. But it moves toward the concreteness of the black-stalked *kuṛiñci*, acting out by analogue the virgin's progress from abstraction to experience. We may remember that this progression (from the basic cosmic elements to the specific component of a landscape) is also the method of the entire intellectual framework behind the poetry: moving from first elements to native elements to human feelings, the poem in the original opens with earth, sky, and water, moves through the native elements of the mountain landscape (slopes, bees, *kuṛiñci*) and ends with a human feeling, *naṭpu*, 'love'.

Evocations designed like these may be seen in poem after poem. *Uḷḷuṛais*—let us call them insets—of the natural scene (somewhat like G. M. Hopkins's inscape) repeat the total action of the poem. Here are two clear examples from a sequence:

What She Said

In his place, mother,
mud-spattered spotted crabs
sneak into holes at the root
of the nightshade.
    O what's the point
    of his marrying me then
    with sweet talk,
    and saying
    these other things now?
In his country,
spotted crabs
born in their mother's death

grow up with crocodiles
that devour their young.

Why is he here now?

And why does he
take those women,
    a jangle of gold bangles
    as they make love,
only to leave them?

Ōrampōkiyār
Aiṅkurunūṟu 22, 24

These are *marutam* poems, poems about infidelity, set in the fertile, well-watered countryside. In the first, he has done to her what the crabs do to the nightshade—sneaked into the hole and gnawed at the root. In the second, the spotted crabs and crocodiles of his region, cannibals all, kill and eat the dear kin they ought to love and protect—like the man himself.

METAPHOR AND METONYMY

A word about the theory of *uḷḷuṟai uvamam* or insets. An inset is an implicit comparison. All explicit markers of comparison are suppressed. The *Tolkāppiyam* says that explicit comparison belongs to worldly usage (*ulakavaḻakku*), whereas implicit metaphor belongs to poetic usage (*ceyyuḷvaḻakku*).

There are other distinctions to be made: (a) An inset is a correlation of the landscapes and their contents (*karu*) to the human scene (*uri*), (b) Unlike metaphor in ordinary language, an inset is a structural feature within the poem; it integrates the different elements of the poem and shapes its message, (c) Unlike metaphor and simile, it often leaves out all the points of comparison and all explicit markers of comparison (e.g., 'like', 'as'); such an omission increases many fold the power of the figure. As we have seen in the poems, image intensifies image, associations flow into each other. These 'montage' and 'dissolve' effects are aided by the flowing syntax of the language, (d) The inset is essentially a 'metonymy',[7] an *in presentia* relationship, where both terms are present, where the signifier and the signified belong to the same universe, share the same 'landscape'. Both are parts of one scene. Such a metonymy, rather than metaphor, is the favorite poetic figure of the classical Tamils. Metaphor implies diversity ('seeing similars in dissimilars' said Aristotle), to be unified by comparison. Poetry for the Tamils does not unify a multiverse but expresses a universe from within, speaking through any of its parts. The man belongs to the scene, the scene represents the man. Adapting a remark of Kenneth Burke's (1945: 6–7) in another context, we may say, 'There is implicit in the quality of a scene the quality of the action implicit in it . . . one could deduce the details of the action from the details of the setting'. This kind of 'metonymous metaphor', based on an entire formal scheme, is a special feature of classical Tamil forms.

But then complex insets are not used everywhere in the poems; they are specifically preferred in the most structured of Tamil poetic genres—the fivefold *akam*; they are not used in the *peruntiḷai* (the mismatched affair), nor preferred in the heroic *puṟam* poems.

The Tamil theory of comparison deserves an essay to itself. I shall content myself here with only one more feature. All comparisons, says the *Tolkāppiyam* (276), whether explicit or implicit, involve terms of comparison. These terms may refer to shape, colour, action, or result. Examples abound in the poems I have quoted. Like the comparisons between crab and lover, that between cobbler and king is based on action; when the bare root of the bean is pink like the leg of a jungle hen, the points of comparison are colour and shape. If we consider colour and shape as special cases of sensory attributes in general, we can include comparisons based on touch, taste, etc., which occur in the poems, e.g., 'sweeter than milk and honey'. Of course, through colour, shape, action, and result, these comparisons convey much more. Usually, several terms are present in any comparison. For instance, in the poem at the beginning of the last section, the emphasis is on the action of the bee and the resulting honey. The shapes of the flower and the bee also suggest obvious sexual images.

THE PERSONAE

The *dramatis personae* in *akam* poems are limited to a small number: the hero, the heroine, the hero's friend(s) or messengers, the heroine's friend and foster-mother, the concubine, and passersby. In the *puram* poems, the poets mostly speak in their own person, though there are a few exceptions.

No *akam* poet speaks in his own voice; and no poem is addressed to a reader. The reader only overhears what the characters say to each other or to themselves or to the moon. A poem in this tradition implies, evokes, enacts a drama in a monologue.

The situations (*tuṛai*) when a hero or heroine or one of their companions may speak out, and to whom, are closely defined. For example,

> The girl friend of the heroine may speak out on the following occasions: when the heroine, left behind by her lover, speaks of her loneliness; when she helps them elope; when she begs the hero to take good care of the heroine; when she tries to dissuade the parents from their search for the runaway couple, or consoles the grieving mother... (*Tol.* 42)

An interesting convention usually restricts the imagery for different speakers within the poems. The heroine's images are mostly confined to what surrounds her house, or to the wonder of discovering his landscape or to hearsay and fantasies about it. The concubine or the heroine's girl friend or foster-mother have more ranging images: they are of a lower class, and their experience is wider. The man's imagery has even greater range. Apparently there are no limits to his experience, and therefore to his imagery. Thus the range of imagery, its quality or content, its very narrowness or width of choice, indirectly characterises speaker and social class.

THE TWO PROPRIETIES

The *Tolkāppiyam* speaks of 'two kinds of proprieties: those of drama and those of the world.' The conventional proprieties outlined so far are of the mode of drama. The situations of real life in the real world are governed by another set of proprieties. The strategy of the poet is to deploy both, to keep the tension between the forms of art and the forms of the world.

A highly formal scheme of landscapes that have neither name nor history bears within it the real land, the vivid particulars of bird, beast, insect, drumbeat, and waterfall.

A little-known book in Tamil by a botanist (Cāmi 1967; see also Varadarajan 1969) documents one's constant sense that these poets knew their fauna and flora; their botanical observations, for instance, are breathtakingly minute and accurate. In these poems, over two hundred plants of all the five Tamil regions are named, described, used in insets and comparisons. Root, stem, bark, bud, petal, inflorescence, seasons, special kinds of pollination, etc., are observed and alluded to. And their properties are aptly used to evoke human relationships.

We may ask, as the Tamil commentators do, why did the poets pick the *kuṟiñci* as the one flower that will name the mountain landscape and the mood of first love? Though such signs are symbols, cultural assignments, arbitrary conventions, they are half-motivated by botanical facts: the *kuṟiñci* plant, of the *Strobilanthes* genus, grows only 6,000 feet above sea level; so it is the mountain flower par excellence. Botanical calendars kept for over a century on South Indian hills like the Nilgiris show that a *kuṟiñci* plant comes to flower only from nine to twelve years after it is planted—this identifies it with the tropical virgin heroine who comes to puberty at the same age.

Kuṟiñci plants flower all at once on the mountain slopes, covering them with millions of blossoms, certainly a great symbol for the suddenness and the overwhelming nature of first love. It is a 'honey' flower, rich in honey. The bees that frequent it frequent no other, thus making what bee-keepers call 'unifloral honey', which is as rich as it is rare and pure. Furthermore, the *kuṟiñci* is fiercely competitive—it permits no other tree to grow in its neighbourhood.

Thus is the real world always kept in sight and included in the symbolic. These poets would have made a modern poet like Marianne

Moore (1951:41) happy: they are 'literalists of the imagination', presenting for inspection in poem after poem 'imaginary gardens with real toads in them.'

A LANGUAGE WITHIN LANGUAGE

In a sense, the tradition of conventions does everything possible to depersonalise the poetry of *akam*. It gives all that can be given to a poet, and makes of poetry a kind of second language.

The poet's language is not only Tamil: landscapes, the personae, the appropriate moods, all become a language within language. Like a native speaker he makes 'infinite use of finite means', to say with familiar words what has never been said before; he can say exactly what he wants to, without even being aware of the ground rules of his grammar. If the world is the vocabulary of the poet, the conventions are his syntax—at least one of the many kinds of poetic syntax.

The lyric poet likes to find ways of saying many things while saying one thing; he would like to suggest an entire astronomy by his specks and flashes. Toward this end, the Tamil poets used a set of five landscapes and formalized the world into a symbolism. By a remarkable consensus, they all spoke this common language of symbols for some five or six generations. Each could make his own poem and by doing so allude to every other poem which had been, was being, or would be written in this symbolic language. Thus poem became relevant to poem, as it they were all written by a single hand. The spurious name *Caṅkam* ('Fraternity,' 'Community') for this poetry was justified not by history but by the poetic practice.

PUṚAM POETRY

The language of *akam* is only half the story. The scheme should include the *puṛam* poems, as well as the mismatched and the one-sided love affairs that define by contrast the tight structure of the fivefold *akam*.

The *puṛam* poems correspond to the *akam* poems in many ways. The *Tolkāppiyam* finds a *puṛam* parallel for every one of the seven genres of *akam*. Six of them are named after a flower or a plant. For instance, *vākai*, the *sirissa* tree of the desert region, lends its name to the *puṟam* genre depicting ideals of achievement—parallel to it is *pālai* in love poetry, which depicts a lover going through the wilderness in search of wealth, fame, etc. Commentators elaborate on the correspondences further. Why should the *kuṛiñci* (union) phase of love correspond to *veṭci* (cattle raids) in war? Because, say the commentators, they both have to do with first encounters, are clandestine, take place at night on hillsides. Chart 2 displays one set of *akam/puṛam* correspondences.

Though these correspondences are in the rhetoric, however, they are not always active in the poetry. The landscapes are not consistently used as 'insets', nor are the distinctions clear. The poem on the cobbler and the king, for instance, is considered a *vākai* poem (in praise of kings, etc.), and is a counterpart of *pālai* (desert: separation, hardship); but the images in the poem do not belong to the desert at all, but to the *mullai* (forest, pasture: waiting, marriage): rains, laburnum, evening, and childbirth. Of course, the colophon could be wrong, or wrongly transmitted, for the *mullai* images could fit very well with the parallel *vañci* (preparation for war). By and large, though, the *puṟam* divisions are not as clear as the ones in *akam*. For instance, the last two classes (*kāñci* and *pāṭān*) are not clearly distinguished from the rest. *Pāṭān* is a large mixed class, and does not bear the name of a tree or flower as the others do. Later writers add more separate classes, include in *puṛam* the classes of mismatched and unrequited love, and add a 'general' class (*porunilai*) to make a twelvefold *puṛam*. By then only the 'ideal fivefold', from *kuṟiñci* to *pālai*, is considered *akam*, 'interior'. Yet in reading *akam* and *puṛam* together one is struck as much by the common world they share as by the differences.

Whereas *akam* poems tend to focus on a single image, *puṛam* images rush and tumble over one another. Yet, as in the following *puṛam* poem, the same flowers and landscapes speak of war and peace, of fertility and desolation:

Chart 2. *Puṟam/Akam* Correspondence

	Akam	*Situation/Theme*	*Puṟam*	*Situation/Theme*	*Common Features*
1.	*kuṟiñci,* a mountain flower	first union	*veṭci*, scarlet ixora	cattle-lifting, prelude to war	night, hillside; clandestine affair
2.	*mullai*, jasmine	separation (patience)	*vañci*, a creeper	preparation for war, invasion	forest, rainy season; separation from loved ones
3.	*marutam*, queen's flower	infidelity (conflict)	*uḻiñai*, a cotton shrub	siege	fertile area (city, etc.), dawn; refusing entry
4.	*neytal*, water lily	separation (anxiety)	*tumpai,* white dead nettle	battle	seashore, open battle-ground, no season; evening; grief
5.	*pālai*, desert tree	elopement, search for wealth, fame, etc.	*vākai*, sirissa tree	ideals of achievement, victory	no particular landscape; praise
6.	*peruntiṇai,*[a] 'major type'	mismatched love	*kāñci*, portia tree	struggle for excellence; endurance	no particular landscape; struggle
7.	*kaikkiḷar*[a] 'base relation'	unrequited love	*pāṭāṇ,*[a] 'praise'	elegy, praise for heroes, asking for gifts, invective	no particular landscape; a one-sided relationship

[a] Not the name of a tree or a flower.

Where the Lilies Were in Flower

Fish leaping
in fields of cattle;

easy unplowed sowing
where the wild boar has rooted;

big-eyed buffalo herds
stopped by fences of lilies
flowering in sugarcane beds:

ancient cows bending their heads
over water flowers
scattered by the busy dancers
swaying with lifted hands;

queen's-flower trees full of bird cries
the rustle of coconut trees,
canals from flowering pools
in countries
with cities sung in song:
    but your anger
    touched them, brought them terror,
    left their beauty in ruins,
    bodies consumed by Death.

The districts are empty, parched;
the waves of sugarcane blossom,
stalks of dry grass.
The thorny babul of the twisted fruit
neck to neck with the giant black babul.

The she-devil with the branching crest
roams
astraddle on her demon,
and the small persistent thorn
is spread in the moving dust
of ashen battlefields.

Not a sound, nothing animal,
not even dung, in the ruins of public places

that kill the hearts of eager men,
chill all courage,
and shake those who remember.

But here,
the sages have sought your woods.
In your open spaces, the fighters play
with bright-jewelled women.

The traveler is safe on the highway.
Sellers of grain shelter their kin
who shelter, in turn, their kin.

The silver star will not go near
the place of the red planet; so it rains
on the thirsty fields.
Hunger has fled
and taken disease with her.

Great one.
Your land blossoms
everywhere.

Kumaṭṭūr Kaṇṇaṉār;
on *Imayavarampaṉ Neṭuñcēralātaṉ*
Patiṟṟupattu 13

The plant names are familiar: e.g., sugarcane, lilies, *marutam* or queen's-flower. The poem clearly falls into two parts, celebrating the destructive and protective functions of a king. The first part celebrates the fertility of the pastoral agricultural, and seashore landscapes (cows, sugarcane, lilies, etc.); the middle part shows how they have been ravaged and turned into a *pālai* wilderness (the thorny babuls, etc.) by the war. The third section praises the king's own flourishing kingdom (forests and fields).

The *akam/puṟam* correspondences are not strict, but still close enough to allow us to integrate the two genres. Such correspondences should not be frozen into an exact taxonomy, for the Tamils never do so—they always make room for 'overlap of classes' (*tiṇaimayakkam*) and 'left-over classes' (e.g., *potunilai*).

Taken in the large, the two genres, poems of love and war—*akam* and *puṛam*—complement one another: contrasted in theme, mood, and structure but unified by imagery. Together, they make the classical, 'bardic' Tamil world. This is why the same poets could write both *akam* and *puṛam* poems. Some poems explicitly place love and war together:

A Leaf in Love and War

The chaste trees, dark-clustered,
blend with the land
that knows no dryness;
the colors on the leaves
mob the eyes.

We've seen those leaves
on jeweled women,
on their mounds
of love.
Now the chaste wreath lies slashed
on the ground, so changed, so mixed
with blood, the vulture snatches
it with its beak,
thinking it raw meat.

We see this too
just because a young man
in love with war
wore it for glory.

Veṛipāṭiya Kāmakkaṉṉiyār
Puṛanāṉūṛu 271

The green leaves of the chaste tree were used as leaf-skirts by women and as laurels by warriors. So it is emblematic of *kuṛiñci* (union) in love and *uḷiñai* (battle) in war; the mere juxtaposition brings the irony home sharply.

One more contrast should be noticed. Through *akam* means 'interior,' *puṛam*, 'exterior,' *akam* poetry, which a modern reader might expect to be the most private and personal expression, is the most formally structured genre in the Tamil tradition; as we know, no names, individuals, or places are usually allowed here, only classes, ideal types; for in this inner world there are no names or individuals. *Puṛam,* the so-called 'public poetry', is allowed names, places, expression of personal circumstances in a real society, a real history, and a certain freedom from the necessities of poetic convention both in insets and in the landscapes. Thus it is the 'public' *puṛam* poetry that becomes the vehicle of personal expression and celebration of historical personages. Indeed, when a woman speaks in her own voice about her love, the poem is placed in a *puṛam* anthology (e.g., p. 119).

LOVE, MISMATCHED

Quite in contrast to both *akam* and *puṛam* genres as we have defined them stands the mismatched affair or *peruntiṇai.* Here is an example from *Kalittokai*, probably the latest of the eight anthologies.

The Hunchback and the Dwarf: A Dialogue

Hunchback woman,
the way you move is gentle
and crooked as a reflection
in the water,
                what good deeds
did you do that I should want you so?
O mother! (she swore to herself) Some
auspicious moment made you dwarf,
so tiny you're almost invisible,
you whelp born to a man-faced owl,
how dare you stop us to say
you want us? Would such midgets
ever get to touch such as us!
Lovely one,
     curvaceous,
                convex
as the blade of a plough,

you strike me with a love
I cannot bear.
    I can live
only by your grace.
    (Look at this creature!)
    You dwarf, standing piece of timber,
    you've yet to learn the right approach
    to girls. In high noon
    you come to hold
    our hand and ask us to your place.
    Have you had any women?

Good woman,
Your waist is higher
than your head, your face a stork,
plucked and skinned,
with a dagger for a beak,
    listen to me.
If I take you in the front, your hump
juts into my chest; if from the back
it'll tickle me in odd places.
    So I'll not
even try it. But come close anyway and let's touch
side to side.
    Chi, you're wicked. Get lost! You half-man!
    As creepers hang on only to the crook of a tree
    there are men who'd love to hold this hunch
    of a body close, though nothing fits. Yet, you lecher,
    you ask for us sideways. What's so wrong
    with us, you ball, you bush of a man.
    Is a gentle hunchback type far worse than a cake
    of black beans?
But I've fallen for you
(he said, and went after her).
O look, my heart,
at the dallying of this hunchback!
    Man, you stand

like a creepy turtle stood up by somebody,
hands flailing in your armpits.
We've told you we're not for you. Yet you hang around.
Look, he walks now like Kama.
Yes, the love-god with arrows, brother to Cama.
Look at this love-god!
Come now, let's find joy,
you in me, me in you; come, let's ask and tell
which parts we touch
I swear by the feet of my king.

All right. O gentle-breasted one. I too will give up mockery.

But I don't want this crowd in the palace
laughing at us, screaming when we do it,
"Hey, hey! Look at them mounting,
leaping like demon on demon!"

O shape
of unbeaten gold, let's get away from the palace
to the wild jasmine bush. Come,
let's touch close, hug hard
and finish the unfinished,
then we'll be
like a gob of wax on a parchment
made out in a court full of wise men,
and stamped
to a seal.
Let's go.

Marutaṉiḷanākaṉār
Kalittokai 94

Note the unheroic, even antiheroic, mock-heroic quality of this unlovely couple, looking not for love but frankly for sex; the folk-like bawdiness, the earthy humour. There are no sunset landscapes, though the poem is classified as *marutam*. Ploughs, herons, turtles and wild jasmine jostle in it. In a single phrase like 'You whelp born to a man-faced owl', many categories are undone. The piece makes comedy and poetry by violating over and over the decorum of *akam* poems. The metaphors are bold, explicit. The two persons are not even young—one of them is 'a stork, plucked and skinned'. This is *peruntiṇai*, the 'major type', depicting the common human condition, love among the misfits with no scruples regarding the niceties of time or landscape; moving from mockery to coupling in the course of a conversation. Their misfit is evident even in their bodies' lack of fit. And they are obviously servants. We have also shifted from the dramatic monologues of *akam* and *puṛam* to dialogue and interaction, from lyric to comic drama. As in drama, the characters and their speech change: the hunchback begins with a royal 'we' in her rejection and ends with an 'I' in yielding; her mocking exclamations to herself drop off.

If the *akam* has the most tightly structured symbolic language, the *peruntiṇai* is free and realistic, with real toads in real cesspools.

We have not spoken of one genre: the *kaikkiḷai*, one-sided or unrequited love. There are not many classical examples of unrequited love. Here is one, from *Kuṛuntokai*:

What He Said

When love is ripe beyond bearing
and goes to seed,
men will ride even palmyra stems
as if they were horses;

will wear on their heads the reeking cones of the *erukkam* bud
as if they were flowers;

will draw to themselves
the laughter of the streets;

and will do worse.

Pēreyin̲ Muruvalār
Kuṛuntokai 17

The most significant observation on *kaikkiḷai* (not found in the *Tolkāppiyam* but in later commentaries) is that such expression of one-sided love is appropriate only to religion. Postclassical Tamil devotees, preoccupied with their unrequited love for their god, in a cloud of unknowing, created the most poignant poems of *kaikkiḷai.*

Thus the four genres (*akam*, *peruntiṇai, kaikkiḷai*, and *puṛam*) cover and formalise the main possibilities of Tamil lyric poetry. They define each other mutually. A great deal of Western love poetry would probably be described by the ancient commentators as the one-sided *kaikkiḷai*; a great deal of modern poetry, fiction, and black comedy as love among the misfits or *peruntiṇai*—exploring the unheroic, the antiheroic, and presenting the ironies of impotence.

Poem becomes relevant to poem within the five *akam* landscapes and across the four genres as well.

AKAM AND *PUṚAM* AS POETIC DEVICES

Akam ('interior') and *puṛam* ('exterior') are not only thematic divisions. The paired opposition is pervasive in Tamil poetry and culture. The two key categories are related to each other by context and by contrast. The various meanings to be found in the Tamil lexicon can be paired as follows:

Akam	*Puṛam*
interior	exterior
heart, mind	body surfaces and extremities, e.g., back, side, arms
self	others
kin	non-kin
house, family	houseyard, field
inland, settlement	area far from dense human habitation, e.g., jungle, desert
earth	farthest ocean
love poems–no names of places or persons	poetry about war and other than (well-matched?) love, a 'public' poetry, with names of real people and places
codes of conduct appropriate to *akam*	codes of conduct appropriate to *puṛam*

The meanings complement each other systematically, as we move from context to context, for each meaning of *akam*, there is a corresponding sense of *puṛam*. It is characteristic of this poetry and its poetics that the meanings seem to expand and contract in concentric circles, with the concrete physical particular at the centre, getting more and more inclusive and abstract as we move outward. The context picks and foregrounds one or another of these circles of meaning

A poem moves along these various senses of *akam* and *puṛam*: this movement is one of the forms of the poem. In the course of such interplay, *akam/puṛam* contrasts such as inner/outer, self/other, nature/culture, household/wilderness become part of the form as well as the content of the poem.

For instance:

What He Said

In this long summer wilderness
    seized and devoured by wildfire,
if I should shut my eyes
    even a wink,
I see
    dead of night, a tall house
    in a cool yard, and the girl
with freckles
    like kino flowers,
hair flowing as with honey,
    her skin a young mango leaf.

Ōtalāntaiyār
Aiṅkuṟuṉūṟu 324

The poem consists of a number of movements from *puṛam* to *akam*, from the faraway wilderness to the inhabited house, from the outer landscape to the fantasy inside him; it also moves from the wildfire and noonday sun (*pālai*, desert, separation) to dead of night, the girl, the yellow kino flowers, and hair glistening as if with honey (all *kuṛiñci* images of lovers' union). Yet the whole poem stays with the *palai* mood of a lover in a desert faraway from his beloved.

Other subtleties should be noted: 'seized and devoured by wildfire', an attribute of the outer wilderness, is also suggestive of the speaker's inner state.

Where he is, is what he is: a scene/agent ratio (in Burke's terms); a metonymy, an *uḷḷuṟai.* He is contained by the wilderness devoured by wildfire; and he also contains it within him. But when he closes his eyes, he contains the house of his beloved in fantasy. We should also remember that *pālai* is one phase of a cycle—he is going away from his woman 'for education, work, earning wealth, war'—all *puṟam* concerns. Among the relations between *akam* and *puṟam*, household and the world, one should include the rhythm of a man going out into the world and coming back into the family. Only a warrior who dies or an ascetic who renounces doesn't return—both are themes for *puṟam* poems. He passes through the *pālai* wilderness on his way to do 'the world's work', and survives by remembering his home and woman, in the heat and wildfire of the outer desert and the inner. Of course, heat and wildfire for the separated lover have sexual overtones.

In reading these poems, one need not explicitly trace *akam/puṟam* shifts. They guide our responses subtly, surprising us often, by turning inside out. *Akam* and *puṟam* are part of the very choreography of poetic moves in Tamil poems. As one learns the 'second language' of these poems, one also learns to sense the 'ins and outs'; one follows the rhythms without labeling them, as one soon learns to read the language of cassias and tigers and waterfalls without running to a glossary of symbols.

Looked at in this way, each poem is a structure and a process. While *akam* and *puṟam*, and the five landscape genres, are opposed to each other as overall genres, and clearly defined as such, within each poem they work as phases, change points. One might even think of the action of each poem as a crossing of thresholds, across genres: the above *pālai* poem crosses from the outer landscape to the interior one, and also from the wilderness to the human settlement. Each of the genres enacts a characteristic crossing of the *akam/puṟam* oppositions.

Typically, the movement of *akam* poems is a crossing from outer to inner; from outer body to the heart within, in memory or imagination (*kuṟiñci*); from sea to land (*neytal*), from warfield to home (*mullai*); from home to wilderness in actuality, from wilderness to home in memory (*pālai*); from the concubine who is no kin, who lives on the town's outskirts, to home, wife, and kin (*marutam*).

Puṟam poems, like the following, tend to start inside a house (*akam*) and move, like the tiger, out into the world (*puṟam*):

You stand against the pillar
of my hut and ask:
    Where is your son?
I don't really know.

My womb was once
a lair
for that tiger.

You can see him now
only in battlefields.

Kāvaṟpeṇṭu
Aiṅkuṟuṉūṟu 86

Often the poetic moment is actually poised on the threshold, though a figure in the poem may move (actually, or in imagination) from outer to inner. Many *marutam* poems are literally enacted at the door which is shut in the face ofthe unfaithful returning husband. The most extraordinary of these 'door-shutting' (*vāyil maṟuttal*) poems moves from *puṟam* to *akam*, from the public realm of townsmen, kinsmen, and the wedding ceremony, step by step to the privacy of the bedroom and finally to the ultimate *akam* or 'interior' of the bride's private parts:

What He Said
after a quarrel, remembering his wedding night

Serving in endless bounty
white rice and meat

cooked to a turn,
    drenched in ghee,
to honored guests,

and when the bird omens were right,
at the perfect junction
of the Wagon Stars with the moon
    shining in a wide soft-lit sky.

wedding site decorated, gods honored,
kettledrum and marriage drum
sounding loud the wedding beat,

the women who'd given her a bridal bath
—piercing eyes looking on, unwinking—
suddenly gone,
her near kin
strung a white thread on her
with the split soft-backed leaves
of the *sirissa*,
and with the *aruku* grass,

    its sacred root a figurine,
    its buds cool, fragrant,
    dark-petaled, blue
    as washed sapphire,

    brought forth by the thundering skies
    of first rains in valleys
    where adolescent calves
    feed on them,
they brought her to me
decked in new clothes,
rousing my desire
even in the wedding canopy,
    wedding noises noisy as pounding rain
on that first night,

and when they wiped her sweat,
and gave her to me,

she splendid with ornament,
I said to her
who was body now to my breath,
chaste without harshness,
wrapped all over in a robe
new, uncrushed,

"It's hot. Sweat is breaking out
on that crescent, your brow.
Open your robe a little,
let the wind cool it,"
and even as I spoke,
my heart hasty with desire,
I pulled it off

and she stood exposed,
her form shining
like a sword unsheathed,
not knowing how to hide herself,
cried Woy!
in shame, then bowed, begged of me,
as she loosened her hair
undoing the thick colorful wreath
of broken lily petals

and, with the darkness of black full tresses,
hand-picked flowers on them
still luring the bees,

hid
her private
parts.

Viṟṟūṟṟu Mūteyiṉaṉār
Akanāṉūṟu 13

Before we leave the manifold of *akam/puṟam*, we must note some more ways in which the two genres differ. Only the full cycle of love between well-matched lovers is called *akam*; all else, including ill-matched love, the life and death of heroes, their relations to land, clan, enemy, and bard, were called *puṟam*. The Tamil world was divided between family, or 'household' (one meaning of *akam*) and the 'kingdom', the outer world. Women were central to the former, as heroes (named kings and chieftains and unnamed warriors) were central to the latter. In an *akam* anthology like *Kuṟuntokai*, only 62 poems are assigned to the man, but 180 to the woman, 140 to her girl-friend, 14 others to women characters like foster-mothers and concubines. In a *puṟam* anthology like *Puṟanāṉūṟu*, hardly a handful are spoken by women—about 18 songs are about or by women characters, mothers, wives, or widows of heroes. I am not counting the songs by women poets, such as the 13 by Auvaiyār (e.g., *Puṟanāṉūṟu* 101–4), which she sings not as a woman but as a bard about her patron.

In many *akam* poems, a woman's body is suggestively present to our senses—the smell or texture of her hair, the shape of her breast, her brow, her mound of love or black-snake pubis, her leaf-skirts, the conch-shell bangles, her teeth like rice sprouts, her skin like young mango leaf, her great shoulders and red-streaked eyes, and in one poem even the taste of her saliva—yet a woman is never described in more than one or two details in each poem. We do not hear much about the man's appearance; we know more about what he has and about his country's scenery than about him. As we hear about her glittering bangles and ornaments, we also hear of his bright spear, his horses, chariots, garlands, anklebands, sometimes a chest enlarged by the drawing of bows. His spouse's chastity and virtue are also a chieftain's ornaments and his magical shields against disaster, as effective as his own 'upright scepter' (*ceṅkōl*, as contrasted with *koṭuṅkōl* 'crooked scepter'). It is significant that in the *akam* poems, rarely is the woman seen as the mature mother of a grown man, as she is in the *puṟam*. As in other heroic milieus, women bards, and poems in women's voices, enlist filial and familial feeling in the cause of war—especially that most compelling of family feelings, a mother's pride (or shame) about her son.

Notes

[Notes 1 and 2 in the original refer to matter not included in this extract, Ed.]

3. This fact adds further subtlety to the symbolism. *Pālai* (wasteland) associated with separation can happen even in the heart of union (*kuṛiñci* or mountain landscape).
4. 'Objective correlatives' (Eliot 1950), and what I have called correlative objects, are very different things: the first are sought and found by individual poets, the latter are given by the culture in which the poets dwell.
5. From now on, I translate *tiṇai* as 'landscape.' But *tiṇai* has several meanings: 'class, genre, type,' as in *akattiṇai* 'the *akam* genre.' In a more specific sense, *tiṇai* is a complex concept defined in the poetics for Tamil poetry: a genre is represented by a region or landscape, its nature and culture, and the human feelings associated with them—in short, an entire ecosystem used for poetic expression. 'Landscape' is a convenient metonymy for the whole cluster of notions. Like the Tamils, we will also use the names *kuṛiñci*, *mullai* etc., for the landscapes and the genres associated with them.
6. This series is clearly reminiscent of the Jain 'ladder of life' of *ekendriya* ('one sense'), *dvendriya* ('two-sense'), etc., all the way to the gods. See Zimmer (1960:277) for an exposition of this Jain system. Though several such Jain elements are found or 'borrowed' in the Tamil texts, their use is not Jain at all; its thrust is not metaphysical, religious, nor does it imply an ethic of nonviolence. Instead, it adds one more 'concrete' figure to the poetry. The subject of Jain ideas in early Tamil literature merits exploration.
7. My use of 'metaphor' and 'metonymy' follows Jakobson (1971: 254–7), whom I find suggestive. As I show below, the categories cannot be mutually exclusive, nor can all figures be divided into these two super-classes. For a cogent criticism, see Genette (1982).

20

Bimal Krishna Matilal

After studying at Calcutta and Harvard, B. K. Matilal (1935–91) taught at the Universities of Toronto, Pennsylvania, Chicago and California (Berkeley). Between 1976 and 1991, the year of his death, he was the Spalding Professor of Eastern Religions and Ethics at Oxford and a Fellow of All Souls College.

Among his more important publications are *Logical and Ethical Issues of Religious Belief* (University of Calcutta, 1982), *Logic, Language and Reality* (Motilal Banarsidass, 1985), *Perception: An Essay on Classical Indian Theories of Knowledge* (Clarendon Press, Oxford, 1986) and *The Word and the World* (Oxford University Press, Delhi, 1990).

Matilal occupies a very important place among academic philosophers dealing with India as a field of study. Unlike his predecessors in the field, Matilal avoids being confined to speculative philosophy alone. In the tradition of Russell and Wittgenstein, he engages his attention in the language of philosophy and the philosophy of language. We see in his work a fruitful combination of profound understanding of modern philosophical schools and methods and an intimate knowledge of Hindu and Buddhist classics. As a result Matilal is able to illuminate modern Western linguistics in the light of Buddhist theories of perception as well as bring back into intellectual currency the *sphoṭa* debate between Bhartṛhari and Nāgarjuna–Dinnāga. The extract reproduced here forms a chapter in Matilal's *The Word and The World* (pp. 84–98).

Bhartṛhari's View of *Sphoṭa*

I

The *sphoṭa* doctrine has been most prominently associated with Bhartṛhari. But scholars have held different views about the exact significance of this concept in Bhartṛhari's thought. The situation if further complicated by the fact that later grammarians attribute a much crystallised and ostensibly different doctrine of *sphoṭa* not only to Bhartṛhari but also to Patanjalī.

Early Indologists (Keith, 1928, 387; De, 1925, 180) described *sphoṭa* as a mysterious or mystical entity, and this was probably due to its association with Bhartṛhari's notion of *śabda-brahman* or the Eternal Verbum (Sastri, 1959). But this was a mistake. In spite of its metaphysical underpinning which M. Biardeau (1964, 268) rightly emphasised, there is a linguistic treatment of the concept well-documented by Bhartṛhari himself, and other grammarians. Brough (1951, 34) and Kunjunni Raja (1969, 97–148) were right to stress the point that *sphoṭa* was not a mysterious entity. There is another dispute that is connected with it; whether the *sphoṭa* in Bhartṛhari is simply the linguistic sign in its aspect of meaning-bearer (Brough, Kunjunni Raja), or whether it represents an abstract class of sounds sorted out and extracted by the listener from gross matter (Moshi, 1967, 40). Cardona (1976, 302) thinks that Brough's thesis should be modified since Bhartṛhari also talks about *varṇa-sphota*, which refers to a sound unit of the language system, not to any meaning-bearing speech unit. Iyer (1969, 158–9) has, however, refuted Joshi's rather sweeping comment that Bhartṛ hari's *sphoṭa* had nothing to do with the meaning-bearing speech unit. In *Mahābhaṣya-dīpikā* Bhartṛhari reinterpreted Patanjalī's use of the word *śabda*. This was noted by Patanjalī as the meaning-bearing element in the *Paspaśā* section. Bhartṛhari glossed this as *sphoṭa* and characterised it as eternal.

II

In *Vākyapadīya* Bhartṛhari clearly develops the threefold doctrine of *sphoṭa* related to letters or phonemes, words and sentences. This is explicitly mentioned in the *Vṛtti*. Sometimes he uses *śabda* and *sphoṭa* interchangeably, which might have been the source of confusion. The *sphoṭa* is further described as partless and indivisible, and as devoid of internal sequence. A *pada-sphoṭa*, i.e., *sphoṭa* identified as a word, seems to be a meaning-bearing unit. But, for Bhartṛhari, the *vākya-sphoṭa*, i.e., the *sphoṭa* in the form of a sentence, is the most important. In the second *kāṇda* of *Vākyapadīya*, he deals with various definitions of the sentences, and finally concludes that a sentence is a sequenceless, partless whole, a *sphoṭa*, that gets 'expressed' or manifested in a sequential and temporary utterance. This is also the primary meaning-bearing element.

For Bhartṛhari, however, this is a wrong term: 'meaning-bearing unit'. *Sphoṭa* is the real substratum, proper linguistic unit, which is identical also with its meaning. Language is not the vehicle of meaning or the conveyor-belt of thought. Thought anchors language and language anchors thought. *Śabdanā*, 'languageing', is thinking; and thought 'vibrates' through language. In this way of looking at things, there cannot be any essential difference between a linguistic unit and its meaning or the thought it conveys. *Sphoṭa* refers to this non-differentiated language-principle. Thus I believe that it is sometimes even incorrect to ask whether *sphoṭa* is or is not the meaning-bearing speech unit in Bhartṛhari's system.

III

Bhartṛhari begins the discussion of his theory by a reference to the distinguishing of the two aspects of language by his predecessors. In verse I.44 he says that the linguists comprehend two types of *śabda* among the *upādāna śabda*, linguistic sound: one is the causal root of its manifestation and the other is applied, being manifested, to convey meaning. Of these two, the second is the linguistic unit properly understood, it is the real language, while the first is what 'manifests' or 'expresses' it. Bhartṛhari, and following him some later grammarians, related this duality to what I shall call the *sphoṭa-nāda* distinction of language. *Nāda* manifests *sphoṭa* and *sphoṭa* conveys meaning. We need to explain such expressions as 'manifests' and 'expresses'. The *sphoṭa* is an indivisible unit, a partless, sequenceless whole, which is connected with the verbal dispositional ability of the speaker or the hearer. For the sake of communication between language-users, *sphoṭa* needs to be made explicit, i.e., potentiality must be actualised, so that the bearer may receive it. This cannot be done without *nāda*, the sequential utterances of sound-elements. This is how the *nāda* becomes the causal factor for making *sphoṭa* explicit. The speaker cannot but utter *nāda* in a particular sequence, and *nāda* therefore reveals *sphoṭa* in this way appears (falsely) to have parts and temporal sequences just as the moon reflected in wavy waters appears to be wavy and disintegrated. Since the *nāda* is also identified with the *sphoṭa*, certain spurious features are superimposed on the *sphoṭa*.

The sounds uttered by the speaker make the real linguistic units, primarily a sentence, explicit, but this is the *sphoṭa* of the speaker. *sphoṭa* is also shared by the hearer, and as a result the hearer's *sphoṭa* is 'awakened' by the utterance of the speaker. This awakening of the hearer's *sphoṭa* is what is called the comprehension by the hearer of the sentence uttered. This is what is meant by the claim that the sentence uttered must 'already be present' in the hearer. From the point of view of the speaker, however, the *sphoṭa* 'already present in him' will be the causal condition for the *nāda* or the sequential word utterance, which will convey the *sphoṭa* to the hearer.

The metaphysical view of Bhartṛhari is that whatever is called *śabda*, language and *artha*, 'meaning', 'thought' or 'things meant', are one and undifferentiated in their pre-verbal or potential state. Before the utterance, it is argued, the language along with whatever it conveys or means is like the yolk of a peahen's egg. In that state all the variegated colours of a full-grown peacock lie dormant in potential form. Later these colours are actualised. Similarly in the self of the speaker or hearer, or whoever is gifted with linguistic capability, all the variety and differentiation of linguistic items and their meanings exist as potentialities, and language and thought are identical at that stage. Bhartṛhari even believes that the nature of the self is nothing but identical with the nature of language-thought. This state of complete identity of language with thought is called the *paśyantī* stage of language. Before the proper articulation of the sound-sequence or utterance, there is another 'intermediate' stage (called *madhyamā vāk*) where the language and the thought it conveys are still one and undifferentiated, but at this 'pre-verbal' stage the speaker sees them as differentiable. In other words, he recognises the verbal part, which he is about to verbalise either to himself or to another, as distinct and separable from the *artha*, meaning or thought'. This perception impels him to speech which results in the *nāda-sphoṭa* differentiation.

It may be useful to quote here some relevant verses of Bhartṛ hari to underline the *sphoṭa-nāda* distinction.

Verse I.44: Linguists (*śabdavidah*) comprehend two types of *śabda* among linguistic *śabda*. One is the *nimitta* of the sound and the other designates the object or meaning.

Commentary: In the sequenceless nature of the speech (*vāk*) both powers, the power to be articulated in sound (audible form) and the power to convey meaning, lie intermixed.

Verse I.46: Just as light/fire (*jyotih*) resides in the *araṇi* stick and (being manifested) becomes the cause for manifesting other objects, *śabda* resides likewise in the Mind (inner faculty, *buddhi*) and (being manifested) becomes separately the cause for manifesting the meaning ('as well as itself' added in the commentary).

Verse I.48: Since *nāda* (sound) arises in sequence, *sphoṭa*, which has neither a former nor a latter stage and which is sequenceless (*akrama*), is apprehended (through *nāda*) and appears to be having a sequence as well as parts.

Verse I.49: (Thus, properties of *nāda* are transferred to the *sphoṭa*.) The reflected image (of the moon, for example) although it resides in a separate location, seems to share the operation (i.e., movement of the waves in water) of objects in a separate location; *sphoṭa* being manifested in *nāda* shares the properties of *nāda* in the same way.

Verse I.52: A figure being grasped by a single awareness is painted on a canvas (part by part) into another complete, unitary figure (for the viewer to grasp it in one sweep). Similarly in *śabda*, too, all these three stages are found.

Verse I.53: The speaker apprehends beforehand the entire *śabda*, with regard to which the hearer's awareness also arises.

Verse I.55: Just as fire has both powers—the power to be the object of manifestation and the agent of manifestation—all *śabdas* individually have both powers likewise. (Fire in manifesting itself manifests others; *śabda*, too, in manifesting itself manifests others.)

Verse I.56: (For this reason) *śabdas* do not convey meaning without themselves being the objects of our awareness. They cannot manifest or reveal the meanings simply by their existence, if they (themselves) remain unapprehended.

Verse I.57: Hence, when from indistinct utterance, the form of the *śabda* is not apprehended, one asks 'what did he say?' But when the senses reveal objects, those senses do not need to be apprehended themselves.

IV

How is the *sphoṭa-nāda* distinction comprehended? Or, we may rephrase the question: how is 'language' comprehended? We have seen that Bhartṛhari has posited three stages of language or speech. The first stage, where there is complete identity of language and thought, is called the *paśyantī* stage; we can call it 'non-verbal'. The 'intermediate' stage, where despite the identity of thought and language their difference is discernible, can be called the 'pre-verbal' stage. And the third, the *vaikharī* stage, can be called the 'verbal' stage. This is how the matter stands from the speaker's point of view. But how does the hearer comprehend it? Bhartṛhari states four different views on this point.

According to some, *sphoṭa* is cognised as identical with the sound or *nāda*. One who grasps the *nāda* grasps the *sphoṭa* at the same time. Since basically the sound or *nāda* is identical with the *sphoṭa*, and they are so to say only two sides of the same coin, the grasping of one cannot be distinguished from that of the other. In other words, he who has not grasped one has not grasped the other. The commentator has supplied a beautiful analogy to elucidate the point. When a piece of crystal is placed near a red *japā* flower, the piece (of crystal) cannot be grasped or perceived without the colour red, for it now certainly appears red because of the proximity of the red flower. The *sphoṭa* is likewise comprehended along with the *nāda* that manifests it, one grasps the bits of language as sound or utterance, i.e., the *sphoṭa* as the *nāda*. It is not clear whether this analogy can be taken to imply that the *nāda* is only a superimposed feature of the *sphoṭa*, the real language. For, the piece of crystal is only apparently red due to the conditional superimposition; in reality it is colourless. If the implicit idea is that the *nāda* or sound is an inessential, conditionally superimposed feature of the real language or the *sphoṭa*, then I do not think this would be in exact accord with the doctrine of Bhartṛhari. Perhaps the analogy is not to be taken too far. It may be that simply the identification of the *nāda* with the *sphoṭa* is what is implied. In that case, this may well be Bhartṛ hari's own view. The analogy between a piece of crystal and a bit of language was again used by Bhartṛhari in *kāṇḍa* 3 of *Vākyapadīya*. But the purpose of that analogy was probably different. It was to illustrate a point of Bhartṛhari's semantics. Objects meant by bits of language are only created by the language, for language is autonomous just as a piece of crystal is believed to be autonomous (according to the pre-scientific theory of light) in the sense that it 'reflects' objects by according an autonomous status to them (the reflector modifies the object in its own way). This analogy has been used with great ingenuity by R. Herzberger in her exposition of Bhartṛhari's semantics (Herzberger, 1986, 50–3). However, in the context of our comprehension of the *sphoṭa* through *nāda*, the 'crystal' analogy might serve a slightly different purpose. We grasp the *sphoṭa* as reflected in the *nāda*, and as almost identical with the *nāda* itself, just as we grasp redness as presented by the piece of crystal, not in any other way.

Bhartṛhari refers to a second view held by some: that the comprehension of the *sphoṭa* does not require the comprehension of sounds or *nāda* as a condition. A tentative argument is given in favour of this view. We know that when we cognize an object, say a pot, through visual perception, we do so through the instrumentality of the faculty of vision, the eye, and it is an established fact that we do not need to know the properties or features of the eye-organ itself. The fact that we have the eye-organ is enough, for this only is relevant for the knowledge of the object. Similarly we comprehend the *sphoṭa* through the instrumentality of *nāda*, sounds. Patanjalī has contended that sound is the attribute of the *sphoṭa*. Now when the *sphoṭa* is presented through sounds, we comprehend it right away even prior to our cognition of all the sound-symbols, though the latter is indicative of the former. In other words, in this view the cognition of the sounds themselves is not needed prior to our cognition of the *sphoṭa*. Bhartṛhari has criticized this view, saying that as long as the sounds are uttered they are also directly perceived by our sense of hearing. Hence it is impossible to comprehend the *sphoṭa* without comprehending the sounds. The view, as it stands, is indeed peculiar. Perhaps the upholders of this view were unconsciously arguing in favour of a distinction between sound-tokens and sound-types, and they accordingly wanted to say that we do not need to cognise the sound-types over and above the sound-tokens prior to our comprehension of the *sphoṭa*. Sometimes, it may be pointed out, we comprehend the *sphoṭa* even when only a part of the relevant sound-token is heard.

The third and fourth views mentioned by Bhartṛhari were also obscure. There were a few thinkers who apparently believed in the metaphysical existence of the *sphoṭa* but maintained that it could not be amenable to perception. The reason adduced further confounds the issue, for it is said that the distance that separates the *sphoṭa* from the cognising hearer makes the *sphoṭa* imperceptible. The upholders of the fourth view understood the matter in another way. Distance cannot make the *sphoṭa* imperceptible but can render it rather indistinguishable! In other words, since distance does not remove the object from the field or perception, it can render the *sphoṭa*, like an object at a distance, indistinguishable from the environment. Thus, we fail to perceive *sphoṭa* as a distinct entity. Bhartṛhari obviously rejected these views, and it is difficult to make sense of their notion of *sphoṭa*.

There is an obvious problem when we say that the sequential and atomic-*nāda* units in combination reveal or manifest the indivisible, impartite *sphoṭa*. The problem is similar to the problem of perception: how do the parts present the whole? If they present it partially, then the whole will never be presented, in one sweep and this will cast doubt upon the contention about the reality of the whole over and above the constituents out of which it is formed. For the grammarians, the *sphoṭa* is a whole and it is a metaphysical entity, neither an object of construction, nor an abstraction. So the question arises: How do we perceive it from the utterance of a divisible and sequential sound-stretch? How is the unity perceived through the presentation of plurality? Thus by stating that the sound-stretch manifests the *sphoṭa* we do not explain much or answer the crucial question: How? For surely separate efforts are required to produce different sounds and they are produced in succession. At which point exactly is the unity that we call *sphoṭa* comprehended? If the unity is cognised at every instant from the beginning, then there is the fault of repetition and redundancy! If it is by the last (utterance of the) sound-unit then all the preceding units (or their utterances) are superfluous, for they have been destroyed at the time of comprehension.

Bhartṛhari answers this objection as follows: For the sake of convenience, let us use the illustration of a word-*sphoṭa* '*gauḥ*' (the cow). There is a unity here, the word. But the four sound-units or letters, *g*, *a*, *u*, and *ḥ*, present the *sphoṭa*, each individually. Bhartṛhari says that each letter here is the medium of manifestation of the unity, the whole *sphoṭa*. The problem of repetitiveness or redundancy is avoided by postulating a difference or a distinct property (*viśeṣa*) each time in the resulting awareness or comprehension. The first letter (or the first sound-unit) shows the whole, but very indistinctly. It becomes gradually clearer and progressively better understood through successive stages until the last unit is uttered. Although the earlier units disappear when the last unit is reached, the memory-impressions left behind by those earlier units are in the hearer and each time there is a qualitative difference in the memory-impression (*saṃskāra*). The *sphoṭa* itself does not admit of any qualitative or quantitative difference, addition or subtraction, but the impression or image of it may be imperfect and different, due to the imperfect nature of the human intellect. Our memory-impression may be dim or partial, clear or unclear, on various occasions, but the object, *sphoṭa*, will always shine in its undimmed glory.

It may be further argued that Bhartṛhari's explanation of the comprehension of *sphoṭa* is unsatisfactory. For certainly the letters of sounds, *g*, *a*, *u* and *h*, reveal themselves only individually. That is, we perceive each unit as it is produced. When we produce *g* or *a*, it must be perceived as *g* or *a*. But *gauh* is not *g* or *a*. The *sphoṭa* is not identical with any of the individual sound-units. To perceive something x as what it is not, is to misperceive x. We call it error. It is somewhat unparsimonious to first postulate an entity like the *sphoṭa* of *gauh* and then claim that it is only misperceived in the first, second or third letter, *g*, *a*, *u*. Besides, each misperception is based upon recognition of some similarity between the object present and the object superimposed. In the present case, it is difficult to obtain any satisfactory account of such a series of misperceptions. Bhartṛhari gives a bold reply to this criticism which also has the metaphysical underpinnings of his *sphoṭa* doctrine. He says that just as the cognition of the lower numbers, 'one' and 'two', is the means for understanding a higher number, say, 'three', although they are each distinct and different, similarly, comprehension of the *sphoṭa*, either a *pada-sphoṭa* or a *vākya-sphoṭa*, is invariably conditioned by the cognition of the so-called constituents, either the sound, *g*, *a*, *u*, *h* or the word-elements 'Devadatta' and 'goes' (in the *sphoṭa* as a sentence 'Devadatta goes'). This presupposes an understanding of the *Vaiśeṣika* theory of numbers. According to this theory, numbers are distinct from one another and they constitute separate entities, and all numbers higher than one are produced by a sort of 'connective-comparative' cognition called *apekṣābuddhi*. This is the notion that brings many unities under one number or another. When two things are present, one cognises both as 'this is one and that is one'. This is the 'connective-comparative' cognition that gives rise to the awareness of 'two' or duality, and similarly with each succeeding number. In this theory understanding of the previous number is the conditioning factor for the awareness of the higher number. Similarly understanding of the distinct sounds or distinct word-elements is the means for the awareness of the combined unity, the *sphoṭa*. Besides, Bhartṛhari claims that for the *sphoṭa*, or what he would call the *real* language, to convey some meaning to the hearer, it is an essential and unavoidable condition that it be made explicit through the sequential and transitory *nāda* elements. Just as an episode of knowledge cannot be known or talked about without any reference to what it represents or what is known by it, similarly the *sphoṭa* cannot communicate or convey any meaning (or be known) without its being manifested through the sequential *nāda* or speech. To have a clear perception of a tree, for example, we must proceed from a distance step by step when the vague and indistinct blur gradually gives way to a distinct shape and identity. Similarly the *sphoṭa*, through steps or sequences, is distinctly understood and identified. Bhartṛhari claims that a man who has mastered the *śabdayoga* or obtained the light of the Eternal Verbum (some sages have apparently succeeded in this) can perceive or understand the *sphoṭa* clearly when the first sound is heard, just as a man with perfect vision or unlimited power of sight (if such a man exists) can see the tree distinctly even from a distance. Comprehension of the *sphoṭa* is equivalent to such a distinct vision of reality.

V

Bhartṛhari has noted also that there is no unanimity among his predecessors regarding the real nature of the *sphoṭa*. He refers to several earlier views. According to one, the *sphoṭa* is the *universal* manifested by the individuals which are *nāda* elements or sounds. The *sphoṭa* is thus the class, of which sounds would be members. The commentary quotes a line from the *Mahābhāṣya* of Patanjali, where the word *sphoṭa* is used in the sense of the universal. It is the universal of the word *gauḥ*, not the universal called word-ness. We may call it the word-form, realized through the sequential utterance of the sounds. Some later commentators (cf. Bhaṭṭoji) apparently have taken the class-*sphoṭa* theory as Bhartṛhari's own. But this is a mistake, and the claim of some modern scholars to the effect that *sphoṭa* is nothing but a postulation of a unitary word-universal should be rejected. Another view mentioned by Bhartṛhari regards *sphoṭa* as an impermanent entity, produced by the initial sounds resulting from the contacts and separations of the vocal organs. The initial sounds themselves constitute the *sphoṭa*, they do not manifest it. But these sounds, despite being momentary, produce further sounds which thus spread in all directions, gradually decreasing in intensity, and reach the hearer's organ as *nāda*. The sound produced initially is the *sphoṭa*, other sounds produced in reverberation are 'sound-produced' sounds (*dhvani* or *nāda*). Another view modifies this position, in that it understands both *sphoṭa* and *nāda* to be produced simultaneously through contacts and disconnection of vocal organs. They are like the flame and the light of a lamp. We produce both the flame and the light at the same time. The light 'travels', so does the reverberation. The flame is fixed in one place, and so is the *sphoṭa*, according to this view. None of these views would be acceptable to Bhartṛhari. His idea of *sphoṭa* is different, as already described.

Bhartṛhari draws another interesting distinction between two types of sounds in this connection. They are called the 'primary' sounds (*prākṛta*) and the 'derived' or 'transformed' sounds (*vaikṛta*). The usual way to take the 'primary' sounds is to refer to the linguistically relevant sound-sequences which the speaker intends to produce and the hearer expects to hear. It is the shared 'speech' which manifests *sphoṭa* (where the *sphoṭa* can be *prakṛti*, the 'original', and hence the *prākṛta* is the manifestor of the 'original'). These primary sounds are not abstractions, but ideal particulars which have sequences, duration and other qualities—all specified by the particular language system. The long sounds should be long, of required length, the short vowels should be short and so on. But this must be conceived as divested of all personal idiosyncrasies or 'mannerisms' of the speaker who utters them. It is the norm. The non-linguistic concomitants of any utterance are to be separated from this notion of 'primary' sound. This type of sound is also said to be identified with the *sphoṭa*, though of course wrongly, for the *sphoṭa* is conceived as a sequenceless, durationless and partless whole. In other words, one (wrongly) cognises the *sphoṭa* as united with this 'primary' sound-series.

The 'secondary' or 'transformed' sounds may therefore be taken to be the individual instances of utterance that either reverberate or continue to show the individual peculiarities of the speakers, various differences in intonation, tempo, pitch, etc. The description here is a bit obscure, for it is also said that the manifestation of the *sphoṭa* still continues to happen or take place (after the first manifestation by the 'primary' sounds) with the help of the 'transformed' or 'secondary' sounds. 'Difference in the speed of utterance' (*vṛttibheda*) is also a factor in the 'transformed' sounds. They continue to manifest the *sphoṭa* again and again uninterruptedly for a longer period. They are said to resemble the light of a lamp which travels and continues to reveal the object as long as the lamp is lit. If this analogy is not very helpful, we may try another characterisation. It is said that the slow utterance of a short *a* sound does not turn it into a long *a* sound, nor does speedy utterance of the latter turn it into the former. The primary sounds *a* or *ā* are unchanged although the speed becomes a factor in the 'transformed' sound. In his commentary on the *Mahābhāṣya*, Bhartṛhari again refers to this distinction, but the matter there is further complicated by a reference to the two kinds of primary sounds (Iyer, 1969, 171). Kunjunni Raja's description of the 'primary' sound as the acoustic image or the abstract sound pattern is much too influenced by a knowledge of modern linguistics (Kunjunni Raja, 1969, 120). That the 'transformed' sound may be just 'reverberations' after the utterance (of the primary sounds) which reveal the *sphoṭa* is a possible interpretation which receives support front Helaraja in his commentary on the third *kāṇḍa* of the *Vākyapadīya*. But by 'reverberation' we need not think of the echo or returning sound but extend its sense to include the continuous producing of the sound-series after the initial sound is produced by the impact of the vocal organs. This may presuppose the *Vaiśeṣika* theory of sound, according to which the first sound is produced by impact, etc., and is believed to be a momentary entity, which dies at the next instant but nevertheless generates another *similar* sound-individual, which in its turn generates another before being destroyed in the next moment, and so on. This process continues for a while and then stops (on reaching the hearer's organ). How long the process will continue and how far it will 'travel', will depend upon the intensity of the originally produced sound. Bhartṛhari does not contribute to the *Vaiśeṣika* theory of sound-production, but it seems that he would accept this process of sound-travel with one crucial change made in the theory—instead of talking about production of a new sound at every moment, we should talk about the new manifestation of the same sound at every moment during its persistence.

VI

Bhartṛhari's philosophy of language is ultimately grounded in a monistic and idealistic metaphysical theory. He speaks of a transcendental word-essence (*śabdatattva*) as the first principle of the universe. His *sphoṭa* doctrine is finally aligned with the ultimate reality called *śabda-brahman.* A self-realised person attains unity with the word-principle—a man of perfect knowledge. There is no thought without language, no knowledge without word in it. Consciousness vibrates through words, and such vibrating consciousness or a particular cognitive mode motivates us to act and obtain results. Hence language offers the substratum upon which human activity is based. Language and meaning are not two separate realities such that one *conveys* the other. They are in essence the two sides of the same coin. The *sphoṭa* is this unitary principle where the symbol and what is signified are one. To understand each other's speech and to communicate, we do separate the inseparable, the sound and its sense. This is only instrumental to our mutual understanding. At the ultimate level, they are one. Bhartṛhari talks about three kinds of *sphoṭa*: letter- or sound-*sphoṭa*, word-*sphoṭa* and sentence-*sphoṭa*, but his primary interest lies with the sentence-*sphoṭa*. He underlines the importance and primacy of the sentence in language analysis in the second *kāṇḍa* of *Vākyapadīya.*

The sentence is the unit of communication. According to Bhartṛ hari it is a unity, a whole, and not the result of joining together smaller units called words. The sentence-meaning is likewise a whole, not constituted by word meanings put together. The *Mīmāṃsakas* apparently believed that the sentence and the sentence-meaning are produced by joining the smaller units, words and word-meanings together. Bhartṛhari examines five different definitions of the sentence put forward by the *Mīmāṃsakas*.

1. The sentence is a 'collection' (*saṃghāta*) or words, and each word has a certain meaning of its own. When it is used in a sentence, it conveys the same meaning. But when the words are linked in a sentence, then, through mutual linkage, an additional meaning is given to the whole unit. Thus the sentence-meaning is the 'mutual linkage' (*saṃsarga*).
2. The sentence is the 'sequence' (*krama*) of words, and the sentence-meaning belongs to this sequence. But since sequence is a property of time, one has to superimpose it upon the linguistic units called words.

Both views uphold an extreme form of atomism and are ascribed, later on in history, to the Bhaṭṭa school of *Mīmāṃsakas*. This Bhaṭṭa theory has been nicknamed *abhihitānvaya*, 'designation followed by (syntactic) connection', theory. In simple language, it means: words designate their meanings and then the meanings are brought together to give the sentence-meanings.

3. A sentence must have a finite verb, and we may even say that the finite verb is the sentence, for all the other words would be required in any case to be connected with the verb. Hence if we understand the verb, we understand the sentence, all the other *kāraka*-words being understood. The sentence-meaning, on this view, is of the nature of an action or process. It is the dependence of the meanings of other words on that of the verb that makes the sentence-meaning possible.
4. Even the very first word can be called the sentence, for the meaning of the sentence is already contained in, though only vaguely or partially expressed by, the first word.
5. A further modification of the above view is that each word in the sentence contains the whole sentence-meaning, though it is only partly revealed by it.

These last three views are supportive of a sort of contextualism. Words may have isolated meanings, but when they are in isolation they cannot express such separate or isolated meanings or meaning-atoms. Each word in connection with another word has a designation (meaning), which we should call 'connected designation'; it designates a connected entity. This is ascribed later on to the Prābhākara school of *Mīmāṃsakas*, and nicknamed *anvitābhidhāna*, 'connected designation'. The idea is that since, in order to talk about a word, we talk about a word used in some sentence or other, its meaning cannot be known in isolation. We must necessarily talk about the word's contextual meaning or rather its meaning in connection with the meanings of other words in the sentence.

Bhartṛhari refutes all these five notions of the sentence, and rejects both atomism and the sort of contextualism that has been defended by the second group of *Mīmāṃsakas*. He puts forward instead a holistic framework and argues that a sentence might be understood as an indivisible *sphoṭa*. The sentences as well as their meanings are indivisible units. It is for the sake of convenience as well as for facilitating our learning and understanding of a language, that we break the wholes into parts and smaller units and correlate words and word-meanings. The indivisible sentence is either internal to the language-user (any member of the speech-community) or external to him. It is externalised through its manifestation in speech or *nāda*. And through such manifestation it appears to have divisions (and this is true of both the sound-aspect and the meaning-aspect), although essentially it remains indivisible. In other words, appearance of divisibility of sentences and sentence-meanings is deceptive. It is like the 'cognition of multiplicity (*citra-jñāna*). Although the cognition in such cases is one and indivisible, one sees plurality in it. A drink from the punch bowl will have a plurality of flavours and tastes, but it is one and a unique drink—a whole.

Bhartṛhari underlines this indivisibility aspect by offering three more definitions of the notion of the sentence in addition to the five already mentioned.

6. The sentence is the class of the sequences of words, or the universal resident in the sequence of words. Or,

7. It is the whole string of words without any divisible part.

Both these definitions refer to what has been called the 'external' *sphoṭa* above. The former regards the sentence as a universal while the later regards it as a particular whole. Technically the later grammarians called them the *jāti-sphoṭa* and the *vyakti-sphoṭa*, respectively.

8. The last definition refers to what has been called 'internal' *sphoṭa*. The sentence is a whole piece of cognitive awareness.

These three so-called definitions may be just recognition of the three different levels of the realisation of the same *sphoṭa* or three different ways of capturing the same reality, *sphoṭa*, the sentence. The sentence-meaning in all these cases is declared to be given by *pratibhā*, i.e., by a 'flash of understanding' of what is being communicated. This flash of understanding is also declared to be holistic. We do not obtain it bit by bit. That is why some people are said to understand the meaning of the sentence even before the utterance of the whole sentence.

Several points are not made clear here. The correlation between the 'external' and the 'internal' *sphoṭa* must be a crucial factor here. For, an ordinary sentence with indexicals, be it in the form of a universal of the sound-sequence or a concrete and particular sound stretch, will have to have a different *sphoṭa* as the speaker, time and place change. This distinction can be maintained by associating the external sound-pattern with the 'internal' *sphoṭa* of the speaker, which reveals itself to him at a particular time and place. This question has not been raised in this way and therefore the answer has not been given or discussed. Besides, if the *sphoṭa* is the *real* language or a particular language system, as Bhartṛhari seems to imply, we must apply the word 'language' in an extended sense, not to a system or string of sound-units having sense, but to what is only made explicit in a system-of-sound-units, not, that is, to the *nāda* exclusively, but to what is 'manifested' by *nāda*, the *sphoṭa*.

Bibliography

Bhaṭṭoji-Dīkṣita. *Śabdakaustubha*, Vol. I, ed. Rāmakṛṣṇa Śāstrī; Vol. II, ed. Vindheśvarī Dvivedin and Gaṇapati Sāstrī Mokate, Chowkhamba Sanskrit Series, Varanasi, 1898–1917.

Biardeau, M. *Theorie de la Connaissance et Philosophic de la Parole dans le Brahmanisme Classique*, Paris, 1964.

Brough, John. 'Theories of General Linguistics in the Sanskrit Grammarians', *Transactions of the Philological Society*, 1951, 21–46.

Cardona, George. *Panini: A Survey of Research*, Mouton & Co., The Hague and Paris, 1976.

De, S. K. *Studies in the History of Sanskrit Poetics*, Luzac & Co., London, 1925.

Herzberger, R. *Bhartṛhari and the Buddhists*, Studies of Classical India Series No. 8, D. Reidel Publishing Co., Holland, 1986.

Iyer, S. *Bhartṛhari*, Deccan College, Poona, 1969.

Joshi, S. D. *The Sphoṭa-nirṇaya of Kaundabhaṭṭa*, Poona, 1967.

Keith, A. B. *A History of Sanskrit Literature*, Oxford University Press, Oxford, 1928.

Kunjunni Raja, K. *Indian Theories of Meaning*, Adyar Library, Madras, 1969.

Sastri, G. A. *The Philosophy of Word and Meaning*, Sanskrit College, Calcutta, 1959.

21

M. Hiriyanna

Ever since Bharata postulated his theory of *rasas*, the exact number of *rasas* has been a debated issue. The more orthodox view has been that there are only eight *rasas*, while another view proposes nine *rasas*. Both these have found able advocates over the centuries. The ninth disputed *rasa* is named the *śāntarasa,* which has been closely analysed by Abhinavagupta in his chapter on that topic. The issue has been raised in the twentieth century once again. The most scholarly commentary on it was written by V. Raghavan in his The *Number of Rasas* (The Adyar Library, Madras, 1940). Raghavan's work is a compendium of views, for and against the inclusion of *śānta* in the gamut of *rasas*. A lucid summary of Raghavan's comments is included in M. Hiriyanna's *Art Experience* (Kavyalaya, Mysore, 1954). An excerpt from it (pp. 62–64) is reproduced here.

The Number of *Rasas*

Owing to the uncertainty of our knowledge of the early phase of Indian classical literature, it is not possible to say when poets began to portray this *rasa*. The ascetic and mystic elements, however, which form its distinctive basis, are very old features of Indian life; and they were highly valued by those who followed the teaching of the Veda as well as by those who did not. So we may assume that the *śānta* attitude found expression in literature quite early; and this is corroborated by the works of Aśvaghoṣa even if, on account of its chronological indefiniteness, we leave out of consideration the *Mahābhārata*, the useful example given of the *śānta rasa*. As regards writers on poetics, the earliest to recognise it definitely, so far as our knowledge at present goes, was Udbhaṭa. Possibly its recognition by them was even earlier. Bharata's view in the matter is somewhat doubtful, by reason of the unsatisfactory character of the *Nāṭyaśāstra* as it has come down to us. Some manuscripts of it mention only eight *rasas*, but others nine. The weight of evidence bearing on the point seems, on the whole, to be on the former side; and Dr Raghavan adduces several convincing arguments to show that the references to this *rasa* in Bharata are all spurious. But it should be added that the *Nāṭyaśāstra* contains nearly all the essential points necessary for a theoretical formulation of it.

Before we pass on to the aesthetic aspect of the question, it is desirable to distinguish the emotive content or theme of a literary work from the aesthetic sentiment which, according to the prevalent Indian view, its idealised presentation evokes in the reader or the spectator. Thus in the case of the *Śākuntala*, Duṣyanta's love for Śakuntalā forms the chief theme while the emotion, which it awakens in us as we witness the drama enacted, is *śṛngāra*. When we ask whether *śānta* can be a *rasa*, we mean whether situations in life involving the quietistic sentiment lend themselves to be similarly dealt with in literature. If they do, then *śānta* is a *rasa*; otherwise it is not. The practice of great poets like Kālidāsa, which is after all the true touchstone in such matters, shows that *śānta* situations can certainly be thus delineated in literary works. In the last act of his play, just alluded to, Kālidāsa describes the tranquility and holiness of Mārica's hermitage in a manner which affects us most profoundly. But, however splendidly depicted, the *śānta rasa* occupies only a subordinate place there; and a doubt may therefore arise whether it can be the leading sentiment in a work, i.e., whether it can be portrayed in such a manner that it will impress us at the end as the predominant element in the unity of *rasas* which, according to the Indian view, every work of art is expected to achieve. Some of the works of Aśvaghoṣa, to whom I have already referred, show that it can be so represented. The *Mahābhārata* also, at any rate in its present form, illustrates the truth, as set forth by Ānandavardhana in his masterly way in the last section of *Dhvanyāloka*.

Yet there were theorists who denied that the *śānta* could be an art emotion. It is hardly necessary to examine their arguments when we have the practice of great poets and the opinion of great art critics to the contrary. But a reference should be made to one of them which appears, at first sight, to possess some force. This argument is that the attitude of mind for which *śānta* stands is altogether a rare one, and that its representation in art cannot therefore appeal to more than a very few. The objection, it is obvious, is based on the supposition that the test of true art is in the wideness of its appeal. The advocates of *śānta* brush this argument aside usually by saying that such questions are not to be decided by a plebiscite; but, by thus admitting the narrowness of its appeal, they seem to give up their position. Their conclusion is that *śānta* as a *rasa* is irresistible. Indeed, it would have been a strange irony of circumstance if Indians, of all, had excluded it from the sphere of art. The way in which this particular objection is met, however, is not satisfactory. May it be that the contention that the appeal of *śānta* is only to a very few is wrong? No unwonted occasion in life—whether it be one of joy or one of sorrow—passes without bringing home to man the supreme desirability of spiritual peace. It means that the need for such peace is fundamental to the human heart; and this conclusion is confirmed by the pure satisfaction which the contemplation, for example, of the images of Buddha in meditative repose brings to many. If so, the *śānta* mood is by no means uncommon; and the *śānta rasa* need not be an exception to the rule that the appeal of art is general. What is uncommon is the capacity in man to capture that mood and cultivate it, so that it may come to prevail over all other moods; but this deficiency does not matter so far as art is concerned, for it has the power of itself to enable him to attain, albeit only for a while, the peace of spirit which, as an old Indian critic has observed, even a *yogin* has to strain himself long to win.

From Art Experience

22

R. B. Patankar

R. B. Patankar, who was Professor of English at the Bombay University till 1986 and taught aesthetics and criticism, is a bilingual critic. His major work is in Marathi and related to Marathi literature and criticism. Two of his monumental books, *Saundaryamimansa* (1972) and *Kantche Saundaryaśastra* (1984) have already acquired the status of critical classics in Marathi. He has a volume of essays in English, *Literature* and *Aesthetics* (1968). Patankar has published some practical criticism too, mainly dealing with modern Marathi fiction.

In three decades of an active critical career, Patankar gave Marathi criticism a certain climate of concerns related to conceptual clarity and terminological and methodological precision. He writes criticism about criticism; and as such, it was natural that he engaged himself in analysing the ideas of Western origin and Indian tradition. The *Saundaryamimansa* is such an examination and re-statement of ideas, concepts and terms.

The most important contribution of Patankar lies in his critique of Marathi literary aesthetics. The essay reproduced here was published in the *Journal of Arts & Ideas* No. 6, January–March 1984. It raises serious and fundamental issues related to the tradition and identity of Indian criticism. These issues have immediate relevance to literatures in other Indian languages too.

Aesthetics: Some Important Problems

Aesthetics is a much-respected, almost awe-inspiring subject in Maharashtra today. People are enthusiastic and inquisitive about it. A large number of articles and books are being written on the subject. Many people have claimed that Marathi writing on aesthetics has a significant contribution to make to world aesthetic thought. Such claims, not infrequently made, are wild. The fact of the matter is that we have not made any contribution to any discipline that is included in the general category known as Humanities. That is why nobody has made similar claims about our contribution to any social science (on the theoretical plane); or to ethics, epistemology, metaphysics. Nobody appears to have evinced the slightest interest in these subjects. It is indeed a great wonder that so much should have been done in aesthetics alone and absolutely nothing in any other field. This is all the more surprising because some of these neglected fields should have been our main preoccupation. But let us pause a little and ask: by what criteria is it to be judged whether we have actually achieved anything significant in the sphere of aesthetics?

To begin with we have to ascertain whether the necessary infra-structure, of the right variety and quality, was already there, to make the emergence of new aesthetic systems possible. This infrastructure has at least three aspects:

(A) There should exist new and powerful movements in different Arts, clamouring for new theoretical formulations which they hope would do better justice to them than the older, outmoded ones. Do such movements exist in today's (or yesterday's) Maharashtra? At least in the field of literature the picture is not very heartening. Absence of greatness in modern Marathi literature is a theme to which critics from B. S. Mardhekar (who, incidentally, was our first modern aesthetician) have repeatedly turned, and nobody has challenged this estimate of modern Marathi literature. This observation has certain theoretical implications. Aesthetic theories are conceived and grow in the womb of a living, developing art tradition. The aesthetician or the theoretical critic cannot take the place of the parents; his is a much humbler task, that of watching the steady growth of the foetus, to help it in this process, till it comes out in the world in a perfectly normal, healthy condition.

(B) Aesthetic theoretical structures are usually present in the language of practical criticism in an implicit form. The second precondition for the emergence of a new aesthetic theory therefore is the existence of a strong critical tradition. If criticism is to be good, the critic must have absorbed his literary tradition and have the ability and the inclination to explore all the minutiae of new literary works which he is faced with. He is expected to have acquired certain intellectual skills, because he has to study the aesthetic data supplied by a work of art and on that basis reason his way to evaluative judgment. From where does a critic get these intellectual skills? Of course, from the community, that is, if there is a strong intellectual tradition in it.

(C) The existence of this tradition is the third precondition that a community which boasts of having created new aesthetic theories must satisfy. Our practical criticism, by and large, has degenerated into smart, verbally titillating chat or verbal pyrotechnics. The content of our critical articles is usually meagre. Very often they tell us more about the critic than about a literary work. Critical articles which combine a comprehensive range and attention to minutiae are already an extinct species. Entertaining chat about books/authors has taken the place of serious articles. Anyway, what can one expect from the butterflies and grasshoppers who today go by the name of literary critics? Things are in very bad shape in the province of intellectual, discursive prose. We just do not have a tradition of intellectual prose. A Lokamanya Tilak here and a Dr Ketkar or Tarkateerth Laxmanshastri Joshi there do not constitute a tradition. Even if we assume that these few are our peaks, we must not forget that peaks by themselves do not constitute a mountain-range. A recent debate among Maharashtrian intellectuals about the merits of a history of Western philosophy in Marathi was both entertaining and saddening. Equally saddening is the Lawande–Patankar–Rege debate about Kant's relationship

> with Expressionism. All the debate shows is that we cannot yet distinguish between instruction and entertainment. The biting, exasperated attacks made by Prof. M. P. Rege on the poor quality of discursive prose in Marathi have had no effect, every writer complacently assuming that it was the others who were being attacked. We are *baddha* and, as always happens, we do not know that we are *buddh*. This intellectual poverty is not restricted to the field of literary criticism and aesthetics; it is present in every academic field.

The conclusion is obvious. If new aesthetic theories of world significance have begun to appear in a cultural group, even in the total absence of relevant traditions in the arts, criticism and discursive prose-writing, we are victims of an illusion. Extreme intellectual naivete alone is responsible for the Marathi fantasy—a world full of aesthetic *Pushpaks*.

Excessive importance is attached in Maharashtra to aesthetics because of an elementary misconception about the nature of the subject. It is believed that man can create an original aesthetic theory even if he is not deeply steeped in any artistic tradition and in all the important material on the subject; what one needs is nothing except original talent. But all this is a big illusion. Most Marathi thinking on the subject takes place within the Western framework. Aesthetics in the West is an age-old game. The first moves were made by Plato and Aristotle; later Kant and Hegel joined the game; it is being played today by people of similar calibre. Aristotle and Kant—or their eastern counterparts, Shankuka and Abhinavagupta—are giants; the present day Marathi theoreticians are to them what pebbles are to mountain peaks. What contribution can we hope to make to a game which was started and kept going by Aristotle and Kant? And this without first acquiring the preparatory materials and skills? We are qualified to make only a hesitant move and retire. If one is deluded into believing that one has done something more than this, one should, as a corrective, carefully read again—or, as would be the case with many, for the first time—Aristotle, Kant, Shankuka, Abhinavagupta. One will then realise that our so-called original theories have been suggested in passing by these great minds. As our scholarship develops, the illusions about our achievements will progressively melt. Once people realise the need for adequate knowledge—of art and theory—they will desist from writing on the subject on the strength of a brief acquaintance with an Osborne or a Santayana.

We shall have to modify a little our earlier statement about the absence of the threefold preparation needed for the creation of an aesthetic system. It is of course a fact, that we do not have any vigorous traditions. However, occasional attempts to move in the right direction appear to have been made. An occasional essay in practical criticism, which is comprehensive and which also goes into minutiae, a good critical survey of the literature of a particular period, an able treatise on a subject like imagery provide some, although meagre, evidence in support of this. But as these attempts try to exceed their present limits, difficulties crop up. For now we arc forced to face questions about our basic conceptual structure. Within which structure have we been functioning? What are our valuational criteria? What is our aesthetic tradition?

Everything that has taken place in India since ancient times obviously does not belong to our (i.e., modern Maharashtrians) *today*. By the twelfth century A.D. the vigorous Sanskrit traditions in imaginative and critical literature dried up. Today's writer cannot claim to have a living and comprehensive relation with them either on the creative or the critical plane. If we try to re-establish a relation with these there are two types of formidable obstacles in the way. It is true that we do now and then come across *Pundits* who discuss the Sanskrit poetic theories on an academic plane. But nobody would analyse a modern Indian play on the basis of the Sanskrit structuring principles of *sandhis* and *sandhvangas*. Nor do we get a detailed analysis and evaluation of a modern play in terms of *ālambana* and *vibhāvas*, *anubhāva*, *uddīpana*, *vyabhicāribhāvas*. Occasionally, we run into a critic who says that a particular novel is suffused with the *karuṇa rasa*. But he does not use the concepts of *vibhāva*, *sthāyibhāva*, *sādharaṇīkarṃa*. If the modern critic's responses do not spontaneously get articulated in the old Sanskrit theories, if these theories are not already there in the womb of the creative and critical processes of a modern man, these theories cannot be legitimately claimed to be part of our *today*. Secondly, the concepts which we spontaneously use today do not appear to have received due attention and emphasis in Sanskrit poetics. Sanskrit theoreticians agree that *rasas* are closely related to *puruśārthas*, the four ultimate goals of life. But Sanskrit poetics does not tell us how to discuss the moral problems presented in a contemporary novel, and, further, how to evaluate that novel in the light of this discussion. A play is today regarded as valuable on the ground that it gives an original and deep insight into life. These evaluations cannot be made from within the framework of Sanskrit Poetics. The above difficulties, it may be noted in passing, are not present, at least not in this degree, in the Greco-Roman framework. There is obviously nothing wrong in being proud of being Indians, but we should be more cautious in making claims on behalf of our Indian heritage. Indianness is a changing concept. We must constantly keep in mind that we are *today's* Indians and bear only a limited resemblance to our forefathers of the ninth or tenth centuries.

From the mid-nineteenth century onwards we imported through the medium of English some Western literary forms. We cultivated them partly in the Western and partly in our own ways, impoverished them and very rarely and in a negligible way enriched them. It was therefore only natural that we used the Western conceptual framework for the analysis and evaluation of literary works produced within these imported structures. These Western conceptual structures in the process of being assimilated in our changing identity, ultimately replaced our older structures. We should therefore frankly admit that today we spontaneously work within the Western framework, both as creative writers and as critics. To ask us to use theories like that of *rasa* will be a form of cultural tyranny. If we spontaneously begin to create literary works similar to those our forefathers created a thousand years ago, we shall equally spontaneously adopt the pre-Mammata critical framework. It will then not be necessary to persuade us to do this; we shall do it because we shall have no other alternative.

We were influenced most by the nineteenth-century—and to some extent by the eighteenth-century—English literature. We read even Shakespeare through nineteenth-century English eyes. The critical theory of this period was part of a long tradition of critical thinking from the Greek days to the modern age. This tradition, it is true, underwent changes, some of them major ones; but at no period was there a complete break. The artistic tradition in whose womb this theoretical tradition grew has also been in existence for over two thousand years. It also underwent major changes; but there was never a *complete break*. It looks as if the Greco-Roman tradition got lost in the Dark Ages. But it will not be a totally unwarranted guess to believe that it must have been alive at the deeper levels, maybe hibernating for a long period. The guess is not wild because if we do not accept it, we cannot explain the energetic re-awakening of the tradition during the Renaissance. There has been an equally long *intellectual tradition* in the West. This shows how the present West enjoys long and vital traditions of art, art-criticism and intellectual efforts in all fields. This explains the advance the West has made in different fields like aesthetics, moral and social philosophy, epistemology, logic, philosophy of science, metaphysics. Had this infrastructure been present in India we would have witnessed an equal advance in these and other fields. There is something to learn from this contrast. If we start in earnest to build the infrastructure today, in due course we shall be able to produce, if not the ethereal *pushpaka*, at least a couple of screws which might perhaps come in handy when we start making an aeroplane.

The first step that we have to take is to reject artificial aesthetic frameworks, accepted or assembled on a rarefied theoretical level, and attempt a spontaneous, undistorted, honest response to a literary work. If we analyse this response we shall begin to discern in it a conceptual structure and corresponding structural principles in its correlative, i.e. the literary work itself. This is sure to happen because the nature of a literary work and our spontaneous response to it are inter-dependent. In the principles underlying these structures there usually is a natural tendency towards universal expansion. To seek unity in multiplicity, to bring the largest possible diversity under a unifying principle is part of an inalienable human nature. One should not therefore feel surprised if a literary theorist who, after discerning expression of emotion as the most prominent feature in some poems, should try to extend it to all literature, and further to all arts. It is precisely here that one needs to exercise extreme caution; the complexity of human life calls for this caution; and yet the temptation not to exercise it is very strong. This reminds one of what Kant calls the transcendental illusion. At the time of sunrise or sunset the sun appears larger than it does at noon. We know that the size of the sun does not really undergo a change at the time it rises or sets. But even when this knowledge is firmly established in us we (including the scientists) continue to see that the size has changed. The theoretician in literature is subject to a similar illusion when he assumes that there must be one principle common to all literature. He has therefore to reconcile the impulse to unity with the awareness of multiplicity.

The insight that people have in the arts, if they have it at all, is usually restricted to one art or one of the varieties of a particular art, rarely to two. Let us suppose that a theoretician has obtained a genuine insight into fiction and drama. The concept of 'Probability' plays a significant role in them—at least in some of their varieties. Probability here is usually taken to mean statistical probability. If out of 100 cases x is followed by y in ninety cases it is taken as very probable that in the 91st case x will be followed by y. In a realistic novel to show that x follows y is to adhere to the principle of probability. In order to adhere to this principle the writer has to compare how things and events are connected in reality and in their literary representation. The claim that a representation of reality approximates truth depends upon whether the representation corresponds to the reality that it purports to represent. When the theoretician wants to extend the principle of probability to a non-literary art, for example, music, he is faced with a problem. How can the structure of a musical piece be compared with the structure of reality? A novel can be, and very often is, realistic. But it cannot be said that a musical piece is realistic. How can the principle of probability be applied to music? How can we decide that at a particular point in a musical piece, A is more *probable* than B? It is sometimes suggested that, between A and B, that which coheres better with the other constituents of the musical piece is more probable than the other. But this sense of probability is different from the sense of probability discussed earlier. Correspondence between reality and the artistic representation of reality appears to have been replaced by internal coherence in the constituents of the artistic whole. Two different theories of truth (correspondence theory and something like coherence theory) are implied in these two contexts and they ought not to be mixed up.

Once we have completely changed the meaning of probability to suit the context of music, can we still apply the term (in its changed sense) to literature? We can use it legitimately in its changed sense only while talking about fairy-tales. If its application is extended to realistic literature there will be chaos. It is possible to argue that the concept of probability in both its senses is applicable to a literary work. Does not Aristotle mention: (a) beginning–middle–end and (b) probability–necessity as two structuring principles in tragedy? Although this may be conceded, it must not be forgotten that dramatic representation can claim to be 'more philosophical than history' *only* on the basis of the second principle mentioned above. What is true of the concept of probability is equally true of the concept of rhythm. Can this concept which has spontaneously emerged in the art of music, and where alone it is certainly legitimate, be really applied in its original sense to the novels of Dostoevsky? One can of course apply it if one has placed a wager to do it and if one is willing to do violence to facts. Anything is possible for a 'clever' or a rash man. Such a man can, for example, prove that one common principle is present in things as different as Napoleon, the blue sky, a stone quarry, and cholera germs. The question is not what we *can* do; it rather is what we naturally, spontaneously do. In most contexts it will be seen that when a concept is transferred from its field of birth to another field it usually involves metaphorical extension of meaning to a large extent. If this is true, what is common to the two fields is only *one word*, but not one self-identical *concept*. To forget this is to extend an invitation to theoretical confusion.

We see here an amazing thing which is perhaps peculiar to a naive community like ours, adding to this confusion. The conceptual structure inherent in music will/can be discerned only by a musician and a discerning music critic. They alone are competent to tell the world what the nature of rhythm is and what its place is in the total conceptual structure underlying the musical world. But in our community it is mostly people whose acquaintance with the world of music is very slight who are found talking eloquently about the principle of rhythm and the nature of music as a whole. The loquacious critics working in the field of literature appear to be talking with equal authority on music, painting, and all the other arts. The musicians and music-critics do not know how to talk glibly about things as literary artists and critics do; they therefore are, or till recently have been, silent about their art. But it is a welcome sign that things are changing. Musicians and music-critics, who alone are competent to talk with authority about music are at last becoming vocal. Let us hope they in their turn do not make the mistake that literary critics have been making all along.

People who have attained some degree of sophistication and discipline in other intellectual fields show a surprising degree of naivete when they deal with concepts pertaining to the arts. That is probably because they do not pay equal attention to all aspects of the function of aesthetics; some are perhaps not aware of all these aspects or their importance. The aim of aesthetics is to analyse the statements which critics make about works of art and the concepts embedded in these statements. This analysis includes the study of (a) the logical peculiarities, and (b) the content/substance of the relevant concepts. Many people ignore (a) altogether and approach (b) directly, but soon get tied up in theoretical knots. It is therefore more fruitful if due attention is paid to (a) right from the beginning.

I shall illustrate my point with the help of a book called *Gārambichā Bāpu*. Soon after we have started reading it we realise that the book is a narrative—but it does not narrate what happened to actual men and women; it narrates fictional happenings; that it is a *novel* and it ought be read as a novel. This shows how classification is present right from the beginning of our process of reading anything. In other words, we do not merely read a book, we read it as a member of some kind/class.

Two questions arise here: the first is about the theoretical legitimacy of the process of classification and the second is about the concept *novel.* Some people hold that classification is in literary criticism only for practical convenience, but that such classification into literary forms or kinds has no *theoretical justification*. Benedetto Croce has taken this extreme position. He holds that the librarian, for his own convenience, classifies books and places them in different cupboards, which are then labelled as *Drama, Novel,* or *Miscellaneous.* Then begins the search of the theoretician who assumed that because all books in a particular cupboard are called 'Novels', they must share some principle or essence in common that needs to be discovered. We should thank our stars that critics have not as yet set out to look for the common essence of books placed in the cupboard labelled 'Miscellaneous'. Croce thus ridicules the concept of literary/artistic classification because, according to him, Art is a Genus which has members in it, but no species. But this is evidently wrong. Just as there cannot be an Indian who is not at the same time a Maharashtrian, a Gujarati, a Rajasthani, there cannot be a work of art which is not at the same time a painting, a literary work, a musical piece; there cannot be a literary work which is not a novel, a lyric, a play. Only a professional philosopher, particularly of the older school, will ask 'how do we identify a work of art, as a work of art'? A non-philosopher reader will ask a more specific question; 'Is the book that I am reading a novel? How can I know for certain that it is one? In some respects it is like *Jādugār, Kulābyāchi Dāndi,* but then...' It is only the latter, the more specific question that is important in the context of our discussion. And it presupposes classification. The problem of literary classification is important for another reason also. When we realise that the book we are reading is a novel a definite range of expectations is created in. us; different expectations are created, if we know that the book is a play; they become more specific if we realise that it is a musical play. Definite expectations are created if we know to which form of literature the book we are reading belongs because definite conventions are associated with definite forms. It is these conventions which, in a sense, define the limits of a form. Although they change in the course of history, it never happens that they are totally absent. Till now we have been considering the problem from the reader's point of view. What is true of a reader is equally true of a writer: By the time a writer is completing the first page of what he is writing he becomes (however vaguely it might be) aware, of the range of the literary kind in which he is writing. To cite an example from another field, a musician does not just begin to sing, he begins to sing a *Khyal* in a particular *Raga*. The process of learning and teaching music presupposes the concept of *Raga*; it is present with different degrees of explicitness in the teacher and the learner. It seems that the concept of a literary kind and a literary work are logically interconnected right from the moment the latter is conceived.

Evaluation of literary works is possible only because certain conventions and certain expectations with regard to them exist in a community. If we know that we are reading a social-realistic novel, we also know what to expect and what not to expect from it. We have already read many novels of the kind, their impressions have been synthesised and ordered in our minds, complex and elastic criteria for judging them have also been formed. This concept–value–criteria complex enables us to read a social-realistic novel as a social-realistic novel, and also judge whether it is successful At the same time we also look for newness, conscious departures from traditional conventions, experiments with regard to the substance, its comprehensiveness and subtlety, the work's organisation, technique, style, diction. For a literary work owes part of its value to its being new, different; both of these concepts (newness and difference) are relative and not absolute. Difference presupposes similarity; and newness implies the existence of conventions, tradition, history.

Awareness of literary classification is a necessary but not a sufficient condition for the production and criticism of a literary work. Our problem is how to accommodate in our conceptual structure both the universal and the particular.

We shall now address ourselves to the second of the two questions raised above. It is about the nature of concepts like that of the novel which a critic cannot avoid using. We must bear in mind the fact that it is far more difficult to decide whether a particular piece of writing is a novel, than to decide whether a particular animal is a dog, because concepts like 'novel', 'play', 'tragedy' are not rigidly closed as the concept 'dog' is. One cannot identify permanently usable criteria of these concepts. It is generally held that the novel as a form emerged in England around the eighteenth century. Right from the start it was not a rigidly closed concept; for one cannot identify an essence common to the earliest well-known novels like *Robinson Crusoe*, *Pamela*, *Tom Jones*, *Roderick Random*, *Tristram Shandy*; they appear to be related to each other by a network of similarities and differences. With the addition of new novels this network became wider and more complex. We cannot predict today how and in what direction this network will grow. A form like the novel becomes complex also on account of the introduction in it of certain features which are more characteristic of other forms. For example, occasionally the presence of dialogue in a novel becomes so pronounced that one is continuously reminded of the concept of drama. The combination of drama and music in Marathi musical plays is well known. Sometimes the element of 'action' in a short story is overwhelmed by that of free meditation, with some event as an excuse, and then it becomes very difficult to decide whether the story is really a story and not a meditative personal essay. This is, of course, a borderline case. The point to remember is that in other, everyday contexts also borderline cases exist, but they do not render the concept of classification invalid or unusable. For example, we can meaningfully use the concept of family-relationship, although it is difficult to decide whether one's second cousin is to be called a family-relation. The elasticity of the concept has proved to be useful, for we can go beyond one's brother and call one's first cousin a relation.

Since concepts like the novel or the drama are open in a large measure, a critic sometimes comes to the conclusion that he can dispense with such concepts altogether. But he soon realises that they are not dispensable. He then goes to the opposite extreme and tries to impose rigid discipline on these relatively open concepts; with a determined will he looks for the differentia of the novel, the drama, etc., and sooner or later announces that he has discovered them. For him all that now needs to be done is to use the differentia in the vast variegated field of concrete literary works. The relationship between theoretical criticism and criticism of particular literary works is conceived here as similar to that between science and technology. But this is a foolish error. The expressions 'practical' or 'applied' criticism commonly used by critics are highly misleading. A critic worth the name does not apply any abstractly conceived principles to concrete literary works. To try to apply such principles is to accept slavishly a discipline imposed from outside. Critics, whatever they may profess on the plane of theory, do not, indeed cannot work under an externally imposed discipline. Things of course work out differently if an extremely clever theoretician meets a group of extremely loyal, but less clever followers. They together can prove to be a disaster. But ordinarily a practising critic accepts complexity as a given fact and deals with it successfully. But the same complexity scares him stiff as soon as he rises to the level of theory. But if he were to study the logical features of the concepts he uses he would realise that all concepts do not have identical logical features. They are useful and usable precisely because of the differences among them. For analysing some concepts the Platonic one-essence model is adequate; for some others the Wittgensteinian family-resemblance model is more suitable. So long as human life continues to be what it is we cannot avoid using different models for analysing different concepts.

Till now, we have been discussing the validity of certain concepts, like kinds of literature and have examined their logical features.

The concepts are being constantly used and they make literary criticism possible. Keeping them at the centre, we shall now try to move a little in two directions. On the one hand we shall consider concepts with scope wider than that of the novel or the drama. At the same time we shall try to evaluate the extent of usefulness of these concepts of ever-widening ranges for the analysis and evaluation of individual literary works.

We shall, however, not look for the most general features of works of art or aesthetic objects as such. The differences among the arts and aesthetic objects will show anybody that our decision is sensible. We shall confine ourselves to concepts of a middle range. Poetry or literature considered as a whole might prove to be a good choice. In modern times some critics have tried to explore and formulate the distinguishing marks and structuring principles of poetry and literature. They have tried to do it in two ways. First, some theoreticians have placed literature in a large class which contains, besides literature proper, such categories as dreams, day-dreams, myths, fairy tales, contents of the racial unconscious, and ritual. That these critics who give great importance to these non-literary products should pay special attention to disciplines like psychology and anthropology, is very natural. There is no doubt that these extra-literary aids are important. But a word of caution is necessary here. We do not need these aids in the case of all literary works. In order to analyse some, we are not required to go beyond the level of everyday consciousness and explanation in terms of established conventions and common sense. The wisest strategy in these cases is not to go beyond these. If in some cases we are required to use extra literary aids we should acquire adequate mastery over them. This needs to be emphasised, for Indians today appear to be averse to scholarship of any kind. Further, in the case of literary works where the use of these aids is found to be indispensable, it is also often discovered to be inadequate. Both *Oedipus Rex* and *Hamlet* are explained with a large amount of success with the help of Freudian theories. Dr Ernest Jones's explanation of Hamlet's delay in avenging his father's murder is much more satisfying than many other explanations offered so far. But it is evident that the theory which explains equally adequately *Oedipus Rex* as well as *Hamlet* cannot by itself explain how they differ from each other. For this purpose, we shall need some other explanation. In order to determine the nature and value of any individual literary work we need not one, but *many principles*, theories and criteria.

We shall now turn to the second of the two above mentioned ways. A school of criticism known as 'New Criticism' was in vogue in the UK and USA for quite some time from the 1920s or 30s. Critics of this school start from the assumption that poetry or literature is a variety of linguistic discourse. In order to identify the nature of this variety, they contrast it with some other readily identifiable variety. Language as it is used in science invariably serves the necessary purpose. Literature evidently does not belong to the scientific variety of discourse. Scientific discourse is then used as a negative analogue to determine the features of literary discourse. For example, consider the dichotomy LA. Richards has arrived at.

Scientific language is used to describe reality; literary (poetic) language is used not to describe anything, but to express and/or induce emotions. When Cleanth Brooks says that the language of paradox is the language of poetry he too has in mind a similar contrast between two varieties of linguistic discourse.

These critics claim to have also discovered the structuring principles peculiar to poetry (literature); these are: reconciliation of opposites, paradox, ambiguity, irony, etc. One does come across literary works characterised by these. But it might prove to be an exaggerated claim that *all* literary works exemplify them. On the other hand it can be shown that these structuring principles are not peculiar to literature alone. For example, one does not find them in many poems of Wordsworth. And, on the other hand, examples of paradox and irony can be seen in plenty outside literature, even in everyday life. Some of these critics see conflict as the central principle of literary works and try to show how the conflict between good and evil, life and death, light and darkness is at the core of different literary works. It is easy enough to show such conflicts in all literary works.

But, if the type of principles mentioned above are treated as the sole differentia of all literature, the differences between various forms of literature are easily lost sight of. If a lyric by Donne, a Shakespearean tragedy like *King Lear*, and a Dostoievskian novel like *The Brothers Karamazov* can be identified with the help of one distinguishing mark alone, where is the need for the existence of different forms such as the lyric, the drama, and the novel? But we have already seen that the differences between forms of literature are important. The critics who recommended and, to some extent practised the above method evidently had in their mind poetry, or, to be more precise, short, lyrical poems. That the lyric is an important form of literature is of course a fact. But to treat it as a paradigm for all literature in all its aspects is patently wrong. If one treats any other form as a paradigm, it will be equally wrong. The above critics gave the central place to lyrical poetry and used the conceptual framework, which is perhaps adequate for it, for the criticism of all literature. But one does not ordinarily find in a lyric such elements as strong characterisation, elaborate plot construction, or descriptions on a large scale. Naturally, elements like imagery take the place of plot, characterisation etc., in lyric. But if we approach a novel like *War and Peace* with a conceptual structure in which imagery occupies the central place, the result will obviously be disastrous.

We discussed above the place in literary criticism of classes broader than the novel. R. S. Crane, a prominent neo-Aristotelian critic, has taken strong exception to the use in criticism of classes with ever-widening scope. In his book *The Language of Criticism and the Structure of Poetry*, Crane maintains that every act of criticism necessarily takes place within a framework; which framework to choose from among the many that are available depends on what the critic is aiming at. If he is aiming at (a) understanding and (b) evaluating *individual* literary works, frameworks which relate to the most general features of literature will be of little use to him. For a critic who has this aim in mind, Crane recommends the Aristotelian framework which will enable him to arrive at the knowledge of the individual literary work, and to grasp its individual structuring principle.

Aristotle himself, in his *Poetics*, has discussed two forms of literature: tragedy and epic. He has analysed tragedy in detail and has thus provided a model for analysing forms of literature. A neo-Aristotelian critic like Crane would not be hostile to the concept of literary forms. But it is probable that he might be opposed to the use of classes with a broader scope. Crane's contention most probably will be that the concept of forms of literature is not useless, but it is inadequate. That Crane is right becomes clear in all contexts where the value of individuality is recognised. Where individuality is not regarded as valuable, classification of individuals is enough. But in the modern concept of man individuality is included as an inalienable constituent. We adopt a similar attitude to a large number of man-made things. This is certainly true about individual literary works. This uniqueness partly constitutes the source of its value.

That every literary work has its own unique, non-repeatable structure and expression is a well-known tenet of the Kant–Hegel aesthetic tradition. Once this is accepted, it follows that the criterion for evaluating a literary work lies within itself. Kant has distinguished between determinate and reflective judgement. The function of judgement is to create unity in diversity. When the synthesising concepts and principles are already given, the judgement is determinate; on the other hand, it is reflective when the unifying principle is still to be discovered. It is the reflective judgement that is operative in aesthetic experience. For, here the unifying principle is not given, it is to be discovered. Every manifold that is to be synthesised will need its own synthesising principle. To operate with a unifying principle common to different manifolds amounts to replacing reflective by determinate judgement. But Kant was determined to avoid this. For otherwise the aesthetic experience would be transformed into cognitive experience, and would lose it autonomy. We experience a peculiar internal tension in the Kantian analysis of aesthetic experience. Kant comes very close to recognising the existence of concepts in aesthetic experience; but till the end he does not explicitly say that concepts are present.

There is only one possible way out of the predicament of the Kantians. They should accept the existence of concepts in the experience of beauty and art, and at the same time assert that these concepts are very often not closed, but admit of openness up to a point. Some of these concepts are rooted in particular arts and are usually confined to them; consider for example, concepts like *Bhairavi, Mālkauns, Khyāl, Thumri, Pancham*, ... It will not always be possible to find concepts which are born in a particular art and are confined to it alone. The possibility of finding them is greater in music than in literature. Once we admit that concepts in the field of art are to some extent open we shall also have to admit that the items which come under them are not exactly identical. Classes here are like families, the members of which are linked together by similarities and differences. It also follows that no two works of art are exactly identical in respect of substance, structuring principle, mode of expression; identity is not expected to be there; and even if we expect it, we shall never succeed in discovering it. Partial similarity is all that we can expect to find; and we do find it. And it is this partial similarity which makes teaching and learning possible within the framework of an art-tradition. If a structuring principle which is really not repeatable in any measure is possible in theory at all, then at least in practice it is well nigh impossible to be able to discern it in any work of art created in the past or to be created in the future. According to Absolute Idealists, if one wants to know the real character of a thing one will have to study all its *relations* with all the other things in the Universe, because the character of the thing we desire to know is determined exactly by these relations. It is theoretically impossible for any man to accomplish this task. The knowledge obtained by any *finite* knower will necessarily be incomplete, so long as he is finite; the object of his knowledge will also be incomplete on account of the same finitencss. This applies to a work of art as it does not to all the other things in the world. A work of art will be incomplete so long as it is finite. It will be complete only when it covers the whole Universe, and paradoxically it is only then that its principle of organisation/expression will be really unique. In order to experience such a work of art the critic will himself have to be the infinite *Brahmānanda* (the blissful experience of total identification with the Universal spirit) or to be *Brahmānanda-sahodara* (the twin-brother of *Brahmānanda*). As knowers, moral agents, and aesthetic appreciators, we are finite; and the objects we deal with are also finite. It is therefore logically impossible to find in the human world a principle of organisation/expression which will get completely absorbed in one work of art. So long as the present situation (created by our finiteness) continues to be the same, the distinctions between concepts and their examples, classes and their members, traditions and individual works of art as well as their interdependence will have to be accepted.

We have been discussing problems pertaining to Form primarily because Marathi critics happen to be preoccupied with them. With all this, their first spontaneous responses to literary works are about the content of these works. Let me illustrate this point with the help of two short stories, both written by one author, sharing an equal degree of technical finesse. The first story depicts a dispute between a group of students and the Hostel Warden. One of the agitating students has gone on a hunger strike; tension is mounting every day. The Warden's wife intervenes at this stage and lovingly coaxes the boy to end the fast. At the same time she prevails upon her husband to give up his office. The second story depicts the mental torture that a woman, caught in a trying situation, is experiencing. She is a married woman and has recently become a mother. In fact this should have been a moment of great satisfaction and joy to her. But it is just at this moment that she comes to know about a hereditary disease in her parents' family—in each generation somebody in the family is afflicted with psychosis. She also realises that she herself has a kink in her personality. This sudden realisation unnerves her. Now the only earnest prayer that she, a mother, wishes to offer is that the child should not be tainted by the hereditary disease in her family, that the child should turn out to be the offspring of her husband alone, that it should belong only to its father's family and inherit nothing from the mother's side. The deeply painful conflict in her mind is powerfully depicted in the story. The first story is escapist like a day-dream and is, on that account, mediocre. The convincing depiction of the heroine's mental anguish makes the second story valuationally superior. We called the first story mediocre and the second story good mainly because the content of the first is, as content, valuationally much inferior to that of the latter. The Marathi reader needs to be reminded that we have called the second story *good* and not *great*. A Marathi critic, who moves about wearing certain theoretical blinkers, does not mind content-oriented criteria for judging *greatness* in literature; but he is opposed to using this variety of criteria for judging *goodness* in literature. When we do not have these blinkers on, we spontaneously give due importance to the content while deciding whether a particular piece of writing is a *good literary* work. But when a critic rises to the theoretical level, he regards as invalid all content-oriented criteria. Kant, while writing about the art of painting in his *Critique of Aesthetic Judgment*, gives all importance to design and almost no importance to the colours; and that was a serious error on his part. A similar, a more serious mistake is being made by contemporary Marathi writers on literary theory when they do not attach due importance to the quality of the content of a literary work in determining whether it belongs to the category of literature and in giving their verdict on its goodness as a literary work; the other aspect of their mistake consists in the excessive importance they give to the structure of a literary work. As a matter of fact a literary work derives its value from various sources such as the merits of the content, diction, style, metre, plot-construction, and so on. It seems Marathi critics are oblivious to this fact. That is why, even after you have analysed and evaluated all the above aspects of a story they will persist in saying: 'all this is very fine; but you have not yet told us what makes this story a *work of art*. At least now you will have to admit the importance of Form. For ultimately it is Form alone which is the deciding factor.'

This argument is based on an assumption whose truth is taken as self-evident. It is assumed that there is a well-demarcated class called Art; that it has a definite distinguishing characteristic to mark it off from all that is not Art. You cannot hope to find it in the aspect of content, because there is little similarity in the content of the different arts. In literature we get content in the sense of *meaning* which is expressed through words. Content *in this sense* is not present in an abstract painting; there, in the place of expressed meaning, what we get is an organisation of colours, etc. On account of such basic differences it is impossible to get at anything common in the content of works of art. The only way out is to concede that the common distinguishing characteristic of all arts can be found only in the aspect of Form; we should therefore look for it only there. As this common characteristic or principle is supposed to cover all works of art it is sure to be extremely abstract. 'Unity in diversity', 'harmony-contrast-balance' can be cited as examples of such abstract, all-comprehensive principles.

One can understand the difficulty before the people who accept the above assumption. They do not feel confident that by concentrating their attention of the content of works of art they will be able to clearly mark off art from non-art. It is, of course, true that the task is difficult; but it is not impossible as they think it to be. If we make a determined effort we shall be able to discover the dividing lines between the two fields. They might not have the certainty and precision that obtain in natural sciences; but they will be found to be adequate for doing practical criticism successfully and fruitfully at least in the case of most literary works. Let us take an example. Suppose that we are reading Laxman Mane's book *Uparā*. Before we had read it we knew almost nothing about the Kaikādi tribe, whose life it depicts. The book has made a substantial addition to our general awareness of tribal life. The range of our experience and understanding has been widened. But that is not all; more important than this is the fact that the structure of our customary emotional and ethical responses has been shaken. We have realised the nature of the high degree of tension and hostility that is generated when an inter-caste marriage takes place; we have also realised how tenaciously the caste-system continues to live on at all levels in our society. This social insight creates in us a mixed response, consisting of indignation, helplessness, a variety of despair, and along with these there is the intense realisation that it is imperative to fight for social justice. This complex response is wholly content-oriented. It is exactly for these content-oriented reasons that we found the book to be so good. A difficulty needs to be taken note of at this stage. *Uparā*, we saw, gives an insight into our social life. Can we not get the same insight elsewhere too, for example through a book on sociology? A sociological book, it will have to be conceded, will certainly give us an insight into society; the insight will be characterised by precision and certainty also, if disciplines like statistics have been made use of. But the insight that a sociological book can give will not be of the same nature as the insight that *Uparā* gives. Sociological studies give us knowledge of reality on the plane of abstraction. Individuals have no room in these studies except as examples. When we read *Uparā* or Daya Pawar's *Balutan* we feel as if we are watching actual actions of real people taking place before our eyes. What we see *suggests* general propositions about our social life. But books like these do not *transcend* individuality of either persons of events in order to give us abstract formulations about reality as scientific books do.

Secondly, the mode of presenting information in a scientific book is not necessarily attractive. In a literary work it is presented in such a way as would create interest even in a common man. Further, the information contained in a scientific treatise is, as far as possible, kept away from emotions and values. These two elements are present in a large measure in most literary works. It is true that some modern writers consciously use an emotionally neutral style in their stories and novels. They rely rather on particular arrangements of the events, characters, situations in their novels to convey to the readers new insights and evaluations. This reliance on particular skilful arrangements of the constituents of literary works to give insights into life can be regarded as one more distinguishing mark of literary works.

We must however never forget that it may prove impossible to discover the principle that makes all literary works beautiful/good/powerful. It may be the case that all literary works do not share any one principle in common; again, if there is one, there may be no unanimity about it among critics. Let us consider a couple of examples. Some of the characteristics which were mentioned above in the context of literary works—e.g., that they are interesting, give importance to the particularity of events and characters—can be found in journalistic writing also. But is the latter, on account of this, to be admitted to the category of literature? But it may be pointed out as negative evidence that most journalistic writing is characterised by sensationalism, use of a cliché-dominated style, a tendency towards simplification, absence of neat organisation, incapacity to provide a broad human context to events. That is why many critics will refuse to give the name of literature to most journalistic writing.

Suppose, following Warren and Wellek, we say that in literature the events, facts, characters all belong to the plane of *fictionality,* and that we make no positive or negative ontological claim about their actual existence. Science and history, on the other hand, give us information about events and facts which actually exist/existed in the real world. This distinction, however, may not be found to have universal applicability. If *fictionality* is regarded as the distinguishing mark of literature, what do we do with an autobiographical literary classic like Laxmibai Tilak's *Smrutichitre*? Some literary theorists try to overcome this difficulty by advising the readers to treat actual facts described in such works as if they were fictions. But then it would amount to conceding that the actual facts in that case have attained literary excellence without belonging to the plane of fictionality.

Till now we have been trying to look for content-oriented criteria of evaluating literary works. If we now turn our attention to the aspect of the expression of this content, we might be able to identify characteristics which will mark off literature from non-literature. It is possible to get a sufficient number of such characteristics if we pay attention to diction, qualities of style like *Prasāda*, *Ojas*, *Mādhurya*, and principles such as *Dhvani*, *Vakrokti* and *Alankāra*. If we are analysing a novel, we should keep in mind the different points of view from which events in a novel can be narrated, and the different ways in which they can be organised. But such comprehensive analysis of literary works has become a rarity during the last many years—perhaps during the last three or four decades.

Adequate knowledge of the individuality of persons, things, and situations can be obtained, valuational decisions in their regard can be made without losing sight of their individuality, if we bring to bear upon them a complex and flexible structure of various concepts and criteria used simultaneously. This is what we actually do in everyday life. In spite of the fact that this way of dealing with things has proved to be successful in our everyday life, we insist on trying to discover and use only one self-identical criterion in the field of literature; there seems to be something very odd about this insistence. It is better to solve a fresh problem in a fresh way with the help of the organised, ordered experiences we have stored in our mind, than to depend on some single so-called distinguishing mark of literature. If we do not want to lose the capacity to appreciate new literary works, we must, with firm determination, set aside the *Essentialist Fallacy* (the one-term one-essence fallacy), and resist the inclination to accept misleading simplifications, in any event to accept the assumption that all works of art have one common essence. If we accept this assumption there is every danger that while looking for the so-called common essence of all art in a literary work, we might forget that it is a literary work.

It should be clear from the general trend of the argument stated so far, that just as we must not fall a prey to the Essentialist Fallacy while thinking about the nature of works of art, we must also protect ourselves from that fallacy while considering the nature of the experiences induced by works of art. That different works of art, in the various fields of art, give rise to experiences which are different, sometimes strikingly different, from one another is a matter of everyday observation. It is therefore very surprising to see how people who are otherwise levelheaded, can readily assume that all art experiences are identical in nature. *Premā Tuzā Rang Kasa*? will create in us a healthy, pleasant mood; we shall find *King Lear* profoundly disturbing; *Antigone* might leave us feeling disturbed and baffled; *The Tempest* will transport us beyond the turmoils of the real world to the peace and tranquillity of a make-believe world. The *Mahābhārata* will create in us *Kshamā* and *Nirveda*, a state of non-attachment with regard to the phenomenal world. There can be no doubt that all these are valid literary experiences. The differences among them are so obvious, that if somebody thinks that he can discern a common principle in all of them he should be regarded as a victim of a conceptual illusion.

Sometimes aestheticians tell us that all art experience is characterised by delight/rapture, detachment and an all-absorbing concentration, verging on identification with the art-object. It is necessary to examine this assertion closely. First of all, all-absorbing concentration is not peculiar to art-experience alone. We can find it in various activities which have nothing to do with art; e.g., in watching a cricket match, working in our garden, playing cards, killing mosquitoes which disturb our sleep.... We know that everyday experiences are pleasurable or non-pleasurable, or they contain both pleasure and non-pleasure. But it is claimed by most Sanskritists, that the *Rasa* experience is necessarily pleasurable. Our own experience while watching plays does not lend support to this. One has only to consider the *Bībhatsa* and *Bhayānaka Rasas* to see why our actual experience cannot support the Sanskritists' claim. It is argued that in the *Rasa* experience, the *Sattva* predominates, and the *Rajas* and *Tamas* are weakened; this inevitably renders the *Rasa* experience pleasurable. This argument is not based on actual experience, but on a particular metaphysical theory. And we need not accept the argument as valid or convincing unless we have already accepted that particular metaphysical theory. Perhaps there is some point in saying that the *Tamas* is weakened while we are watching a work of art. This is likely to happen because we are on the conscious plane and are all the while alert. But this point needs deeper probing. It is very likely that the *Tamas* is in ascendence when we are reading an escapist romance which takes us away from reality. Again, we cannot assert with certainty the *Rajas,* the principle at the basis of all our actions, is weakened in a literary experience. We shall return to this point later in the context of our discussion of the concept of Detachment.

A mention has already been made in this paper of the ontological status of a work of art and an aesthetic object. According to Kant in the context of aesthetic experience we are not supposed to claim that the object of our experience actually exists. This Kantian view seems to have been accepted by a large number of the later aestheticians. So far as the aesthetic experience is concerned, it makes no difference whether the aesthetic object actually exists or is only an illusion, an appearance. Once a person accepts this Kantian position, i.e. once he withholds the ontological claim he thinks that he has thereby ruled out the possibility of any commerce with the aesthetic object from the cognitive and the practical points of view; he cannot now look upon it even as something agreeable. Once he has excluded these approaches, it follows that in the aesthetic context his attitude is, and can only be, that of detached contemplation.

This line of thinking is convincing only up to a point. As there is no ontological continuity between the art world and our everyday world, we (who belong to the everyday world) cannot touch anything that belongs to the art world. But the converse is not true, at least not true in all respects. Things in the art world can, and often do, affect us, despite the ontological difference between the two worlds. Things in the art world do move us emotionally, and, to a certain extent, move us as practical agents also. To cite an example, we cannot dissuade Othello from killing Desdemona; but at the same time it is true that we are as much disturbed by the murder of the innocent Desdemona as we would be by the murder of an innocent woman in the actual world. This shows that characters in a play have the capacity to induce in us real-life emotions. Secondly, our response is not merely emotional. In the context of many literary works our response includes different elements such as our capacities to know, to think, to act, and to act morally; it comprehends our total value-system. And in the context of these literary works 'detachment' merely means absence of overt action with regard to the characters in literary works, and perhaps also non-involvement of the empirical self.

Let us probe further the concept of Detachment. In the context of many literary works 'detachment' signifies only absence of overt action with regard to the characters in a literary work. Action is closely related to desires. Desires are of two types. One type of desire can be satisfied only if items of a definite class are made available; for example, thirst can be quenched only with water or liquids which resemble it in relevant respects; nothing else will serve the purpose. On the other hand certain elastic desires are satisfied by a very wide range of heterogeneous objects. Love (*Rati*) is one such desire; the range of its objects includes union with the beloved as well as separation from her and the poignant lamenting over the separation. That is why Sanskritists mention *Vipralambha Shringāra* along with *Sambhoga Shringāra*. The actual presence of the beloved, her memory, her image, a handkerchief presented by her, thinking about her, thinking about even a fictional character can satisfy *Rati* in varying degrees. The escapist romantic literature that appears in popular magazines available in circulating libraries will bear ample testimony to this. The satisfaction of desires is thus seen not to have been ruled out by the ontological difference mentioned above. The problem of the cognitive aspect of literary experience will have to be tackled in a slightly different way. If the elements in a literary work and the organisational principles which synthesise them are similar to their counterparts in actuality (in spite of the ontological difference between them) we shall obtain an insight into reality through a literary work. This will naturally awaken our cognitive faculty and also our faculty of moral judgement.

Judgements such as '*Uparā* has given a new social awareness', '*Koslā* has given us an insight into the mind of a whole generation', 'when we saw the recent film *Ākrosh* we were convinced that it is imperative to fight against the present social structure although it is extremely difficult to undertake this fight', 'the universal destruction shown in the *Mahābhārata* fills our mind with despair' are regarded as valid critical judgements only because we accept the validity of content-oriented criteria of literary excellence. Moral, cognitive, and intellectual elements spontaneously enter these judgements and their legitimacy is not ordinarily challenged. But it is not enough to say only this; it is necessary to go a step further. In the context of some literary works it is necessary that these elements should find a place in our judgements about them. If, while reading some of the stories in *Maraṇ Swasta Hot Āhe,* the value structure of the reader is not even slightly disturbed, it will have to be said that his response falls short of completeness. An analogy might help us here. Suppose a film director has to decide whether to give the role of a particular character to a certain actor; the character is to be shown as drowning in a river and crying out for help; if the actor's urgent appeal for help proves to be effective the film director will give him the role. This is all that is expected from the director in the present context. But suppose the same director is strolling along the bank of a river and he hears the same appeal for help from a man who is really drowning. If, in this changed context also, the director's response does not go beyond, 'excellent performance; he should get an assignment in the new film', it will have to be regarded as a response which is totally irrelevant and incomplete in the changed context. Only if he had rushed to the rescue of the drowning man would the response have been relevant and adequate. The relevance and adequacy of the response depends upon the context in which it is made. Just as this is true about real life contexts, it is true also about literary contexts. A particular story by Baburao Bagul gives a jolt to our value-structure. Its excellence as a good story lies precisely in its capacity to give this sort of jolt. And in feeling this jolt lies, in a very large measure, the fullness and the relevance of our response as a literary response. On the other hand the excellence of an *Abhang* sung by Bhimsen Joshi early in the morning lies in its capacity to create in us mental repose; and in the context of such an *Abhang* the mental repose constitutes the fullness and relevance of our response. It may be appropriate, relevant, and valid to approach works of art of certain types only with one aspect of our personality; on the other hand, it will be appropriate, valid and relevant to approach with our total personality some other types of works of art. We can keep our ethical value-structure outside an art gallery and enjoy an exhibition of abstract paintings. But, if we keep our value-structure out, it may turn out to be impossible to read *Koslā* and to respond to it adequately. If reading *Koslā* does not affect our general view of reality and our value-structure, it only proves that we have read the novel as a proof-corrector reads any printed material.

It should be evident from the above analysis that so far as novels, stories, plays are concerned, our spontaneous and almost entire response is often content-oriented. But this does mean that the consideration of form plays no part in the process of reading and evaluating a literary work. At some stage or the other in our content-oriented study of a literary work we are inevitably led to the analysis of form. Here we should bear in mind two points. Firstly, how much importance form has in comparison with content depends upon the particular Art, the particular province in that art, and the particular work of art we have in mind. Secondly, 'form' does not only mean the principle of organisation of a work of art as it is generally taken to mean in Marathi today. Form has other meanings as well; e.g., form of literature, expression (of some semantic content), arrangement of the elements of a plot.

According to some so-called Formalists in Marathi a work of art becomes a work of art only on account of its form, by which they mean some specific principle of organisation. It has already been suggested above that this view cannot be accepted in the context of literature. We shall now discuss in some detail the reasons for saying so. While talking about an abstract musical composition we need not go beyond sound-units and their organisation. But this cannot be the case with literature, our response to which, as we saw earlier, is mainly content-oriented. In the context of literature we have to consider two different concept-pairs: (a) semantic content and its expression, and (b) constituents like character, situation, events, ideas, emotions, etc., and their organisation. Let us remind ourselves of one point before we proceed further. A literary work owes its existence as a literary work in a large measure to a content of a certain quality that it embodies. While we are looking for the features of the form of a literary work we shall have to keep this fact constantly in mind. To forget the demands of the content will be a big blunder.

B. S. Mardhekar has argued that emotive meaning is the medium of literature. Let us grant for the sake of discussion that this is true. According to Mardhekar the literary artist's aim is to create a beautiful work of art in this medium; in other words the literary artist aims at organising emotive meanings in accordance with the three laws of rhythm, viz., harmony, contrast, and balance, which, Mardhekar claims, constitute beauty in art and nature. Generally, other relations (e.g., psychological) also exist between emotive statements. We take them for granted and do not take special note of them in the aesthetic context. Mardhekar has not shown any logical connection between these other relations and the three laws referred to above. We may therefore ignore the former and concentrate on the organisation of emotive meanings in accordance with three Mardhekarian laws. Let us now consider the following passage from *Gārambicha Bāpu,* the famous novel already referred to above: 'And they were then laughing with abandon . . . their eyes dimmed, their ears felt slapped and they felt faint at that sight. . . . Excessive enthusiasm, excessive attachment, attraction without a cause, despair and pain also without any cause . . . see how happy Bapu is; he has no recollection; no pain.' Mardhekarians will point out that the first two sentences are related by contrast; the third on one side and the fourth and the fifth on the other are also linked by contrast. If we take the group of the first two sentences and the group of the next three sentences, we will discern the relation of balance between them. Besides, the three units in the second sentence are linked together by harmony; the first three units of the third sentence have one, and the last two units of the same sentence have an additional relation of harmony. The first three units and the last two units in the same sentence are held together by the relation of contrast. As the organisation of the different sentences in the passage is in accordance with the laws of harmony, contrast, and balance, it inevitably follows that the passage is a beautiful configuration.

But, to be honest, the above sentences are not taken from one single passage at all. But if they are read together it is possible that they might appear to be interrelated according to some laws e.g. by logical or psychological laws and create an impression that they constitute one passage. If we want to keep the laws of beauty completely separated from laws irrelevant to beauty, we must see to it from the beginning that these non-aesthetic laws do not get a chance to enter the aesthetic experience at all. Is not this separation artificial? Perhaps, yes. But we have a good precedent. In his discussion of Hedonism, Plato has made a distinction—which also looks artificial—between pleasure and consciousness of pleasure. There should be no logical difficulty if, following Plato's example, we isolated the three aesthetic laws from other, i.e. non-aesthetic laws. As an experiment let us consider the following sentences in which this separation has been consciously made: 'Kakasaheb looked very angrily at the clerk. Elizabeth glanced at Browning with smiling eyes. Justice Ranade and others sent petitions to the kindly government. The Peshwas rejected outright the Nizam's proposal regarding a treaty'. There is contrast between the first two sentences, and also in the next two sentences. There is balance between the first two and the latter two sentences. Again there is harmony in the first and the fourth, and also in the second and the third ... all this can be shown. The Marathi Formalist will be immediately convinced that the above four sentences constitute a beautiful configuration. The real question is about the response and judgement of readers like us who do not wear the Mardhekarian theoretical blinkers. We shall certainly refuse to look upon this group of sentences as beautiful; we shall also go further and regard this attempt at bringing these four disconnected sentences together as the height of folly. So far as literature is concerned, content is not something whose presence is to be taken for granted only to be conveniently forgotten while formulating an aesthetic theory. Whatever may be true of other arts, form cannot be the only necessary pre-condition of the existence of the literary art; the presence of content of a certain quality is a much more important pre-condition. Finally, it must never be forgotten that 'form' must not be narrowly interpreted as Mardhekarians tend to do. Our critics, let us hope, will also turn their attention to the other things signified by 'Form'; this is most likely to happen as the study of forms of literature and stylistics strikes deeper roots in our soil.

There is perhaps one difficulty in Marathi critics' admitting the importance of content in literature. At least on the plane of theory this difficulty appears to be formidable. Giving importance to content, some critics feel, will lead to the devaluation of literature as art. The content of a literary work brings with it values of our everyday life, thus lowering art to the position of an instrument to establish and promote these life-values. We shall see that this fear is baseless if we consider the question not in the context of particular values like Plato's Wisdom, Courage, Temperance, Justice, but in the context of a larger and more general question: what makes life as a whole valuable? There are many possible answers to the above question. Suppose we accept the theory of value advocated by the utilitarians and I. A. Richards; the life in which the largest number of important impulses are satisfied, and which involves the least frustration of them, will then become the most valuable. Now suppose that we are able to prove that while reading literature that maximum number of important impulses are satisfied and the minimum number of them are frustrated. It will follow from this that reading literature does not lead to valuable life; it is in itself a way of living valuable life. Here we are making use of valuable life as a criterion of literary excellence; but that does not make us advocates of didactic literature. Suppose knowledge is an inalienable part of valuable life. If literature gives insights into different sides of life, it automatically becomes valuable on that account. If we accept that the knowledge that literature gives is different from—not higher or lower than—the knowledge that science gives, the cognitive aspect of literature will be seen to possess intrinsic (and not instrumental) value. From this it should be clear that by bringing Art close to life we do not devalue art. Some arts can be completely divorced from life (e.g., abstract designing); they might consequently claim and enjoy autonomy. Literature can never get the autonomy that these arts can claim and get. So long as literature cannot be deconceptualised, the present situation will not change. Literature need not be given the lowest position in the hierarchy of Arts on this account. To be fraught with concepts is just a peculiarity and not a defect of literature. If we avoid the Essentialist Fallacy we shall realise that literature is only different from other arts in some respects; it is neither superior nor inferior to other arts.

So far we were doing two things. We were studying some important problems in aesthetics. We were also considering the step that the Marathi critics and aestheticians have to take in order to make a genuine contribution to this discipline. We saw at the outset that aesthetics is the study of the logical features and the content of the concepts which spontaneously appear in our critical judgements. We discussed (a) whether concepts are present in our experience of works of art, (b) whether they are closed or open concepts; (c) how they are related to evaluation. We also discussed the nature of some important concepts in the context of literature. We considered the similarities and differences between literature and the other arts, the relation between content and form in literature, the importance of content in literary works, the problem of the autonomy of literature, and other similar substantive questions. Literature being life-values-oriented, we discussed in some detail the nature of the content-aspect of literature.

Now that we know something definite about the nature of aesthetics, it should not be difficult for us to see and evaluate what the Marathi critics and aestheticians have been able to do, and what they have not been able to do. Theories of beauty grow in the womb of art-traditions, they begin to become explicit in criticism, and if there is a strong intellectual tradition in the community, they can be formulated with logical rigour. If we resist the temptation of indulging in self-glorification and decide to face reality, we shall have to admit that nothing significant has been done in any of the three fields: aesthetics, criticism and creative writing. It is a saddening realisation that this all-round poverty is not a recent phenomenon in Maharashtra; it has been there for decades That there should spring into existence new aesthetic theories in this atmosphere of poverty seems to be almost impossible. We shall have to come to the same conclusion about all disciplines that are given the general name of 'Humanities'. It is only when society is vibrating with life and vigour in all its aspects, traditions and institutions that the possibility is created for the emergence of new theoretical systems. Great problems arise only in such a living society; and the traditions in that society throw up great men endowed with genius to tackle them. No such problems have arisen in our art-tradition; and we have not produced great geniuses to tackle them.

To be honest, we shall have to begin at the beginning. Artists should try to be conscious of what they are trying to do; while they are endeavouring to attain self-awareness as artists, they should also communicate their findings to society. On the other hand, the art-critics must put away blinkers of arbitrary theories and examine their genuine and spontaneous responses to works of art. Mere enthusiasm is not an adequate equipment for art-critics; they must also have a well cultivated sensibility, necessary scholarship, tenacity and seriousness of purpose. They must acquire the intellectual skills necessary for formulating their responses explicitly and with logical precision. Criticism should be directed to a work of art and neither to the artist nor to the critic. It is necessary to examine carefully the complex theoretical structure that emerges from what the self-conscious artists and well-equipped critics say about works of art; one must do this with deft fingers, and while doing this delicate operation one must scrupulously avoid using the clumsy instrument called 'one-art one-essence fallacy'. We must explore whether the same or analogous concepts are found to exist in different arts. It is needless to emphasise the importance of academic integrity in the whole process. It is here that we can hope to get much help from the Western aesthetic theories. We must of course resist the temptation to rely only on somebody like Clive Bell or Collingwood or Osborne, just because their books are easily accessible. The Western aesthetic structure is very comprehensive, complex, and well-built. It has received solid support from art-tradition on the one hand and the tradition of philosophical thinking on the other. It is necessary to study in detail the different constituents of this vast structure, to evaluate them, to examine their mutual bearings with regard to one another, to construct a conceptual map. It is for them to ascertain where we and *our theories* can be placed on this map. All this will require a long time. We shall need, besides untiring patience, a well-developed ability to think on the abstract, philosophical plane. The number of people gifted with this specific ability is much smaller than we suppose. It is certainly not universal; further, it is not necessarily seen in people who are intelligent in other ways. No single individual will be able to cope with all the tasks listed above. It is in fact a sort of project that only a group of researchers, scholars, critics, philosophers can tackle. While this work is being done on the plane of theory, we must at the same time maintain continuous and direct grass-root contacts with literature, by functioning as practical critics with all the necessary equipment and substantial help from our native common sense.

That Maharashtrian critics and aestheticians should have wasted about thirty years in dealing with a particularly weak, small branch of the great tree of the aesthetics of the Kantian-Hegelian tradition bears ample testimony to their naïveté and all-round ignorance. They were deluded into believing that this weak branch has great importance in world aesthetic thought. To give it a slight jolt was thought to be an event of international significance; to give it some support was also regarded as an equally significant event. If we had devoted even half of this time to the study of the Kantian-Hegelian tree itself perhaps we would have been able to produce a small corpus of theoretical writing of good quality. Thirty years is a small period in the entire history of Maharashtra. If we have our feet planted firmly in reality, and if we make all-round, honest, and determined efforts along proper lines, it is probable that an aesthetic theory which we can legitimately call *our own* may emerge in the next fifty or hundred years. When we call an aesthetic theory our own, it is implied that it is the creation not of any one individual, however brilliant he may be, but of a whole art tradition, a whole socio-cultural group. Let us hope that during this period an equal amount of work of good quality will have been done in natural sciences and humanities, and all sensible people will have been convinced that these other fields of inquiry are more important than aesthetics. Aesthetics will then get its due place; even if it turns out to be low, it will be its legitimate place.